STO

ALLEN COUNTY PUBLIC LIBRARY

ACPL ITEM
DISCARDED

33
Br
1927-

THE FIELD OF SOCIA
INVESTMENT

S0-BWM-472

DO NOT REMOVE
CARDS FROM POCKET

ALLEN COUNTY PUBLIC LIBRARY

FORT WAYNE, INDIANA 46802

You may return this book to any agency, branch,
or bookmobile of the Allen County Public Library.

**The Arnold and Caroline Rose Monograph Series
of the American Sociological Association**

The field of social investment

The field of financial investment is undergoing a quiet revolution
as fiduciaries are beginning to use social criteria in allocating
capital in the U.S. economy. This social practice is authorized by
pension funds, churches, universities, insurance companies,
banks, and mutual funds, as well as wealthy individuals. Social
investment of this kind alters the traditional reasons for allocating
capital, and the professional basis for investment decision-making
can therefore no longer be rooted solely in the disciplines of
economics and finance: it now requires the addition of sociology
and related social sciences. It is such an addition that Severyn
Bruyn undertakes in this book.

The book is concerned with the theory and practice of social
investment as a profession. Professor Bruyn interprets the
meaning of social investment, describes current investment
practices, and proposes a theory of social investment based on
these practices. He reviews empirical studies supporting new
directions in investment policies, and shows how they affect
developing countries. He also provides guidelines for fiduciaries,
based on the best available knowledge of corporate behavior, and
presents researchers with key hypotheses to follow in gathering
data for the evaluation of social investment norms.

The study uniquely offers a basis for defining social investment
as a field of knowledge, and will interest all readers concerned
with its practice or analysis.

The Rose Monograph Series was established in 1968 in honor of the distinguished sociologists Arnold and Caroline Rose whose bequest makes the Series possible. The sole criterion for publication in the Series is that a manuscript contribute to knowledge in the discipline of sociology in a systematic and substantial manner. All areas of the discipline and all established and promising modes of inquiry are equally eligible for consideration. The Rose Monograph Series is an official publication of the American Sociological Association.

Editor: Ernest Q. Campbell

Editorial Board:

Andrew Cherlin	Robert Hauser
Daniel Chirot	Virginia Hiday
Phillips Cutright	Teresa Sullivan
Kai Erikson	Jonathan Turner

The Editor and Board of Editors gratefully acknowledge the contributions of William F. Whyte of Cornell University and Tom Koenig of Northeastern University as expert reviewers of this book in manuscript.

The field of social investment

Severyn T. Bruyn

Boston College

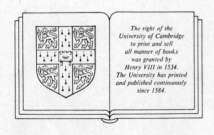

The right of the
University of Cambridge
to print and sell
all manner of books
was granted by
Henry VIII in 1534.
The University has printed
and published continuously
since 1584.

Cambridge University Press

Cambridge
London   New York   New Rochelle
Melbourne   Sydney

Published by the Press Syndicate of the University of Cambridge
The Pitt Building, Trumpington Street, Cambridge, CB2 1RP
32 East 57th Street, New York, NY 10022, USA
10 Stamford Road, Oakleigh, Melbourne 3166, Australia

© Cambridge University Press 1987

First published 1987

Printed in Great Britain by
Redwood Burn Limited, Trowbridge, Wiltshire

British Library cataloguing in publication data
Bruyn, Severyn T.
The field of social investment. –
(The Arnold and Caroline Rose monograph series of
the American Sociological Association)
1. Investments – Social aspects
2. Investments – Economic aspects
I. Title   II. Series
332.6   HG4515

Library of Congress cataloguing in publication data
Bruyn, Severyn Ten Haut, 1927–
The field of social investment.
(The Arnold and Caroline Rose monograph series of
the American Sociological Association)
Bibliography
1. Investments – Social aspects – United States.
2. Investments, American – Social aspects.
3. Industry – Social aspects – United States.
I. Title.   II. Title: Social investment.   III.Series.
HG4910.B77   1987   332.6   86–26393

ISBN 0 521 33292 3

Allen County Public Library
Ft. Wayne, Indiana

RB.

Contents

Preface

The field of financial investment is undergoing a quiet revolution as fiduciaries are beginning to use social criteria in decisions concerning the allocation of capital in the U.S. economy. This social practice is authorized by churches, universities, unions, insurance companies, banks, and mutual funds as well as wealthy individuals. The significance of this trend is indicated by the amount of money that is socially invested today and by signs that still more funds will be so directed in the future. For example, pension funds constitute over $1 trillion today and are expected to reach over $4 trillion in the 1990s. The AFL–CIO has mounted a campaign to persuade members to increase their control over the social direction of these funds. But there are billions of dollars in other institutions whose fiduciaries are becoming conscious of "the social factor" in the economic allocation of funds. The amount of capital involved suggests the potential power of social investors to alter the shape of the economy in the decades ahead.

This book is about the theory and practice of social investment as a profession. Its purpose is to offer a conceptual foundation for investment policy and research. It contains guidelines for fiduciaries based on the best available knowledge of corporate behavior in the context of society. For researchers, it contains key hypotheses to follow in gathering data for the evaluation of social investment norms.

Social investment alters the traditional reasons for allocating capital. The professional basis for decision making can no longer be rooted solely in the disciplines of economics and finance; the new dimension of investment policy requires the addition of sociology and related social sciences. The rationale for financial decisions now requires social theory supported by empirical research.

The book has three parts. The first part is designed to interpret the meaning of social investment, describe current investment practices, and propose a theory of social investment based on these practices. The second part interprets this theory and practice more systematically at different levels of the economy and points to empirical research supporting the new direction in investment policy. The third part reviews empirical studies that assess the impact of international investment policies on developing countries. We combine the results of these studies with our principles of social investment to recommend guidelines for investment at the global level. Finally, the epilogue is a review of the trend toward social investment and its relationship to solving problems in the U.S. economy. Our assessment of this trend becomes the basis for suggesting new financial and governmental policies to treat these problems in the coming decade.

Part I: The idea of social investment

The first chapter examines the meaning and legal framework of social investment within which capital is allocated in the United States, providing the background for chapter 2, which reviews the practices of social investors of different interests and values. Chapter 3 draws on ideas from these investment practices to advance a theory guiding investment decisions from a broader perspective. The theory is formulated around the idea that the economy is socially governed at different levels of organization: the workshop, the corporation, the industry, and the economy as a whole; the global economy and the local community are variations. A basic assumption is that each level is in the process of social development. The key hypothesis is that the corporate economy is evolving a social foundation to govern itself relatively independently of outside controls at each level, but the foundation has only begun to develop and is not yet sufficiently stable to be reliable over time. The business economy experiences cycles of depression and inflation that make it vulnerable to government intervention and controls. Providing a more secure foundation for social self-regulation requires a process of social-economic development promoted by investment policies.

Social-economic development is a complex process that calls for innovative theory and research, and the cultivation of both human and material resources within the levels of the corporate economy. At the level of the firm, development can mean cultivating new skills and responsible authority among people in departments, office systems, and workshops. At the level of an industry, it can mean promoting creative relationships between trade associations in the public interest and between labor and management. At the international level, it can mean helping to build a social foundation for the economy of a developing nation. Development, then, demands not only the best investment wisdom but also long-range research to anticipate the impact of decisions on people and the economy. This is the reason for constructing a professional field of social investment.

Part II: Social criteria and research

The second part of the book describes how social investors can begin to apply the normative principles underlying the theory at different levels of the economy. The chapters review policies of investment based on current empirical studies at the level of the corporation, the industry, and the community.

The most significant idea for social investors and researchers may be what William Foote Whyte has called "social inventions." Social inventions occur when a new element in organizational or interorganizational structures is established, when new social procedures are formulated, or when a new set of roles is formulated in a social system. Social inventions can make a difference in corporate productivity and profits and also in terms of fulfilling human values and social development in the economy. Investors have always looked toward technological inventions that promise profits and new directions for economic development, but now investors can add social inventions to enhance the probability that human values can be cultivated in the process. New patterns of social development become a critical part of the subject matter of this new field of financial investment.

The theory of social investment is conservative in its goal of reducing government regulations while enhancing self-regulation, but it is also paradoxically liberal and radical in its methods. For example, in chapter 4 the theory supports liberal investors who are recommending that corporations consider their "stakeholders" to be as important as their stockholders. The argument is that stakeholders who are affected by the firm – labor, management, consumers, and local citizens – are closely related to the firm's capacity to be productive and make profits. Social investors are therefore interested not only in how managers maintain profits by keeping an eye on the market and the development of new technology but also on how they remain accountable to their constituencies. The theory is thus in concert with current policies of investment that stress corporate accountability. Chapter 4 outlines a "social frontier" for radical alternatives in corporate development. This frontier involves experimenting with new structures of social accountability in keeping with economic efficiency that guide the private firm to function increasingly in the public interest without government controls.

Although social investors do not normally support whole industries today, a concern has developed in this direction through unions and the use of pension funds. The concern has also arisen among economists who have witnessed the destructive impact of declining industries on employment and the economy. Industrial decline has been studied by economists of different persuasions, such as Lester Thurow, Barry Bluestone, Charles Reich, Samuel Bowles, and Paul Lawrence. In chapter 5 we interpret their findings within a sociological framework and recommend a new pattern of investment policy to treat the social and economic problems of industrial decline.

The criteria for investment at the industrial level are sufficiently complex that we take chapter 6 to discuss directions for social research on these issues. Special attention is given to the role of nonprofit federations in providing the basis for industries to thrive with a minimum of government controls. One proposition offered is that institutional investors can encourage corporate leaders to experiment with new systems of legislative and judicial practice within the private sector to avoid government intervention. The conceptual framework leads investors to think about a creative mix of values in the ideologies of laissez-faire and economic democracy.

The basis for utilizing social criteria to invest in local communities is dealt with in chapter 7. Using the "frontier" criteria described earlier, we formulate a conceptual framework for investing in a decentralized economy. Social investment policy at this level would strengthen local economies while avoiding problems of provincialism and local elitism. The proposed policy includes experimenting with socio-legal inventions like land trusts, worker-owned firms, community banks, and community development corporations. Such entities democratically increase the power of local people to manage their own affairs without government controls while at the same time offering opportunities for trade at national and global levels. The final issue is how future economies can become local and global at the same time. The answer suggested is through social inventions that federate firms and optimize local power in the context of the larger corporate community.

Part III: Global social investment

The need for social investment at the global level is most dramatically demonstrated by the failure of international banks to solve poverty and hunger in Third World nations. These problems persist despite enormous amounts of capital spent to eliminate them. Chapter 8 contends that the reason rests in the continued use of solely economic criteria in banking policies. Our argument is that the economic problems underlying hunger and poverty are caused by social problems that need to be addressed directly in banking policies. In chapter 9 we provide examples of social investment criteria for the World Bank, multinational corporations, and international funding agencies.

In sum, this book provides a conceptual framework for the study and practice of social investment. It offers a basis for developing a professional field of study that integrates social and economic criteria in the practice of financial investment. It is designed to be of practical use to investors and at the same time to serve as a guide to social scientists and economists who must conduct the critical research needed to correct and redirect the investment process.

I want to thank my colleagues in the department of sociology at Boston College for their helpful conversations and their support of the graduate Program in Social Economy and Social Policy, where this book achieved its inspiration. Special thanks to Professor Charles Derber for commenting on some draft chapters and to Professor Ritchie Lowry for his interest in discussing ideas in this field as well as his persistence in the practice of social investment in his own corporation. I also want to thank the graduate students in this Program for the opportunity to share ideas with them and a special thanks to James Meehan for typing some chapters with a fine editorial eye. The professional editorial assistance of Betty Seaver was extraordinarily helpful, as was the assistance of Cambridge University Press. Finally, I want to express my appreciation to all the social investors who are challenging tradition and making innovations in this field of finance. Without their courage and imagination, this book could not have been written.

Part I   The idea of social investment

1 The meaning of social investment

We are accustomed in our society to the idea of making economic investments, but not to the idea of making social investments. Social investments introduce noneconomic criteria into investment decisions and thus change the order of business. Social investors are interested in the impact of their investment on people as well as in making a profit. They believe they can maintain economic returns on their capital while expressing a social concern about corporate conduct; that by investing only in socially responsible companies they can have an effect on corporate behavior; and that social criteria can provide incentives for business to function more reliably in the public interest. Other investors hold that social investments will help business become more self-regulating. Still others contend that investments should be directed toward the cultivation of social objectives within the economy. At a more theoretical level, we might say that they are all interested in social development while remaining steadfastly committed to economic development and financial returns on their investment. They all seek to encourage the development of social values within the free enterprise system.

The origins of the movement are hard to trace, but the use of social criteria became visible among large organizations in the 1960s during a period of urban unrest. In 1967 the Ford Foundation, stimulated by a concern already being expressed by church and university leaders, announced that social investments would become part of its philanthropic program. It hoped to increase the impact of its giving by making higher-risk, lower-return investments in minority businesses, housing, and conservation projects.[1]

Churches also took a turn toward social investment during the 1960s. Although it might be said that they have the oldest tradition in this field because some churches refrained from investing in companies producing liquor and tobacco in the nineteenth century, now the churches became interested in a great variety of corporate activities. The National Committee on Tithing in Investments recommended investing in open

1

(integrated) housing and avoiding investment in South Africa. The Cooperative Assistance Fund, initiated by the Taconic Foundation, welcomed social investing by churches. It agreed to assess the likelihood that a company would "show reasonable security and economic return" and "produce institutional change." In 1968 the General Assembly of the Presbyterian Church established an independent corporation, the Presbyterian Economic Development Corporation, to manage the church's unrestricted funds, which were to be spent in higher-risk lower-return ventures in the public interest. One-fifth of the investments and loans went toward housing; two-fifths toward minority economic development; and two-fifths into securities of banks with strong minority-loan records.[2]

More recently, mutual funds, pension funds, and banks have begun utilizing social criteria for directing their stock purchases. The Dreyfus Third Century Fund, for example, is a mutual fund that has set up a special arrangement for its customers to invest with human concern. U.S. Trust, a major bank in Boston, has several officers working with investors on issues of social investment. The Teachers Insurance and Annuity Association and College Retirement Equities Fund (TIAA-CREF), an employee retirement plan with assets of about $9 billion, has been utilizing social criteria in making its investment decisions. The AFL-CIO has established a national committee to develop social criteria for investing its pension funds. Other investment corporations, such as Shearson American Express, Drexel, Burnham Lambert, Travelers Corporation, the Calvert Social Investment Fund, Franklin Research, the New Alternative Fund, the Pioneer Fund, and Pax World Fund, are utilizing social criteria. Numerous universities have been making social investments and are studying the social criteria most appropriate for their portfolios. Indeed, a new field of study is evolving around the proper mix of social and economic criteria for investment.

Investment analysts are interested in developing systematic studies of social criteria to determine their reliability and validity. They are also interested in evaluating the social impact of their investments on investees and evaluating their own efforts on a larger scale of values. There is no systematic theory guiding these separate efforts to utilize social criteria for investments, and almost no empirical research on the issues. The problems in the field have yet to be clarified and formulated for systematic criticism. Indeed, there is need for developing a social science of investment that can track and study these new financial interests.

The traditional field of investment is a well-established course of study in schools of business, but the introduction of social criteria radically changes its conceptual foundation and renders the area of inquiry immensely broad and complex. Yet some investors argue that this step could make it easier to anticipate investment outcomes and make the study of investments more logically complete because social variables have always existed in investment but have generally been left unobserved and unmeasured. By taking account of this larger universe, analysts say they can better predict the results of their investments.

Our purpose here is to clarify the major problems that must be addressed so that systematic studies can begin. The problems are interdisciplinary and need to be confronted by behavioral scientists, corporate lawyers, social investors, and business scholars. The problems are the following. First, we want to clarify the kind of institutional power exercised by investors and the abuses that may exist in the investment field. This tells us something about the type of research needed and any relationship it may have to the public interest. It also tells us how investment analysts must be properly informed in making decisions and how researchers must take account of the interdisciplinary nature of their studies. Second, we want to define the meaning of *social investment*. It is important to find a common concept for the construction of a theory and the conduct of empirical studies.

The problem of power

It has become important to consider social investment today partly because staggering amounts of money are becoming concentrated in fiduciary institutions with an extraordinary power to control investment capital. Public and private employee pension fund assets, for example, are over $1 trillion in the United States, and are expected to reach $4 trillion in the 1990s. The nation's three major religions – Protestant, Catholic, and Jewish – have invested billions in the stock market and other types of securities as well as directly in commercial businesses. In 1970 religious organizations had over $22 billion in the stock market alone. The Corporate Information Center of the National Council of Churches studied ten denominations with portfolios totaling $1.5 billion. Universities have invested still more billions and, like churches and unions, have become interested in the social direction of their investments. The significance of these astronomical sums is that they are in the hands of a relatively small number of trustees. This fact leads to questions of public policy in regard to control and raises issues about the direction of investments.

The control of securities by trustees in financial institutions has been heavily criticized by unions. In 1975 the hundred largest banks managed over $145 billion in pension funds; Bankers' Trust and Morgan Guaranty each managed nearly $15 billion. Unions are protesting on the grounds that pension funds are legally "employees' money."[3]

The House Banking and Currency Committee has documented many abuses in the use of managed funds, including undue pressure by fund managers on big corporations through "self dealing" (favouring stock investment in the bank's best loan-customers). Banks have developed interlocking directorates that allow them to pyramid control over sectors of the economy, an illegal practice that may result in government action. Also, bank trustees may hold stock in declining companies in which they also have loans because the bank fears large loan losses, but such support can be detrimental to fund beneficiaries, who stand to lose when a company finally goes under.[4]

The return on pension funds administered by the banks is very low, so low that many fiduciaries have raised questions about prudence and legality. *Fortune* describes the situation: "During the five years ending in 1975, the total return (i.e., including dividends, which are assumed to be reinvested) on the Standard & Poor's 500 . . . was 3.3. percent. The median rate of return for managed pension fund stock portfolios over those ten years was only 1.6 percent."[5] During this same period FHA and VA federally guaranteed home mortgages were paying 8 and 9 per cent; passbook accounts, 4 and 5 per cent. Managed pension funds could have been socially directed and received a higher rate of return. The trustees could have invested more profitably in low-income housing and even charitable enterprises.

Trade unions have learned that trustees not only lose pension money but also invest in corporations opposed to union interests. For example, trustees may invest in conglomerate corporations that move plants overseas. They may invest in businesses where their union is fighting nonunion employers. Pension trustees have also invested heavily in the South, where companies have relocated to avoid unions.[6] In the face of these realities, the AFL-CIO has begun to look into the possibilities of obtaining greater control over pension funds and of utilizing investment criteria that would be in unions' interest.

The AFL-CIO Executive Council in 1980 adopted a broad policy regarding the investment objectives of union-negotiated pension funds. The policy was based on a Department of Labor study showing that pension funds in the private sector will own between 54 per cent and 60 per cent of all corporate stock by 1995. State and local government pension funds were not included in the study, but estimates suggest that they will own 10 per cent to 15 per cent of the corporate stock. In the manufacturing industries, the funds will amount to over $2 trillion; in transportation, to over $400 billion; in the service sector, to almost $400 billion; in the construction industry, to about $300 billion; and in the financial sector, to some $200 billion. The council's social criteria for investment included job creation through reindustrialization, advancing "social purposes such as worker housing and health centers," improving "the ability of workers to exercise their rights as share-holders in a coordinated fashion," and excluding "from union pension plan investment portfolios companies whose policies are hostiile to workers' rights."[7]

The council further recommended that the AFL-CIO work toward the establishment of an independent institution to facilitate the investment of pension funds for reindustrializing the nation's economic base. "The new institution should be directed by a tripartite board of directors, equally representing the labor movement, employers and the public. To assure that the interests of the pensioners are protected, the government should guarantee a minimum return on the invested funds." The council proposed that the institution be created by Congress, and that it be given specific responsibilities and authority to pool monies, grant guarantees, and negotiate investments.

Pension funds supply the principal part of corporate equity and bond purchases in the United States. In the 1970s, corporate pension funds alone brought more than half of all new equity issues. Pension funds normally provide about three quarters of net corporate bond purchases. Employee pension funds are therefore critical to the operations of the basic financial institutions which, in turn, control the formation of capital in the United States.

Financial institutions utilize both voluntary and forced savings in the formation of capital. Among voluntary household savings, between one-fifth and one-quarter goes into insurance and pension fund plans. This pool of capital becomes available to financial institutions who use it to purchase equities (or make bond loans) to the largest 500 corporations. Forty per cent of the remaining voluntary household savings goes into accounts at commercial and savings banks to finance housing, small businesses and durable consumer purchases. The remaining twenty-five per cent is directed toward the purchase of corporate equity. The main form of forced saving in the United States is pension fund contributions made as a commitment to retirement income. These forced savings come under the management of insurance companies, bank trust departments, or the corporate employers' own investment department.[8]

Corporations have increasingly become indebted to outside sources of funding and the irony is that the outside sources are funded by the corporations themselves through pension payments. The credit market supplied over 50 per cent of total capital expenditure of the non-financial corporate sector in 1979. The credit markets (bond and equity shares), in turn, are dominated by the pension funds and the insurance companies that represent them.[9]

Pension funds are thus critical to the process of capital formation in the United States. They are organized in both the private and public sector.

Private sector pension plans are trusteed and subject to the Employee Retirement Investment Security Act regulations. Under the authority of this Act the employer establishes the fund. Unions cannot be sole administrators of these plans, but they can jointly administer them with management if they win this arrangement through collective bargaining. At present over $100 billion of pension assets is jointly trusteed. But few unions have really chosen to exercise their power over specific investment decisions.

Public sector pension plans operate under various government rules. The Federal government pension system can be held only in the form of federal government securities. Most state and local government plans are also trusteed under state laws, with standards and restrictions on trustee behavior varying between states. Employees frequently have some representation on these trustee boards but joint control is not guaranteed (see figure 1.1).

Financial institutions normally adhere to a "Wall-Street Rule" in exercising their voting rights. This means that institutional investors agree informally not to take an active role in pressing for change in the corporations in which they invest. They prefer to pass the proxies to management. If they disagree with management, they tend to sell their shares. An important control is exercised by these institutions, however, through creditor relationships and the placement of appropriate persons on the board of directors in sympathy with their interests. This policy is followed because the key decisions flow from the boards themselves. The boards determine the rate of profit retention, the rate of borrowing, the rate of share issuance, the location of plants, and the rate of net investment.

Unions have begun to bargain special arrangements for what are called "target investments." For example, the UAW does not have a joint trusteeship, but in the 1979 round of bargaining it won a set-aside of 10 per cent of pension fund growth. This set-aside is to be invested under the advice of a joint UAW-Chrysler Investment Advisory Committee, in mortgage programs and in nonprofit organizations such as nursing homes, nursery schools, and HMOs (Health Maintenance Organizations) in the communities where UAW members live.

The pooling "set-aside" is seen to minimize the risk of utilizing target criteria. In this way no single pension fund risks a significant portion of its portfolio and no individual worker's pension is greatly jeopardized.

The trade unions have a legal case for exercising greater control over the investment of their funds because they are legally defined as "deferred

Figure 1.1
PENSION FUND SIZE AND SCOPE

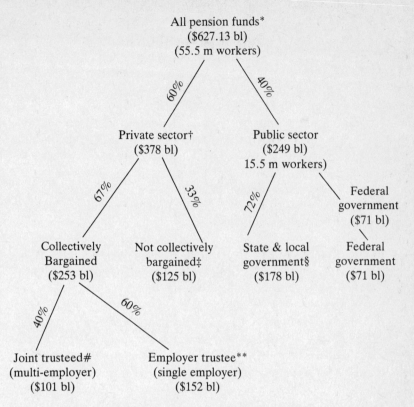

All pension funds*
($627.13 bl)
(55.5 m workers)

60% / 40%

Private sector†   Public sector
($378 bl)   ($249 bl)
                         15.5 m workers)

67% / 33%   72% / Federal government ($71 bl)

Collectively   Not collectively   State & local   Federal
Bargained   bargained‡   government§   government
($253 bl)   ($125 bl)   ($178 bl)   ($71 bl)

40% / 60%

Joint trusteed#   Employer trustee**
(multi-employer)   (single employer)
($101 bl)   ($152 bl)

* Dollar estimates, 1980. Employment estimates, 1978.
† All of these are trusteed and covered by ERISA. 1970 BLS estimates are that 79% are non-contributory for workers.
‡ Most of these are turned over to banks and insurance companies to manage, or the benefits are contracted to an insurance company directly. Large ones are likely to be managed "in house" by the corporate asset management department.
§ Virtually all defined benefit plans, subject to state legislation. They are *usually* joint contribution, with some worker representation on the controlling boards. Assets can only be invested in federal government securities.
\# Largely defined contribution plans, generally in the building and needle trades.
** Largely defined benefit plans, bargained by industrial unions, such as the UAW, Steelworkers, CWA. (ERISA provides that even if unions do not negotiate joint trusteeships, they are entitled to disclosure of portfolio information.)

Source: Jocelyn Gutchess, update of Ruttenberg et al., *AFL–CIO Pension Fund Investment Study*, August 20, 1980. Quoted in Carol Cleireacain, "Towards Democratic Control of Capital Formation in the United States," in Nancy Lieber, ed., *Eurosocialism and America*, (Phila.: Temple University Press, (1982) p. 52.

wages" rather than as a "gratuity" provided by the company. In 1949 the Supreme Court upheld and quoted with approval the National Labor Relations Board contention that "realistically viewed, this type of wage enhancement or increase, no less than any other, becomes an integral part of the entire wage structure, and the character of the employee representative's interest in it, and the terms of its grant, is no different than any other case where a change in the wage structure is affected."[10] Subsequent Court decisions have taken the position that pension contributions by employers must be viewed as part of wages. Once a contribution has been made to the fund, the money no longer belongs to the employer. The tax laws strengthen the argument by making pensions tax exempt. Union leaders point out that employees pay income tax when they receive their pension benefits. The issue of who holds the final authority over the investment of pension funds is still under study, but the unions clearly have a strong legal position.

Who should exercise power over pension funds and the billions of dollars channeled through mutual funds and banks from other sources will be a major legal issue in the future. Capital can be invested only through a legal framework, and the legal framework is currently bound by the assumption that investments are made in the economic interest of investors, not primarily in the interest of investees or the public. It is therefore essential to examine investment law because the new investors are beginning to create a process of investment that is on the legal borderline. They open a new frontier for sociological research: "public interest" law.

The legal framework

A major question for socially oriented investors concerns the "prudent-man" ruling in 1830 by a Massachusetts court in *Harvard College* v. *Amory*. Harvard College and Massachusetts General Hospital were to be beneficiaries of $50,000, a sum that Francis Amory was to manage. Amory lost $20,000 while managing the trust and was sued by Harvard College on the count that he invested not in public securities and conservative stocks but in manufacturing and insurance stocks that were considered not safe. Amory argued that he handled the trust in good faith, and the court ruled in his favor:

All that can be required of a trustee to invest is, that he shall conduct himself faithfully and exercise a sound discretion. He is to observe how men of prudence, discretion and intelligence manage their own affairs, not in regard to speculation, but in regard to the permanent disposition of their funds, considering probable income, as well as the probable safety of the capital to be invested.[11]

The argument against social investments originates with this historic ruling that asserts that trustees must be guided primarily by the economic interests of the beneficiaries and the safety of the money. Many state statutes provide lists of permissible investments (e.g., government securities, first mortgages on land, high-quality bonds) for public monies, which place still more restrictions on the options of trustees. Public pension funds have over $200 billion in assets and represent almost one-third of all pension investments. The rulings and the statutes hence have a significant impact on the direction of investment.

Michael T. Leibig makes a strong argument that social investments are permissible and even mandatory under conditions in which beneficiaries claim that social criteria should be used in investment. He points to a variety of decisions in which exceptions were made to the prudent-man rule. Recent cases include *Blankenship* v. *Boyle*, in which a union invested in public utility companies. The companies benefited the United Mine Workers because they bought coal produced by the workers. Subsequent decisions have upheld this principle that a union could receive "collateral benefits" from its investment. For example, in *Withers* v. *Teachers' Retirement System of the City of New York*, the court decided that a nontraditional investment decision of the union to invest in municipal securities at a time when the city was in severe financial crisis was acceptable and did not involve "self-dealing." The teachers, of course, benefited by helping to pull the city out of the crisis. The court said that it was acceptable for a union to invest in a corporation that might enhance the interests of the union as long as there were no self-dealing interests on the part of the executors of the fund to place the principal at undue risk.[12]

Leibig's argument rests on an analysis of the Employee Retirement Income Security Act of 1974 (ERISA), which governs pension investing. Leibig points out that the Act (Section 404(a) (1)) and its legal precedent point to such prudent rules as investing with an eye to the "overall portfolio," "diversifying assets," "looking to the benefit of the participants and the beneficiaries," "avoidance of self dealing," and "taking account of the intent of the plan and the documents" behind the investment. Each rule gives credibility to using social criteria within the law.

In responding to these guidelines on behalf of the social investor, Leibig shows first how the "overall portfolio" may be given greater weight under ERISA than under the common law rule, which had required almost completely separate consideration of each investment. This guideline then is actually conducive to socially beneficial investment policies applied within the context of the overall portfolio. The overall portfolio is judged for its percentage of economic return rather than for each of its consitituent parts.

Second, the principle of "diversifying assets" makes it easier to invest a percentage of the plan's assets in socially desirable investments. The diversification can be made with social criteria. Third, the social investment can benefit the beneficiaries without executor "self-dealing," that is, investments can be made in collateral investments, as in the case of the coal miners and the teachers in New York City. Fourth, the rule that the investment is intended to aid "participants and beneficiaries" could be interpreted to mean current employees of the firm in which the investment is made. An Employee Stock Ownership Plan in which employees are also beneficiaries is particularly applicable to this interpretation. Fifth, the rule that self-dealing cannot enter into investments as a motive is actually on the side of the social investor whose investments are guided not by self-dealing but by social principles and can be justified on that account. Such investments are therefore not prohibited by this rule. Finally, Leibig points out that the beneficiaries are always important to the investment decision. If investments do not give full consideration to the interests of the beneficiaries and participants, the fiduciaries can be held in violation of the trust. Clearly, then, if beneficiaries mandate social criteria for their investments, the fiduciary is obligated to follow that mandate.

Other questions concerning the right of investors to use social criteria involves the Internal Revenue Service. In 1970 a taxpayer asked whether an amendment to an unemployment benefit trust permitting low-risk income-producing investments that served a social purpose would affect the tax-exempt status of the trust. The Internal Revenue Service approved the amendment with the following statement:

Although the proposed amendment expands the factors that may be considered by the trust in formulating its investment policy, the amendment does not affect the purpose of the trust ... low-risk investments that produce income and also serve a social purpose will not be considered a diversion of the corpus or income from the trust's purpose even though such investments yield a rate of return lower than that in the current market.[13]

Clearly, there are some legal risks that attend social investment, but social investment can be made properly without penalty under the right conditions. We must now determine the exact meaning of social investment.

The concept of social investment

The scientific meaning of investment focuses on its economic functions.

Economists generally distinguish between the "aggregate investment function" and the "individual investment decision." *Aggregate function* refers to the relation of the producers' net acquisition of capital goods (buildings, equipment, and inventories) to the process of production in the economy as a whole. It has a twofold importance to economists. First, it means economic growth, that is, increase in the rate of output. This was studied by the classical and neoclassical economists under the designation *capital accumulation*, and by Karl Marx. Second, it means the maintenance of full employment and the full utilization of existing resources. The second aspect has received attention largely because of the influence of John Maynard Keynes.[14]

The individual investment decision by economic agents is often construed as a present sacrifice for future benefit. The investment can be variously reasoned but is always toward an economic end.

Investment decisions of economic agents include an individual's buying a bond, planting a seed, or undertaking a course of training; a firm's purchasing a machine or constructing a building; and a government agency's building a dam. Productive investments (such as planting a seed) necessitate a social sacrifice of current consumption and may be distinguished from financial investments (such as purchase of a bond), which reduce to an exchange of titles to consumption between two economic agents.[15]

Economic definitions of investment generally ignore the social factor. The result is a distortion of reality and a lack of precision in predicting investment outcomes. For example, economists usually disregard the social fact that the "rate of production" is highly interdependent with types of labor-management organization within industry. To neglect a fact like this, of course, means losing track of a large part of reality and then suffering the consequences in poor predictions. Also, the maintenance of full employment is generally considered an outcome of economic variables, but it also happens to be a social goal that was introduced as a "function" in Keynesian economics. It actually represents only one social outcome (goal) of investment among many others, as we shall see. Such functions are simply not recognized as "social" in economics. Finally, the individual investment decision is also conceived in purely economic terms, entirely omitting social goals. But social investors are now creating social goals and making the social factor more obvious.

The concept of social investment does not have a history behind it as does economic investment. Its definitions are quite current and are debated in the field. They begin by differentiating social investments from economic investments. For example, James Hutchinson and Charles Cole offer three categories defining investment. The first category is "totally neutral investment alternatives," by which is meant an economic investment without noneconomic considerations. The second is "socially sensitive investment policies," which involves a social criterion introduced after the traditional economic criteria are considered. The third is "socially directed investment policies," which includes those permitting the "sacrifice of safety, return, diversification, or marketability" or those that consider an objective not clearly "related to the interest of plan participants or beneficiaries as such." The authors approve of investments in the first category; they tentatively approve of those in the second category; and they disapprove of those in the third category.[16]

Hutchinson and Cole's viewpoint is debatable because it assumes that economic investments are neutral, that they have no inherent social preference or social value. It misses the fact that all economic investments include a social factor. For example, an economic investment of pension funds is structured for social purposes; retirement can be a social goal. But this is not an isolated case. Investment in transportation, food, or communications industries also involves social goals. Social factors exist in all business investments: the whole investment process has a social foundation.

Hutchinson and Cole's viewpoint implies that a gradient-priority exists from the purely neutral (economic) investment to the purely social (noneconomic) investment. Put another way, they believe that economic criteria have priority over social criteria. Furthermore, the viewpoint assumes that by increasing attention to social values in making an investment, we automatically diminish economic values (profits). These assumptions are not necessarily warranted, and they actually misconceive the social investment process.

In reality, social considerations in the investment process can actually enhance the possibilities of economic return. The fact is that the two values (social and economic) are not necessarily exclusive. Social and economic values can be maximized together, and this creative synergism is the practical direction taken by social investors today. Research has shown that the combination of these two factors can enhance investment. Instead of each detracting from the other, a synergy can occur in their joint application. Social investment has outperformed traditional investment designed to maximize profits alone. The reason may be that the search for information on the social factor increases the expertise of the investor in predicting the behavior of the firm.

Two facts stand out from the current evidence. First, social criteria that traditional investors say lessen profits have instead increased profits. For example, although social investors have been severely criticized for not investing in nuclear facilities, a *New York Times* comparison of the stock performance of nuclear and nonnuclear electric utilities revealed that the latter won easily. Also, social investors have been told that they would lose profits by avoiding companies doing business in South Africa, yet a major bank's analysis of the performance of Fortune 500 companies between 1977 and 1982 found that those not operating in South Africa outperformed the others in eighteen of twenty quarters.[17]

Second, social investors seem to be earning better profits than are traditional investors in overall performance. Between 1974 and 1982 investment in the social fund of Dreyfus Third Century returned 373 per cent, compared with 110 per cent for investment in the Dow Jones Industrial Index. The Pax Fund's net asset value per share rose approximately 61 per cent between 1975 and 1980, a bad period for mutual funds and the economy as a whole. In 1983 Pax provided a total return (capital gains plus income) of 22.9 per cent. The ethical accounts of Franklin Research were up over 50 per cent from mid 1982 through mid 1983; the Dow was up only 44 per cent.[18] These cases do not prove that social investments always outperform conventional investments, but they do demonstrate that they can perform better. Indeed, these cases even suggest that further research might indicate social investment could outperform conventional investment on a regular basis.

The definition of social investment

Social investment has a meaning at different levels of interpretation. We shall call them *descriptive, normative, analytical and theoretical*.

Descriptively, *social investment is the allocation of capital to organizations in the context of society with the purpose of making economic returns*. This is a fact about all investment activity, which is always conducted in a social context with the intention of financial returns. Private investors do not normally take social factors into account, but they are still there and important for our purposes to assess what happens. Our argument is that all capital allocations designed for economic returns to the investors take place factually in the context of society and are therefore technically social investments. This includes all business investments.

Normatively, *social investment is the allocation of capital to advance the social and economic well-being of people*. Social investors are interested in their own economic well-being as well as the well-being of those in whom they invest; they expect some return for their money but they differ from traditional investors in being conscious of and selective of the social factors they want to include in their decision making. They also differ because they are interested in the economic well-being of their investees. Traditional investors may be interested only in their profit. Put another way, social investors have an interest in the personal and economic welfare of their investees as well as in their own economic interest. Their purpose is to advance the well-being both of themselves and of recipients in the context of advancing the larger interests of the society.

Analytically, *the allocation of capital has a social framework:* social factors enter into every economic decision. For example, every profit-oriented investor must take account of the social organization of a targeted business so as to predict financial outcome. Profit-conscious investors at best assess the stability of labor–management relations in a company in estimating its profitability. Labor unrest is a social factor that can vitally affect company profits; a major strike could severely damage returns. Also, traditional investors may assess the likelihood that a company will become embroiled in a court case contesting product safety; stock dividends depend upon avoiding criminal liabilities. Moreover, it may be important in some instances for profit-oriented investors to evaluate the probability of a company's foreign subsidiaries being nationalized; foreign assets lost thereby can be considerable. The list of noneconomic factors affecting the economic outlook of a company is a lengthy one, but the point is that *the social behavior of the company is critical to the assessment of any economic investment.* In the final analysis social criteria always interconnect with economic criteria, and make it important for all investors to be interested in social studies of a company. As economic investors come to see the interdependence of the social and economic well-being of a company, they may begin to act normatively like social investors. They might, say, look closely at the quality of working life and the accountable behavior of a company because such factors bear so strongly on the company's productivity and capacity to make profits.

Theoretically, the allocation of capital affects the power and values of people in society in various ways. The nature of the impact is the subject of social theory. The *Britannica World Language Dictionary* defines *investment* in economic terms as "the placing ... of money ... to gain a profit" but does not stop there. The dictionary also notes that *investment* means "to give power, authority or rank to." Here we see the sociological implications of investment. Capital investment is the conferring of power and value on people and organizations in society. The political issue of investment in the economy in this case then becomes, who should get the power and how can value be properly achieved by this investment?

In theory, investment can do the following: it can retard or advance progress: it can perpetuate corporate dominance or it can provide the ground for greater corporate freedom and equity in the economy; it can increase or reduce government controls over the economy; it can destroy people's lives or it can give life to people. The societal impact of investment is multifaceted. Investment, therefore, requires study regarding its relationship to "class structure," "community," "power," and "culture." Investment is a social activity because it vitally affects so many aspects of the corporate system and may even determine the whole course of society.

Our primary interest is in normative investments made in the private sector of business. Our task is to develop a theory and recommend research based on this unique practice. Social investors are similar in many ways to traditional investors in that capital is allocated without any reference to a theory of societal development. A social theory is not available to investors so that its propositions can be refuted or substantiated by empirical studies. There is no sufficient body of knowledge that can adequately guide either the social or business investor to allocate capital in the interest of the larger society. There are thus limitations on the ability of all investors to judge adequately the full impact and meaning of their decisions in a societal context. This is the reason for creating a scientific foundation for professional studies in this field. Our purpose here is to examine the current activities of investors so as to forge a better framework for evaluating financial decisions in the interest of all parties affected by the transaction.

We will now consider how investors make decisions about investments, and how social and economic factors interconnect in the decision-making process. The actual investment activity can then provide the information we need to develop a theory of social investment and lay the foundations for future research in this field.

2 The activity of social investment

The field of social investment is the study and the practice of making financial decisions in the context of society. Our interest here is the way various types of investors make decisions with a social purpose, with special emphasis on how they integrate social and economic criteria of investment.[1]

Social investors in the United States may be divided into two groups: (1) direct investors, and (2) stock market investors. The distinction between the two types is not always sharp, but in general direct investors place funds into nonprofit corporations or socially structured corporations, seeking a direct impact on the development of social values in the corporations. Direct investors may aim to solve social problems through such organizations or help them realize social goals by supplying capital to them. These investors include business corporations that give directly from their pretax profits for "charitable purposes", corporations making low-interest loans to assist in community development, and nonprofit foundations designed especially to invest for social (educational, religious, and health) purposes.

Stock market investors differ from direct investors in that they purchase shares selectively in profit enterprises listed on the New York and American stock exchanges. They invest for economic gain but utilize social criteria in making their decisions. They do not always exercise direct influence on the corporations, nor do they seek to contribute directly to the welfare of a particular community. In some cases they have a direct influence on a specific type of corporate policy, as we shall see, but on the whole their power has rested in their general influence on the direction of profit enterprises through their use of social criteria. They choose their investments according to an openly communicated set of ethical guidelines. They seek to sensitize business leaders to social issues. The amount of influence they exert is problematic. The amount of stock they own in a corporation is usually a small percentage of the total, but it can have a significant effect on the decisions of some executives, although other executives successfully fight or ignore their efforts. Let us now look at the decision-making patterns of each type of investor.

Direct investors

Business corporations were not permitted to spend funds for social (noneconomic) purposes until 1935, but since then they have gradually been increasing this activity. In 1980 businesses gave $2.5 billion, manifestly for charitable purposes, mainly to education and secondarily to health and welfare programs. They are permitted to contribute up to 10 per cent of their pretax profits but normally do not do so.[2]

According to a study commissioned by the Council on Foundations and conducted by the research firm of Yankelovich, Skelly and White, Inc., chief executive officers (CEOs) of the Fortune 1300 corporations were favorable to corporate donations. The study involved interviews with 220 CEOs from a cross-section of major industries. Approximately 90 per cent of the companies represented had made monetary contributions to nonprofit organizations in the previous fiscal year and practically all claimed a history of such giving. On the average the companies made contributions of 1.1 per cent of pretax net income. Companies of intermediate size (annual sales ranging from $50 to $100 million) gave 1.3 per cent of their pretax income; smaller companies, 1.7 per cent. About six in ten planned to increase their contributions in the next few years.[3]

Private funds spent directly for charitable purposes are considerable. In 1980 private foundations, corporations, organizations, and individuals spent $47.74 billion. Of this amount, $49.93 million was contributed by individuals, mostly to religious institutions. The next-largest recipient was education, followed by health, sciences, welfare, and the humanities. The 21,600 private foundations organized for philanthropic purposes (about 1,500 company foundations and about 22,000 family foundations) spent $2.4 billion. There were also 245 community foundations, with assets of $1.52 billion.[4]

Investments made by organizations for social purposes have been supported from conservative, liberal, and "alternative" standpoints. The theory behind the politics of investment has yet to be scientifically tested, but the arguments are important to follow. From a conservative view, business investments are designed for social purposes in some cases, to increase profit in other cases, and to reduce the necessity for the government to control sectors of the economy in still other cases. The idea is that voluntary charitable investment by business reduces the need for government expenditure and intervention: if business participates to a greater extent in the support of community causes, in addition to acting in its own profit interest, there is less necessity for government to meet community needs, and thus fewer government controls.

Liberal investors have similar interests, but they are more willing to make concessions on profits, and in some cases may even accept financial losses to achieve social goals. They want to help to solve community problems such as crime, bad housing, and drug addiction, in the belief that the investment will aid business in the long run. For example, they might take a loss by investing in low-income housing to relieve a crowded tenement district partly because the investment may be repaid by a better pool of employees. They will occasionally place more emphasis on the total well-being of the community than do conservative investors.

Alternative investors are also interested in integrating social and economic criteria, but their main purpose is to alter the structure of business so that it does not cause social problems. In other words, the structure is to be accountable to its constituencies "automatically" and will operate by its nature in the public interest. Alternative investors have been supporting worker-owned and -managed firms, cooperative credit unions, community development corporations, land trusts, and consumer cooperatives in the private sector. Alternative investors sometimes envision such businesses as forming the social foundation of the economy.

Let us consider these three approaches to investment in order to examine the relevance of their separate policies to a theory of social investment.

The conservative approach

The President's Task Force on Private Sector Initiatives, introduced by the Reagan administration, has set special goals for business. First, it has recommended that by 1986 business should contribute at least 2 per cent of pretax net income to charitable nonprofit organizations. Second, business should double corporate community activities by helping employees use their volunteer potential and by finding new avenues for giving. Third, business should reassess its pattern of cash contributions and other forms of public involvement to ensure that the most pressing community needs are being addressed. The task force recommendations simply seek to increase an activity that has already been evident to some degree in the business community.

Government leaders know that business often makes a social investment in its own economic interest. In this case, they point to the fact that business can invest to its own advantage in community development in many different ways.

First, a company may want to provide financial assistance for community development while making a profit. For example, Consolidated Edison of New York has sponsored a ten-year program of special electric rates to commercial and industrial businesses that locate or expand their activities in several depressed areas of the city where less than 50 per cent of Edison's electric distribution capacity is utilized. The rate incentives could increase the company's profits and could also lower charges to customers. In addition, the lowered rates could help create jobs if the program succeeds in returning the use of electrical distribution facilities to their previous maximum levels. The idea is that everybody can win by Edison's cost reduction. The policy is a social investment in the interest of both the company and the community.

Second, corporate gifts or low-interest loans can upgrade the public image of a conservative company (a very large gift or a very low-interest loan would signify a more liberal approach to social investment) even as they aid the community. For example, for sixteen years Eastman Kodak Company in Rochester, New York, has funded Teens on Patrol, who help local police in parks, recreation areas, and housing projects. The program started in 1967 when the company was seeking more effective channels of communication with the city's minorities and has contributed to the community and to the company's public relations.

Third, a company may act in the public interest and at the same time in its own marketing interests. An instance: ITT Continental Baking Company has launched a nationwide three-year project, based on scientific research and directed toward health professionals, to improve the nutritional status of citizens over sixty-five years of age. Continental earmarked $200,000 in starter grants for university and professional research on the relationship between eating patterns and the aging process. It has worked in conjunction with the American Association of Retired Persons and instituted a national survey to measure the opinions, attitudes, and habits of the elderly in regard to nutrition. This type of investment pays off for the company through what some observers call "political marketing": the company seeks scientific knowledge on nutrition for the elderly, who are one of its key markets, and at the same time establishes very important contacts with professionals who help "legitimate" its business.[5]

Fourth, companies may take advantage of special tax incentives available for community development projects, such as the neighborhood assistance programs. The programs are supported by state tax laws that encourage private-sector participation in the redevelopment of low-income neighborhoods. The programs vary in different states, but most of the projects eligible for neighborhood assistance tax credits include employment and training, educational assistance, medical assistance, and crime reduction.[6]

Fifth, the conservative approach to social investment includes the work of business leaders who make a special effort to meet human needs: many business people work within the profit framework of enterprise but emphasize "community service." An illustration is James W. Rouse, who has been meeting housing needs for decades with new patterns of community development, and who represents the borderline between the conservative and liberal approaches to investment.

Since the 1950s Rouse has worked on slum renewal and planned communities that take account of human needs. During the time of the civil rights movement he put together the Columbia project, a 17,000-acre, racially integrated community with innovative social services. More recently he launched an attack on slum housing, beginning with the dilapidated Adams-Morgan section of Washington D.C., where he renovated a tenement and introduced a set of human services as part of the project. The housing complex is now owned by Jubilee Housing, a church-affiliated, not-for-profit organization, which operates a clinic and job-placement service, provides drug abuse counseling, and helps tenants manage the building. Rouse is now seeking to duplicate this success story in other city slums. His aim is to provide desirable housing for people with incomes of less than $9,000, and he has organized the not-for-profit Enterprise Foundation, which will build on ideas from the Jubilee project. Long-term funding will come from a taxable profit-motivated real estate subsidiary of Enterprise, which will develop festival marketplaces in small cities (the Faneuil Hall Market Place in Boston is an example of a former such activity of Rouse's). Investors have begun to rally around the idea with $15 million in donations and challenge grants. The Equitable Life Assurance Society is providing below-market-rate loans as part of its social investment program, and Rouse has already put some money to work to obtain favorable project terms. Enterprise has deposited $100,000 with the United Virginia Bank at 6 per cent interest, for which the bank will provide a mortgage at 9 per cent for a Lynchburg, Virginia project. So far the average Enterprise apartment rents at under $200 per month. Rouse's work is an example of social programs designed innovatively within the enterprise system. It is supported by church and business groups seeking to invest with a social purpose, and is often connected with what we are describing as the liberal approach to investment.[7]

Conservative business leaders are becoming interested in socially directed investments because they believe that business can do well and "do good" at the same time. They recognize that business and society are interdependent, and that the success and safe operation of business are dependent upon support from the community and the building of a common social foundation. Many companies have developed social policies based on this political philosophy.

The liberal approach

While conservative investors develop social goals and maximize their profits, liberal investors make concessions when it comes to profits and in some cases may even take short-term losses to combine public relations with social objectives. They hope generally to optimize (not maximize) profits in the long run, and are sometimes willing to sacrifice economic returns so as to realize their social purposes. Careful studies are needed to evaluate fully the liberality of a corporate investment, but we will nevertheless attempt to illustrate the kind of corporate action that suggests a liberal character in the following examples.

Aetna Life Insurance set a target of $30 million in social purpose investments for 1982 and authorized rate concessions of up to 5 per cent on social investments. Chemical Bank created its Urban Housing Unit to stimulate housing construction in low and moderate-income neighborhoods in New York, and to respond to minority-owned businesses, while realizing that it might only break even in this experiment. Cigna established an annual budgeted target for social investments expressed in terms of interest-rate concessions. Citibank, a subsidiary of Citicorp, has developed a number of high-risk, low-return lending programs to help create jobs and revitalize neighborhoods threatened with economic decline. Morgan Guaranty Trust organized its Community Relations Department to handle social investments in large-scale enterprises and minority-owned financial institutions. Prudential has geared its social investments toward neighborhood projects, such as the $1.4 million loan to the O Street Market in Washington, D.C., and the $2 million investment to assist the Local Initiatives Support Corporation to provide decentralized funds toward residential, commercial, and industrial redevelopment nationwide. All the above corporate actions are suggestive of liberal investments, even though in other cases some of the same firms have acted quite conservatively. Such social investments have economic purposes but are distinguished by a conscious plan to meet social needs: investors plan for a reduction in profits as part of the investment. They may not see a way to maximize social and economic factors together in one decision.

Aetna Life experimented briefly in 1981 with a system designed to measure the degree of difference between what we are calling conservative and liberal investments in real estate. It developed the following format:

Part I: Basic Positive Value of Normal Real Estate Investment – e.g. creates employment, contributes to local tax base [conservative];

Part II: Avoidance of Undesirable Impacts Upon Environment – e.g. conforms to existing zoning regulations, building codes and pollution standards; does not generate excessive traffic [conservative];

Part III: Achievement of Special Social Responsibility Objectives – e.g. minority employment, increase in low-moderate income housing, assistance to the elderly [conservative – liberal borderline];

Part IV: Sacrifices Required to Achieve Social Responsibility Objectives – e.g., sacrifice of risk-avoidance for rate of return standards [liberal].[8]

The format is biased because it ignores the negative end of the continuum, that is, the degree to which the real estate industry exploits people and the land, but the point is that there is a gradation in the norms of social investment. Real estate investment generally makes some social contribution – if only by paying taxes and creating employment opportunities for the community – but the further it goes in sacrificing economic returns, the more the social motive dominates its character. Certain investors accent social over economic returns, although the norm is to integrate these values.

Industries differ in the degree to which they are involved in liberal investment. The life and health insurance industry has been significantly involved in liberally oriented social investments and gifts. In 1982 it reported on a "decade of social progress," noting that in 1972, 147 insurance companies had participated in the first "Social Reporting Program"; in 1982, 228. In 1972, the reporting companies had contributed $418.6 million for community and charitable causes; a decade later, $71.6 million. In 1972 social investment loans totaled $449.2 million; in 1982, $1.3 billion.[9]

Corporate gifts to community causes in 1982 included such categories as arts and cultural programs, minority affairs, programs for the handicapped, local health, community improvement, housing, crime prevention, drug and alcohol abuse programs, day care, antipollution, safety programs, and many others.

Social investment loans are carefully reviewed by companies for their potential environmental impact and community value as well as for *financial* safety and return. Investment in housing facilities represented roughly a third of all reported investments; investment in the environment and in health facilities follows. Examples of specific investments include the following:

A consortium of 10 North Central Insurance companies, both large and small, pooled their resources – funds, skills and manpower – to make loans totaling nearly $1 million to eight community-based businesses.

Over $4 million was made available by a Northeastern company to help finance a badly needed mental health clinic for a depressed urban area.

A $3 million low-interest loan was made to a minority entrepreneur for development of a cable television company.

A $15 million loan to an auto parts plants, which was about to close, saved 1,200 jobs and had a major impact on stabilizing an area characterized by high unemployment.[10]

The terms *loans* and *gifts* are separated for statistical purposes, but analytically speaking even a gift can carry the premise that it is "socially empowering" to the people receiving it. It also has the potential of an economic return; it can be a social investment.

Churches have been engaged in liberal approaches to social investment as well as in alternative approaches. A mixture of social and economic criteria is often utilized by churches in deciding on the direction of their overall investments. They balance the profits they make in commercial enterprises (for example steel companies and parking garages) against their losses from service enterprises with social goals, which include educational institutions, publishing houses, retirement homes, and community development corporations. For example, the United Church of Christ has a large retirement home in Phoenix, Arizona, that represents an investment of about $5 million and at times has lost money. Churches often lose money on such investments but maintain them to fulfill their social values, and counterbalance them by investments in commercial enterprises with high economic returns. The Trinity Episcopal Church on Wall Street in New York, for instance, has commercial assets of more than $50 million. It owns eighteen major business buildings in the city, including the seventeen-story Standard and Poor building. The returns on such properties compensate for losses on its charitable social investments.[11]

The attempt to create a balance between social and economic returns in church investment is similar to the attempts of many social investors in the stock market today, who are able thus to stay within the "prudent-man" ruling stressed in some court decisions. The investment portfolio is evaluated for its total economic returns rather than for each investment.

The distinction between "conservative" and "liberal" investors may occasionally seem to blur, but they both contrast with "alternative" investors on how business should be organized. The aim of alternative investors is to build structures of accountability into the business organization itself so that *social problems are solved in the process of doing business*.

The alternative approach

Some social investors have become aware that business can be structured to be accountable to its constituencies, which reduces the need for government regulations. Its constituencies include employees, customers, buyers, sellers, owners, and citizens in the communities on which business has a powerful impact. Many investors have therefore been encouraging business to bring these constituencies into the decision-making process. For example, investors believe that labor is less likely to rebel or be exploited when it is included in the structure of business management; customers are less likely to go to court or be duped when they become part of the advisory powers and management of a company. For these reasons, many investors have been investing in companies organized in such a way that labor and consumers participate in the direction of the companies.

Other types of business structures have also been found to be of social value. Community development corporations (CDCs), for instance, have been encouraged by investors because they include citizens on their board of directors. CDCs create products and services in the interest of the whole community and can balance high profits made from the sale of one product against losses in another service area that contributes to community development. In the interest of community development, a profitable business in electrical supplies, say, can be balanced against a losing enterprise in housing for the elderly for the locality. Other innovative businesses include *community development credit unions*, which provide low-interest loans to socially oriented businesses; *land trusts* to protect land from exploitation; and *business cooperatives* structured to be accountable to their customers and employees.

Lynn Rhenisch studied the decision-making process of alternative investors to determine the criteria utilized in providing capital to new enterprises. The investors included the Campaign for Human Development, the National Rural Development Finance Corporation, the Sisters of Charity of Cincinnati, Hilltown Community Development Corporation, the Institute for Community Economics, the Reformed Church of America, and the Industrial Cooperative Association. She found them interested in supporting enterprises that show a high degree of employee ownership and participation in management, community support behind the enterprise, a company structure responsive to employees, intentions of locating in low-income neighborhoods, and the potential to contribute directly to community needs. Each investor differed in regard to the emphasis given to these factors, but they were all interested in the development of socially structured businesses. Rhenisch generalized from their individual priorities to determine the types of social and business criteria that were held in common (see list below).[12]

Types of criteria used in making socially responsible investments:

Social criteria
1. Democratic nature of enterprise.
2. Types of products or services delivered and their relation to social needs.
3. Degree of community representation.
4. Constituency served (e.g., low income).
5. Relationship with the community.
6. Structure of organization (e.g., non-bureaucratic).
7. Nature of profit distribution (e.g., equitable).
8. Type of ownership (e.g., worker, consumer).
9. Environmental impact.
10. Status of workers: working conditions, benefits and degree of participation.
11. Impact on community employment, capital flows and neighborhood development.
12. Sensitivity to cultural and ethnic characteristics of the community.
13. Potential for furthering economic democracy and similar forms of social change.

Business criteria
1. Degree of financing needed (partial/total).
2. Readiness of group to handle financing.
3. Management experience and skill.
4. Legal status.
5. Organizational structure and management–employee relationships.
6. Strength of business plan (prospects for profitability and self-sufficiency).
7. Type of market (social/geographic considerations) and marketing plan.
8. Access to other resources of capital (banks, finance corporations, government, other lenders).
9. Access to and need for technical assistance.
10. Relationship to competitors.
11. Past performance.
12. Credit history.
13. Current assets and liabilities.
14. Type and amount of collateral available.

The Rhenisch study reports that the Institute for Community Economics has a revolving loan fund for direct loans to low-income communities for the "acquisition or improvement of land by community land trusts, new housing, cooperative commercial development, and the purchase of tools and supplies." Its emphasis is on the development of community land trusts and limited-equity cooperatives to provide land, housing, and productive resources for low-income people.

The Campaign for Human Development is a federated arm of the Catholic Church in America and provides $5 million annually to socially accountable enterprises. It emphasizes "work owned and managed businesses" that produce and process manufactured goods. It also supports "tribally-owned businesses which are worker-managed enterprises: innovative businesses that are created and wholly owned by non-profit community organizations which have significant worker and resident participation; innovative consumer cooperatives, where the business is owned by consumer members."

It is noteworthy that although in the past these foundations have been described as "alternative" in their emphasis on creating business "structured" to be accountable to their constituencies, such investments are becoming more commonplace in the conservative business community. For example, Prudential recently made a $25 million investment to assist 1,200 employees of General Motors to acquire a GM bearing plant in Clark, New Jersey, that GM had intended to close. The employees sought to own and operate the plant through an employee ownership trust.

In the cases studied by Rhenisch, investors assessed social and economic risks together before investing in the companies. The investors wanted to know, for instance, how much experience the entrepreneurs had with employee ownership and self-management so that they could predict entrepreneurial success. The investors asked employees about their "social plans" as well as their "financial plans." They considered the availability of experts in employee ownership in the area should the new entrepreneurs need assistance in troubled times, just as they would judge the availability of experts in finance and marketing through programs of the Small Business Administration. The investors saw that the criteria for evaluating the risk of a social return depended upon the organizational skills of the entrepreneurs in the same way that evaluating the risk of economic returns depended on business skills.

Alternative investors often take higher risks and lower returns on their investment than traditional investors, but this need not be the case. For example, an investment in the Self-Help Credit Union in North Carolina is insured up to $100,000; no risk is involved. The union was started to provide loans at reasonable interest rates to worker-owners.

Low- and middle-income workers can borrow up to $45,000 each to start a worker cooperative, convert a traditional business to a cooperative, or invest in an existing cooperative. The credit union can also make loans directly to democratically structured organizations. It is a vehicle for churches and nonprofit organizations that need security but still want to make an alternative investment.

The National Federation of Community Development Credit Unions

(NFCDCU) is an organization of 100 low-income, financial cooperatives in thirty-four states. The Community Development Credit Union is a customer-owned bank, and provides technical assistance to credit unions. Deposits are insured up to $100,000 per depositor. Again, it is a no-risk alternative investment.

Many charitable foundations – among them the Vanguard Public Foundation, the Haymarket People's Fund, and the Liberty Hill Foundation – make gifts to socially structured enterprises and thus contribute toward the social development of the economy. They are *not* investments in the sense of providing an economic return, but when directed toward the development of such enterprises, the gifts take on one of the traits of social investment.

Affirmative Investments is an alternative investment advisory service, organized as an independent for-profit corporation and capitalized by three public foundations and the United States Trust Company Bank in Boston. It advises on investments that are not conventionally marketed on the stock exchange and extends special consideration to disadvantaged groups and communities.

The activity of direct investors differs from that of stock market investors, although the social criteria can sometimes be the same. Stock market investors have more difficulty influencing established corporations where the percentage of their shares is small. They are normally working with very large companies; their tactics and strategies for social development are therefore different and require special attention.

Stock market investors

The character of the stock market has changed markedly in the past forty years. Before the middle of this century, market customers were wealthy individuals for the most part, but in the succeeding decades they have been gradually replaced by institutional investors. Adolf Berle first noted this shift in *Power without Property* (1959). He saw the big fiduciary institutions such as pension funds, insurance companies, and mutual funds beginning to take over the stock market, and expressed concern about their new power. The trend has continued so that today two-thirds of market customers are institutional investors and one-third are individuals. Typical trading is now by large-block purchases, and new records for volume trading continue to be established.

Institutional managers reported equity assets of nearly $250 billion in the last quarter of 1978. In that year only 10 per cent of the typical U.S. family's investment was in stocks. Further, only a few of the largest corporations were still owned by individual investors. The following table illustrates how institutional funds' assets have come to surpass family wealth.[13]

Social investment brokers deal almost exclusively with conventional stock, bond, and money market investments. They differ from traditional brokers in that they maintain social screens. Examples are presented below.

The United States Trust Company of Boston has been providing comprehensive portfolio management to socially concerned individual and institutional investors nationwide for more than ten years. It maintains an active research program on corporate social performance. A reasonable minimum new account size is about $750,000. In the seven years ending December 1986, the median account had an 18 per cent compound annual return.

The Franklin Research and Development Corporation is structured as a cooperative and gives participants a share of the profits and a voice in management. Investments are made with a computerized social screen developed over a four-year period. The screen lists about 1,100 companies and deals with ten social issues. An advisory letter is periodically sent to all clients.

Shearson/American Express has a special staff to give advice to union pension funds and individual portfolios based on social criteria. It specializes in building portfolios without securities in companies involved in South Africa, the weapons industry, and nuclear power.

Mosely, Hallgarten, Estabrook and Weeden has a staff person to advise on social investments. Assistance is provided with regard to stocks and bonds, retirement plans, tax-advantaged investments, and portfolio management.

The Calvert Social Investment Fund is a large mutual fund that uses a comprehensive program in selecting securities. It invests in companies according to their record for product quality, environmental responsibility, participatory management, equal employment opportunity, and workplace safety. The fund is also concerned about issues of nuclear power, armaments manufacture, and investment in countries ruled by repressive regimes, such as South Africa.

Calvert's Money Market Portfolio invests in U.S. government agency securities such as the Student Loan Marketing Association, the Federal Farm Credit Association, and the Bank for Cooperatives, as well as other agencies that meet the social criteria of its mutual fund. The money market portfolio provides for automatic cash withdrawals and check writing in amounts of $250 and above.

The Working Assets Money Fund is a money market fund with an investment adviser dedicated exclusively to managing socially responsible invest-

Table 2.1. *Estimated Concentration of Wealth In the United States, 1979*

Family or institutions	Estimated wealth and worth (billions of dollars)
California State Public Employee and Teachers Retirement System	13.3
TIAA–CREF (Private College and University Retirement Plan)	9.4
New York Life Insurance Company Investments	9.1
New York State Common Retirement Fund	6.8
New York City Employees Retirement System	6.7
New York State Teachers Retirement System	5.8
United States Steel Employees Pension Plan	4.1
duPont Family Investments	4.0
Mellon Family Investments	4.0
General Motors Retirement Program for Salaried Employees	4.0
New Jersey State Common Pension Funds	4.0
Wisconsin State Board of Investment	3.8
General Motors Hourly-Rate Employees Pension Plan	3.7
General Electric Pension Plan	3.6
Ohio State Teachers Retirement System	3.4
Texas Teachers Retirement System	3.4
New York City Teachers Retirement System	3.3
Ford Motor General Retirement Plan	1.8
Harvard University Portfolio	1.5
Ford Family Investments	1.5
Getty Family Investments	1.5
Hunt Family Investments	1.5
Rockefeller Family Investments	1.5
ATT Bell System Savings Plan for Salaried Employees	1.5
Eastman Kodak Retirement Income Plan	1.4
Bethlehem Steel and Subsidiary Companies Pension Plan	1.1
Union Carbide Retirement Program for Employees	1.0
Pennsylvania Bell Telephone Plan for Employees Pension Benefits	.6
Tennessee Valley Authority Retirement System	.5
Yale University Portfolio	.4
Grumman Corporation Employees Retirement Plan	.4
Kennedy Family Investments	.4
International Paper Company Employee Retirement Plan	.3
Goodrich (B.F.) Pension Plan	.3
Sears Roebuck Employees Savings and Profit Sharing Plan	.2
Delta Pilots Retirement Plan	.2
United Mine Workers 1974 Pension Plan	.2
Sheet Metal Workers National Pension Plan	.1
Carpenters Pension Plan of Ohio	.1

Primary source: Pension Investments: A Social Audit (New York: Corporate Data Exchange, 1979), adapted by Ritchie Lowry.

ments. It invests in money market instruments that finance housing, small business, renewable energy, higher education, and family farms. It avoids financing enterprises that pollute, build weapons, discriminate against women or minorities, produce nuclear power, treat employees unfairly, support repressive foreign regimes, or shut down plants in the U.S. and shift jobs abroad.

A recent survey of the attitudes and practices of institutional investors by the Investor Responsibility Research Center provides data on the values and norms guiding institutional decisions. The Center found that among these investors certain criteria offer reasons for investing in selected corporations and other criteria offer reasons not to do so. Favored investments included corporations with *good records of equal employment opportunity, occupational health and safety, environmental protection, product quality and safety, fair labor practices, job creation,* and *a willingness to disclose information on those matters.* Some of the social criteria employed to preclude investment were more controversial. They excluded corporations *that were located in South Africa, that produced nuclear weapons, expressed antiunion policies, exploited consumers, exploited developing countries, or engaged in producing or selling liquor, tobacco, or gambling devices.*[14]

Mutual funds and banks depend for the selection of social criteria upon wealthy customers such as unions, churches, universities, and other institutions as well as rich individuals. Examples of how fiduciaries and their customers have chosen various criteria are noted in Table 2.2. These represent only recent trends in priorities for investment at the corporate level. Other criteria are developing for investors as new dimensions of social responsibility are seen to be compatible.

When unions control their own pension funds, they have often used social criteria for their investment. Preliminary investigation shows that investments favored by unions include companies showing a good record of *job creation and housing construction,* and companies *directly engaged in social services,* such as health centers. Unions have avoided investing in companies that *violate regulations of the National Labor Relations Board, are involved in South Africa, discriminate against minorities and women, violate health and safety regulations, engage in community redlining and foster urban decay, pollute the environment, participate in the nuclear power industry, relocate factories overseas, and are nonunionized.*[15]

A variety of approaches

Theodore Purcell studied the 1970s increase in stockholder resolutions to a point that 112 corporations were presented with 130 shareholder resol-

Table 2.2. Social criteria utilized by selected companies (examples)

	Favor						Avoid		
	Equal employer	Occupational safety	Environmental protection	Product quality	Community development	Worker ownership / Community participation	Nuclear plants	Nuclear weapons	South Africa
Mutual Funds									
Working Assets	X	X	X	X	X	X	X	X	X
Calvert Soc. Inv. Fund	X	X	X	X		X	X	X	X
Dreyfus	X	X	X	X					
Parnassus	X	X	X	X	X	X			
Pax World	X		X					X	
New Alternatives			X				X	X	X
Investment Advisers*									
FDRC	X	X	X	X		X	X	X	X
U.S. Trust			X	X	X	X	X	X	X
Affirmative Investments†	X	X			X	X			
Corporations									
Aetna Life	X		X				X		
Travelers Corp.		X	X	X					X
Control Data	X	X	X						

* Investment advisers such as Franklin Research Development Corporation (FRDC) have a social screen policy within which clients are offered choices. Screening is able to be done on any issue. The same policy applies to brokers, such as Robert Schwartz at Shearson/American Express, Mark Fisher at Lehman Brothers, and Susan Hickenlooper at Bartlett & Co., as well as a number of other brokers and advisers.

† Affirmative Investments advises only on non-marketable securities, i.e. limited partnerships and venture capital. My thanks to Ami Domini and Patrick McVeigh for assisting me with this information.

utions on questions of social responsibility. Twenty-eight resolutions were withdrawn in 1979 following an agreement between the proponents and the companies involved. The remaining 102 resolutions were brought to a vote at annual meetings, at which forty-six survived to be considered again the next year. To survive, the resolutions had to receive 3 per cent of the vote to come up again the second year and 6 per cent for the third year. The main concerns were *business investments in South Africa, trade with repressive governments other than South Africa, nuclear power plants, redlining and community reinvestment, domestic political activities, employment of former government officials, domestic labor practices, and proposals to military contractors for converting to peacetime production.*

Most of the shareholder resolutions were coordinated with the aid of the Interfaith Center on Corporate Responsibility (ICCR), an organization connected with the National Council of Churches. The Council includes seventeen Protestant denominations and 170 Roman Catholic religious orders and dioceses. Church shareholders alone presented more than eighty-two resolutions in 1979 to sixty-one U.S. corporations, among them thirty on South Africa. The ICCR also sought support from other institutional investors for the resolutions introduced by its members.

Dr Ritchie Lowry, in a study of different strategies used by stock market investors, classifies their actions as "passive" or "active" with varying substrategies in the "selecting, avoiding, and encouraging" methods of investors. For example, a passive investor simply chooses stock in a company with a desirable record without any further action; some fiduciary companies, like Aetna Life and Casualty, may appoint executives specifically for this purpose. An active investor, on the other hand, targets firms in order to act directly on company policy, attempting to influence policy through stockholder resolutions and personal contacts with top executives. An example would be the church-related stockholders who negotiated with First National Corporation of Boston, and whose efforts resulted in the corporation's agreeing not to renew existing loans to the South African government and not to make new loans.

A passive investor avoids certain stocks and takes no other action, as for example, when TIAA-CREF, a pension fund, in 1978 did not invest in companies conducting a major portion of their business in liquor or tobacco industries. On the other hand, an active investor winnows stock by diversifying ownership in firms when they do not respond to stockholder actions. Smith College, for instance, sold its share of Firestone in 1977 after no satisfactory answers were received to its inquiries about the company's activities in South Africa.[16]

The activity of the stock market investor in shaping company policy has been debated for its legality and its effectiveness. The effectiveness of stockholder investments is, of course, highly interdependent with its legality. To illustrate: when Protestant churches in Puerto Rico sought to place stockholder resolutions on the ballot for the annual meeting of Kennecott Copper in 1971 with the aim of requiring the corporation to submit a plan on how it would protect the island environment during excavation, management refused permission. The churches protested to the Securities Exchange Commission, only to find that the SEC supported management's stand. The SEC based its decision on Rule 14a–8 of the 1934 SEC Act, which gave the right to turn aside proposals "submitted primarily for the purpose of promoting general social, economic or political causes not related to the company's business." The churches lost the stockholder battle, but succeeded in raising island resistance to the copper negotiations – which have not yet been concluded, partly because of the issues raised earlier.[17]

A number of changes in SEC rules have broadened the opportunity for stockholder protest. One recent case involves the Sisters of Loretto, a teaching order of the Catholic church that became concerned about the rights of miners working for the Blue Diamond Coal Company, who asked 300 individuals to buy one share of stock as a basis for monitoring the activities of the company. Blue Diamond would not register the stock of the new purchasers, arguing that such purchases should be made only for profit motives, whereupon the Monitoring Project sued Blue Diamond. In early 1982 the court ruled in favor of the project: "Shareholders have the inherent right to assert their individual interests within their Company, however bizarre, unpopular, or unusual they may be."[18] It also directed the company to pay the legal fees involved.

Shareholder resolutions have increased since the first socially related shareholder resolution, filed with Dow Chemical in 1969, questioned the morality of producing napalm. By 1982 shareholder activists had filed hundreds of resolutions related to all kinds of social issues, and on behalf of small shareholders on such issues as cumulative voting and executive compensation. Still, the SEC continues to act largely in favor of management by proposing new shareholder rules that may slow down or deter proposals from social investors.[19] As a consequence, some stock market investors have looked into the feasibility of exercising a controlling interest in selected cases by taking bolder steps toward controlling votes to change the board of directors directly.

Pension fund executors have the capital to exercise this type of control over corporate behavior, and some pension authorities have begun to move in this direction, for example, the appointment in 1980 of a governor's task force to look into the proper role of investment for the pension funds of the state of California. The result was establishment of the Pension Investment Unit (PIU), which the task force instructed to identify potential invest-ments that would (1) promote economic development within the state while not simply displacing existing capital investment; (2) earn competitive yields and thus insure beneficiaries' retirement income, and (3) meet socially responsible criteria. Noting that pension fund liquidity require-ments are lower than those of other investors, the task force held that pen-sion funds are uniquely suited to investments that promise good long-term returns, and therefore recommended establishing a relationship between pension fund capital and such spearhead industries as semiconductors, com-puters, telecommunications, and bio-engineering. It also recommended that all public retirement funds adopt the State Teachers Retirement System Guidelines for a responsible investment policy that avoids actions or investments that "serve to undermine basic human rights or dignities." This could be done by a proxy voting strategy in favor of resolutions that "prevent, reduce, or eliminate social injury," and by exercising other share-holder rights.[20]

Here we see a policy that supports stock market investments to obtain direct control over corporate policies so as to promote economic growth and employment in a state, and at the same time selectively to persuade companies to improve their policies on human rights. This is a mixed case of social investment policy aiming both for direct control of companies, and for influencing firms through stock market investments guided by social cri-teria. It may be a future trend in the field of social investment.

The mix is especially evident in the management of pension funds. The Taft-Hartley Act banned establishment of funds managed solely by unions (except when negotiated through collective bargaining) but permitted exist-ing union-controlled funds to continue. At present there are 9,000 joint trusts with $50 billion available for investment. The AFL-CIO is currently negotiating to obtain more union control over pension funds and the direc-tion of investments.

In San Francisco the Building Trades Council has already established a foundation to act as a conduit between the unions' pension funds and build-ing projects. Elsewhere the marine engineers are using their pension fund not only to *construct union-built ships* but to form a *union-pension-owned company to operate ships crewed by union members*. In the Twin Cities, a group of union pension funds has joined local governments and private mortgage bankers to set up the *Family Housing Fund for low- and moderate-income families*; the pension funds are guaranteed a 13 per cent return on investment. Unions are clearly on the move to direct investments along lines that will benefit their interests, and they remain open to broader government policies to direct investments in the public interest.[21]

Professional associations have also taken strong positions on social accountability in business as the basis for judging investments. For example, the National Association of Accountants appointed a committee in 1974 to develop a list of taxonomic categories on "corporate social performance." The key categories were: human resources, community involvement, physical resources and environment contributions, and product or service contributions. Each was subdivided into a list of social concerns, such as "providing equal job opportunities for all persons" and "providing warranties for product." A survey of 261 accounting leaders ascertained opinion on whether each of the concerns was important enough to be ranked and distributed in an information system.[22]

Terry McAdam surveyed opinions by business executives, corporate lawyers, and union leaders to devise an independent set of social categories for judging corporate performance. His detailed list of social criteria for investors can be summarized as follows: product safety, ethical marketing practices, employee education and training, corporate philanthropy, environmental control, external relations (including community development, government relations, disclosure of information, and international operations), employee relations (benefits and satisfaction with work), minority and women employment and advancement, and employee safety and health.

An important point is how investors balance the social and economic risks in investing. There is an expectation in social investments – unlike that in conventional investments – that the entrepreneurs will achieve their social objectives and that there will therefore be a "social return," a risk that must be balanced against economic returns. Social investors are assisted in their decision making by research organizations and information networks, of which the following are examples.

The *Council on Economic Priorities* conducts research regularly on the social performance of business corporations and publishes its findings in monographs and newsletters. It focuses especially on military spending, energy resources, fair employment practices, and environmental impact. Council staff testify before congressional committees, and the national press reports regularly on their findings.

The *Interfaith Center on Corporate Responsibility* coordinates church investment studies and advises on stockholder resolutions. It coordinates more than 100 resolutions each year on such issues as plant closings, nuclear weapons contracts, export of dangerous pesticides and drugs, investment in South Africa, and nuclear energy. It also maintains the Clearinghouse on

Alternative Investments and publishes information on corporate conduct as well as a monthly newsletter, the *Corporate Examiner*.

Still others: The National Action/Research on the Military Industrial Complex (NARMIC) publishes lists of U.S. corporations with subsidiaries in South Africa, manufacturers of nuclear weapons, and the top hundred defense contractors; and *Good Money*, a bimonthly newsletter of information on social investment and independent research monographs. *Resource Publishing Group, Inc.*, publishes the *Concerned Investors Guide*, which provides a five-year performance history of over 1,400 New York stock exchange companies in the areas of environment, fair labor practices, product safety, occupational safety and health, antitrust actions, nuclear industry, South Africa, and weapons contractors.[23]

Stock market investors continue to expand the criteria they deem important for investment. In a recent newsletter from the investment firm of Franklin Research, Milton Moskowitz includes the following questions in a checklist for the evaluation of companies.

1. Does the company contribute more than 1 percent of pre-tax profits to charity?
2. How many minority group members work for the company – and how does that compare to minority representation in their main employment centers?
3. Does the board of directors have a black and a female member?
4. Is there a profit-sharing plan?
5. Is the company noted for its nauseating commercials?
6. Is employee turnover high?
7. Has the company been cited regularly by the Federal Trade Commission for misleading and/or false advertising?
8. If the company is active in South Africa, has it signed the Sullivan Principles?[24]
9. Is the company always acquiring other companies?
10. Did the company cave in to the Arab boycott?
11. Did the company cave in to the Moral Majority and act as a censor of TV programs?

These questions are designed for social investors, but they raise still larger questions for research on public policy. What political philosophies motivate social investors? What do they see for the future? How far can social investors go in controlling – not simply recommending – standards for corporate conduct? What will happen to the free enterprise system if control over stocks becomes still more centralized in fiduciaries? The answers to these questions depend upon surveys and studies about what is happening in the investment field today.

Other questions follow for purposes of scientific research. Is a theory of investment emerging from the practices of social investors? Is it possible to formulate a theory of investment that takes into account the values of democracy and justice in a free enterprise system? How can social theory provide guidelines for empirical research in this field?

The answers to these questions are the subject of our next chapter. We shall find that the former questions on public policy and the latter questions on scientific research are closely intertwined.

3 A theory of social investment

The practice of social investment is so varied and the interests of institutional investors so diverse that it would seem impossible to devise a social logic that would characterize social investing as a profession. Most fiduciaries today argue that it is quite inappropriate to develop a social theory. Nevertheless, this is our task. We want to broaden our understanding of social investment as a practice by formulating a conceptual framework to account for it. This framework, essential in building a foundation for social investment as a professional field of knowledge, can then be utilized for empirical research as well as for critical judgments about investment practice.

A theory of social investment is valuable to investors in three ways. *First*, it provides insight into the complex nature of investment within the context of society by broadening the vision of investors and encouraging them to take more factors into account, which should in turn increase their capacity to predict the outcome of their decisions. *Second*, a theory provides testable propositions for social research. Such research should yield facts that improve the accuracy and the wisdom of investments. *Third*, the insights gained from theory and research should encourage investors to become more self-critical about investment as an institutional activity. Impartial studies of investment outcomes should quicken the ability of fiduciaries to discern whether investments function in the public interest as well as in the interest of their clients.[1]

Our purpose is to initiate a conceptual foundation for investment theory starting with the concepts of sociology and related disciplines. We propose to identify key variables explaining the direction of capital allocation as a guide both to investors and researchers. We will focus on concepts of social governance and distinguish our position from a statist approach to financial investment.

A sociological perspective

The master concept for investment theory was formulated in the origins of

38

sociology as a discipline. Sociology emerged in the nineteenth century with the concept of "society" as distinguished from the "state," "church," "business," and other related organizations. "Society" was conceived as generic to these organizations, and now becomes a fundamental concept in a theory of social investment.[2]

Other concepts arose in such disciplines as psychology, anthropology, and political science, and each discipline had its own central concepts, such as "self," "culture," and "government." Each developed its own conceptual language as part of the new social sciences. Economics developed separately from the other social sciences and evolved its own analytical terms. It was founded upon the premise that certain laws of the capitalist system could be studied and analyzed without reference to a concept of "society" or the "self." Its academic language was drawn primarily from an interpretation of how the business system operated according to natural law. Its concepts revolved around profits, wages, supply and demand, market forces, interest rates, and so on without systematic study of the social foundation upon which they rested.[3] The history of economics shows intellectual trends in which the concept of society was introduced (e.g., institutional economics) but economists as a rule have studied market "regularities"; studies are confined largely to the conceptual universe of economics without a sociological framework.[4]

A sociological framework is important because it bears on the outcome of investment policy and research. The economy in this framework is conceived not as a separate entity without social foundations but as an institutional part of society. In this view society is more generic than the economy. It is the highest unit of analysis and therefore contains the higher analytical value.[5] Let us now examine the meaning of the economy as a part of society and look at the economy as a social phenomenon.

The social economy

Some scholars define the economy as a system within which people compete for economic advantages. Others define it as a system characterized by *profit-seeking firms operating in a competitive market.* Still others define it as a system for *allocating scarce means whose ends are determined by society.* The ends, of course, are not within the scope of economics.[6] These textbook definitions represent part but not all of the reality. Our scope of social inquiry is broader and in some ways more complex. It includes these attributes and much more in what we may best denominate the social economy.

The social economy refers to the human organization of production and allocation of goods and services in society. In this picture, the economy is socially constructed and is composed of human institutions and values. It is regulated by folkways, customs, and values, as well as by the government and private interests, and has a culture that changes and develops over time. The economy is socially designed at its roots and is not simply an expression of natural law outside society.[7]

This concept of the social economy includes *the allocation of abundant means* as well as scarce means; it involves *cooperation* as well as competition, *social advantages* as well as economic advantages, *nonprofit firms* as well as profit firms. It includes all income-producing firms showing value in their dimensions of production, distribution, and consumption in society. These additional factors, though they may be ignored by financial analysts, are important to social investors. Farm goods can be *abundant* and be allowed to rot in government storehouses. This is a concern to social investors; the problem is political and not merely economic. Enterprises are engaged in *cooperation* as much as in competition, and cooperation can be more important than competition in determining the size of profits. Enterprises express *social advantages* as well as economic advantages, and can be vital to productivity.

Many businesses compete for social advantages through their quality of working life and find that higher quality pays off in financial returns. They compete through better safety, and health and recreational opportunities for employees. High-tech firms offer competing programs in tuition-free education; auto firms compete for the best safety devices; and so forth. Interdependent with economic advantages are social advantages, which interest investors because they express human values.

Social investors have shown a strong interest in supporting *human values* in the economy. The enterprise system is founded on such great values as freedom, justice, and democracy. They are vital to the well-being of the economy, even though economists do not normally study them as part of their discipline. The value of *freedom* is bred into the system in multifaceted ways; it is supported by common law and by statutes that protect business from state controls. The value of *justice* is formally expressed and interpreted daily in the work of the Antitrust Division of the Justice Department and regulatory commissions of the government as well as in the ethical codes of trade associations. The value of *democracy* is formally expressed in the organization of consumer federations, farm marketing associations, and trade unions as well as in business law. The Labor–Management Reporting and Disclosure Act specifies how democratic practices are to be followed by trade unions. These values are an unstudied part of economics and finance, and yet they are fundamental to the practice of social investment.

Social investors have shown that the economy in which they invest cannot be defined only in terms of profit corporations. *Nonprofit corporations* are equally important. Gifts and loans are transferred daily from profit to non-profit universities and hospitals. Business itself contributes directly to education and health institutions. In turn, universities and churches invest regularly in the stock market for their own profit, and utilize their profit to advance their own educational and religious values. The social economy is in this way a complex set of interdependent corporations designed to promote human values as well as self-interests. Thus we shall argue that the investor is involved in the social development of the economy and that sociological theory can give direction to investment policy and research.

Social development

A concept of social development was an implicit part of nineteenth century thought. It can be discerned in the work of such contrasting sociologists as Karl Marx and Herbert Spencer, for whom development was a part of social evolution. It had a progressive meaning in which the state played a secondary role in the context of society. For Marx, society was the modern battleground for proletariat and bourgeoisie. He saw a revolutionary transformation developing in which the state would eventually "wither away," but only after major social changes in the economic order that would dissolve the basis for a class structure. For Herbert Spencer, development was explained by the principles of differentiation and integration. Social institutions become more individuated, and each stage of institutional development requires a greater degree of differentiation and then a higher form of social integration.[8] Marx and Spencer were miles apart in most of their thinking, but they both viewed social development as the redirection of human resources toward a higher expression of social life.

This early sociological perspective became a background for studies spanning more than a century. The intellectual effort to explore the social and economic forces of development includes the work of such scholars as R. H. Tawney, Joseph Schumpeter, John R. Commons, Wesley Mitchell, John Maurice Clark, John A. Hobson, Selig Perlman, John Bates Clark, A. C. Pigou, Thorstein Veblen, Vilfredo Pareto, Talcott Parsons, Neil Smelser, Arthur Stinchcombe, and many others. They have worked in subdisciplines called economic sociology, institutional economics, and social economics, and their work there has yet to be related to the emerging field of social investment.

Let us now identify key issues in the field of social investment that have been a part of the subdisciplines connecting sociology and economics. We want to make specific assertions about the nature of development that are directly relevant to decision making in social investment.

Creative conflict

We begin with the broad assertion that development has the quality of a dialectic: it consists of opposing forces that clash and differentiate and finally integrate into new forms. This assertion is related, of course, to the great dialectical questions of Hegel and Marx in the nineteenth century, but it is not our task here to explore these connections. It is our task to show that social investment is part of a process of creative conflict, that is, a process of integrating social and economic criteria for the allocation of capital in the social economy.[9]

Social investors face a conflict between ideologies, but they also must translate the conflict into the theoretical arguments of the profession. For example, they have the mandate to resolve legitimate differences between social and economic development, to reconcile the opposition between fulfilling individual and community needs, and to find a reasonable solution between the needs of investors to make money and the potentially oppressive impact of their investment on people. The trustees of capital are thus engaged in a daily process of conflict resolution. They may at times attack the problem of class structure directly in their decisions, and at other times simply advance a new level of consciousness for investors in regard to the way human development can provide profits for everyone. We have seen social fiduciaries invest in the rehabilitation of slums in ways that pay dividends for both investors and investees. They show the potential to alter the self-paralyzing conditions of capitalism and lay the seeds for a new system of enterprise. They are a new breed who believe that it is possible to enhance both human and material resources together.[10]

Let us look at the dialectical forces at work and the possibilities for creative resolution in the field of social investment.

Human vs. material resources

Human resources are the basic elements of life that sustain our capacity to survive in society. They include knowledge, imagination, sensitivity, feelings, authority, skills, and intelligence. Cultivating resources within society requires educational systems, governments, religious organizations, business enterprises, art associations, scientific organizations, and so forth.

Social development means increasing the use of these resources by bringing them to a higher level of expression.

Material resources are represented by natural properties in the earth, water, air and in human properties such as technology and modern factories. An increase in material resources is often measured by productivity and profits in the business system. These resources co-exist and act interdependently with human resources.

Social development is the cultivation of human and material resources together. Each separate resource, human (social) and material (economic), then becomes a part of the master dialectic of development.

```
                    ——— Social development ———
Material resources ————————————————————————— Human resources
```

The integration of these polar resources is the overriding dialectical problem for the investor. Every decision for allocating capital should contain this question: how does this investment enhance human and material resources at the same time? Put another way, how can the cultivation of one resource advance the development of the other? A specific example: how can the earth be cultivated with care while people share equitably in an increase of productivity and economic returns? How can new technology advance economic returns and simultaneously develop human imagination and help build social institutions? These are the kinds of questions that social investors have already begun to raise. This does not mean that they can be answered fully in every investment, but it does indicate a principle in decision making that cannot be ignored. It is our task to clarify the meaning of this dialectic in a theory of organizational development.

For the moment we move selectively along one side of the master dialectic. We will examine only the development of human resources and then only the problem of social organization within this focus. We will not examine the complex interplay between human and material development, that is, the process of combining social and economic notices together in decision making, the problem of combining economic development with organizational development, and the impact of investment on the social economy of investees. Nor will we pursue the issues that exist in the cultural content of social investment, judgments about allocating capital differently to educational, religious, scientific, political and recreational institutions. Similarly, we will not examine the problem of investing differently in select industries such as energy, food, and transportation or the issues of investing in sunset versus sunrise industries, or even the question of investing in "industry" versus the "service economy." All these issues become part of a theory of social investment in the long haul, but are set aside for our im-

mediate purposes. We will examine only the social organization of the economy. We will sketch the theoretical issues briefly, but we give them priority
because social organization is a substructural problem, critically positioned
as a theory within the larger problem of cultivating human resources, and
fundamentally related to the development of a social economy.

Our primary task is to identify opposing principles involved in the development of human organization. We shall examine most carefully those contradictions in the "social factor" while keeping in mind that investment
always includes the economic factor and the material well-being of society.

Self-governance vs. command governance

A dialectic operates continuously to transform the governance of economic
life. The economy is based on a system of social governance beset with contradictory principles. *Social governance* refers to the way people manage
their affairs, conscious of one another as part of an interdependent system.
It is a descriptive term but social governance itself plays a role in explaining
the norms of development. It harbors the dialectical principles of organization called self-governance and command governance.

Self-governance refers to the capacity of people to solve their own problems apart from outside controls. This is a most critical principle of social
development, and is based on the assumption that there is a need for
greater expression of self-direction and independence among people at
every level of organization. Command governance, on the other hand,
refers to the resolution of problems through a system of hierarchy and obedience and is the main organizing principle today in the corporate system. It
rests on the assumption that there is a need for order and specialization
among people at every level of organization. These two principles of
governance are central to the dialectical development of a social economy.

Our proposition is that the resolution of the contradiction between these
two principles – self-direction and external control – is the introduction of a
third organizing principle called mutual governance. *Mutual governance*
refers to the capacity of people to resolve their problems through reciprocal
action, which grows from social accountability and equitable participation
in the governance of the economy. The activation of this principle demands
the development of human resources.

The economy has been developing historically through the action of this
principle of mutuality. It can be seen in the early decades of this century in
the rise of the trade unionism; labor gradually acquired new degrees of
equality with management by participating in collective bargaining. It can
be seen in the organization of personnel departments and pension plans in

business corporations; business began to show greater social accountability to employees. It can be observed in the changes wrought by the human relations movement as workers began to participate more in decision making with management. It is evident in profit-sharing plans and labor–management committees that provide oversight in the production process. It is visible in the development of democratic federations, such as trade associations, cooperative leagues, consumer councils, and trade unions. It has developed along with self-governance as an organizing principle of the social economy.

Self-governance is apparent to some degree at every command level of the corporate economy. It exists among laborers in workshops where they have a measure of self-direction. It applies by degree to higher levels of departments and divisions that have autonomy within the firm. It applies most notably to the corporation itself as it takes its own direction independently in the market place. It also applies to industries that are known to be self-regulating in some measure outside the aegis of the state. It applies finally, in relative degree, to the whole economy.

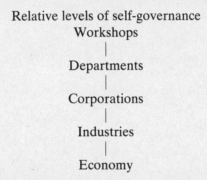

Relative levels of self-governance
Workshops
|
Departments
|
Corporations
|
Industries
|
Economy

The corporation operates typically on a command system but it is also maintained through principles of self-governance and mutual governance. These latter principles are critical to observe, because this is the direction of social development for the future.

The future can be anticipated partly in the way some social investors have encouraged the development of producer cooperatives, community development corporations, consumer cooperatives, community credit unions, and land trusts. The future is more complex than these present firms indicate, but we can see how they maximize self-governance and mutuality at the same time. The election of worker representatives to the board of directors of a firm, or the placement of consumer representatives on the board of a credit union necessarily increases the representatives' formal power. A major development of human resources (e.g., new management skills) is necessary along with the development of material resources for more people in a more accountable manner. The command system does not disappear even in these extreme examples of social governance; it simply readjusts. It becomes more sensitive to corporate constituencies because of the new structure of governance.

We have four principles explaining the governance of the economy:

Figure 3.1 *The governance of the economy*

In sum, *social governance* is a master concept explaining the nature of corporate systems composed of interdependent parts. The successful management of any system requires a conscious recognition of the interdependence of its separate units. *Self-governance* refers to systems based on some measure of autonomy among the separate units. Every system contains parts with people expressing variable degrees of self-direction and independence. *Command governance* refers to systems based on a hierarchy of superordinate and subordinate offices; such organization is based on the principle that people have some measure of dependence on a higher authority. *Mutual governance* refers to the degree that an organization allows for equity in the reciprocal action of its members. Every system expresses some degree of equity and accountability for members at some level of organization.

The organizing principles operate together in the process of development. The problem for investors is to find their creative connection in the development of a social economy. Our assertion is that the principles of self-governance and mutual governance provide the leading edge of development. People strive normally to find higher degrees of self-governance and relatedly, greater self-direction in their organization. They can also show resistance to self-governance because of the tradition of command and the complexities of personal involvement. Our argument is that the resistance is short run; the long-run tendency is to overcome the traditional forms of hierarchy in the quest for higher levels of self-development.

We propose that the principle of mutual governance becomes the mediating action in the strain toward self-governance. It is through new arrangements incorporating accountability and equity that higher levels of self-governance are achieved. The arrangements of mutuality then replace older parts of the command structure without totally displacing it. As new degrees of self-management are established at different levels of organization, the system becomes more socially oriented. People in it become more aware of their interdependence and more conscious of the ways in which they can operate effectively together.

The promotion of effective forms of self-governance and mutuality in modern development becomes the task of social investors. It is combined, of course, with the development of economic resources. The larger problem for the investor is always to combine financial returns with the principle of social governance. The economy and its productivity remains central to all investors.

Cooperation vs. competition

The principle of social governance becomes visible in what may be called the processes of development. Social processes are methods by which people relate to one another to achieve their ends. The most notable process in the capitalist system is competition, but other processes are equally important even though they are less visible. We shall add here *cooperation* and *conflict*, recognizing that there are still other processes that are important to study but that lie beyond our immediate scope.

Competition refers to the way people act against one another within a set of rules to obtain *scarce ends* (goods). *Cooperation* refers to how people act together to achieve *common ends*. *Conflict* refers to how people oppose each other for *exclusive ends*. In competition, some people, but not everyone, normally win some scarce goods; in cooperation, everyone normally wins but not always; in conflict, only one party normally wins but all parties can also lose. These processes operate at all levels of the economy: workshops, departments, corporations, and industries.

In the command hierarchy of a firm, cooperation is usually emphasized among unequals, but more recently management has added competition to promote innovation. This is an important observation for corporate sociologists because consultants argue that competition is the fashion in the best companies today; it was a key attribute reported in Peters and Waterman's *In Search of Excellence.*[11]

Other consultants say that the path to success is the promotion of cooperation and a sense of community in the corporation – a primary argument of William Ouchi in *Theory Z*. Drawing upon a Japanese model of management, many consultants assert that the process of cooperation and community building is the most important attribute of successful firms in the United States.[12] Which process is most important to social investors?

Our position is that competition and cooperation are intricately involved in every organization, but cooperation provides the leading edge in development. Cooperation offers the basis for cultivating the self-governance and mutuality that fulfill human values in enterprise organization. Mutuality leads towards a sense of *community* within a firm, and self-governance leads toward *individuality*. Both attributes are prized by students of organizational development and can be evoked through cooperation. Competition remains important in the strain toward self-development, but there is still the question of whether effective forms of cooperation cannot achieve the same ends. The problem may be solved by learning the most effective methods of cooperation.

Competition among firms is the norm in the capitalist system and is associated with self-direction. Less visible is the fact that they cooperate to promote their self-direction: they cooperate to set the rules for competition. Furthermore, cooperation provides the ground for competing in the public interest. The challenge in promoting cooperation is to avoid collusion and to encourage a higher dynamic in the productivity of industry.

Intense competition among firms leads to corporate conflict and eventually monopoly or oligopoly, wherein a few firms dominate the market. At this point the government intervenes and industry tends to lose its power of self-governance. The task is to learn how government intervention can lead toward self-regulation. Government regulations in some cases can diminish social development. The key question becomes, how can investors help increase the power of self-regulation within industries? The answer lies in supporting firms that cooperate in the public interest and trade associations that set rules for fair competition. Trade associations, for example, have established ethical codes, tribunals, and product standardization in ways that can operate in the interest of the larger society, and reduce the need for government regulations and intervention. Trade associations are grounded in cooperative development; they are mutual aid corporations. Although they have operated against the public interest many times, in the long run they are needed for advancing industrial self-regulation. They are governed formally on the principles of mutuality and self-governance, and provide a basis for building toward a social economy.[13]

Let us examine how the principles of governance combine to advance social development at the separate levels of the corporation and the industry.

The governance of corporations

Max Weber described the governance of corporations in terms of (1) autonomy and (2) autocephaly. By *autonomy* he meant that the "order governing the organization has been established by its own members on their own' authority" as opposed to "heteronomy," that is, imposed by an outside agency. By *autocephaly* he meant that the "chief and his staff" are elected according to the "autonomous order of the organization itself" as opposed to "heterocephaly," that is, a staff appointed by outsiders. Weber described the capitalist system as composed of corporations based on autonomy and autocephaly.[14]

Weber's concepts express the general nature of self-governance in modern business, but they are not adequate to explain the complexity of social development. Private firms are autonomous in the sense that the order of business is established by its own members, but they are not autonomous in the sense that government agencies, trade unions, consumer groups, and powerful competitors may dominate and control their behaviour. They are autocephalous in the sense that the "chief" is selected by the order of the organization itself but not in respect to who "elects" the chief within that governing order. These are the critical questions of development that we want to address.

Internal self-governance

The typical firm is governed by a command system, but simultaneously, as we have said, self-governance operates in the organization of its workshop, assembly line, departments, and divisions. Most important, management consultants have been introducing greater degrees of autonomy at each level and changing the order of command. Similarly, the strain toward establishing new systems of accountability has also been evident by changes in the character of command hierarchy. The changes have been brought about not only by consultants, but also unions, social researchers, and executives themselves interested in a more productive and humane form of corporate bureaucracy.

The process of development toward higher levels of self-governance is normally gradual rather than revolutionary. It has meant accenting new modes of cooperation that change the direction of competition. Internal competition, for example, has been increasingly directed away from self-advancement in a strict line of command toward the larger interests of the firm.

Recent management policies have accented internal competition to promote innovation and greater self-direction on the job. Procter and Gamble, for example, promotes brand competition among its managers to promote higher quality and durability for its products. IBM encourages competition for ideas about new products and then conducts performance "shoot-outs" among competing groups to bring about innovation. General Motors fosters competition among its divisions to obtain better-performing automobiles. Buyers and merchandising vice presidents at Bloomingdale's fight for floor space, and this results in more effective use of the building. An internally competitive process, then, seems to move toward breaking down the more rigid forms of bureaucracy, destroying overly rigid systems of command and obedience, and promoting a greater degree of individuality and self-reliance in the work system.[15]

Some consultants declare that competition tends to bring about domination and alienation in the firm. Procter and Gamble says that it promotes internal competition to "keep from being too clumsy" but that when it goes too far, such competition becomes destructive. Brand managers are then not given adequate information on what other firm brands are doing. Competition by itself breeds what Rosabeth Kanter has described as "segmentation," which keeps departments from engaging in a more useful activity called "lateral communication," a form of "reciprocity" between departments and divisions. Promoting lateral communication allows employees to get essential information about the whole firm and leads eventually to higher levels of innovation and effective management of the firm.[16]

Steps toward greater degrees of reciprocity and equity in a firm can begin in the formal or informal organization. For example, Intell Corporation has experimented with various methods of overcoming the fixed character of its hierarchy by establishing networks of authority in which workers have several bosses, with the purpose of fostering a greater degree of self-management on the job. Intell employees are encouraged to dress informally and to avoid the trappings of status. Most importantly, employees also participate on management councils in an advisory capacity. Tandem Computer Company has flexible work hours, Friday afternoon beer parties, employee stock options, and sabbatical leaves. Polaroid's 14,500 employees have representatives on committees that hear complaints about management policy. Honeywell has 350 quality circles that involve employees in management. The American Center for the Quality of Work-life records two hundred firms with quality circles. In the pyramid structure these are small changes that may seem superficial but are nevertheless experiments that embody the principle of mutuality. They are contemporary expressions of what has been a sea change in employer accountability during the past century, signs of a movement from vertical toward horizontal authority.[17]

We have noted many new systems in this century that involve increased accountability in corporate life so as to correct inequities. They are based on new forms of cooperation and include collective bargaining, pension plans, labor–management committees, grievance committees, auditing procedures, conciliation boards, social auditing, and most recently, new systems of employee ownership and management. The latest development probably represents the most radical departure from the past. Corporations have begun to develop employee ownership and to seat labor representatives on boards of directors. Such self-management requires special attention by social investors. It also requires a new concept of social authority by researchers and theorists because of its critical connection to cooperation and competition.

Weber's definition of authority is important to explain the direction of the latest development in self-management. His concept of authority, *Herrschaft*, expresses a notion of legitimacy that explains best what is happening. *Herrschaft* has been translated at some times as "domination," at other times as "imperial control," but most scholars believe that its true meaning is "rightful rule." Weber intended to say that a command bureaucracy could function effectively only when it was deemed right, fair, or just, and thus legitimate by its members.[18]

A new concept of rightful rule is developing in corporate life, and is beginning to be debated as a result of new legislation called the Employees Stock Ownership Plan (ESOP). Over 8,000 corporations are participating today under an ESOP, and many more can be expected to do so. An ESOP offers the right of employee equity in the firm but does not normally supply the right to vote for the firm's board; it creates a split between the right to ownership and the right to vote stock. It radically alters the concept of corporate authority.

The meaning of stock ownership has changed frequently in the last century. It was once associated with the right to vote for board members and thus the right to influence corporate policy, but it has increasingly meant simply the opportunity to trade for capital gains on the stock market. ESOPs dramatize a major change in the meaning of corporate authority today. Let us look at one example of its impact. The employees of the South Bend Lathe Corporation, a machine tool firm, found themselves its owners through an ESOP but discovered that they had no right to elect the board of directors. They did not object until an important issue arose concerning pension plans, when they became upset about their lack of voting power and went on strike. The irony of workers striking against their company points up the significance of this change in the nature of corporate authority.[19]

What does the change mean for investment research? It means studying corporate experiments in worker ownership, especially when they are combined with training for employee management. Researchers need to find effective connections between new levels of employee ownership and management, between worker self-management and productivity.[20]

Increasing formal modes of employee authority require careful study for their impact on the personal lives of workers. Some research shows that establishing employee ownership can have many positive consequences for employees, and that electing labor representatives to the board can have many positive outcomes. But the process clearly requires special training programs to operate effectively.[21]

What does the change in the nature of corporate authority mean for social investors? It means looking carefully at the process by which worker self-management takes place. Financial investors can make a mistake if they invest in companies claiming formal worker ownership and labor management without also carefully examining the quality of life in the firm. The way in which people relate to one another inside the firm makes a difference in the success of the firm.[22]

What does the change in the nature of corporate authority mean for investment theorists? It means formulating a new concept of authority that includes its inner meaning as well as its outer meaning. The concept of *Herrschaft* refers to an outer authority; for Weber, the forms of rulership through bureaucracy, charismatic leadership, and tradition, are all outer-directed. In bureaucracy, people look for an external command or a rule to guide their conduct; in a charismatic leader, they look for outward signs of what is right or wrong; in tradition, such as the Ten Commandments or the Bible, they look literally for signs of correct behavior. The new concept in worker self-management requires the development of an inner *authority*. It requires new levels of inner direction and self-reliance.

To be effective, this inner development will require cooperation for self-management and a new matrix of lateral relationships that are mutually supportive. It involves a new interpretation of social authority. The data for such an interpretation are present in management theory today.[23]

Rosabeth Kanter found that the most innovative and self-directing firms had cooperative linkages within their governing systems that encouraged employees to form an integrative outlook on their company. The most effective firms developed what she calls a "parallel organization" that coexisted and yet contrasted with the "maintenance organization." The parallel organization accented "problem-solving" (not simply routine operations), focused on "organizational development" (not only production), provided expandable opportunities for employee participation in management task forces (not simply staying on fixed jobs), maintained a short, not long, chain of command, and drew leadership from every level of hierarchy (not simply the high level). The parallel organization could be said to increase in social authority as it decentralizes power and cultivates leadership from the middle and bottom levels of the corporate hierarchy.

The parallel organization may be the basis for instituting what is called "corporate self-studies." Self-studies provide the training for developing a new system of ownership and authority in the firm. A self-study can make major changes take place more effectively if the study committee comprises employees representative of all levels of the corporation. Aided by professional consultants, the committee collects data about the corporation and examines the hierarchy and "corporate culture." Its purpose is to ascertain what steps can be taken to create higher levels of self-development. Employees together with management and owners make the decisions, moving consciously and conscientiously toward shared ownership and higher levels of self-management.[24]

External governance

Attempts to govern corporations from the outside have a history that interconnects with employee ownership. Employee ownership is only a recent example of a century-long struggle to establish internal corporate controls. In the early nineteenth century state controls over corporations were evident and pervasive. States set limits on the corporation's assets, its type of commerce, and the extent of marketing between states. After the Civil War states began to compete with one another for corporate charters and the right to control corporate conduct, and demands for control were extensively lowered. The New Jersey general corporation law in 1875 offered much wider powers to incorporators, and after that date permission to incorporate for "any lawful purpose" was common nationwide.

By the end of the century the governance of large corporations was in the hands of industrial barons, and ownership in the hands of a relatively few individuals and their families. This pattern continues in many firms, but it is no longer typical for large corporations.

After the turn of the century corporate stock began to be sold to the public, and more individuals competed for control. As the amount of stock sold increased, the power of individual stockholders diminished. Outside stockholders were too great in number and too unorganized to exercise direct authority over corporate policy, and accordingly turned their attention toward the stock market itself and away from management. Actual control over the corporation then shifted again, this time to inside executives and managers. Adolf Berle and Gardiner Means documented this shift in authority in the 1930s.

At mid-century, Berle restudied corporate ownership and concluded that control was going outside again, to "institutional investors." Pension funds, mutual funds, and insurance companies were purchasing stocks in large quantities; Berle saw this as threatening to the authority of corporate excecutives. This pattern is still evident today, and social investors are part of it. But we have posited that the effort to increase human resources by promoting greater degrees of employee authority is the leading edge of corporate development for the future.

Figure 3.2
Historic trends in influence over corporate direction

States $\rightarrow$ Families $\rightarrow$ Individuals $\rightarrow$ Managers $\rightarrow$ Institutions $\rightarrow$ Employees
1840   1890   1910   1930   1960   2000

Investment policy is best directed toward decentralizing authority in the firm. This means funding experimental steps toward employee self-management that augments the productive and profit-making capacity of the firm. Employee management is complex, involving the development of a judicial system and work councils organized appropriately at different levels of hierarchy. It involves advancing new systems of lateral communication and employee rights, and can involve new levels of corporate accountability to the community. This type of investment policy is at the heart of dialectical development: simultaneously increasing the capacity of firms to be productive and profitable, and increasing their capacity to be accountable to employees in the context of the community.[25]

The governance of industry

A key problem for industries is developing a capacity for self-governance. To do this effectively they must solve problems in developing productivity, maintaining profit levels, expanding markets, and many other important associated activities. Our special concern, however, is with their capacity to govern themselves socially so as to avoid government intervention. One way to accomplish this end is to promote systems of accountability among the *stakeholders* of the corporation.[26]

Stakeholders of the corporation are people who are affected by corporate policy. They are *direct competitors*, *buyers*, *sellers*, *employees*, *consumers*, *stockholders*, and the community at large. Stakeholders have a special interest in maximizing their economic benefits and in some cases in simply protecting themselves from corporate activity. Some business scholars have asserted that certain stakeholders have a greater interest in shaping corporate policy than do stockholders. Stockholders are usually more interested in the stock market than in the corporation, and are only one "stakeholder" concerned about the direction of corporate policy.

By developing systems of mutuality for stakeholders within the organization of industry, firms can provide the basis for self-governance. By developing measures of accountability for stakeholders at certain junctures of competition, they can reduce the necessity for government regulation. Put another way, the chief end of social investment is to establish self-regulatory patterns among competing stakeholders, thereby transferring the regulatory powers of government to private industry while maintaining a productive free enterprise system.

Our task now is to examine the patterns of opposition and mutuality that have developed among the various stakeholders and to suggest a basis for self-development at the level of industrial associations.

Competitors vs. competitors

According to *Webster's Dictionary*, *mutual governance* exists when two or more associations "have the same or equal claims or in which they have an equal interest and participation." Trade associations fit the bill. They developed in the nineteenth century as a method by which business competitors could advance their common interests: better product promotion, protection from excessive competition, and improving community relations. By organizing democratically, businesses gained in survival ability. Local, state, regional, and national associations together grew in number from 800 in 1910 to 12,000 in 1950; national and state associations alone, from 100 in 1900 to 3,200 in 1980. They appear in almost every trade and professional field of business.[27]

Trade associations seek government protection, especially in the area of export and import. They lobby extensively for tariffs on textiles and apparel, export subsidies in agriculture and aerospace, and at times seek legislation to protect against competition. But trade associations on the whole are antiregulation. They have often organized against government regulations, and their primary interest is to find ways to promote their industries through self-regulation.[28]

Examples of how trade associations reduce the need for government regulation are plentiful. The American Standards Association, for example, standardizes competitive products and thus lessens the likelihood of the expansion of the Federal Bureau of Standards in the Commerce Department. Through its efforts, it is possible for a manufacturer in New York to produce a light bulb that fits a socket in Los Angeles, for a manufacturer in New England to produce a size 5 shoe that fits a size 5 foot in New Orleans, and for a doctor in Pittsburgh to write a prescription that can be filled safely in Denver. The activities of such trade associations are thus a substitute for government regulation.

Studies by the National Chamber of Commerce show hundreds of trade associations engaged in some form of commercial arbitration. The establishment of arbitration boards by trade federations reduces the cost of federal courts and the need for government arbitration.[29]

The cooperative activities of business competitors in trade associations include studying unfair competition, establishing consumer affairs departments, creating uniform cost accounting, collaborative advertising and marketing, encouraging product uniformity in the public interest, creating common product standards, simplifying products, engaging in commercial arbitration, sharing engineering services and research and development facilities, holding trade conferences, political lobbying, and many others.

Trade associations are complex entities that can oppose everything we have proposed as desirable in social development. They can inhibit the self-governing powers of their members, promote government regulations, and act against the public interest. Yet, they also serve as "functional substitutes" for government bureaus, and cautiously considered, they become a part of the social foundation of a self-governing economy.

Buyers vs. sellers

Industry is usually defined as a set of business competitors in the same product line. Its popular meaning refers to competitors in the same stage of product development. For example, *automobile industries* would suggest a specific set of direct competitors, namely General Motors, the Ford Motor Company, and Chrysler Motors. They have their own trade association. But an industry can also be defined as a whole range of suppliers, producers, wholesalers, and retailers in one product line. In this sense *automobile industry* refers to all firms buying and selling products related to automobiles, and would include steel and petroleum firms as well as supply manufacturers, auto dealers, repair shops, and gas station owners. This larger concept affords a different picture of how self-regulation operates: it involves a continuum of sellers and buyers from supply to production to retail. This picture is part of the social constitution of a self-governing economy.

Many trade associations are composed of corporations that are competitively interdependent as buyers and sellers. Conflicts among them may lead to government intervention, but they also have developed systems of accountability that eliminate the government as an outside authority and rule-maker. It is this pattern of social and economic exchange among buyers and sellers that is essential to the social construction of self-regulation in the economy as a whole.

Most people think that a monopoly in the automobile industry means that General Motors has overcome Ford and Chrysler in the marketplace, but this set of manufacturers is only a small part of the larger system of competing corporations. The manufacturers themselves can collectively dominate the remaining infrastructure of suppliers and dealers. The auto dealers, for example, have fought long and hard against the manufacturers as a monopoly that has dominated and not infrequently exploited the dealers for many decades. The dealers organized a national trade association and were then able to establish regulatory agreements in their own self-interest as customers, which reduced the necessity for government intervention on their behalf. The power of the dealers diminished somewhat the need for the government to regulate the conduct of manufacturers.

Trade associations develop norms and regulatory activities in the context of the marketplace. The system is too complex to define in any detail but it can be discussed in principle, with illustrations suggesting the direction of development.

Our theory is based on three assumptions. First, self-regulation works best when opposing buyer–seller federations are relatively equal in power. If one federation is weaker – as were the auto dealers before the mid-century – an industry monopoly sector develops. The economic exchange between the associations is affected by the unequal social exchange; the weak–dominant relationship leads toward economic exploitation and eventually government intervention. Second, self-regulation works best when the two opposing federations have developed techniques of conflict resolution as well as systems of accountability to resolve their problems. If they do not have these systems, government will eventually regulate them in some measure. Third, to be fully functional, the conditions of equality in power and mutual accountability must exist from one end of the industry to the other, from the stage of raw supply for production to the final stage of consumption:

Figure 3.3
Equality and mutual accountability of federations

Raw supplier → Producer → Distributor/Wholesaler → Retailer → Consumer
(federation)   (federation)   (federation)   (federation) (federation)

In the textile industry the American Textile Manufacturers Institute (ATMI) has 300 business members and fifty-five staff employees. It is a federation that includes other federations, such as the National Federation of Textiles, the National Association of Finishers of Textiles, the Textile Data Processing Associations, and the National Association of Wool Manufacturers. ATMI has committees on consumer affairs, environmental preservation, and employee benefits, and other committees operating with a semipublic interest.[30] It is a powerful producer federation that needs counterbalancing at the wholesale and retail ends of the continuum.

Federations in production have a long history of exchange with retail associations interested in self-regulation. As far back as 1937, the National Retail Dry Goods Association proposed a program for coordinated standards, grades, and labels among manufacturers in order to make consumer goods uniform in the public interest. The program had eight principal activities: elimination of misleading information; development of a plan to provide truthful and factual information: cooperation among manufacturers, retailers, and consumer representatives in developing standard terminology; cooperation in the generation of standards for performance, durability, measurement, composition, and fiber content; definition of advertising standards; encouragement of manufacturer standards; and independent certification of tested materials. Retail associations tend to work in the interest of the consumer in the context of their "buyer" opposition to production and wholesaling.[31] A self-regulating economy requires this balance.

Another example of how trade associations operate is in the footwear industry. Shoe manufacturers have been interested in protecting their industry against cheap imports, but their lobbying effort does not necessarily speak for consumers interested in low prices. The Footwear Retailers of America opposed any relief for domestic shoe manufacturers in hearings of the U.S. International Trade Commission (ITC). The Footwear Retailers, representing about thirty shoe store chains, argued that "quotas could cost American consumers $3 billion each year in additional cost for their shoes." The ITC then had to decide whether to salvage the domestic production of shoes; it opted for limited quotas that might help maintain the self-governing capacity of the industry while admitting enough foreign imports to stimulate manufacturers to develop new technologies for domestic production.[32]

One more illustration: The pharmaceutical industry has shown a great propensity for conflict between manufacturers (sellers) and retail druggists (buyers). Nevertheless, the National Association of Retail Druggists and the Pharmaceutical Manufacturers Association have found it possible to resolve many of their problems in the public interest. A recent conflict involved "generic labeling" of products. Pharmaceutical firms have opposed generic drugs, which compete on the market with products that may contain exactly the same ingredients and yet are promoted differently through the firms' self-interest. Retail Druggists carried the argument for generic labelling into discussions with the Pharmaceutical Association and was able to resolve many of the issues through joint agreements. Because these two opposing federations have developed positions of equal power at the national level, and have sought to resolve their disputes amicably between themselves, they have tended at times to function in the interest of the larger society.

Our theory is that competing federations can work together in the public interest, but they also need public recognition and support to develop more adequate systems of communication and reconciliation. When opposing federations develop this capacity to be self-regulatory, they provide the social foundation for government de-regulation.

Employees vs. stockholders

The history of corporate development recounts the struggle between outsiders and insiders to control the corporation. We have argued that social development favors the evolution of inside control by employees who undergo training in management. Outside social investors have a role in aiding self-rule in the firm, but as this new system of authority develops, their power as stockholders will diminish over time. During the slow transition, however, they can still have a role in supporting greater accountability to other stakeholders, such as consumers and the local communities in which firms reside. The future role of stockholders and consumers is discussed in more detail in the epilogue.

Trade unions also influence corporate governance from the outside, but they are changing their role with the advent of employee ownership. Union leaders are becoming interested in assisting firms to become worker-owned, and have begun to do this in such industries as steel, automobiles, meat packing, and food production and distribution. Economists interested in self-managed firms argue that newly formed democratic firms need trade union consultants to defend the rights of workers in establishing the proper mechanisms of development, such as grievance committees, work councils, judicial systems, "internal accounts" guaranteeing profit sharing, and proper representation on the board of directors.[33]

The process of development is complex. Although major corporations like Weirton Steel (7,000 employees) and important subsidiaries like Hyatt-Clark (formerly of General Motors) took significant steps toward worker-ownership and management, the process is described as "partial" by self-management consultants. Employees own stock in the conventional sense and thus vote per share rather than per person; and they participate only to a limited degree in management at different levels of organization. Consultants believe that adjustments toward greater equity and responsibility for employees are likely to come about.[34]

The prototype of employee-owned firms seems to be the producer (or worker) cooperative in which all employees have one vote. Self-management economists see this as the future direction of corporate development in the United States.[35]

Business vs. consumers

Milton Friedman declares that the doctrine of corporate social responsibility is a "fundamentally subversive doctrine," and that there is "only one social responsibility in business – to use its resources and engage in activities designed to increase its profits so long as it stays within the rules of the game, which is to say, engages in open and free competition without deception or fraud." Friedman ignores the causes of the development of a labor movement, consumer organizations, and government regulations. He opposes the right of business leaders to assume these social responsibilities in their own firms and for stockholders to assume their same rights in shaping responsible corporate policy. Ami Domini points out the contradiction between Friedman's position and business law, which supports the right of stockholders to assert social concerns within a company.[36]

Friedman also argues that the consumer is so well protected by competition that consumer organizations have a hard time prospering. Consumers' Research, started in 1928, publishes *Consumers' Research* magazine, and Consumers' Union, started in 1935, publishes *Consumer*

Reports. Both seek to protect the consumer against exploitation by business. Friedman says that they have not been able to attract more than 1 or 2 per cent of the potential clientele. Consumers' Union, the larger firm, has about 2 million members. Friedman, of course, does not measure the impact that these organizations have on business conduct. Nor does he count the customers who consult these magazines in libraries at the time they choose a new product or who ask retailers for reprints of the sections of magazines dealing with the research on their contemplated purchase. We count these firms as businesses themselves that are helping to complete a circuit of social justice in the system. We are interested in studying the degree to which such research firms help keep the system honest while making their own profit.[37]

We might add that other groups act for the consumer on a national scale because the problem of exploitation is so widespread. These groups include Action for the Prevention of Burn Injuries to Children, the American Council on Consumer Interests, Common Cause, Consumer Action, Consumer Federation of America, the Environmental Defense Fund, the Federation of Homemakers, the National Consumers' League, the National Fire Protection Association, the National Home Economics Association, the National Resources Defense Council Petroleum Watchdog, the Public Interest Research Group, the Sierra Club, Truth in Advertising, and a host of others working on behalf of the consumer in the public interest. They should be on the list of investment priorities.

It is important to acknowledge the role of manufacturers themselves in providing measures of accountability, which also requires support. Many trade associations organize certification programs to guarantee product standards. For example, the Association of Home Appliances Manufacturers (AHAM) contains more than 100 member firms. It has developed product standards and tests models for compliance to the standards for such products as electric ranges, air conditioners, dishwashers, humidifiers, and refrigerators. By a seal of certification AHAM guarantees that a model's performance ability has been stated accurately and meets AHAM expectations. The program is voluntary but usage is widespread; for instance, every room air conditioner sold in the U.S. is certified by AHAM.

The consumer, then, is protected in part by an infrastructure of institutional activities that have evolved within the private sector. The infrastructure includes not only trade association activity and consumer organizations but also "consumer reporting" on local and national television networks, warranties and guarantees of products, and other efforts by business itself through Better Business Bureaus and committees of local Chambers of Commerce.

The social investor must stay alert to the balance of competing interests. In spite of important efforts of conventional business organizations to act on behalf of the consumer, it is important to invest in structural alternatives such as consumer cooperatives, community credit unions, and community development corporations at the local level. A theory of social development favors a balance in the powers of corporations from supply and production to retail and consumer-based firms (see figure 3.4). We discuss these issues in more detail in chapters 5 and 6.

Figure 3.4

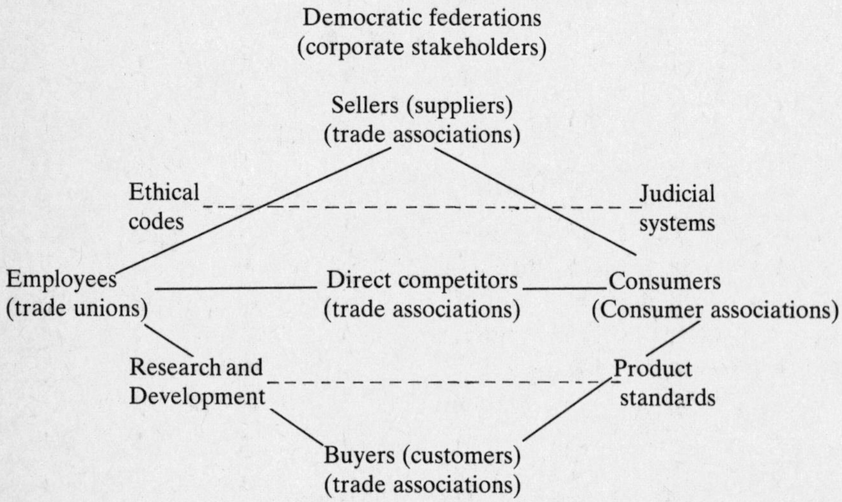

The role of government

Our argument is that the business system has helped cause government regulations and services to grow because the system has not organized to be accountable to the people it affects, to those we describe as stakeholders. The government has had to protect consumers, labor, direct competitors, buyers, sellers, and the community environment through legislation and regulatory agencies.

The task of government in this theory of development is to provide the incentives for industry to become socially self-governing. It is not our purpose to develop a tax plan and incentive system within the infrastructure of federal and local governments toward this end, but it is important to distinguish our conception of this role as a part of investment policy.

Our approach to social development harmonizes with certain interests of all parties across the political spectrum, but it is not in full agreement with any of them. It harmonizes with selected interests of political conservatives seeking to reduce the size of government, lower taxes, and promote deregulation, but it differs radically in arguing that tax incentives should be designed to promote social accountability as well as productivity in the private sector. Our idea of development also harmonizes with liberal interests insofar as it calls for social responsibility within business, but it does not fit the tradition of asking government to provide regulations and services when they can be constructed within the nonstatist sector of the economy. This proposal for development should also draw interest from the extreme right and left – libertarians and anarchists – who hold that government should virtually disappear in favor of individual sovereignty, but it also avoids certain extremes in these positions by arguing that a system of social governance must be developed within the economy from top to bottom so as to provide a basis to work toward that sovereignty in the framework of community life.

The political traditions of liberalism and conservatism seek to sustain the private sector, but neither tradition has a theory of the dynamics underlying the evolution of business. Keynesian theorists sought to save the business system through government fiscal controls, and supply side economists seek to preserve the system by eliminating those controls. The theory of neither group offers insight into what Joseph Schumpeter once called the "creative destruction" of capitalism.

The neo-Marxist tradition does perceive destructive forces operating in state capitalism, even though it is flawed in its conception of economic alternatives and the meaning of social investment. Marxist thought today is directed toward explaining how the state is engaged in a self-paralyzing relationship with business. In this theory, *social investment* is defined as "government outlays" for "expansion and or enhancement" of highways, communications, transportation, and civilian research and development. Marxists then argue that the impetus behind such government expenditure is to increase profitability within the private sector by shifting "constant capital" costs to the state. Thus, "state managers ensure private accumulation, placate competing classes and factions, and acquiesce to or rebuff demands by mass insurgents – all within the context of tenuously legitimate electoral institutions and a fragile social order." Marxists see fiscal policy as a "politicized vehicle" by which the state insures and protects the capitalist system. But there is much more to the dynamics. According to James O'Connor, the state absorbs basic training and human maintenance costs –

such as education and health expenditure – to its own detriment. The costs of private capital are "externalized" in the state. But the problem is that the costs of state "welfare and warfare" keep mounting, and are leading to a major fiscal crisis, whereby the state capitalist system is doomed to collapse. Other Marxists see other contradictions but propose no solutions. Economic alternatives are not carefully studied; the accent of Marxist literature is on "critique" without systematically pursuing solutions.[38]

Our approach accepts the idea that contradictions exist in the modern state, but we believe that social investment can play a constructive role in changing its self-paralyzing course. Our argument is that an investment alternative is already developing within the current social order of enterprise.

Our interpretation of *social investment* differs markedly from O'Connor's definition, even though it finds a certain resonance with it. O'Connor holds that government outlays for such programs as highway construction are "social investments," a term loosely similar to popular usages that hold that government expenditures toward medicare and education are social investments. But these social expenditures are really subsidies, not investments, which we have defined as involving a financial return to the investor on the allocation of capital. Welfare systems do not provide financial returns to the government but are in one sense props for the business system. Business does not have to provide retraining programs or be accountable to the people laid off. In this sense we can resonate with the Marxist interpretation, but we go on to argue that investments are best designed to stimulate socially self-governing entities. Truly to invest in the welfare of the unemployed, the government would develop a totally different policy based on principles of self-development.

An investment differs from a subsidy; a subsidy is like a gift. A gift can approach the character of an investment in our theoretical framework if it is offered to stimulate self-governing enterprises accountable to constituencies. The gift can then obtain a social return even though it does not obtain an immediate economic return. Such gifts can be a part of government policy, just as they have been a part of the policy of certain private foundations supporting "alternative investments."

When a government really *invests* in social welfare (meaning: development), it provides funds toward self-employment. It helps the private sector organize firms that supply steady jobs to the unemployed. It would offer low-interest loans to socially accountable firms like community development corporations (CDCs) to perform the task of organizing firms in the locality. A CDC could be mandated to help develop the skills of welfare recipients, and to conduct market research for new enterprises with the participation of the unemployed. There are many ways in which government can fund new enterprises selectively for welfare recipients. It is not our task to pursue a concept of eliminating the welfare system, but it is important to point out the policy principle of social development within the enterprise system.[39]

The Reagan administration has begun to put in place a piece of this new puzzle of social development in its promotion of tax cuts and deregulation, even though it has severely retarded development on other counts. The Reagan policies have radically altered the outlook of local officials. Local officials had previously sought to expand their political bases by expanding government services with the help of funds from the federal government; now, because federal funds are drying up, they have begun to turn over government functions to the private sector. Lydia Manchester of the International City Management Association says that city officials are redefining their role from simply delivering services to seeking the basis for them in the private sector. Governor Mario Cuomo of New York has said, "It is not government's obligation to provide the services, but to see that they're provided." A survey financed by the Department of Housing and Urban Development showed that private industry has begun to provide local governments with a significant fraction of government functions. These newly privatized functions include *waste collection, street-light operation, vehicle towing and storage, ambulance services, parks maintenance, fleet management and maintenance, labor relations, data processing, personnel services, secretarial services, jails*, and much more.[40]

We shall not pursue the subject of destatification, but the implications of our theory should be clear for a government policy based on social investment. The task of the government – like that of the social investor – is to construct a social foundation for a self-regulating economy. This means cultivating a new concept of the private sector capable of undergoing social development. Investors need a concept of the private sector as social, that is, based on a system of cooperation and human values as well as on competition and private interests. The social sector should be rooted in a notion of economic exchange that operates more effectively in the public interest, and reduces the necessity for government regulations.

The social sector

The social sector is a *nonstatist system of production and exchange in which firms operate competitively and cooperatively in the context of society.* This is a descriptive statement of what already exists as the private sector, but we now want to add facts about it to create an image that will help us know better how to invest in social development.[41]

The social sector is distinguished first from the state sector by its institutional character. The state is the only institution in society with the power to coerce people to act against their will. No corporation in the social sector has the power to tax its members or force them to go to jail or to go to work.

The social sector is composed of profit and nonprofit firms in a system of social and economic exchange. The firms exchange socioeconomically through gifts and stock purchases; they also exchange members of their boards of directors and are becoming closely linked in ways that need to be carefully examined. Profit and nonprofit firms are beginning to look like one another. The Boston Pops and the Boston Symphony are separate entities but they are both chartered as one nonprofit corporation. The Pops maximizes its profits while the Symphony continually loses money; the profits and losses balance on the final account sheet. The Symphony could not survive without its profit-maximizing partner. The same experience of profits and losses occurs in divisions of profit corporations. The difference between the profit and nonprofit firm is that the nonprofit firm will normally tolerate the losses in its subsidiary for a longer period of time.[42]

Lawyers admit that they have trouble distinguishing between profit and nonprofit firms. Profit firms look like nonprofits when they add systems of accountability and their executives speak openly about their intent to operate in the public interest. Nonprofits look more like conventional businesses when they hire market analysts and engage in commercial transactions. Both are part of the social sector, a social-economic system of exchange that differs markedly from the state sector.[43] We have said that the state sector is not actually removed from the influence of "social development." Government agencies – hospitals, social work departments, schools, medical clinics, libraries, police – are becoming socialized as part of the private (social) sector.

The process of destatification is one piece of the new development design, but much more must be done to create a social foundation for these private enterprises – former government agencies – to work in the public interest. For example, private enterprises need encouragement to develop social audits and social constitutions that require them to act responsibly toward their constituencies. The social audit is a planning device in the corporation that functions alongside the financial audit. It calls for management to target social goals for the corporation and requires an annual review by the board of directors of the extent to which those goals have been met. Social audits are not yet frequent among firms, but dozens of corporations have adopted them and they serve as a model for social investors to examine and for governments to require when functions are turned over to private business.[44] The social constitution has to do with the way the firm is organized to respond to its constituencies. It begins with a statement of social purposes recorded in the state charter and is elaborated in the by-laws of the firm. It depicts the division of authority and accountability of the firm to workers, customers, and the community. Democratic by-laws and social constitutions are customary in nonprofit corporations like many churches, trade associations, unions, the YMCA, and the Boy Scouts, but they have yet to develop in conventional business. They should be of interest to governments that seek to transfer their functions to the private sector. Social investors could include social audits and constitutions in their screens to foster this development.[45]

A social picture of the so-called private sector is critical to investment policy. Investors need to examine the meaning of this sector as profit and nonprofit entities begin to look alike. On the negative side: nonprofits can so accent a profit orientation that they lose their social and cultural values. The Episcopal Church and the YWCA can begin to look like IBM. The Reverend Moon's Unification Church is an extreme example of how a nonprofit corporation can take on a profit orientation and engage in exploitative activities while espousing religious ideals. On the positive side: some dying nonprofit corporations have begun to survive economically with their ideals intact while stressing better business management. The question is how the social values that nonprofit firms have emphasized in the past may integrate with the economic values they are now cultivating, and conversely, how business may develop new social values.

The new picture requires taking another look at industries as part of the social sector. The health industry, for example, is composed not only of profit-minded pharmaceutical firms, drug stores, and their trade federations but also of many nonprofit firms designed to be accountable to their constituencies. The industry is sustained by professional organizations like the American Medical Association and dozens of other professional groups with member tribunals and is grounded in ethical codes of conduct. It contains medical clinics in which physicians collaborate on an equal basis in ownership and management. It involves both nonprofit and profit hospitals, nursing homes, and medical schools, and includes mutual insurance firms, nursing associations, and a host of publically oriented educational institutions. All are part of the health industry within the social sector and are generally dedicated to advancing not simply profits but also people's physical and personal well-being. Public norms, professional ethics, and mutually agreed upon standards of practice and technology are a constituent part of the governance of this industry. The message to investors is that they can best direct their capital toward the development of those social dimensions of private industry. The role of the social investor – and of the government – is to provide incentives for this matrix of organizations to co-operate more fully in the public interest and in the interest of their communities. The task is to identify cooperative linkages among the competing firms that lead toward the advancement of human values at every self-governing level of the industry.

This picture of the social sector should not omit the reality of greed, violent conflict, egotism, and the quest for corporate power that exists in both profit and nonprofit corporations. Nonprofit corporations such as churches, libraries, universities, and hospitals seem to operate in a benign culture compared to the competitive life of business, but such is not always the case. The struggle for power among competing factions of the Southern Baptists at their 1985 national convention was not unlike a corporate take-over: it was filled with strife and bitterness. The confrontation in the General Assembly of the Presbyterian Church (USA) over abortion rights at times resembled the vicious verbal attacks of labor and management in the business sector. But the battleground was the floor of a democratic assembly, and the voting was based on the importance of the individual rather than the monetary power of shares in a business corporation. There is a difference in the structure of many nonprofit corporations that investors need to examine for its relevance in building the social sector.

The overall picture

We have described the economy as an institutional part of society with potential in the economic order for social development, and have suggested a basis for developing human values in the midst of human conflict and competitive self-interest. In this framework, the cultivation of human resources is considered a vital task along with the cultivation of material resources.

We interpreted social investment theory as having the quality of a dialectic consisting of *opposing principles* in policy decisions and *opposing associations* in the business system that are critical to its evolution. We argued that opposing principles were in balance with one another – human vs. material resources, social vs. economic factors, self-governance vs. command governance, cooperation vs. competition – but that in the long run the first-named principle in each polarity was the leading edge of development. The social investor must integrate the opposing principles in actual decisions while keeping in mind the overriding value of the human factor.

Advancing the human factor means developing self-governance at every level of command hierarchy in the economy. The achievement of higher

degrees of self-governance requires supporting systems of social accountability, human equity, and the increase of responsible participation by labor
in the governance of the economy. Social development means overcoming
ineffective modes of command bureaucracy and replacing them with new
modes of self-direction and self-reliance, with the result of a higher level of
social governance in a competitive economy.

We interpreted the governance of industries as a function of its major
stakeholders, who are represented in social federations that become the
basis for industrial self-governance. Through the creative opposition of
these federations, we foresee a system of social self-regulation emerging for
the economy as a whole.

We discuss the implications of this theoretical view of social development in the chapters that follow. We look further at what social investors
have begun to do and what researchers can do to obtain the essential facts
about corporate and industrial governance.

The resolution of these contradictory and complementary interests res-
ides finally in community development. The development of opposing
interests in the context of the community becomes the ultimate test of success for investors who apply principles of social development in the larger
economy.

Our discussion in Part III follows the theoretical framework and principles of development outlined here but applies them to the political economy of world banking and multinational corporations. Our focus is on the
use of social criteria in treating the problems of hunger and poverty in Third
World nations, but our theoretical framework is directed in this case to both
socialist and capitalist nations. The investment theory we have been formulating in the context of domestic policies has significance for its application
to international policies of social development.

Part II   Social criteria and research

4 Social investment in business corporations

Having set a general framework that explains the development of a social (nonstatist) economy, we can now look at the norms guiding investors at the corporate level, and translate the general concept of social development into a more specific framework of normative investment policy.

We begin with a review of research on corporate goals to assist the social analysts interested in finding a synthesis of social and economic goals. We then list social criteria used by fiduciaries as the basis for investment, and add another list of those generally considered to be on the "social frontier." The latter criteria (or norms) point to the creative edge of organizational development in corporate life, an edge represented by democratic experiments in business enterprise. We conclude by discussing some of the problems of corporate development and community relations that democratically oriented companies share with conventional ones. We point to some of the dangers and pitfalls of the investment process.

Our purpose is to look for a connection between the practice of social investment and substantiating empirical evidence. Social investors are increasingly interested in how the results of scientific research can become a basic part of the guidelines for decision making.

Research on corporate goals

Organizational researchers have shown that social and economic factors in corporate goals are closely intertwined. The classical interpretation of business behavior declared only one goal: profit maximization. And it assumed that there were only single owners who managed the firm for a profit. This classical interpretation is now seen as inapplicable to the whole business economy; it is better restricted to certain sectors. In the main, business corporations can best be understood when viewed as having many goals and many stakeholders who together define the goals.

The erosion of the classical interpretation of "profit maximization" by single owners began with repeated attempts to study what actually happens

71

in a firm. Among the first challengers were Adolf Berle and Gardiner Means in their famous 1932 study, *The Modern Corporation and Private Property*; their research revealed how owners were multiplying and becoming disassociated from the practice of management. They believed that the motives of managers – who were coming to control the corporation – were moving toward a wider set of interests than profit maximizing, and that the corporation was beginning to act in the public interest as well as in its own self-interest.[1] Indeed, the fight by managers to obtain the right of corporations to give part of their profits to charities in the 1930s was one example of the shift.[2]

Further research revealed other problems with classic interpretation, problems involving the time frame for maximizing profits. First, should profits be maximized in the short run or the long run? The traditional answer was the short run, but we know today that entrepreneurs differ on this question. Some executives want to limit short-run profits for various reasons, for example, to maintain a long-term customer interest by holding prices down. They may want simply to stabilize their market and to optimize their profits.[3]

Researchers also found that it was extremely difficult to "operationalize" profit maximization because *it did not exist in reality*. They found executives playing golf, lunching at fancy restaurants, taking afternoon naps, purchasing expensive paintings for offices, going on extended "business vacations," and so on – activities that did not always represent the ideal of profit maximizing. In fact, the need to work hard in companies that were secure in the marketplace was not so pressing as the need in companies engaged in a price war. The habits and customs of business executives differed markedly among industries.[4]

The "logic" of profit maximization was then challenged in the business literature. The issue of whether it should even be considered an ideal in the system became a question, and researchers found that the norms of business practice were changing so rapidly that new social interests and legal concerns were increasingly favored over profit goals. Some scholars summarize the reasoning like this: The ideal of "maximizing profits" led business managers to act in a manner that the public came to describe as tyrannical behavior and legislators to describe as "unfair competition." Pursuing profits as the single ideal meant that managers should use every trick in the book to keep wage and fringe benefits down, extract every last dollar from the consumer, sell as low-quality a product as possible, disclaim any responsibility to the community and its environment, and obtain the lowest possible price from vendors regardless of the effect upon them. All these "profitizing" directions had been tried in the past, but the laws, mores, and norms were changing the ethics of doing business. Over time, the attitude of business managers themselves changed. While nineteenth-century business could act this way, twentieth century business could not (and should not) without suffering serious consequences.[5]

Corporate executives began to realize that they must take into account a complex human environment in order to operate successfully. By the middle of the twentieth century a social concern on the part of many business executives had become a part of the framework for seeking profits.

A significant shift in the theory of the firm began at about the same time, a shift recorded in business education when Herbert Simon suggested that the concept of profit maximization be dropped in favor of multiple goals. The corporation was acting under a number of constraints and therefore "satisficed" rather than "maximized" profits. March and J. G. Simon, writing in the same vein, discussed five major constituents in the firm whose interests needed to be satisfied: employees, investors, suppliers, distributors, and consumers. The concept of corporate goals was thus shifting toward a consideration of *groups* affected by the corporation. Each participant had a stake in the well-being of the corporation; furthermore, each participant sought inducements in return for its contributions. There was now an exchange relationship between the corporation and its constituencies, and the interests of all these groups had to be satisfied in the context of the exchange. Profit making was only *one exchange*, and took place with only *one constituency*, the investor.[6]

Cyert and March continued the argument when they wrote that a coalition of individuals existed together to determine the corporate goals. Instead of a single authority at the top of the corporation following the single goal of profit, multiple authorities joined in setting goals. The employees, for example, were one group who now took their position along with others in decision making, and their interests were no less important than those of the owners. *The firm could not operate without workers and wages any more than it could operate without owners and profits. The firm could no longer be seen as an entity operating simply by top-down decision-making.*[7]

The direction of the research was becoming more evident. Behavioral scientists were beginning to develop a sociological conception of firm behavior as that of multiple actors determining multiple goals together. Goals were set not only by workers in unions but also in various departments, such as engineering, sales, and production. The separate goals had to be coordinated in the overall interest of the company, but profit making was not always the winner. In industries with a strong union, for instance, the wages of workers became more important than profits. Collective bargaining took away some of the profits from owners: the interest of the owners was still in the decision making but so was that of the workers. In failing industries, the goals of engineers in research and development became more important than those of the workers or the owners because the survival of the firm depended upon new technology. *The engineering department, therefore, received more priority for money than the workers, the shareholders, or the sales department.*

The corporation is best seen today as a social-economic entity in a complex environment with many goals and interest groups. Keeping in mind the need for the corporation to maintain profits, social investors have been increasingly interested in the way profit making can become the basis for the development of human resources, and conversely, in the way developing human resources contributes to higher profits. The development of human resources has therefore become an important motif in the modern corporation.

Experiments in the development of human resources

Social investors have taken note of recent experiments by management to increase the level of worker participation in the governance of their jobs. The first steps taken in this direction began in the 1970s through experiments in the quality of working life (QWL).

General Motors was one of the leaders in the experimental QWL movement. In 1974 Local 664 and GM's Tarrytown management decided to launch a formal QWL project and by late 1975 had formalized it. A joint labor–management program was constituted, led by the plant manager, the production manager, the personnel manager, the union's top officers, and two QWL coordinators. Believing it was important to keep the process voluntary, a committee surveyed 600 workers in two departments and found that 95 per cent wanted to be in the program. By 1977 the economic performance of the Tarrytown plant, as measured by the GM Assembly Division performance index, had moved up from sixteenth to first among eighteen plants nationwide. That fall the plant began taking fifty workers per week through three days of paid training in the QWL concept. Absenteeism dropped from over 7 per cent to between 2 and 3 per cent. In December 1978 there were only 32 grievances as opposed to a previous 2,000. By 1980 Tarrytown had become a model for managers of other companies looking for ways to improve productivity.

Then a most interesting decision was made. The chief of QWL experiments at GM's Gear plant began an experiment with 7,000 employees that involved a radical shift in the organizational structure. He sought to abolish the hierarchical pyramid by developing a technical team of advisers as re-source people to self-governing circles of employees serving as business teams. The advisers helped coordinate action among the business teams and provided help in management planning. Group leaders of the teams were chosen by employees. By March 1982 52 per cent of the employees were in the circles. After two months of operation, a circle in Plant One had reduced its scrap cost by 50 per cent, a saving of $250 a day. Absenteeism went from 7 per cent to 4.2 per cent. There was a 12 per cent increase in pro-ductivity on the axle assembly line, and repairs on finished products from circles decreased by 90 per cent.[8]

Experiments in QWL are now going on in many corporations. They vary considerably and have yet to be looked at systematically for results, but studies so far have shown that they have generally been instrumental in rais-ing productivity and adding profits. Observers report that their real value rests in the degree of personal development that usually occurs among employees, development that tends to take place with each advance in group autonomy and self-management. QWL experiments differ in the degree of autonomy offered by management, but there is evidence that those that enhance the autonomy of workers have contributed most to both the social and the economic well-being of firms.[9] For this reason, social investors have taken them seriously as a criterion of investment.

Social investors have also given attention to other policies of employee development in the firm. For example, they are interested in corporate poli-cies that provide equal job and advancement opportunities for all workers, new training programs for employees to increase their job skills, safe work-ing conditions, good fringe benefits, and intentional efforts to avoid layoffs.

Consumers and communities

The development of human resources is not the only concern of social investors as they choose corporations in which to invest. They look for firms that are attentive to the consumer in regard to product quality and safety, packaging, informative labeling, and complaints, and that grant the con-sumer advisory status. They also are alert to the impact of the firm on the community in connection with environmental protection, welfare needs, day-care facilities, employee transportation and parking facilities.

The following list, compiled through discussions with social investors, reveals and summarizes the varying criteria of social investors with these categories in mind.

I. **Labor: development of human resources**

A. Employment practices
1. Providing equal job opportunities for all persons.
2. Creating summer job opportunities for students.
3. Recruiting workers from minority groups and the handicapped.

B. Training programs
1. Providing training for all employees to increase their skills, their earning potential, and their job satisfaction.
2. Providing scholarship opportunities for workers to continue their education while employed.
3. Providing retraining programs for workers laid off by automation, and designing training for specific jobs that will be available to them.

C. Promotion policies
1. Providing equal opportunities for advancement.
2. Creating positions for newly trained employees (e.g., higher-paid technical positions for secretaries learning word-processing and computer techniques).

D. Quality of working life programs
1. Providing the most meaningful and personally rewarding work practical for all employees.
2. Introducing new dimensions to old routine jobs through experiments in job enrichment, job enlargement, and job rotation.

E. Worker participation and responsibility
1. Introducing experiments in quality circles and relatively autonomous groups.
2. Organizing labor–management committees to connect the success in work-efficiency experiments to profit sharing (e.g. Scanlon Plan).

F. Employment continuity
1. Scheduling production to minimize layoffs and recalls.
2. Maintaining facilities in efficient operating condition so they do not need to be abandoned.
3. Consulting with labor on impending plant shutdowns and offering opportunities for joint employee ownership where feasible.
4. Maintaining research and development on new technology to keep up with the competition and avoid plant shutdowns.

G. Remuneration
1. Maintaining a system of payments linked to profits by a negotiated percentage so that the economic advantages of the company are justly returned to the employees.
2. Maintaining a level of remuneration that is not totally inconsistent with other types of income in the community or industry.
3. Developing a system of remuneration in which the top salary is not absurdly out of line with the bottom wages.
4. Offering opportunities for employees, and not exclusively for top executives, to purchase stock in the company.

H. Working conditions
1. Providing safe, healthful, and pleasant working conditions.

    2. Offering periodic surveys for employees to express their opinion on working conditions.

I.   Communications

    1. Maintaining two-way communication among levels of employees to secure suggestions, provide information as to what the company is actually doing and how each department's activities relate to the total corporate activity.

    2. Offering opportunities for employees to be elected to an editorial board guiding the policy of company newsletters.

J.   Fringe benefits

    1. Providing adequate pension plans, insurance and health programs.

    2. Offering clinical services for treatment of alcoholism and narcotic addiction.

II.   Consumer: product and service quality

A.   Completeness and clarity of labeling, packaging, and marketing representation – assurance that labeling and representation as to methods of use, limitations on use, hazards of use, and quality of contents cannot be misunderstood.

B.   Warranty provisions – adherence to all stated or implied warranties of a product with implementations through timely recalls, repairs, or replacements.

C.   Responsiveness to consumer complaints – prompt and complete responses to all complaints, with remedial action where appropriate.

D.   Consumer education – literature and media programs to keep consumers informed of product or service characteristics, methods and areas of use or products, and of planned product changes or discontinuances.

E.   Product quality assurance through adequate control, so that quality is at least equal to what customers may reasonably expect on the basis of what the company represents.

F.   Product safety – design or formulation and packaging of products to minimize possibilities of harm or injury in product use.

G.   Content and frequency of advertising – giving full consideration to the omission of any material that may be offensive and the avoidance of so much repetition that it becomes repugnant.

H.   Constructive research – orienting technical and market research to meet defined social needs and to avoid creating environmental problems.

I.   Clear explanations of credit terms and purchase price.

III.   Citizen: community impact

A.   Investment practices

    1. Insuring equal opportunity before locating new facilities.

    2. Identifying opportunites to serve community needs through business expansion (e.g., housing rehabilitation or teaching machines).

    3. Placing funds in minority banks without undue imbalance in local banking.

B.   Municipal relations

    1. Providing corporate expertise for research on public policy.

    2. Disclosure of information in the public interest while maintaining confidentiality in personnel data.

C.   Family relations

    1. Provision of day-care facilities on a no-cost or break-even basis.

    2. Arrangement of transportation and parking facilities for employees without interference with community needs.

D.   Environmental protection

    1. Air – timely meeting of the law and going beyond the law by avoiding the creation of or by eliminating pollutants.

    2. Water – avoiding the creation of pollutants.

    3. Sound – similarly, avoiding the creation of and eliminating pollution.

    4. Solid waste – disposal of waste so as to minimize contamination, reduce bulk, minimize waste.

    5. Use of scarce resources – the conservation of existing energy sources, the development of new energy sources, and the conservation of scarce materials.

    6. Aesthetics – the design and location of facilities that harmonize with the physical surroundings through pleasing architecture and landscaping.

The history behind the development of the social norms noted above cannot be traced in detail here, but some reference can be made to their significance. For instance, although not many companies actually retrain employees who are laid off because of automation, Armour, Swift, and Cudahy in the meatpacking industry are early examples of companies that did. The significance of this norm rests in the assumption that the more companies actually do this, the less needed is government expenditure on training programs and welfare. The corporate system thus takes a small step toward self-governance.

Investment norms in connection with consumer and community relations have a long and complex history, but the trends in the direction of accountability are clearly documented.[10] Corporate executives have become very aware of the social implications of environmental pollution and the importance of taking the community into account. The business corporation has come a long way from the company town in which citizens were virtually under the gun of corporate owners.

The clarification of social goals as related to the economic goals of the firm is still going on, but an investment frontier is opening up through a new approach to the cultivation of human resources. It is a social frontier in business that requires careful study.

The social frontier

The recent appearance of many cases in which workers have assumed a position of ownership and management in their own corporations can be confusing to investors, but they deserve priority for their bearing on social development. The rash of employee ownership has come about partly through the stimulus of legislation originally enacted by Congress in 1974, called the Employee Stock Ownership Plan (ESOP). It is a method by which management can obtain a tax break by borrowing money while providing corporate stock to the employees. The law is complex and has had positive and negative outcomes. It can lend itself to shrewd manipulation by managers at the same time that it can raise work motivation and productivity in the firm. One outcome occurred in the case of a South Bend lathe company that used an ESOP to avert a shutdown. Voting shares were weighted in favor of management and a strike followed. Another instance had to do with the Rath Meatpacking Company of Waterloo, Iowa. It, too, was about to shut down, partly because of a poor market. Union officers took the lead to buy the company by means of an ESOP, but this time the voting procedures were amended to give the 2,000 employees representation on the board. The market, however, continued downward. Rath's pension funds were exhausted in the salvage attempt, and the workers took two pay cuts before the firm's bankruptcy.

It is important to examine the positive outcomes because over 8,000 companies have followed it, and preliminary studies suggest that they have thereby bettered themselves. In 1981 a survey of 1,400 firms with ESOPs reported that they experienced "improved productivity between 1975 and 1979, as contrasted with a decline for the average non-ESOP company in the same period and industry." A third of the companies with ESOPs over three years old showed a reduction in employee turnover and greater employee morale and interest in company progress. A study of ninety-eight firms by the U.S. Senate found that profits of firms with ESOPs averaged 50 per cent higher than those of firms without ESOPs in the same industry. Another survey revealed that the more stock equity the employees owned, the greater the company profits.[11]

Social investors interested in observing and encouraging these recent trends will want to examine the literature on the subject,[12] but should be cautious in their interpretations. The studies suggest only that employee ownership does not necessarily lead toward a lessening of productivity and profits. They refute the stereotype that employee ownership can never work effectively; however, the process to bring about success is more complex than the preliminary studies indicate. The ESOP law itself can be misleading in many ways and is still being evaluated to ascertain its value to employees and businesses.

Executives who introduce an ESOP know that they must also educate employees as to its meaning. Some executives have found it desirable to train employees in management so that by the time they acquire stock, they will have achieved the skills necessary to vote knowledgeably for their board of directors. Some executives have also found it desirable to bring workers into management committees at middle levels as well as lower workshop levels. These aspects of worker participation constitute notable innovations in business administration but the issues remain complex.

Investors have tended to react to ESOPs either with a romantic idealism that treats them as signposts toward a utopian society or with an extreme cynicism that denies that they may represent progress. Let us look at reactions to some recent cases and then distinguish them from what we would call serious research.

Recent cases

People Express is an airline company that celebrates itself as worker-owned and -managed. The company has very low fares and seems responsive to consumer needs. The *idealist* speaks of the ethical principles now being applied in management. New employees buy their ownership in the firm with 100 shares of stock at a cost of about $1,000, can purchase additional shares at slightly below market price, and receive yearly profit-sharing bonuses. These facts show accountability to the workers. Further, salaries do not show a large differential; they begin at $17,000, rise to $22,000 for pilots, and end with a little over $60,000 for top officers – a sharp contrast with salary ranges in conventional firms, whose executives may receive over $1,000,000. Moreover, there is no line-management hierarchy. Employees are expected to rotate their work so that everyone spends some time on direct customer service. No one has a secretary. All participate at some level in corporate planning. The idealist says: "This is a dream company."

The *cynic* says, "Not so fast." The low fares are really a smart marketing strategy and not to be associated with concern for customers. In fact, customers can get less attention on People Express than on other airlines. Certain employees are not owners: maintenance crews, baggage attendants, and telephone reservation clerks. Only a third of the employees are owners, and they vote "per share" rather than "per person." As for job rotation, we find that employees tend to stick to one job; rotation actually caused problems in management because not all skills could be quickly learned. Rotation exists to some extent, but many employees found that familiarizing themselves with another job on a one-day-a-week basis was overly demanding. Also, many people have never become attuned to the whole idea of modest salaries. Many pilots, for example, would prefer the pay their counterparts earn at conventional airlines. Finally nothing is said publicly about the deep disagreements that have developed among People Express managers, or about the fact that the firm could be easily purchased by another company. So much for idealism.

The *idealist* turns to Weirton Steel in West Virginia, where we find total worker ownership with about 7,500 employees. Weirton formerly was a division of National Steel making about 1 per cent return on sales but not enough profit for its owner-conglomerate to want to keep it. National Steel wanted to close the plant or sell it, but the $800 million or so tied up in pension liabilities and severance benefits made it an attractive offering to potential buyers. Facing shutdown, the Independent Steelworkers, a company union, bought the plant. Our idealist points out that the jobs were saved, the plant is now more profitable than ever, and the union has representatives on the board of directors to help direct policy. This is a real case of worker control.

Our *cynic* points out that real power at Weirton continues to be held by managers and bankers. Salvaging the company required deep wage cuts as a trade-off for ownership. There is a modest form of participatory management but on the whole the old management system prevails. Workers do not get full voting rights on their stock for five years, and further, voting is based on number of shares owned rather than on the individual. The voting pattern favors management. It is true that the union has three members on the board, but it is a fourteen-member board; the union can be outvoted by outside directors appointed by the consulting company.

Our *idealist* remains undaunted. Many companies are fully owned and managed by the workers on the basis of one person, one vote. One example is the O and O (Owned and Operated) stores in Philadelphia that came into being when A&P decided to shut down an entire division. At that time Local 1357 of the United Food and Commercial Workers, assisted by the Philadelphia Association for Cooperative Enterprise (PACE), helped the A&P employees buy two large supermarkets. Sales have since gone up dramatically, and labor costs are running at 9 per cent of gross sales, compared to about 15 per cent under A&P ownership. The sales-per-person index is about 20 per cent above the industry average. The O and O stores are planning to develop five similar stores by the end of 1986. Employees elect their board of directors and then hire a store manager; they participate in management committees and make all decisions regarding marketing, purchasing, recruiting, finances, business planning, and capital investment. Workers pay an equity share of $45,000, a sum they can borrow if necessary from the local's credit union and repay via payroll deductions. When the worker retires, the co-op buys back his or her share. The stores are an un-equivocal success.

The *cynic* is now ready for the kill. These are "mom-and-pop" stores. Co-operatives have always been a part of U.S. business but they have never amounted to anything. You could probably count no more than a few hundred worker co-ops in the United States today among millions of enter-prises. Furthermore, these small companies are vulnerable to big market changes. Corporations have to be big to survive in a capitalist society.

The *idealist* may now retort with cases of large-scale co-ops and the evol-utionary time necessary for new organizations to arise. But the argument will continue because each investor is dead set on an ideological position. The real question is, how can these enterprises be studied? We need to know what facts have been accumulated in this field, and why these inno-vations should be considered a frontier for investors.

The pattern of research findings

Social investors can see the significance of worker-owned enterprises in various organizational studies. Studies have shown the highly negative effects of hierarchy on people in lower-strata positions in corporations. Labor-managed firms tend to flatten hierarchy and to change the meaning of jobs in the firm, transforming the negative effects into positive effects for employees.

Research indicates that individuals at upper levels of the corporation have more control over their work than do those at lower levels, with a cor-responding impact on job satisfaction. Additionally, lower- and middle-level employees are most likely to feel that they lack authority in their work.[13] Research consistently finds a positive relationship between job sat-isfaction and amount of control exercised.[14] When employees have some influence in shaping their daily work, it increases their feelings of identity, personal commitment, and responsibility.[15]

Status in the corporation has varying effects. Employees at higher levels are of course formally assigned higher status: they are generally considered more important individuals; they are given greater responsibility, respect, and social recognition; they earn more money and are given more perquis-ites, such as stock options, longer vacations, and paid sick leave. All these elements contribute to self-esteem and job satisfaction. In contrast, employees in lower positions experience a sense of relative deprivation, which can adversely affect their physical and mental health.[16]

Work at the higher levels is usually more interesting and challenging, less repetitious, routinized, and fractionated. It permits greater discretion and choice, individuality, and opportunity for self-fulfillment. On the other hand, work at the lower levels does not allow for realization of potential or outlet for real abilities.[17]

The value of the pioneering steps in worker self-management is that when the level of participation in company management is increased, workers may also be able to grow personally in the new environment. They may gain more job satisfaction, self-esteem, and social recognition. And by acquiring skills that were heretofore out of bounds, they add to their sense of responsibility by serving on the top board or a middle-management committee.

In sum, the more democratic structure of worker-owned businesses appears to add opportunities for employees to grow and to increase their capacity for self-direction on the job.[18] At the same time employee identity and loyalty to the company tends to increase. Such changes could be one reason that productivity has risen under these conditions.[19]

Income equity

Some worker-managed firms tend to encourage income equity among employees, and a few rare firms have taken radical steps toward income equality, believing strongly in eliminating the negative effects of hierarchy. The most radical action has been by plywood cooperatives in Oregon, where workers have reduced differences in the wage scale to zero. All employees in firms of about 200 employees receive the same pay; however, to make certain of having managers with top skills, some companies hire outside professionals at higher salaries. To offset problems in regard to employees with higher responsibilities who might be unhappy about their equal pay, some companies train for job rotation, which helps to increase the sense of community among employees who would otherwise resent company policy.

Most worker-managed companies do not radically attempt to equalize wages, but they do tend to have smaller income differentials than conventional firms. The ratio of the highest-paid to lowest-paid employees in some business cooperatives is 5 to 1, in contrast to traditional firms, which run 50 to 1 and higher. No studies have been made of the wage policies of worker-owned companies.

Internal structure

Social investors may do well to examine the internal structure of worker-owned firms to try to foresee the kinds of problems they may encounter in the future.

Voting rights in traditional companies are located in shares sold individually to anyone, including employees. In a worker-owned company employees may sell their acquired shares to outsiders and thus destroy the basis of worker ownership. This is what happened in the case of a mining company, the Vermont Asbestos Group, and the *Kansas City Star*. Accordingly, worker-management consultants argue the importance of separating "membership rights" from "ownership rights." The concept of ownership rights can then be "repackaged" as personal (or human) rights attached to the role of workers in the firm, and the capital portion can be structured into internal capital accounts. Thus, in a self-managed firm, the workers do not have property rights that extend to buying and selling their shares, but they do have personal rights in the firm, such as voting privileges and the right to a general assembly. The legal separation protects the firm from being "sold out" by individual workers who could make a profit from their stock and destroy worker ownership. Instead, workers see themselves as "members," similar to members of a trade union or a church. Social investors are still able to support these firms through loans or secondary debentures without voting rights.

According to David Ellerman, it is important for a labor-managed firm to classify equity according to individual accounts separate from collective accounts. Part of the balance in an individual account is "paid-in capital," which comes from a membership fee, and part is "retained earnings" from past operations of the business. The capital represented in the individual and collective accounts should be legally available "for any and all corporate purposes." The individual accounts, however, are maintained as all savings accounts in a bank; a cash reserve is kept to cover withdrawals. For example, an individual account may be withdrawn when a worker retires; a retiree cannot sell his or her stock but can close out an individual account, which can be a part of the pension plan. In effect, a pension fund allows workers to continue to maintain an income after they leave a firm.[20] The literature on self-management contains details on these structures and is open to examination by social investors seeking to advance this particular frontier of "human resource development" in the firm.[21]

Middle management resistance

Among the pitfalls in converting a company to worker ownership and management is the resistance of middle management. The redesigning of a firm to high worker participation often puts into jeopardy the positions of foremen, forewomen, and supervisors, who in consequence fear dismissal or loss of authority. Generally in a "line organization" and accustomed to command, they may not welcome the change.

Illustrative of the opposition possible in a move to worker ownership and management were the difficulties in organizing self-governing committees at General Foods in Topeka, Kansas, and at the General Motors Tarrytown plant. The introduction of equality into the occupational hierarchy threatened the positions of corporate technicians, the plant line manager, quality control personnel, and industrial engineers. The democratic reorganization of one plant among the many plants of corporation can result in foot dragging by both professionals and top supervisors.[22] It is patent that steps toward worker management could beneficially include corporate self-studies that include middle-management in the planning process.

Unions

The role of unions in worker-managed companies is complex and potentially troublesome because the organization of a democratic company can threaten their traditional role in collective bargaining. Union leaders are accustomed to confrontations rather than cooperation with management or even participation in management. Nevertheless, some unions have acted positively in the development of worker-owned companies.

Experience suggests that unions under sympathetic and forceful officers make important contributions in regard to worker ownership. *First, a union can aid in the creation of employee ownership in a firm.* For example, union leaders participated in the reorganization of Chrysler Motors; Douglas Fraser, president of the United Auto Workers, helped establish an ESOP and then served on the board of directors. Union leadership went even further at Weirton Steel in Virginia and the Rath meatpacking plant in Iowa in negotiating voting rights and representation on the board of directors. *Second, a union can represent workers in collective bargaining* when an adequate adjudication system has yet to be set up in a new worker-owned company. This was the case when the employees purchased shares in the Vermont Asbestos Plant. During the extended purchase process, employees had no way to handle their complaints on the job except through the union. *Third, a union can support a pension plan that a worker-managed company by itself cannot afford*, as happened in the Hyatt Plant of General Motors. The United Auto Workers supplied a pension plan while the workers purchased the company subsidiary. The union, then, can be "out in front" when leaders value the transformation to worker ownership.[23]

Organizational development

The worker-owned and -managed company has many advantages when it is organized effectively, but it can face the same bureaucratic problems of development that plague the conventional corporation. The advantages lie in the expansion of responsibilities and vision for employees such that they can grow personally in the process. Yet the firm may take on the shape and characteristic of a large bureaucracy when business expands: diversification, hierarchy, and impersonal authority. These attributes pose extreme challenges to the workers, who seek to maintain democratic ideals and a sense of equity among themselves.

It has been shown that *innovation in products* is a powerful strategy for increasing an organization's *rate of growth*.[24] A major innovation can entail major internal changes that have mixed effects on employees. In reviewing the relevant literature Hage and Aiken found that seven organizational properties were associated with innovation in products and services: a high range of professional specialists; decentralization; low formalization (codification of jobs and rules); low stratification; absence of high-volume production; relatively low emphasis on cost reduction; and high job satisfaction.[25]

The tendency toward decentralization, low formalization, and low stratification is very much in line with the purpose of the worker self-managed firm. The goal of such a firm is to increase gradually the responsibility, authority, and skills of all employees while maintaining identification with and commitment to the corporate community. The investor interested in the growth of self-managed firms can, on the basis of this evidence, encourage innovative steps taken by them.[26]

At the time of innovation, however, the increase in number of specialists and professionals in the firm sets in motion a restructuring that is often difficult to manage. The recruits tend to become a new class, an elite group within the firm that is in conflict with the democratic ideals of the firm, and the resulting friction can slow down worker efficiency.

The social investor in this case may well support what many firms are doing in the face of organizational conflict: the initiation of a corporate self-study, in which all employees are involved, in consultation with an outside professional who understands the democratic purposes of the firm. Together they examine the changes in corporate structure, the role of the newcomers, the stereotyping that has begun, the tendencies of professionals to make key decisions, the jealousies arising from new salary differentials, the special privileges that often develop automatically in higher offices. They then draw their own conclusions and formulate methods for dealing with these factors.[27]

As a company grows and develops new technologies, its organizational complexity increases both vertically and horizontally, making it more and more difficult to maintain cohesion. The following negative consequences have been observed by researchers: serious problems in managerial overhead, communication distortion, and poor morale among lower-level personnel.[28] These can occur, of course, in a worker-controlled firm.

Ulgor is an excellent illustration of how a democratically organized firm can become large and still overcome the growth-associated problems. A producer cooperative in the Basque region of Spain, Ulgor in 1968 had 2,000 employees. Employee-elected representatives sat on the board of directors, and human relations in the firm seemed good. Then suddenly Ulgor faced a strike organized by a few dissident employees, in the wake of inauguration of a resented pattern of close supervision. The workers believed they had eliminated the need for strikes by placing representatives on the board, but the company had developed a bureaucratic command system that placed workers at the bottom at a great distance from controlling policy. The result of the strike was that the board spun off five separately owned enterprises, a federation they called Ularco. Two members of each firm's board together constitute the board of the federation, and today employees in the new firms have much more control over their management than they did in the former large corporation.

Investing successfully in companies experimenting with democratic forms of corporate governance necessitates scrutiny of the process by which the innovations are made. When the process is voluntary and jointly planned by employees, there is a higher likelihood of management success and a resulting likelihood of financial return for the investor. The following list of normative trends in innovative firms represents a social frontier today for investors.

Frontier development (human resources)
A.   Worker ownership and participation
   1. Experimenting with employee ownership under a plan that includes educating workers over time to gain appropriate managerial skills.
   2. Experimenting with worker-elected boards of directors.
   3. Organizing worker councils at middle-management and workshop levels of administration.
   4. Developing a plan for worker ownership that eventuates in one person, one vote instead of the conventional voting pattern based on number of shares owned by each employee.
B.   Remuneration
   1. Introducing discussions among employees on the subject of eliminating privileged differences between "salaries" and "wages", and then establishing a consistent system of payment as well as "continuity of employment" as operating principles.
   2. Discussing the idea within management of reducing income differential so that over time the corporate income ratio of 90:1 might be reduced to 70:1, and moving on toward greater equity while still rewarding differences in competence.
C.   Employee human rights
   1. Forming a labor–management committee to study human rights for employees in such areas as

         a. free speech regarding the quality and
           safety of corporate products;
         b. free assembly of employees under specified conditions.
      2. Providing an opportunity for employees to be heard by a jury of peers in cases when higher management has exercised severe penalties.

D.   Union–management relations
      1. Encouraging unions to participate and help plan programs of employee participation in higher management.
      2. Maintaining effective relationships with unions under employee ownership plans so that continuity can be preserved in such areas as pension funds, grievance committees, union fees.

E.   Disclosure of information
      1. Providing all information about the company requested by workers that does not endanger the competitive edge of the firm in the marketplace; providing even that proprietary information to a representative group of workers under oath of confidentiality.
      2. Establishing a labor–management committee to define information most relevant to employee decision making so that it can be properly disseminated to all employees.

F.   Fringe benefits
      1. Providing opportunities for employees to select social criteria for their pension-fund investment without interfering with prudent administration.
      2. Establishing recreational facilities in the firm and opportunities to increase the cultural life of employees in such fields as science, literature, and drama.

Community relations

It is important to follow the way in which worker self-managed firms develop a relationship with the communities in which they reside. Social investors need to know what problems can arise and which worker-managed firms have made special contributions to community life.

Some producer cooperatives have invited community representatives on the board of directors. Some retail cooperatives have found that the advice of local customers is useful in the purchase of goods for the store; a customer-representative on the board even offers a political advantage in marketing and public relations. Some industrial cooperatives have also included community representatives on the board because of the negative impact the factory may have on the local environment. In both types of cases, however, self-management theorists argue that the power of employees should remain dominant on the board.

The major question in these cases is the proper extent of community control over the internal life of the firm: how much power from the community is appropriate on the board? Although there have been no studies made of this matter, self-management theorists usually answer on principle that the local community may have some influence over the company insofar as its policies affect the community (e.g., air pollution or product safety) but that the workers should retain full authority over the internal management of the firm.

Labor-managed firms have shown a tendency to contribute a portion of their profits to community development. For example, the English firm Scott-Bader gives 20 per cent of its profits to the community; 60 per cent is turned back to the firm, and 20 per cent is added as a reward to salaries.[29] The Mondragon cooperative enterprises allocate 10 per cent to 15 per cent to a reserve fund for retirement, 70 per cent to employees in proportion to hours worked and wage rate, and 15 per cent to 20 per cent to the community. Their community contributions are often geared toward other self-managed enterprises and the support of schools that teach students about self-management.[30]

In conclusion

The key to success of worker-managed firms is the *process* by which they are organized: it should be voluntary and jointly planned through labor–management committees, and not imposed by management. The critical points to observe in the development of a democratic firm are (1) the clarification of social and economic goals; (2) the selection of leaders who are skillful in their jobs and responsive to workers; (3) the redesign of responsibility for middle managers so that they do not fear losing status or being dismissed; (4) the continued decentralization through innovations; (5) the timely initiation of worker retraining programs and corporate self-studies; (6) the construction of a new relationship with union leaders so they can be of assistance.

Executives of pension funds may develop a special interest in this social frontier. Union-negotiated pension funds in the private sector total about $300 billion, of which over $60 billion is jointly controlled by union and management trustees. The size of the funds and the growing interest of unions in employee self-management may be an incentive to foster this form of labor development.

Public pension funds also may become involved in utilizing "frontier" criteria. California's Public Employee Retirement System is seeking seats on the boards of directors of companies in which it has substantial investments. Such a role could foster consideration of new structures of accountability for workers and the community.

Social investment cannot be restricted solely to the level of individual corporations, important as that may be. The individual corporation is embedded in a system of *industrial governance* that can strongly affect its behavior; each firm is part of an industrial community with its own collective norms and trade practices that could lead it to be exploitive or, conversely, to work in the public interest as well as in its own. It is therefore important to consider the placement of capital for the social and economic development of firms in entire industries.

5 Social investment in industry: a new social policy

U.S. industries have been lagging behind those of other nations in economic performance, and economists have begun to focus on the problem. Lester Thurow, for example, asserts that the huge technological superiority of the U.S. in the 1950s and 1960s is gone. Our competitors have not only matched our achievements but may be moving ahead of us (table 5.1).

Table 5.1. *Manufacturing productivity 1982*

Country	Output per hour of work* (1975 prices)	Rate of growth 1977–82†
United States	$11.20	0.6%
Germany	12.39	2.1
France	11.96	3.0
Italy	11.29	3.6
Japan	10.63	3.4
Canada	10.21	−0.3
United Kingdom	6.85	2.7

* Roger Brinner and Nigel Gault, "U.S. Manufacturing Costs and International Competition," *Data Resources Review* (October 1983), p. 1.15.
† U.S. Department of Commerce, International Economic Indicators (September 1983), p. 64.
Adapted from Lester Thurow, *California Management Review*, vol. xxvii, no. 1, Fall 1984, p. 10.

Thurow noted that from 1972 to 1978, industrial productivity rose 1 per cent per year in the U.S., almost 4 per cent in West Germany, and over 5 per cent in Japan. West Germany and Japan have been introducing new products and improving the making of old products more rapidly than the United States, and have made major market inroads that threaten U.S. industries. The United States has slipped from having the world's highest standard of living to now standing behind Switzerland, Denmark, West Germany, and Sweden in per capita GNP. The U.S. GNP has never grown half as rapidly as Japan's which is now growing and which is only 7 per cent lower per capita than the U.S. GNP and expected to surpass it soon. If these trends continue, Thurow concludes, we shall become like Egypt, Greece, Italy, Portugal, and Spain, all of which once led the world.[1]

Robert Reich of the Kennedy School at Harvard reinforces Thurow when he writes that the proportion of U.S. manufacturing capacity employed in production averaged around 80 per cent during the 1970s and fell to less than 70 per cent by 1982. Only 3.5 per cent of the labor force was jobless in 1969; thereafter unemployment climbed steadily, reaching approximately 10 per cent in 1983. By the 1980s, the core industries of the management era – steel, automobiles, petrochemicals, textiles, consumer electronics, electrical machinery, metal-forming machinery – were in trouble.[2]

Some critics of U.S. industrial performance go further, saying that U.S. industries have also shown major shortcomings in social performance. The consequences of the lack of social accountability are, among other things, environmental pollution, massive unemployment and associated welfare costs, consumer exploitation, runaway factories, workplace danger, and labor–management conflict. Public response has been to act through government to create regulatory and protective agencies. Some observers argue that the proliferation of agencies that deal directly with the economy has also been caused by the lack of accountability. Corporations and industries are not organized to protect the people they affect. In the interest of stripping government growth we must scrutinize the accountability structures of business.[3]

Many congressional leaders believe that some action at the national level is necessary to halt industrial decline. It has been argued that in spite of some industrial recoveries a *cyclic effect is inherent in the business system and that the next slump in the economy could be more disastrous*. Hence, a method of national planning and a new system of investment are required.

Felix G. Rohatyn, chairman of New York City's Municipal Assistance Corporation, has declared that the establishment of a federal bank could ensure that industries follow government mandates to correct their problems. Aid would be conditional on management and labor's making the concessions that are necessary for the viability of business. The federal bank, similar to the Reconstruction Finance Corporation, would function like an old-time investment bank and have the clout to force those involved to make tough decisions, as was done in the Chrysler Corporation and New York City bailouts. The bank would require that private investors put up at least 50 per cent to make sure that the idea had the backing of the market.

In 1983 Congressman John LaFalce (D–N.Y.) began his House Banking Subcommittee on Economic Stabilization hearings on an industrial policy bill. LaFalce asserted that what is needed is a "coordinative mechanism" to help in the transition to a postindustrial society. At the same time, a number of other House Democrats, including Stanley Lundine of New York and David Bonior of Michigan, proposed the National Industrial Strategy Act to create an economic cooperation council through which the government, business, and labor would collect and analyze data and recommend steps to improve competitiveness. The Act would also create a national industrial development bank with authority to lend $12 billion over four years and to grant an additional $24 billion in loan guarantees. Richard Ottinger (D–N.Y.) led a National Recovery Project backed by 150 Democrats, to develop a "high production strategy." A Senate Democratic Policy Committee task force worked up a similar package for Edward M. Kennedy (D–Mass.).

In concert with this movement, the AFL–CIO was saying that its pension funds should be used for investment in the revitalization of industry:

All of these proposals have one thing in common; they require vast sums of money. Massive capital investments will be needed as our society adjusts to the fundamental changes that have occurred in the American and world economies. This investment capital will come from the savings of individuals and corporations, and will be used, along with huge projected government expenditures, to help corporations retool, develop new technologies and find new sources of energy.

Pension and other benefit funds are major, and growing repositories of these savings. This year, $69 to $70 billion in the "deferred wages" of 50 million workers will be deposited into these funds, which are the nation's largest form of individual savings today . . .

The simple fact is that pension funds will provide much of the investment capital for reindustrializing this country and the investment policies that they pursue will play a vital role in shaping the American economic future.[4]

In the light of a Labor Department study showing that private-sector pension funds will be worth some $3 trillion by 1995, the Executive Council of the AFL–CIO had recommended that the labor organization work for establishment of an independent entity to facilitate their investment in reindustrialization. "The new institution should be directed by a tripartite board of directors, equally representing the labor movement, employers and the public. To assure that the interests of the pensioners are protected, the government should guarantee a minimum return on the invested funds."[5]

There are, then, indicators that a national investment policy may be forthcoming, and it behooves us to examine current theories of industrial decline. The effectiveness of a new policy is dependent in part upon the causes of decline and the availability of supportive information. Studies on industrial problems are too many to review properly here, but we can examine four contrasting approaches to illustrate the main dimensions of the argument regarding national policy.

The orientation of these studies tends to be toward economics and finance. Our thinking is that they can best be viewed from a sociological perspective, because economic analysis has not saved key industries whose problems continue in spite of the economic recovery, and also because without such a perspective the overall decline is likely to continue. It is important to consider theories of decline from a more comprehensive perspective that recognizes that decline is cyclical and rooted in the social organization of business. Avoidance of economic stagnation mandates implementation of a new policy of social investment.

Theories of industrial decline and revitalization

Theory of information complexity (IC) and resource scarcity (RS)

The research of Paul Lawrence and Davis Dyer suggests that the causes of industrial decline can best be considered under two categories: information complexity (IC) and resource scarcity (RS). IC is measured by the number and variety of such factors as competitors, customers, technologies, products, and government regulations. When the factors become too complex in an industry, corporations lose their vitality. RS consists of the raw materials, capital, and people needed in production. Lawrence and Dyer find that when these resources become too scarce, the industry also declines.

In Lawrence and Dyer's study key measures of economic revitalization are the degree of efficiency and innovation within firms. When firms are both efficient and innovative, they show vitality. Too much IC, however, can overload the capacity of managers to remain efficient; too little IC cannot provide the diversity that stimulates creative thinking. Extremes at either end of the continuum discourage the learning necessary for high innovation and efficiency. Similarly, too little RS reduces the motivation to seek efficiency, and too much RS means that resources are lacking to achieve high innovation and efficiency. It is intermediate amounts of IC and RS that leads to the earning and striving necessary for high performance.

It is not enough for management alone to be engaged in learning efficiency and striving for innovation; all employees should be involved. The "entire membership" should become aware of "the broad purpose, ethical standards, and operating principles of the firm with emphasis given throughout to the value of both efficiency and innovation."[6]

Lawrence and Dyer assess industries on the basis of their degree of IC and RS (high, intermediate, and low). For example, steel, autos, and coal today have a high RS and a low IC; they have tended to develop a "machine bureaucracy," and have lost their capacity for innovation. The authors say that certain industries need "de-concentration" to increase IC; in other industries there is a need for "de-regulation" to help decrease IC. Still other industries require some government protection while they make the transition to new technologies. They must give more attention to long-term versus short-term profits. At the same time, all industries should focus more sharply on research and development. In general, the authors suggest that new links can be formed between trade associations, trade unions, and government agencies for industrial revitalization.

Theory of supply-side economics

George Gilder, a leading exponent of supply-side economics, declares that government policies have created the problem of industrial decline by accenting demand as the basis for capital growth. He believes that economists have become mistakenly fascinated with demand curves, which are only an epiphenomenon of supply, and that it is supply curves that register the real efforts and sacrifices of producers – the key to economic growth.

Gilder says that the worst thing for an economic system is the diversion of money from productive use. The sinking of money into "sumps of wealth," like gold, art, and "collectibles," represents a major loss to the productive engines of the economy. Other "sumps" would be money itself when hoarded, or government spending on unproductive social services. Gilder sees government as one of the biggest sink holes in the economy.[7]

Supply-siders advocate a reduction in taxes to stimulate production, as well as deregulation of government controls to reduce the cost and tyranny of government agencies. Their motto is "The less government, the better," and they hold that many government services should be "devolved" to private enterprise. Their crucial concept for revitalizing industry is to remove government from the economy and let business operate fully in the marketplace.

Theory of flexible systems

Robert Reich argues that *the way production is organized* is the key to economic failure or success. He rejects other causes that economists associate with decline: excessive government regulations, inadequate capital formation, the entrance of women and young people into the labor force, and the unfair trade practices of foreign manufacturers. These elements explain only a small portion of the steady U.S. decline relative to other industrial nations.

The central problem, according to Reich, is that the U.S. has not moved quickly enough out of high-volume, standardized production. U.S. industry had achieved its stunning success by producing "ever larger volumes of standardized goods at even lower unit costs." Today, it is the developing countries that excel at the routinization of work and the standardization of technology. They can easily use mass-production techniques and far lower labor costs to compete aggressively against the U.S. and are bound to win. The development of automation overseas also means that high-volume production is easy to export. Hence, U.S. steel will continue to fall victim to South Korean steel, U.S. clothing to Hong Kong apparel, and U.S. autos to Japanese cars.

Another reason for industrial decline is U.S. firms' loss of their original innovative fire in production; they have instead become wedded to innovation through financial manipulations which Reich calls "paper entrepreneuralism."[8] Assets are rearranged on paper to improve cash flow or defer payments, tax rules are finessed, tax returns are manipulated, additional companies are purchased unnecessarily, accounting rules are changed, and numbers on balance sheets are arranged to look better to stockholders. Reich argues that in the long run the firms lose productivity. His solution is to move from "mass production" to "flexible systems" of production. To do so effectively, highly skilled workers must use computerized techniques for producing products based on precision engineering, custom tailoring, and rapidly developing technologies. The new products will come from such emerging industries as biotechnology and robotics, as well as from special segments of old industries.

Reich also argues that a new method of work organization is required in the "flexible systems." It will flatten out traditional hierarchies of work and introduce some degree of management democracy. There can be "no hierarchy to problem solving"; solutions should come "from anyone, anywhere" in the labor force.

Many economists see value in Reich's arguments against paper entrepreneuralism as a drag on productivity, and for a major shift toward flexible systems. Yet, such systems seem most appropriate only for certain industries; not all can move profitably in this direction. Many social economists, therefore, have also considered other insightful theories to round out the picture.

Theory of economic democracy

An important study of the causes of industrial decline has been made by economists Samuel Bowles, David Gordon, and Thomas Weiskopf.[9] They argue that the causes are rooted in three major institutional complexes that supported high economic performance in the first two decades after the Second World War but then began to break down.

The first institutional complex was in the development of a *Pax Americana* and a military–industrial complex following the Second World War. The new power position of the U.S. after the war was a major factor in vitalizing the economy in the late 1940s and the 1950s. In the next two decades overseas business was increasingly beset by Third World rebellions, and domestic business by competition from exporting firms in advanced countries. Profits began to decline markedly.

The second institutional complex is found in a "capital–labor accord" that began in the immediate postwar period but also fell apart in succeeding decades because of the Vietnam war, labor unrest, and the civil rights movement. There were significantly more strikes and greater labor resistance to management policy. The authors found a major increase in the ratio of supervisors to nonsupervisory personnel between 1960 and 1966, an increase they attribute to an attempt by management to regain control over the labor force. This only raised costs and worsened the decline in productivity.

The third institutional complex was the "capitalist–citizen accord" that was maintained successfully in the late 1940s and the 1950s but lost out during the late 1960s and the 1970s. In the postwar period the major decisions of economic life – technology, product design, industrial location, occupational health and safety, environmental balance – were "problems of the market." The accord disappeared in the 1970s, with the rise of a consumer movement that challenged the right of business to control areas affecting citizens' lives, and that raised questions about such issues as environment and product safety. The breakdown in the accord was accompanied by restrictive legislation and a decline in profits during the last two decades.

For these economist-researchers, the solution to the breakdown of the accords is to create grounds for a new accord based on institutions operating in the public interest. This means the establishment of new systems of social accountability in each institutional complex. In overseas operations, it means new methods for establishing social justice in the structure of multinational corporations; in labor relations, new arrangements of worker participation and ownership in industry; in the community, new types of social enterprise, such as community development corporations, that can reestablish the trust needed between citizens and the business system. The authors recommend a twenty-four-point economic bill of rights that includes tax-based price controls to deal with inflation, programs to increase worker participation and productivity, the encouragement of social services (e.g., day-care centers) to help make full employment possible, nationalizing banking institutions to democratize the investment process, and the formation of community-based enterprises to bring the business system into greater harmony with citizens and consumers.

These studies discussed above indicate the range of current interpretations of industrial problems. We could not cover their rich detail, nor could we discuss the important contributions of others. Our purpose was to point to basic positions and to argue from these that an integral perspective could be developed within a sociological framework. Without trying to fulfill that mission, we here suggest the grounds on which others might begin. We argue that this economic research is largely concerned with the social governance of industrial life, the central issue of a new industrial policy.

The conclusions of these authors and others to be touched upon suggest that a sociological interpretation is needed. Economic decline is not explained solely in terms of economics or finance. The problem and its solutions are to be found more fundamentally in the sociology of industry. These studies make it clear that business rests on a social foundation that creates the difference between success and failure. They show that *profits and productivity are functions of the social organization of business*.

This is not a radical concept for interpreting industrial studies; rather, it represents a deeper understanding of the essential factors underlying industrial behavior. The conservative George Gilder, for example, is taking a sociological perspective when he makes his case for business operating on a nonstatist foundation. When he proposes that the social relations of business provide a sounder basis for managing an economy than government controls, his essential argument is based not on economics but on the distinctions and functions of major institutions of society. Gilder believes that the institutional separation of the state and the economy offers greater values than the dominance of one by the other; that the production of goods and services cannot be run efficiently by a state bureaucracy; and that a greater degree of individual freedom is achieved by the separation of institutions. His argument for efficiency bears on a value of economics. The overall argument, however, is essentially sociological.[10]

Most of the studies we discussed stressed how important worker involvement in corporate management is to morale, productivity, and profits. This is indeed a matter of economics, but its essence lies in the sociology of the enterprise. Each study points to a problem related to economics but is primarily an issue in the social organization of industrial firms.

The same point can be made for studies by other economists. Lester Thurow, for example, argues in effect that the social organization of the economy functions like a zero-sum game in which losses equal winnings because every economic decision produces losers as well as winners. But the social rules and the organization of industry could be changed. Thurow says that a redistribution of income is an essential part of that change. Changing the income (class) structure is an important part of the resolution of economic stagnation and for avoiding the zero-sum game. The new industrial policy should include a new tax program. It should also include repeal of the antitrust laws in the light of the pressure by foreign competition. Such a policy is, of course, open to debate, but it is grounded on complex assumptions about the way industry can govern itself successfully outside government regulation.

Barry Bluestone and Bennett Harrison declare that industry has not governed itself well by closing factories and rapidly diversifying the management of corporations into bumbling conglomerates. The impact of runaway plants and capital flight overseas has been devastating for the U.S. economy. Bluestone and Harrison conclude that an increase in the social accountability of firms to their constituencies is necessary.[11]

These studies are all concerned with the way industry is governed. Their integral underlying concept – even when not explicitly mentioned – is social (self-) governance: *the way industry governs itself as a social system*. It is important to underline this fact because it is not a normal part of economic research, and it has consequences in public policy. Because industry is not analyzed by economists as a problem in social governance, legislators do not recognize that business decline and business cycles are caused by the social organization of business. Mainstream economists define problems typically in terms of interest rates, wage structure, or profits. Because studies of business are normally conducted from the standpoint of economics, solutions are usually stated in economic, not social, terms.

Our argument is that industry is institutionally underdeveloped. Economic factors are partly the effects of a contradictory and poorly developed infrastructure within industry. Economic remedies such as lower interest rates, lower wages, higher capital investment, and so on are not by themselves the real solution. They are simply Band-Aid remedies that allow the underlying organizational problems to continue unabated.

The proper identification of the primary problem is important because it tells us where to formulate solutions. For example, to identify the decline of the steel industry in only economic terms (e.g., high wages) leads to an economic solution (e.g., lower wages), but to identify it as a social problem (e.g., worker alienation) leads to a social solution (e.g., worker participation and ownership). Both social and economic factors are correlated with the decline of steel, but their priority in terms of the primary cause of the problem has not been clearly identified. This may be because it is much easier to act on only the economic factors, that is, to lower wages, to lay off workers, or to file for bankruptcy, rather than combine social and economic factors. Yet we know that it is possible to do the latter and change the organizational climate of firms in troubled industries.

Such combining was done at Eastern Airlines in the midst of a financial crisis. Management at first defined the problem solely in financial terms; it was facing major losses, paying out high wages, and anticipating the costs of an impending labor strike. The logical solution was to file for bankruptcy proceedings, but at the last minute, the problem was redefined as one of labor–management relations and governance of the firm. The solution was a trade-off between wage reductions and a new system of co-management in the corporation. Labor and management agreed to a process of joint decision making on policy, and they have been developing a new method of corporate governance: labor representatives must acquire skills in higher management and union representatives are seated on the board of directors. Labor had to give up some income to lower corporate costs but is compensated with stock ownership. Labor agreed to improve productivity; management agreed to share financial information on the company with the unions. The final steps to a successful conclusion at Eastern involve first, creating a special training program for top management and union leaders that encourages them to accommodate their traditional differences within a new administrative structure. The key players, Frank Borman, Chairman of the Board, and Charles Bryan, President of Eastern's International Association of Machinists and Aerospace Workers, have yet to reconcile personal differences rooted in part in the historic differences of the labor–management structure. Second, it involves altering the organization of share ownership so that stock cannot be purchased by outsiders except by consent of the employees. If this is not done, the failing-or-successful firm becomes vulnerable to outside buyers. A failing firm can be purchased quickly by a conglomerate seeking a tax write-off. Successful, employee-owned firms – like the *Kansas City Star* and the Vermont Asbestos Group – are soon purchased by wealthy outsiders to expand their power and control over the market.

A social solution was devised at Weirton Steel (7,000 employees), where workers were offered ownership and participation in management in return for a reduction in wages. Weirton needed to lower its labor costs by 32 per cent. Employees were offered stock in partial compensation for a direct pay cut. The creative combination of wage cuts, participation, and ownership has worked so far. Weirton Steel is making healthy profits while other steel companies are still attempting to recover from the industrial decline.

The problem of industrial decline and more broadly of business cycles could be defined as a problem in social development. Correction means not only retooling of equipment and refinancing of some failing firms but reorganization of industry. It does not mean that some firms must not die, but does suggest a new look at industrial relations. Industrial relations includes labor and management and also the involvement of trade associations, consumer organizations, professional associations, and research institutes. It means social inventions that can improve the productivity of industry, and a new system of governance for the infrastructure of industrial life.

Let us look at a new industrial relations and some of its components. Its social dimensions can be an important guide to investors. It will emphasize social policies that have not been fully developed in recent studies.

Social policy: investment guidelines

Productivity and corporate governance: the collaboration of labor and management

One of the factors to which industrial decline is attributed is reduction in productivity. The seriousness of lessened productivity is debated – it varies by industry – but its importance to industrial policy is widely acknowledged. Its causes are complex, but a major element is the adversary nature of the labor–management relationship.[12] Studies show that the adversary structure creates more problems than it solves, and that it served well from the thirties to the sixties but today is a hindrance to production. It leads periodically to costly strikes, wage-price spirals, inflation, unnecessary court battles, featherbedding, inappropriate work rules, collective hostility, and resistance to change. The ultimate cost is diminished productivity and a host of government regulations, laws, and monitoring agencies. Business leaders, union leaders, economists, and social scientists have begun to call for a basic change in the relationship of labor and management. They argue that a different kind of relationship could be more effective in fulfilling the purposes of industry.[13]

The replacement of the contemporary labor–management relationship would be a complex process but would not require increasing government controls over industry or abandoning union organization. In fact, it actually could lead to fewer controls and a strengthening of labor participation in the economy. It does mean encouraging experiments that have already begun in many industries. The experiments indicate that greater labor participation in management via union cooperation can result in an environment more conducive to productivity and profit making. The experiments also suggest *how* we may replace the adversary structure with a system beneficial to labor and management, and in the public interest.

We have said that labor and management have been experimenting with worker self-management at all levels, including, first, quality-of-working-life projects and union involvement at low levels of job control through workshop committees; second, middle-level administration through labor–management committees; and third, at the top level, labor participation on the board of directors.[14] The results show relatively consistent correlations between increased employee participation in management and higher productivity.[15] The reason, partly, is that in joint endeavour there is a tendency for each side to trust the other and a greater desire to fulfill goals together. There is mounting evidence that co-management in regard to policies at all levels is the direction in which the new human relations of industry is taking us.[16]

We have discussed problems of some firms becoming employee owned without self-management, but here we want to summarize arguments on the advantages of fully developed (worker owned-and-managed) firms to industrial planning. These firms are important to consider in making investment decisions when business is expected to be socially accountable and self-regulatory as well as economically productive.

Consultants present evidence suggesting that fully developed self-managed firms can be more effective than conventional firms because they are more likely[17] to (1) stay in business during recessions and when profits are low since they can more easily reduce salaries, adjust vacation times, and deploy internal capital for emergencies in their collective interest; (2) decide not to run away to other regions to avoid unions or raise profit levels; thus saving local communities from unemployment and the social costs of crime, drugs, and mental illness as well as government costs in jails, welfare, and rehabilitation; (3) keep capital circulating in localities (since they do not run away) through taxes and employee income spent locally, thus helping maintain other local institutions; (4) stimulate the personal growth of employees who train for higher levels of responsibility in the firm; (5) add to the effectiveness of employees as voting citizens because training inside the plant increases their interest in the democratic process; (6) develop a greater sense of belonging and meaningfulness at work; (7) reduce absenteeism, labor turnover, sickness, and tardiness of employees; (8) eliminate store theft because of peer pressure on fellow-workers to maintain a pattern of probity in their own firm; (9) reduce strikes and the costs of annual collective bargaining and government mediation; (10) increase productivity; and (11) reduce corporate costs by eliminating the need for middle managers and supervisors.[18] The evidence is still being gathered and evaluated, but social investors need to keep abreast of the compelling findings on the advantages of these firms.[19]

Investing in plants where workers are trained to participate effectively at top levels of management appears today to be sound industrial policy. U.S. corporations operating with subsidiaries in West Germany are evidence of this fact. Labor participates with management on boards of directors and on worker councils operating at middle-management levels. Codetermination has been shown to reduce strikes and thus save an industry from the enormous burden of lost working days. The European Economic Community is therefore taking the model of codetermination as the basis for policy in all its member nations.[20]

The important point in recent studies is the discovery that altering the structure of corporate governance improves the economics of industry. Including labor effectively saves the cost of maintaining middle-management supervisors. The study by Bowles, Gordon, and Weiskopf found that inordinate numbers of supervisors contributed to the causes of lower productivity and profits in industry. And John Simmons and William Mares ascertained that when the degree of self-management in corporations is increased, many supervisory personnel are not needed.[21] Add to this financial saving the welfare costs and unemployment compensation that are *eliminated* in instances where workers are able to purchase plants that might otherwise go out of production. We can then see a strong economic argument for training labor to participate in governance of the corporation.

The social and economic factors involved in discarding old patterns of labor management relations are complexly interrelated. The introduction of labor into the operations of management is effective only under the right economic conditions. One such condition is the retention of adequate profit levels of the company as part of the process. Another economic factor involves the stability of the market. At the same time the success of training for management is also dependent upon many social factors, including the readiness of employees to engage in it and positive attitudes among union leaders and top management. Both labor and management have at different times supported or resisted the process of increasing the responsibility of labor in the governance of the corporation; nevertheless, a whole range of new patterns of participation have been conducted effectively through their cooperation.

It is important to learn about the problems and the pitfalls of these changes as well as their potential for social development so that they contribute to the goals of the economy. For example, in the automobile industry, union leaders and executives in the three major companies are radically changing the structure of labor relations. First, the manufacturers have offered workers opportunities to buy subsidiaries in trouble.

Employees rejected a proposal by the Ford Motor Company that they buy a subsidiary in Louisiana, but accepted a proposal by General Motors in New Jersey. The technical details of this process of employee takeover merit study. It requires a basic change in labor attitudes and an innovative pattern of new investments to save a plant from closure.[22] Second, the government insisted that Chrysler during the bailout period offer its stock to employees through an ESOP, and the president of the United Auto Workers went on its board of directors. If we can ascertain where this venture has failed and where it has succeeded, a revised plan could be part of an investment package to help revitalize other industries.[23] Third, the auto companies and the United Auto Workers have initiated a major turnaround in their relationship. New steps toward mutual governance are underway in Mutual Growth Forums and the Saturn project. One legitimate subject is the governance of the corporation at different administrative levels.

In other industries there are also signs of new patterns of worker ownership, with labor participating on company boards. They foretell the creative destruction of the traditional conflict between labor and management, signs of a new social structure of corporate governance.[24]

> *Research and technology: collaboration between industry and universities*

Among the causes of the decline in productivity is outmoded technology. Many industries have fallen behind in their capacity to introduce new technology and adapt to changing times. Some researchers say that the reasons this is so is that some corporations have become bureaucratic and institutionalized. Executives began to slumber, secure in their imperial control over monopoly markets, and it required foreign competition to wake them. The notion may be partly true, but another view is that industries are not socially organized to keep pace with ever-new technology. Should networks of corporations within industries keep obsolescence at bay with assistance from organized labour and universities?

One part of the question is being answered today: corporations are beginning to seek out closer associations with engineering schools and institutes of technology as a way of keeping abreast of current developments. Top executives can thus maintain a dialogue with engineers and scientists and even anticipate major breakthroughs. Because markets are increasingly worldwide, such informational ties are necessary to compete successfully in the international arena.

Steps have already been taken by business to work with universities in high tech and robotics. Recently nineteen companies in computers and electronics contributed $750,000 each ($14.25 million) to Stanford University toward a research center for integrated systems. The companies are paying for construction of a building to which they will have access for research funded largely by federal agencies. One purpose of the combined efforts is to reduce duplication and faster efficiency in research. The venture is, of course, not without major risks. If a corporate representative develops a patentable product jointly with a Stanford professor or student, the company may ask that Stanford withhold the information up to ninety days until the patent is filed; the company gets free but nonexclusive rights to exploit the product. A danger in the arrangement for the university is the potential threat to its autonomy. The funding supplied by industry and the federal government could begin to shape the direction and the values of the university.[25]

This type of cooperative research is growing rapidly. A survey by the Center for Science and Technology Policy at New York University's Graduate School of Business Administration shows five major categories of organizations that engage in cooperative research:

1. Trade associations, such as the Chemical Manufacturers Association and the American Petroleum Institute.
2. Industry associations established specifically to fund or conduct research programs; these include the Semi-conductor Research Corp. of Research Triangle Park, N.C., and the Electric Power Research Institute (EPRI) based in Palo Alto.
3. Subject-specific centers based at universities and using seed money from the federal government, such as the Center for Research on Polymers at the University of Massachusetts, or from interested companies, such as the Stanford University Center for Integrated Systems.
4. Independent research institutes funded by companies to make nonproprietary technical advances and apply research related to "the public welfare." The Sulphur Institute and the Chemical Industry Institute of Toxicology are examples.
5. Independent institutes with a dual focus on education and research, established by an industry to address its labor needs and to do nonproprietary research. The Institute of Paper Chemistry, an accredited degree-granting institution, and the Textile Research Institute affiliated with Princeton University are examples.

Lawrence J. White, a professor of economics at New York University, while cautious about cooperative modes of research, finds certain advantages to them. They can lead "to lower prices, better service, more variety in quality levels, greater efficiency and lower costs in production, and larger output." They have an "economy of scale" that is advantageous to small firms. Industry associations such as the American Egg Board, the American Soybean Association and Development Fund, and the National Livestock and Meat Board fund research efforts that are beyond the capabilities of small firms. At the same time, the likelihood of noncompetitive behavior can increase, a possibility that requires careful attention.[26]

A key question in collaboration concerns the participation of labor and management in the planning of new technology. The argument is that the collaboration of trade associations and labor unions for industrial planning need not involve the federal government and need not interfere with fair trade. The inclusion of labor in industrywide plans for introducing technology enhances the possibility of success, in part through the establishment of joint committees between trade unions and trade associations. This could also be done through the creation of industry councils that could reduce the likelihood of labor resistance and conflict during the process of collaboration with management. Councils are an important part of a new system of governance.

Industry councils: collaboration of trade associations and trade unions

The idea of establishing industry councils has been floating around for decades in the United States but has not yet been implemented. The Industry Council Plan was annually approved by C.I.O. conventions from 1941 to 1955, always by unanimous vote. The 1948 proceedings state: "An Industry Council [would be] composed of representatives of organized labor, industrial management and government, and where possible of ultimate consumers." Further, "There should be a National Production Board on which there would be representatives of organized labor, farmers, consumers, industrial management and government." Finally, "The planning and administrative process should involve an interchange of ideas and decisions between the Industry Councils and the National Production Board in order that a general national plan may be evolved by democratic methods, and adjusted and perfected constantly over a period of years." Each industry – such as auto, steel, building construction – would have its own council.[27]

The International Association of Machinists recently formulated a plan for rebuilding industry, whose purpose is "to promote full employment, economic growth and price stability" by "establishing an independent Labor Industrial Sector Board to develop, coordinate and direct a national investment and industrial production program," a "Domestic Investment and Production Office," and a "Federal Pension Fund Development Bank." The chair of each industrial sector would select respective vice-chairs from among union members, business or industrial management personnel, and professionals who have had significant experience with each respective industry.[28]

Trade unions generally participate in the determination of national policies in European countries. In the United Kingdom, representatives of the Trades Union Congress serve on the National Development Council jointly with management. In Sweden union representatives sit on the Labor Market Board, which determines the timing of private investment decisions. French unions participate in the National Economic Council as well as many modernization committees that set investment, export, and other targets. Dutch unions are represented in the Labor Foundation and the Social and Economic Council, which are concerned with wage and price policies.

Councils can be democratically organized, with representatives appointed by trade associations and trade unions in each industry. They may be formed by consensus without government participation for the purpose of gathering basic information about the industry. Councils can be staffed with researchers to supplement the work of trade associations and trade unions in gathering data on such matters as productivity, strike costs, litigation costs, profit levels, health and safety records, and environmental costs. The collaboration of labor and management staff in this regard signally reduces the conflict that develops around statistics and data on industrial performance.

As labor and management become comfortable with council arrangements, it is possible to strengthen the councils by adding to the number of functions performed. For example, councils could engage in *labour mediation*, provide *final arbitration procedures*, offer *worker retraining programs*, *settle problems in pension liabilities*, experiment with *quality-of-working-life projects*, provide *training programs for labor participation in management, coordinate the resolution of interindustry and interunion conflict*, and develop *institutes on research and development* along with studies on the *impact of new technology* on the work force. Government legislation sympathetic to such purposes could provide incentives for labor and management to move rapidly in this direction.

Industry councils make good economic sense. They should be the type of organizations that help alleviate the "information complexity" and "resource scarcity" so important to industries in the findings of Lawrence and Dyer. This means that they contribute to the profit-making capacity of firms. Social planning in the councils should enhance the technical position of industries competing on the world market. Councils should also help management and workers conduct feasibility studies for the purchase of ailing plants, thereby reducing government costs in welfare for the unem-

Social criteria and research

ployed. They might even establish retraining programs for employees seeking to manage shut-down plants. Councils might also help to eliminate labor unrest by studying the impact of new technology on the work force. In these and similar activities economic benefits should easily outweigh what is spent on council administration.

The central problem in establishing councils is as much social as economic; it is to overcome the antagonism between labor and management. Part of the answer could lie in devising an educational method of industrial self-studies with University consultation that does not require government oversight. But it is clear that industrial economics would be vastly improved by a new pattern of cooperation between trade associations and trade unions.

Decentralizing conglomerates: collaboration of autonomous companies

Studies have shown that large conglomerates, by virtue of their power over the market, become sluggish in productivity and bogged down in the red tape of their own bureaucracies. This is what Max Weber described euphemistically as the rationalization of power. He proclaimed the value of bureaucracy as rational organization but also declaimed its shortcomings to be commanding size and impersonality. In fact, he feared the growing dominance of bureaucracy, that it would end up dominating both capitalist and socialist states. The only remedy he could suggest was a reversion to small-scale organization, what today we might call debureaucratization.

Weber never explored the process he called reversion to small-scale organization.[29] He assumed that the trends toward bureaucracy were too great to overcome in our time. But tendencies toward such a reversion should still be noted, and in the field of business management we can see small steps in this direction. They are important to witness for their relevance to our theory of self-development in the governance of industries.

Peter Drucker has counseled decentralizing big corporations to increase their vitality and flexibility in meeting market demands. This means adding to the autonomy of divisions (or departments) so that they have a greater decision-making power. In some cases, corporations have made subsidiaries into profit centers where gains and losses are calculated in a manner similar to the central administration. Subsidiaries are given major powers in sales, hiring and firing, and even in some cases the distribution of their own profits. Drucker describes this as "federalizing the corporation," by which he does not mean taking the final step of converting the corporation into a federation of companies, but the prospects are there and the economic advantages could be significant. Although he does not discuss the human value of increasing authority and self-direction among employees, he implies it. His policy increases the self-governing powers of managers in the corporation.[30]

The *Milwaukee Journal* is a special case in the newspaper industry. The story of its problems and its reorganization as a federation is of interest here. The *Journal* was incorporated in 1883 and began to prosper later under Harry J. Grant. Grant believed that "it is the right of men and women whose lives go into building a newspaper to have a share in its ownership," and in 1943 he proposed a plan for distributing stock to employees and for organizing the Unitholders (employee stockholders) Council of twenty-four members to represent the employee–owners. Council members were unitholders elected by departmental groups to two-year terms. Each group elected four members, who served with twelve unitholder company directors, one from each major department. The council variously encouraged understanding of democratic management and of company problems. From 1943 to 1980 more than 450 employee-owners were members of the council and 228 were members of the board of directors. The total number of employees grew to 1,800.

The company expanded and diversified rapidly in the last decade and ran into bureaucratic trouble. It purchased new companies in the conventional manner and did not include them in the democratic structure of the corporation. It began to design itself like a business conglomerate with many subsidiaries. New employees complained that they had no representation, and top management then saw its error. It had begun to function like an impersonal command bureaucracy. The company adjusted to the concerns of the workers in its subsidiaries by a restructuring of its original council, the addition of other councils, and increased attention to governance matters.[31] Thus, the *Journal* has become a social federation that seems to be a natural outcome of employee ownership. The personal authority of employees in each subsidiary is increased by the altered organization, which should be reflected in an enhanced capacity of the firm to be internally self-governing. It represents a choice for social development among conglomerate companies initiating patterns of worker self-governance within industries.[32]

Restructuring the multinational corporations: collaboration of autonomous companies

Some industries are deeply involved in overseas operations through multinational corporations (MNCs). MNCs have made high profits on their foreign investments in the past but Bowles and his associates show a period of decline caused by social and political problems. Executives in certain cases have engaged in political payoffs and transfer pricing, and have taken advantage of unequal wages and pricing in host and home countries in ways that have raised doubts about the ethics and wisdom of their practices. In turn, MNCs in various instances have faced production slowdowns, open rebellion in subsidiaries, nationalization, and political revolutions that have destroyed their operations. It has been asked whether the structure of multinational operations can be altered so that justice can reign and profits can be made for all parties in the relationship.

Executives in multinational corporations have become increasingly aware of the political repercussions of their command system and their overinvolvement in a hostile or unstable environment. They have been encouraging greater degrees of local participation. Social and economic factors are closely linked in these cases. It is cost effective and politically astute to reduce the number of U.S. managers in foreign subsidiaries and to increase the number of host-country managers. Executives have also found it worthwhile to raise the level of equity and stockholder participation for host-country citizens and workers, thus raising the level of self-reliance of nationals of the host society and simultaneously economizing in the operations. This is the beginning of the basis for a new contract for social development overseas.[33]

A whole new set of relationships is emerging as MNCs socially adjust to new leadership in host societies taking steps toward self-direction. For example, instead of the MNC providing the capital, technology, personnel, and managerial expertise to build and run a new factory, these elements of industrial expansion have been divided among foreign firms, consultants, and banks on the one hand, and the local government and local private firms on the other. Instead of inviting a big MNC like Xerox or General Motors to buy land and establish a subsidiary, the host society purchases the know-how from the U.S. firm, buys the necessary equipment from a number of different suppliers, hires foreign consultants to help set up the project, and uses domestic resources – such as private suppliers and a local training program – to help develop the new establishment. U.S. business is finding arrangements with host enterprises based on a new set of contracts, but even these changes do not foretell the fundamental restructuring taking place in the MNC itself.

The MNC is becoming more decentralized and socially effective in the current transitional stage. It is taking a federated form in some of its relationships with foreign enterprise, a change that began when the MNC became engaged in joint enterprises with foreign owners where its stock approximated 50 per cent. But the MNC has also changed qualitatively as it engages with nations where host labor serves on the board of directors of the subsidiary. We have noted that host workers are represented on the board of multinational subsidiaries in West Germany, and are in a position to influence the direction of local profits for the mutual advantage of both nations. The practice of codetermination exists in major subsidiaries of U.S. companies like Xerox and General Motors that operate in West Germany. The joint arrangement then redirects certain benefits and profits for international use.

The MNC has thus become a more democratic enterprise in certain instances. A new model is developing in which the board of directors can be composed of employee representatives as well as the company's representatives overseas. Some MNCs have even moved toward becoming a democratic federation. Indeed, federal structures have developed profitably in the organization of *multinational cooperatives*. In effect, the cooperative is an international federation of autonomous firms. The subsidiary companies are fully participating democratic units collaborating in the governance of this international enterprise.[34]

In sum, the MNC is finding a more democratic basis for making profits. It is developing a greater degree of cooperative governance overseas as executives recognize the importance of negotiating reciprocal benefits among the parties with opposing interests. This is a new direction for social investment because it also places MNCs on a much sounder economic basis. If they continue in this direction, they can provide opportunity for social development as well as a more reliable profit base for themselves.

A question remains as to whether the problem of runaway plants and capital flight promoted by MNCs can be treated. We have noted that capital flight is deplored by Bluestone and Harrison because of its devastating deindustrializing effects. When MNCs take their factories overseas, they deplete both labor and capital in the U.S. Yet it is accepted as a normal course of business by Robert Reich, who suggests that mass assembly lines and "fixed production" can go overseas without a loss as long as business can create new forms of flexible production in the U.S. He argues that mass assembly lines can be developed overseas with cheaper labor and that new craft-line production should begin in specialty areas within the United States. But he says nothing about what Bluestone and Harrison deplore: the unemployment thereby created in U.S. communities and the self-destructive patterns of business overseas.

A social policy should integrate the opposing ideas in these studies and bring us toward a creative solution to these problems. Let us construct an imaginary case for the future.

It is possible through tax incentives to encourage U.S. companies to de-

velop factories overseas under contract for future host–employee ownership. A company might contract with host investors to build a
mass-assembly plant that over time would become vested with employee
stock. Developing nations can use the economic advantage of such a plant.
The company would *gain its fair economic returns over a contracted period*
of five to ten years, during which the host company would develop its own
self-direction and its own contracts for international marketing. Under
these arrangements, the company is able to contribute to social and economic development overseas on terms that are just and economically
rewarding.

Simultaneously, the company plans for a domestic changeover to flexible
production so there are no worker layoffs. As it builds its plant overseas, it
also plans with its U.S. workers to build a new market in a specialty industry
recommended by university laboratories with which it has contracts. It
plans with unions to direct pension-fund capital toward a new product in the
industry, and then develops a retraining program in collaboration with
labor or an industry council. It introduces participatory management and
teaches employees new technical skills, very much in the Reichian model.
The company, then, has taken steps to overcome economic and social
underdevelopment abroad and at home. It has come of age in the new economics and sociology of industry.

Using pension funds: collaboration of industry and the government

Industry analysts assert that one economic cause of decline is the lack of
investment capital for industrial development. To that supply-side economists reply that lower taxes would give companies greater reserves for
investment. Such a solution is based on certain social assumptions about the
way business executives make decisions. One is that the money will be
invested in accordance with supply siders' thinking, but as many studies
show, business does not behave as expected with its capital reserves.
Another assumption is that lowering taxes will not result in a large government debt, but here the attitudes of politicians play a key role. If the debt
increases significantly, it kicks back against industrial vitality with higher interest rates. Again, the economic solutions are intimately linked to social
and political research.

We could explain a lack of capital from a sociological perspective and
find another source of funding. We could define the problem as embedded
in the institutional conflict between labor and management and the control
of pension funds. Some analysts find it ironical that billions are available for

investment through pension funds while their use for industrial recovery and stabilization is ignored. This is a problem in their mutual governance.

The use of pension funds demonstrates the sensitive interdependence of labor and management in industry. The funds are in trouble if the industries in which they are invested do not maintain a suitable and reliable profit return. Yet the funds are managed largely by banks and fiduciaries whose own special interests may sometimes take precedence over labor-oriented prudence. Imprudence can arise if a bank takes advantage of fund-managing power to protect its customers; for instance, banks invest funds in a business of which it is a creditor, a manifest conflict of interests. Further, a bank may seek to control corporate policies of its investees through interlocking directorates, and in consequence may keep fund investments in failing companies even when the rate of return is very low to save the company and thereby the loan. We noted earlier that pension funds are not always invested prudently. One ten-year study found the annual returns on pension fund investments to be far below the average annual returns of Standard and Poor's index stocks. The trustees could have done better by investing in union-built housing for the poor at low interest rates.[35]

Still more shocking in the use of these funds is their diversion to competing foreign companies. They are a factor in the failure of U.S. companies and thus the cause of mass layoffs in which workers can lose *pensions as well as jobs*. To illustrate: pension funds in the steel industry have been invested in Japanese steel and support its competitive advancement. U.S. Steel has been falling behind Japan technologically and has laid off thousands of employees. Such a turn of events might have been avoided through the collaboration of labor and management and the investment of pension funds in new technology.[36]

The typical pension fund takes in much more than it pays out in benefits and expenses. Only a relatively small portion of pension assets needs to be invested in high liquid securities that can be sold on very short notice to raise cash. At least some portion, then, of the aggregate pool of more than $1 trillion could be invested in new plant technology. All told, the pool is a powerful investment source because of its flexibility.

Many parties have a stake in the investment of pension funds. The federal government has a stake because it is ultimately responsible for the welfare of major industries and the security of its citizens; such a massive amount of capital can seriously affect the direction of the economy. Management has a stake because it contributes to the funds and its companies are the recipients of the investments. Employees have a stake because the quality of their working lives is dependent on these investments. Trade unions have a stake because their members are the beneficiaries, and fund investments are often inimical to their interests.[37] And the separate *states and cities* have an interest in public pension funds because their money may be invested in companies that shut down plants and leave their jurisdictions in dire straits.[38]

These parties are beginning to use social criteria in overseeing pension fund investments. Among unions, the building trades have taken the greatest initiative. Building trade unions in Southern California have joined in a foundation to facilitate investments in union-built structures. The Milwaukee building trades combine 20 per cent of their assets in pension funds toward union construction. The International Brotherhood of Electrical Workers has placed over 40 per cent of its assets toward mortgages related largely to housing. In the public sector seven states have directed their pension funds toward home mortgages within their boundaries. New York City has a proposal before it for a $100 million program of pension investment in housing rehabilitation and small business development within the city.[39]

A new sense of values is developing in the recent efforts of organizations to direct pension investments, but there remains the problem of private power. An inequality in power develops in the investment process when the more conscious, coordinated, and financially endowed organizations begin to win in the private use of funds. The remaining question is how to provide a national basis for fair investment in the interest of everyone.

One suggestion is that a tripartite commission of labor, management, and government try to arrive at the proper social foundation for a new investment policy. The basis for investment in a balanced development of industry from supply and production to wholesale and retail outlets requires systematic study and oversight at the top governing levels of the corporate economy. The answers, of course, cannot be reached only through the fields of finance and economics, important as they may be in understanding the problems. The problems are political and social as much as financial and economic. They are political, because pension funds are defined by law as "deferred wages," and it is not yet clear how this translates into pension control by contributors and beneficiaries. The interest of labor is critical to the direction in which funds go but there are legal issues to be settled in the pattern of organizational control. And the problems are social because labor, management, and government, each with a stake in the investment, do not have a mechanism by which they can cooperate to make investment decisions.

The proper social foundation for investment policy becomes, then, a matter of interest to social scientists in that social criteria need to be combined with economic criteria to guide the investment process. This requires data from social research with interpretations for an industrial policy.

Hence social scientists should be included with economists and financiers as advisers regarding investment decisions. Indeed, a new investment policy will require not only a basic change in the traditional labor–management patterns but the involvement of social scientists in financial institutions and investment decisions.

In summary

Many economists are concerned that U.S. industries are lagging behind industries in other nations. Their studies show that social factors are intricately involved with economic factors in industrial problems, and suggest that a policy for industrial development should be informed by a sociological perspective. From this viewpoint we have offered policy recommendations oriented toward a new system of governance for industry.

First, new methods for cooperation between labor and management are essential to the effective governance of corporations. Labor participation in management is proving to be "better economics" for various reasons. For example, we know that labor participation in management decisions can reduce the cost of strikes and labor unrest. We know also that labor participation in middle management can contribute to higher morale and higher productivity. Further, labor participation permits the salvaging of corporations through worker ownership and reduces the costs of welfare and unemployment compensation. We know too that labor self-management provides the basis for doing away with a vast body of middle-level supervisors added by management to deal with unmotivated workers.

Second, the lag in technical development and the challenge of foreign competition require new methods of collaboration between industries and universities. Research technology now involves not only firms but also labor unions in joint projects with institutes of technology and engineering schools. It can mean as well the participation of an industry council representing everyone potentially affected.

Third, it is important for trade associations and trade unions to find a basis for collaboration in the study of their industry. We have suggested the formation of industry councils to examine current social and economic problems, and, among other things, to promote retraining programs and develop policies for pension investments.

Fourth, multinational corporations are developing new methods of social governance with their affiliates overseas and have already instituted adjustments that have included divestment of foreign ownership from host countries. We believe MNCs can go still further toward becoming more stable and viable investments. All things being equal – including management and marketing effectiveness – our hypothesis is that a federation of companies under shared governance is the most dependable and "just" form of MNC, and would be the most profitable to all parties in the long run.

Fifth, a tripartite (labor, management, government) commission should be established to study and recommend a social foundation for an investment policy for pension fund capital that would take into account the public interest as well as the interest of beneficiaries. Such a policy would mean combining social criteria and economic criteria in the investment process.

In conclusion, the social development of industry is a critical aspect of business revitalization and stability today. *Socioeconomic research* into corporate systems and the governing infrastructure of industry is fundamental to the promotion of future policies, and accordingly is given special attention in the next chapter. If such research is adequately supported and attended to, Congress should be less likely to repeat the mistakes of the past and more likely to lay solid groundwork for industrial development in the last years of this century.

6 Social research on industrial policy

A new industrial policy is best grounded in a theory whose propositions can be tested and evaluated through empirical research. We have no such theory and little research activity to evaluate the consequences of implementing a new industrial policy. Our purpose here is to initiate steps in this direction, to develop the conceptual basis for a research paradigm that provides an integral view of the social and economic factors operating to affect the performance of industries. A theory is implicit in the conceptual foundation of this paradigm, and the propositions we suggest can be tested by following its guidelines.

We want to create a design for studying industrial performance that also provides insight into social self-regulation. Our task begins with a theoretical orientation that justifies trade groups as important to shaping industrial performance and providing a basis for self-regulation. Second, we outline a research paradigm that includes trade groups as one of many variables predictive of industrial performance. Third, in the light of our paradigm, we suggest hypotheses for the causes of high or low performance in particular industries. We are interested in how experiments could be conducted by social investors to reduce the necessity for government regulation. Then, we examine how paradigm studies could lead toward a theory of the public good. We come face to face with Adam Smith's concept of the invisible hand and the eighteenth-century argument for laissez-faire. We conclude with a discussion of how the private sector has been developing its own "invisible hand" to regulate the economy toward the larger public good.

Theoretical orientation

Many theories on industrial policy have been advanced but the clearest controversy is between the supply-side economists represented by George Gilder and the radical economists represented by Samuel Bowles. Gilder on the "political right" aims to eliminate taxes and federal regulation without changing the system of business. Bowles on the "political left" aims

117

to change the system by developing economic democracy through government participation and regulation. The normal assumption is that one position must be wrong, the other right. In reality, the theories are much more complexly related.[1]

To assume that the two theories are incompatible diverts us from the real task of research, which is to assess the degree of truth in each. Our best assumption is that each has some validity and that their opposing positions should be integral to our research paradigm. We suggest that their key goals and most persuasive ideas can be studied and tested together. For example, we would start with the proposition that certain key goals of each theory can coexist in the same economic system, that Gilder's goal of developing free enterprise and reducing government regulations can coexist with Bowles's goal of developing economic democracy and social justice. We are not trying to formulate a theoretical synthesis but, rather, to point toward a methodology for testing the empirical integration of their ideas in the development of industry.

There are certain broad assumptions implicit in the paradigm. First, we assume that it is possible to increase democratic practices in the private economy in experimental cases in a manner that enables business to regulate itself with less need for government controls. Second, we assume that it is possible to take experimental steps toward democratic accountability while maintaining an optimum level of productivity and profits in the industry. In sum, we propose to test whether business can become relatively democratic, self-regulatory, productive, and profitable at the same time.

We make these broad statements about the direction of investment and research knowing that success depends very much on particular steps taken at each level of the economy. Not all the methods for achieving these goals are fully known. Therefore, to contribute toward a greater understanding of the developmental process, we want to add some missing links that will become central variables for us in evaluating experiments in the development of a social economy, one based on cooperative as well as competitive processes of economic exchange, as we shall see.

Missing links: the democratic federation

The missing links in the developmental process can be found conceptually in the democratic federations that already play a key role in reducing government regulation. Federations of competing businesses and their relations to one another as buyers and sellers are often overlooked by industrial theorists. They need to be recognized not only for their contribution toward maintaining productivity but also for establishing self-regulation and self-resolution of problems even while their members compete with one another in the marketplace.

The federations not only have been critical for the development of self-regulation but have helped make possible the degree of freedom and social justice that exists in the business system. We want to know how these federations contribute toward the creation of democratic values within the competitive order of business, and how they may utilize capital to advance the values in a system of industrial self-governance. The answers can become the basis for establishing criteria for social investment and designing empirical studies that can test movement toward the goals of Gilder and Bowles.

Let us look at the democratic federations to see how they resolve their own problems without government intervention. They are not an official part of the economy any more than political parties are a constitutional part of the political order, yet the system could not operate effectively without them.

Federations of competing firms

We have noted that trade associations are nonprofit federations of business competitors to advance their common interests, and they exist in great variety nationwide.[2] They are organized horizontally and vertically. A horizontal association's members are in the same field; for instance, the Rubber Manufacturers Association's members are manufacturers of rubber products. Vertical associations are fewer in number and consist of buyers and sellers, for example, the Better Vision Institute, which includes manufacturers, distributors, and service people in the optical products field. Associations can be classified functionally and geographically as well as by trade (table 6.1).

Trade associations solve many social problems that develop between competing member firms and also create other problems. They solve problems by cooperating to develop ethical codes, create product standards, establish arbitration boards, organize trade fairs, collaborate on research and development, and formulate standards for advertising, and by engaging in many other activities designed to advance their particular industries in the context of society.

But the associations have been subject to their own faults in structure and leadership. Some of them are undemocratic and exploitative. Like trade unions, their power to create democratic structures varies. Some are dominated by a few firms and others by a few leaders. A few have inhibited new firms from entering their industry. They are generally designed first to

Table 6.1. *Functional and geographic groupings of trade and professional associations*

Manufacturing	Distributive	Service	Professional
	National		
Automobile Manufacturers Association	Association of Food Chains	Linen Supply Association of America	American Institute of Architects
	Regional		
Southern Brick and Tile Manufacturers Association, Inc.	Southern Industrial Distributors Association	Southwest Warehouse and Transfermen's Association	Western Society of Engineers
	State		
Pennsylvania Bakers' Association	Texas Butane Dealers Association	Oklahoma Restaurant Association	California Osteopathic Association
	Local		
St Louis Association of Ice Industries	Chicago Association of Tobacco Distributors	Laundryowner's Bureau of Boston	Los Angeles County Medical Association

serve the pragmatic needs of their members and only secondarily to express human values and the public interest. The associations are complex entities that need to be studied further to ascertain in what ways they function directly in the public interest as well as in their own interest, and how investors can help them become more democratic and effective in their essential task of self-regulation.

Federations of buyers and sellers

The conflicts arising between buyers and sellers are resolved through joint committees and communication between associations. We can illustrate briefly how this is done in nine industries that were studied for their capacity to resolve conflicts in the distribution of their products. Researchers found that democratic federations of manufacturers, wholesalers, and retailers collaborated extensively to resolve their problems without government intervention and without illegal collusion. In such contrasting industries as *automobiles*, *petroleum*, *food*, *electrical products*, *television receivers*, *pesticides*, *pharmaceuticals*, *liquor*, and *farm equipment*, the trade associations advanced the common interests of their members even as the members of each were in a competitive (and conflictive) relationship.

The countervailing federations organized judicial systems, set up joint committees for communications, issued publications, established product standardization, devised common accounting procedures, and engaged in many other common activities while maximizing members' separate self-interests.[3]

We noted in chapter 3 that automobile manufacturers and dealers were in perpetual conflict at midcentury. The former dominated the marketplace and could treat dealers unfairly without much fear of legal recourse. The dealers then organized the National Automobile Dealers Association (NADA) in an effort to match the national strength of manufacturers, and NADA began to negotiate resolutions to problems with the "Big Three" car makers. The first dramatic evidence of change came in the 1950s. Partly in response to congressional pressure initiated by NADA, GM established a tribunal to hear cases having to do with alleged violations by GM of contracts with dealers. Subsequent studies suggest that the tribunal has acted fairly and objectively.[4]

NADA and the big manufacturers have since agreed upon uniformities in "posted prices" for automobiles as a measure of protection against unfair competition. They have also agreed on how dealers are to receive a number of vehicles corresponding to the sales potential of their areas. Such resolutions have had positive outcomes for manufacturers and dealers, but customers have also had to organize on their own behalf. Customer power is still relatively weak, even though it has begun to grow through such agencies as the Center for Auto Safety and the American Automobile Association.

The petroleum industry would require more government regulation than exists today were it not for its organized buyers and sellers. The American Petroleum Institute (API), the National Commission on Petroleum (NCPR), and the National Oil Jobbers Council (NOJC) have worked on many issues. For example, price discrimination by refiners has led to many price wars whose intensity caused retailers to break away from the NOJC because of its lack of support for stabilization. They formed the NCPR in 1947, to provide support for the Robinson-Patman Act. Subsequently, the price war situation was gradually resolved, and other problems began to find easier resolution. The NCPR and NOJC have formed a liaison committee to organize joint activities on "dealer management" and to sponsor sessions with refiners to voice complaints. The API, with NCPR support, has asked its member refiners to inform dealers concerning conflicts over "station management," "cost accounting," and "promotional procedures."

Other industries show comparable records of cooperation and accountability in the public interest while they compete in their own private interest. In the food industry, chains and independents have jointly studied pricing practices and cost structures. In the electrical industry, manufacturers co-operate with the National Association of Electric Distributors in publishing distribution policies concerning mutual obligations, discount structures, pricing policies, inventory requirements, advertising service, and representational policies. In the television-receiver industry, the National Appliance and Radio-TV Dealers Association (NARDA) initiated discussions with manufacturers on the "bypassing of dealers and sales through supermarkets" and came to what it believes to be a fair resolution. NARDA has also worked with manufacturers on mutually beneficial warranty policies, and has invited manufacturers to become members as a means of improving communications (twelve major manufacturers have done so). In the farm equipment industry dealers and manufacturers communicate through Dealer Councils, a system supported by the National Farm and Power Equipment Dealers Association. Problems of inventory control and service and warranty claims have been worked out.

Many trade associations have developed codes of ethics for their members, which are enforceable within the limited power under their constitutions to censure and expel members. The codes thus function as another self-regulatory system, reducing the necessity for government controls. For example, the Professional Standards Committee of the National Association of Realtors interprets and administers a code of ethics. The association has held thousands of disciplinary and arbitration hearings. Over 120 cases of discipline are used precedentially, in essence as "common law" for professional conduct.[5]

The consumer may be the most "unorganized" among the buyers and sellers of the economy. Nevertheless, the field of retailing has in many cases acted responsively to consumers because it is in its own interest to do so. The National Consumer Retailer Council was formed to improve relations between consumers and retailers to the advantage of both. Various trade associations and major retail stores have developed customer affairs departments to respond to complaints.

Consumer federations have developed to act across industries. Consumer organizations forced the Bank Marketing Association to enact a Financial Advertising Code of Ethics (FACE), which guides banks in making full disclosures and in conducting advertising. FACE asserts that consumers should be able to grasp essential information in an advertisement without reading every word of the fine print. Some observers believe the code has been an effective force for self-regulation in the banking field.[6] But FACE by itself would not be effective without consumer federations continuing to act. The Consumer Federation of America, composed of 220 nonprofit organizations representing over 30 million consumers, has been active in the banking field as well as in other industries. In April 1977 it chastised the Federal Reserve Bank for not enforcing the Equal Credit Act, and has met consistently with the House Banking and Finance Committee on advertising issues. As a countervailing power to banking federations, it supported the creation of a national consumer bank that would finance consumer credit unions as another countervailing power. It has often won its points on legislation protecting the consumer over the opposition of banking associations.

Other consumer organizations are also active in the banking field. Consumer Action is a San Francisco-based group of 4,000 families that has published *Break the Banks* and *It's in Your Interest*. The latter book compares passbook rates of forty-seven institutions and warns of bank malpractices. Consumer Action campaigned successfully for a consumer disclosure law that requires banks to provide customers with complete breakdowns of charges, interest rates, and methods by which rates are computed. It was able to force Bank of America to withdraw advertisements for automobile loans that it thought were misleading; the bank's three-year loan rate dropped from 13.26 to 12.39 per cent. Consumer Action also surveyed ninety-six advertisements in thirteen cities and reported unsubstantiated use of superlatives, distorted use of the word *free*, and failure to state clearly the conditions for receiving gifts. Further, it brought a suit against the Federal Reserve to force release of the data used in developing its monthly survey of consumer interest rates.

Trade unions are also part of the buyer–seller relationship even though they have other important functions than do trade associations and may have a different destiny. The relationship is more than by analogy. In effect, members sell their labor to corporations and negotiate that sale through collective bargaining. Insofar as trade union activity is successful, it has reduced the need for government intervention to protect workers from employer exploitation. The trend toward cooperative relationships between buyer–seller federations is visible in the recent trend toward worker participation and ownership. Union leaders have collaborated with management in various cases to avoid layoffs and to salvage failing firms, and have also organized tribunals and ethical codes for their members.

In sum, these various federations of buyers and sellers deserve attention for the key role they play in reducing the need for government controls.

Research guidelines

We can now reformulate the goals of Gilder and Bowles in terms of broad hypotheses about social development in industry. First, we propose that self-regulation is relatively advanced in industry when competing firms become organized democratically in trade associations. The cooperative relationship advances self-regulation as it provides opportunities for a nonstatist system to institute measures of relative justice for intensely competing firms. Second, we can say that self-regulation is partially advanced when federations of buyers and sellers (from producers to consumers) are equitably related in a system of social and economic exchange. In other words, deregulation can happen more easily when federations of buyers and sellers express an equitable balance of power and provide measures of social accountability in their exchange relationship. Self-regulation occurs when they are able to work together to solve their own problems.

These federations are the basis through which human values begin to be expressed by transcending the jungle of competition.[7] They are the structures by which social accountability can become institutionalized. Although the motive of self-interest is retained and the spirit of competition is kept alive, a type of cooperation between competitors can offer an opportunity to gain economic stability yet not sacrifice profitability. This can provide the grounds for achieving degrees of democracy and justice within a free market otherwise beset with conflict and the need for government intervention.

In search of a paradigm

Trade associations play a role in realizing the goals of Gilder and Bowles. They are the collective dimension of individual enterprise and serve as a force affecting the performance of an industry. They are formally *democratic structures* created within the system of *free enterprise* and in some measure express integrally the values of both theorists. We include trade associations now as one variable in our research paradigm.

We want to study the degree to which the broad goals of "enterprise freedom" (Gilder) and "social democracy" (Bowles) can be factored into industrial studies. The strength of free enterprise at this collective level is measured in such variables as the effectiveness of trade associations in achieving association goals, their access to market information, and their capacity to advance technological research (research and development expenditure). These variables are included in a category we call economic autonomy. They help us identify the causes of levels of *economic* performance within specific industries.

The strength of social democracy can be measured by such variables as degree of worker participation, power of consumer organization, balance of power between buyers and sellers, and the structure of employee ownership. We call this category structures of social accountability. These variables allow us to order and identify the causes of levels of *social* performance in an industry.

We assume that the causes of industrial performance can be found in the structure of the private sector. Let us now define the variables in our paradigm.

First, we will look at statistical indexes that measure the *social* and *economic* performance of an industry. Our assumption is that researchers can begin to measure both types of performance. Indeed, the measure of performance should become sophisticated enough to anticipate industrial problems well ahead of forecasts by business leaders. Our social researchers then become both fact assemblers and scholarly analysts of industrial development.

Second, we will look at what *causes* high or low performance within industries. We will identify measures that appear to cause changes in both *economic* and *social* performance. Once we have a set of indexes measuring the performance of industries and another set measuring the causes for that performance, we can begin to formulate hypotheses regarding the relationship between them.

This paradigm is intended for researchers testing propositions about the relationship between the social organization of industry and its performance. In chapter 3 we gave priority to a theory on the social organization of the economy because it was critical to understand the larger questions of social development. In chapter 5, we argued specifically that the poor performance of industries originated in problems in their social organization and governance. We asserted that social and economic factors were intertwined in the assessment of industrial performance and offered examples of their connection in specific cases. Now we seek an instrument for testing industrial performance with these factors in mind. Research based on this paradigm should tell us more clearly how the social organization of industry is related to its performance. Research should also help us to determine how industry can better govern itself. Put another way, this paradigm proposes that a causal relationship exists between social and economic factors in the performance of firms. Its framework is more comprehensive than current management theories and should therefore improve our capacity to predict performance with more accuracy. It should also increase our understanding of the social problems underlying the governance of industry. Researchers can select empirical questions to study within the paradigm and cumulatively build a factual foundation for guiding industrial policy.

We will provide examples of empirical questions to study in connection with the governance of industry after we define key categories of research in the paradigm. Developing an outline of the social-economic variables that affect industrial performance is complex, but it is time that we began the task even within this crude state of the art.

Measures of economic and social performance

Economic performance (Indexes)

The indexes we have selected below for measuring economic performance are useful by themselves in many ways. First, they can be used statistically to compare economic performance in the same industry from decade to decade. The cyclical character of the industry can be studied over time. Second, they can be used to compare the performance of one industry with another. The economic problems of a particular industry (e.g., newspapers) can thus be assessed in relationship to problems in comparable industries (e.g., television). Third, the indexes for one industry can be juxtaposed against national averages for all industries, and in this way an industry's lag in economic performance can be assessed in relationship to the performance of the larger economy. It is important to recall our argument that the indexes are the dependent variables in this research design. They are dependent upon the "structures" of autonomy and accountability in the industry, that is, upon the way industry is socially organized.[8]

The most common measure of economic performance is the *profit* of the firms, averaged for the whole industry. Second, *productivity* is important; it is measured as the real output per hour of work in all the firms of the industry. Third, the *business failure rate* is noteworthy for several reasons. A high rate generally signifies poor industrial performance, but it may also suggest that much innovation is occurring. Bowles et al. suggest it as a measure of innovative pressure, assuming that high-cost businesses are going under because of it. Fourth, the *vitalization ratio* serves as a counter-check on business failures; it expresses the relation between deaths and births of companies in the industry, and can indicate that an industry is economically self-perpetuating in spite of its business failures. Fifth, *capital intensity* is important in that it measures the annual percentage of growth of capital stock per hour. It indicates whether a capital shortage is causing the industrial decline. Sixth, the growth of *hourly income* is represented in the average annual percentage of change in the real net industry income per hour. It can be measured as a ratio of national income per hour, and thus becomes a measure of overall performance of an industry relative to the nation as a whole, and is closely related to the index of productivity. Seventh, the *utilization of productive capacity* is important because it affects the level of real output produced per hour of work. Low rates can discourage new capital formation and technological innovation as well as foretell a slowdown in the rate of productivity. Eighth, the *trade balance* is important to record as a ratio of export prices to import prices. Ninth, *import competition* is a closely related measure, expressing imports as a percentage of gross domestic products. Bowles et al. take these two last measures as signs of the degree to which Third World challenges and foreign competition could precipitate a decline in profits and productivity within the economy. All of these indexes are interrelated and closely interdependent with indexes of social performance.

Social performance (indexes)

Measures of social performance are difficult to obtain because they have not been considered important in the records of private industry, but most of them can be located in the records of government. We are looking at how people are affected by the conduct of firms in an industry, that is, employees, buyers, sellers, owners, and citizens in communities where the firms operate.

The corporate record of performance for employees should include the following data from government agencies: *job safety* (Occupational, Safety, and Health); *discrimination* (Equal Employment Office), *ratio of white/ black female earnings* (Labor Department); *strikes* according to their number, costs, and ratio in relation to union membership in the industry; *health and pension benefits*, *wages*, *'real spendable earnings,'* *quit frequencies*, *layoffs*, and *federal mediation* (Labor Department).

The data on the performance of industries in regard to consumers and the communities in which they reside are also obtainable: for example, data on *product safety* (Consumer Product Safety Commission) and the number of *advertising violations* (Food and Drug Administration and the Federal Trade Commission). There are *price indexes* in different phases of buying and selling that measure the cost to "customers" in the industry. The record of *environmental pollution* (Environmental Protection Agency) is critical for certain industries. It is also of interest to determine the extent of local *philanthropy* and management involvement in the life of local communities.

It is desirable to assess the performance of competing firms in relation to one another within an industry. A record of unfair competition and monopolistic behavior leads to government regulation and court costs. Therefore, we look first for the number of *arbitration cases* settled, distinguishing government mediation from private arbitration, and the ratio of the former to the latter. Private mediation and arbitration are indicators of more cases resolved in such fashion, that is, the more the industry is providing its own basis for conflict resolution. There are numerous private associations engaged in this activity, including the American Arbitration Association.[9]

Second, we look for the number of *violations of fair trade* recorded by the Federal Trade Commission, the Justice Department, and other regulatory agencies. It is possible to "detail" these statistics with different data on the number of violations and the amount of penalties attached to them.

We are omitting measures of the overseas performance of multinational firms at this point because of their complexity. Such measures of course could include percentages of change toward worker ownership and management in host subsidiaries.

Finally, it is important to determine the impact of various ownership structures on corporate owners. Here we record the *rate of dividend returns* in the industry and compare them with other industries. They become a measure of management responsibility to owners and a sign of how workers themselves may benefit through internal accounts if the firms choose to move toward employee ownership in the cooperative tradition. Employees benefit from dividends that support pension funds. These indexes may show low dividends in periods of corporation expansion and technical innovations but it is over the long term that dividends are important for employee owners. We also note the number of stockholder resolutions protesting corporate conduct. The percentage accepted and the percentage passed by management is significant, as is the record of appeals made to the Securities Exchange Commission.

Structures causing high performance: autonomy and accountability

Our next task is to classify the potential causes of high or low performance records (tables 6.2-3). Relevant research is scarce, and so our steps are exploratory; we can only offer hypotheses for investigation into the type of structures in an industry that lead to high or low performance. Our basic hypothesis is that industries with structures supporting institutional autonomy show high economic performance, and industries with structures supporting social accountability show high social performance.

Structures causing high economic performance: autonomy

An industry achieves autonomy in society partly by institutionalizing methods to protect itself from being taken over by the government and other industries. Its economic performance is closely related to its capacity to be institutionally independent. The structures it creates to maintain autonomy are therefore directly connected with its economic performance. One major structure supporting the economic performance of firms is the *trade association*. Other conditions being equal, we hypothesize that a strong trade association leads toward industry high economic performance; a weak trade association, generally low economic performance. The strength of a trade association is assessed by the way it is organized. This is where our studies of economic decline are helpful.

The authors of all our reported studies of economic decline press the point that technological innovation is critical to the capacity of firms to revitalize themselves. A key department to examine in the trade association is, therefore, *research and development*. It is not the only indicator, for we know that the level of competition and the degree of differentiation (specialists, technicians) within firms also play a central role, but the extent to which firms combine their funds with the common purpose of advancing the technology within their industry is an important factor in economic performance. For instance, the success of the plywood cooperation has been attributed in part to the extensive research and development efforts of the Plywood Manufacturers Trade Association that spare members these expenses.

Supply-side economists suggest that a principal cause of economic decline has been a multiplicity of government regulations and commissions. Bowles et al. say not, but admit it can be a factor in certain industries. Here we look to the trade association's department of *governmental relations* and the degree to which it has acted to eliminate government controls as opposed to increasing them. The trade association exists in part to protect its members from government regulation and intrusions into their business. We have stressed that trade associations are also responsible for creating government controls in their own interest, but their primary task is to create conditions conducive to maintaining members' autonomy.

Another key trade association department is sometimes called *clearing-house and communications*. It deals with "information complexity" (IC), which Lawrence and Dyer emphasize as important to success, and keeps member firms aware of trade activities by distributing news and information on government legislation, trade conferences, staff projects, and company members.

Table 6.2. *Measures of industrial self-governance: selected examples*

I. ECONOMIC MEASURES

(Independent variables)	(Dependent variables)
Structures of economic auatonomy	**Indicators of economic performance**
1. Trade association (strength)	1. Profits
a. Major departments (advertising, R and D, public relations, sales promotion, trade conferences)	2. Productivity
b. Staff expertise (degree/experience)	3. Business failure rate
2. Intermediate IC and RS	4. Vitalization ratio
3. Ratio of R and D expenditure of industry to national R and D expenditure	5. Capital intensity
4. Investment rate	6. Hourly income
5. Flexible systems	7. Utilization of productive capacity
6. Government policies	
a. *Tariffs*	8. Trade balance
b. *Taxes*	9. Import competition
c. *Subsidies*	

One more critical trade association department is *trade relations*, which searches for new markets and coordinates firms' advertising. Still another is the *trade conferences and sales promotion* department, whose staff help develop management skills, know-how about financial controls and sales techniques. Other activities include advancing common interests in standardization, simplification of products, legal advice to members and so on.

The trade association is a vehicle through which corporations in an industry can take action to improve their performance. For this reason they are important independent variables, but they are not easily quantified. There are other more quantifiable indicators of the structures causing high or low performance that should reflect trade association activities.

We may hypothesize that all industries showing an *Intermediate IC* and an *Intermediate RS* should show high economic performance.[10] The study of Lawrence and Dyer suggests that extreme indexes of information complexity or resource scarcity should lead to poor performance. The trade association helps to eliminate these extremes in some cases through its communications and trade-relations functions.

Another important index is the *R and D expenditures* of the industry as a proportion of the economy's total expenditure on R and D. The index also allows comparison with R and D rates in other industries. Again, the trade association should help to enhance the capacity for R and D in the industry.

Still another index is the *investment rate*, a measure of the net investment in an industry as a percentage of the net national product. It tells us the extent to which low investment may be a cause of low performance, and could lead to a new investment policy improving conditions in the industry.

The corporate members of trade associations may encourage the adoption of Robert Reich's "flexible systems" in the industry. Reich sees systems of flexible management as critical to high performance, and identifies these systems by the following criteria (our summary):

1 Product quality more important than quantity.
2 Close working relationships among employees.
3 High skills of employees.
4 Quick adaptation of product to consumer demand.
5 Flattened hierarchy; everyone participates in solutions.
6 Few middle managers.
7 No industrial superstructure controlling firms.
8 Informal authority system in firms.
9 Small salary differential.
10 Employee managed.[11]

These criteria stand opposed to the standardized mass-production system. They represent current guidelines for effective management and high economic performance, and they also blend with criteria for social accountability to employees within the firms of an industry.

The government can act to encourage industrial autonomy through various policies on *import/export tariffs*, *taxes*, and *subsidies*. The extent to which these policies encourage industrial autonomy, which in turn becomes related to performance, becomes a measure by itself. But these measures – as important as they may be to industrial performance – are not themselves a part of the infrastructure of industry as a self-governing system. They are therefore simply noted in italics to be observed in the analysis of autonomous forces that can lead to high performance.

Structures causing high social performance: accountability

Structures of accountability refers to the patterns of organization that have developed among workers, consumers, businesses, and owners to advance their own interests and to work together as a self-governing system. The way in which participants in the economy are organized expresses their degree of power and authority in gaining what they want, and has a great deal to do with the performance of an industry.

Labor organization is an important factor in assessing social performance, but the connection is complex. When unions are strong, they should cause a high social performance in specific areas in the industry, such as job safety, wages, and pension plans, and this helps an industry obtain a high performance score. At the same time, their strength may lead toward a high number of strikes, which could mean that labor is in transition toward a new accord with management.

The comparison of performance among industries can be complex because of opposition groups. A sudden rise in the power of the opposition (e.g., labor and consumers) can raise problems, that result in a low performance score and may not indicate any change in corporate behavior. This is simply a situation in which the opposition has been able to draw attention to a problem or an injury that heretofore it had not been strong enough to do. It is a period of consciousness raising. For this reason, it is important to pay special attention to the connection between the rise of an organized opposition and the subsequent rise in a business's social violations and low performance. The business practice of dominance, previously accepted, suddenly becomes violative.

In the case of strikes it is important to include a measure on the ratio of union members to all employees in the industry. This can aid in assessing the role of unions in causing a low performance score around the criterion of strikes.

The key measures of accountability to labor are found in the methods of increasing employee participation and responsibility in the firm, such as the degree to which firms have introduced labor-oriented programs in skill training, quality-of-working-life, and profit sharing, Scanlon plans, and labor representation on boards of directors. Further, labor decision making regarding the investment of pension funds within an industry should be noted; its extent denotes the responsibility of labor in controlling the wealth it helped produce.

The true measure of social accountability for labor rests in the effective skill training that makes possible a higher level of the precision work that Reich describes as well as a higher level of responsibility in corporate management. As labor participation increases, we can expect the salary range between top and bottom employees in firms to narrow. We are also likely to see a higher educational attainment level among all employees in the industry. It is customary today for large corporations to send top management back to school for higher degrees because they see the value of this for improving economic performance. It is conceivable that in the future this privilege may be extended to middle- and lower-management employees, and even blue-collar workers.

As we indicated earlier, it is highly desirable to distinguish the number of cases in which mediation between labor and management is a private as opposed to a government activity. The more that an industry is able to count on *private mediation* to settle its problems, the more it has learned to become self-governing. It is also important to test union democracy, that is, the extent to which a union acts and its own democratic principles. The 1959 Labor–Management Reporting and Disclosure Act requires unions to engage in democratic voting procedures, to maintain a constitution and by-laws, and to disclose specific information concerning the amounts of union funds and the uses to which they are put. Violations of the Act can be interpreted as part of a low performance score in the industry.

It is also critical to examine *consumer organization* within the industry. The strength of consumer federations designed to monitor the industry is important to social performance. The consumer organizations mentioned above and many other associations are vital to the maintenance of social accountability within industries. Because different consumer groups monitor different industries, classification of their importance as a countervailing power is dependent upon which industries are being studied for investment.

As we have indicated, in any industry the balance of power among *buyers and sellers* moving a product from its raw state to its finished, retail form is a significant factor. Any imbalance can result in exploitation of the weaker parties, with the likely consequence of more government regulation. The alternative is for the weaker parties to invest in better organization and develop themselves as a countervailing power and thereby avoid calling upon the government for protection. For example, when farmers sold their goods individually to big corporations, they became vulnerable to exploitation, and their vulnerability is one reason that farmers have organized so many marketing cooperatives. They needed to gain corporate power to protect themselves.

The relative concentration of power among buyers and sellers (measured by size and funding power) is a crucial issue for consumers and local communities. A power imbalance affects not only consumers but also the structure of the industry rather rapidly. Big buyers can cause a weakening of sellers, which in turn is followed by conglomerate buyouts of firms. The problem can nevertheless be anticipated by observing measures of the competing power of firms and their trade associations.

Lawrence White finds that noncompetitive (collusive) behavior increases with

the fewer the number of firms in a market
the greater the differences in the firms' sizes
the greater the difficulty of new firms in entering the market and that of existing (especially small) sellers in expanding their share
the larger the number of buyers, and the lower the concentration among them
the greater the standardization and simplicity of the product.[12]

The impact of business on localities may also be anticipated in the extent to which retail corporations are decentralized and thus responsive to local communities and customers. The amount of authority (in hiring, firing,

Table 6.3. *Measures of industrial self-governance: selected examples*

II. SOCIAL MEASURES

Structures of social accountability

1. Labor organization
   a. Union vs. nonunion employees
   b. Salary range (e.g., 1/40)
   c. Percentage of union control over pension funds
   d. Percentage of firms in worker participation programs (QWL, Scanlon plan, labor–management committees)
   e. Federal vs. private mediation
   f. Educational attainment of employees
   g. Union democracy
2. Consumer organization (CO)
   a. Number of COs active in the industry (size/funds).
   b. Ratio of consumers represented to number of employees
3. Buyer/seller concentration
   a. Balance of power (size/funds) between buyers and sellers
   b. Concentration ratio of firms between buyers and sellers
   c. Decentralization of industry firms
4. Inter-firm structure
   a. Concentration ratio
   b. Government vs. private Arbitration ratio
   c. Trade association practices
      (1) Relevant departments (trade practices, ethical codes, standardization, arbitration, customer community)
      (2) Democratic organization (one vote per member, fair dues structure)
5. Ownership structure
   a. Partnerships (percentage of total)
   b. Public stock (average median number of owners per firm)
   c. Government (percentage of firms)
   d. Community (CDC citizen control)
   e. ESOPs
      (1) ESOP/total firms (ratio)
      (2) Total ESOP employees/total employees
   f. Producer cooperatives

Indicators of social performance

1. Labor
   a. Strikes (number, ratio, cost)
   b. Job safety (violations)
   c. Discrimination (violations)
   d. Ratio of black/white/female
   e. Wages/real spendable hourly earning
   f. Quit frequencies
   g. Federal mediation (cost)
   h. Labor–Management Reporting and Disclosure Act (violations)
2. Consumers
   a. Advertising (violations)
   b. Product safety (violations)
   c. Customer price index
3. Communities
   a. Pollution (violations)
   b. Percentage of ideal-giving vs. profits
   c. Local charitable contributions
4. Inter-firm relations
   a. Fair trade (violations)
   b. Government arbitration
   c. Justice Department (violations)
5. Ownership
   a. Dividend returns
   b. Number of shareholder resolutions
      (1) Percentage accepted by management
      (2) Percentage passed by owner

sales, purchasing, gifts, and so on) that is effectively given to local subsidiaries can make a difference in their ability to respond to customers and to their labor problems. But the degree to which small corporations are integrated into community life, that is, provide leadership in voluntary associations and donate to local foundations, is a complex matter of accountability. Business integration could be a sign of local dominance. The real meaning of accountability is their support for constituencies and constructive action in the interest of the community. We may hypothesize that bureaucratic firms with headquarters in distant cities tend to exhibit an insensitivity toward local employees, customers, and communities. The more sensitive indicators that tell us about how business affects the local community are outside our paradigm on industrial research and are discussed in the next chapter.

A trade association can support social accountability by the way it is organized. As we have noted, some trade associations have departments of *customer relations* that help settle problems between their member firms and customers. Many associations have a department of *trade practices* in which the staff monitor unfair competition in the industry. An association may develop a code of business ethics, which can be influential in stopping breaches of contract, encouraging warranties, eliminating the use of blacklists, avoiding defamation of competition, and the like. Legal enforcement of some aspects of a code must be carried out by the Federal Trade Commission, but the formulation of the code and surveillance by the staff of an association goes far toward obtaining firms' voluntary compliance. Trade associations often promote *product standardization* practices; these operate in the self-interest of firms (helping to reduce unfair competition) and at the same time function in the public interest. A larger number of associations maintain systems of *arbitration and mediation* that reduce recourse to the civil courts. Associations can maintain excellent *democratic practices* among their members and in subtle ways reduce the tendencies of their large member firms toward hegemony. Certain industries have developed strong *warranty standards* that help protect firms from litigation by customers and help protect the customers from being exploited by firms.

Other structures outside the trade association are important to observe as causes of high social performance. A *medium concentration ratio* of firms should correlate with intermediate IC and RS and result in lower prices for customers. Such a ratio means an industry is not dominated by a few firms and that the competitive tendency should work in the interest of the public. This by itself does not tell the whole story because we must balance the value of moderate competition against the trade association's cooperative practices in ethical codes and standardization. But a high concentration ratio, indicating the existence of an oligopoly or a monopoly, does not often lead toward a high social performance without other checks on corporate behavior.

Trade associations – like trade unions – do not always practice social democracy even though they are chartered to do so.[13] It is important, therefore, to examine the pattern of voting and the dues structure of an association to ascertain the extent to which it is following its own ideals. Industries with many firms but with only a few dominating the market appear to have the most trouble with fairness in their trade associations. Industries with a greater balance of power among firms should be more likely to provide a greater degree of equity through their common practices. Maintenance of uniform accounting, sharing of trade information, the practice of product standardization, pooling funds for research and development, and many other activities provide a strain toward equality among competing member firms. Trade associations may also provide private arbitration opportunities for members, reducing the necessity for government activity and enhancing self-governing power.

The *ownership structure* should be identified in a research paradigm because it affects performance. For example, the opportunity for workers to own corporate stock in their firms through employee stock ownership plans (ESOPs) has correlated with an increase in productivity and profits. Researchers have proposed that a causal relationship exists between employee ownership and motivation to work.[14] We have suggested that these studies are too preliminary to draw conclusions, and that much more research is needed. Thus, we want to count the breeds of ownership that exist in producer cooperatives, community development corporations, and public authorities, as well as partnerships and public stock companies. The prominence of an ownership type in any industry (for instance, public authorities in "utilities") can make a significant difference in its performance.

Reasonable hypotheses

The task of social research is to compare industries for their performance scores in relation to the social structures that may correlate with them. The following are examples of hypotheses that could be tested:

1   A strong union (structure) within an industry should correlate well with high performances on job safety, wages, and pension funds.
2   Industries with strong trade association departments in customer relations should correlate with high performance scores in product safety and fair advertising.
3   Industries with a recent increase in worker participation programs (QWL, job rotation, Scanlon plans) should have an increase in productivity and a worker satisfaction (no strikes).
4   Industries with a balance of power between buyers and sellers and with private arbitration systems operating effectively within them should show a high performance score on interfirm relations.

Many such hypotheses could be formulated, but the most exciting area of research is the connection with investment policy. Investors who want to provide incentives for designing social self-regulation can be followed by researchers seeking to test the outcome. Let us look at some hypotheses that could be initiated by investors.

Policy research

First, investors might offer incentives for companies to experiment with employee-ownership plans in the cooperative tradition and with new patterns of worker self-management at levels of administration acceptable to both labor and management in an industry with a poor social performance. If incentives are provided and the experiment is conducted, researchers can follow up on the outcome. Hypotheses:

1   The experiment should reduce strikes, increase job safety, and eliminate quit frequencies.
2   The experiment should increase productivity.
3   The experiment should reduce the cost of government involvement in the industry through the Labor Department and the National Labor Relations Board.

Second, investors could offer funding support to start nonprofit enterprises jointly managed by representatives from opposing federations. The purpose of the enterprises would be to *reduce the need for staff in a government agency and thus reduce taxes and outside regulations*. They would conduct research in the public interest, monitor particular products for durability, safety, and quality, make public recommendations on the improvement of products to manufacturers, and keep an appropriate government agency aware of how the industry is doing.

Several examples: a nonprofit enterprise might be chartered with representatives from the automobile manufacturers and consumer organizations like the American Automobile Association. Such an enterprise could coordinate with the Department of Transportation for the purpose of eliminating some of its tasks in testing safety devices on automobiles. The department could reduce its costs by transferring specific functions to this publicly structured private organization, and could maintain a staff member on the board of the enterprise to monitor its activities. Another nonprofit enterprise might include representatives from an appropriate textile association, retail association, and a consumer organization like the Cooperative League of the U.S.A., whose members include consumer cooperatives. It would work toward replacing selected activities of the U.S. Consumer Product Safety Commission. The same could be done in lumber and wood products, and in petroleum and coal products as their representatives joined with environmental organizations like the Sierra Club and Nader's Public Interest Research Groups to reduce specific tasks of the Environmental Protection Agency. Similar action could take place with the food and pharmaceutical industries in reference to replacing staff in the Food and Drug Administration. The test of the nongovernmental nonprofit enterprises would be whether they could become self-funded in the private sector, and whether they could actually perform a public service that would supplant government responsibility.

Third, investors could collaborate with a trade association to study an ethical code that is difficult to enforce. The investors could support a professional monitoring committee to strengthen the hand of the trade association without interfering with fair trade practices. The assumption is that the public visibility of corporate offenders (made possible by the professional committee) would be sufficient to keep firms in line without court action. If new monitoring techniques were successful, the trade association might want to give financial support toward continuance of the committee. Some industries have been relatively successful in maintaining ethical codes (for example, newspapers and orthopedic appliances), but new experiments could add information on enforcement effectiveness without constant lawsuits. The final issues for researchers of this experiment would be whether the new structure actually *reduces the need for action by the Federal Trade Commission*.

Fourth, investors could encourage a retail trade association with poor social performance to experiment with a customer-relations department and with consumer representatives on its board of directors (the Direct Sellers Association has actually considered this as a trade practice). The research question is whether this new structure would be an effective influence on the selling practices of firms and thus *reduce the need for consumer departments in government to become engaged in expensive litigation*, that is, the extent to which self-monitoring could develop successfully without the need for government agencies.

These types of experiments could be enumerated extensively because the problems in the business system are extensive. For example, we could hypothesize that investments to encourage imperially managed unions to improve their voting practices in certain ways would reduce the need for government enforcement of the provisions of the Labor–Management Reporting and Disclosure Act. We could hypothesize that select investments in trade associations of weak industries could lead them toward new technological research and patterns of organizational development that would keep them from lagging behind other industries. Each hypothesis leads to a theory of the public good that has not been fully articulated. This theory is latent in our research paradigm and could supply a direction for future studies in development.

A theory of the public good

We have discussed a theory of development in the social organization of industry but have not related it to a concept of the public good. Social investors have indicated an interest in promoting the public good but we have not extended this idea into a conceptual framework. This paradigm, then, could be the background for testing the degree to which social advantages and values, in sum, the public good, can become realizable in the development of the economy.

The public good is that which is produced in the interest of the whole society. It can be a work system enhancing the well-being of employees or a product created for the general welfare. Partial expressions of the public good would be the creation of noninjurious and useful products like clothing and nutritious food, but also would be work systems expressing human values, such as a safe workplace, a clean environment, and broadly, freedom and justice within the system of enterprises. The goods can occur at any stage of production and exchange in the economy, but we have argued that the possibility of their occurring is higher when systems of self-governance and mutuality are established.

A theory of the public good is concerned in part with the degree of corporate responsiveness and accountability provided by the people involved in the economy. It begins with the assertion that corporations operate most effectively toward the public good when they are *accountable to their employees* in the workplace. We have noted that only a limited degree of accountability exists today, but that corporations have come a long way in this direction within this century. Conversely, *employees have a responsibility to the corporation* in which they work. When these opposite motifs are integrated, a system of mutuality develops, as we have indicated. The mutuality continues horizontally in some measure within the local economy, as we discuss in the next chapter, but it also continues on the vertical line of governance within industry.

We assume that the *self-interests of employees* are best fulfilled and muted in the democratic corporation. They are altered and transformed through the self-managed activity of departments. Theoretically, the corporation fulfills certain employee interests while muting others that may be destructive to other employees and alters and transforms some of these interests toward the public good. We can say that employees gain a measure of the public good when they produce something of collective value. The product of the corporation normally has some relative value to the larger society. Corporate power then becomes defined in reference to the public good. Corporate power is not monopoly in this theory but rather "the ability to mobilize and utilize human resources for the development of goods having collective value."[15]

Corporate self-interests then gain a measure of the public good when they are properly fulfilled, muted, altered, and transformed democratically in the activity of the trade association. The association acts to advance the interests of its member firms, but also theoretically constrains excessive rivalries through legally acceptable tribunal action, ethical codes, and joint commercial ventures for the public interest. When this joint action happens effectively, associations can act together in the public welfare. This happens in specific cases in which corporations have transformed their self-interests through associations meeting the larger interests of society.

The trade association by itself is not systematically organized to operate on behalf of the public good, even though it synthesizes competing corporate interests toward broader goals. We have noted how each industry stands in competition with other industries to energize their interests separately. The silk industry competes with the chemical industry and the railroad industry competes with the airline industry. Their competitive actions may not always result in the public good, even though they have transcended their corporate self-interests in some measure. They require a more transcendent relationship so as to achieve this end to a greater degree.

Our theory of accountability and responsiveness continues upward on a vertical line. We have discussed another step taken in the public interest when these competing associations negotiate and transcend their differences. In certain cases interindustry committees help to resolve conflicts that are destructive to the public welfare as well as their own trade interests. We have given numerous examples of how this action transcends the self-interest of specific industries without interfering with the competitive system.[16]

This stage of social development – as much as it may contribute toward building a public orientation within the private sector – is not enough. We have suggested that the public good is advanced most significantly by ongoing interindustry councils operating between competing trade associations from the stage of supply and production to retail and consumption. This systematic linkage should offer a still higher probability that the economy will be responsive and accountable nationally to the people it affects. But are interindustry councils sufficient in theory to resolve corporate issues without government intervention? Can they be the "summit" in the transformation of corporate and industrial self-interests (see table 6.3).

Table 6.3. *Toward the Public Good*

transformation of self-interests into social values
Peak organizations (Societal interests)
Interindustry councils (Regional interests)
Trade associations (Industry interests)
Corporations (Enterprise interests)
Employees (Individual interests)

A peak organization

Some business scholars argue that one more step is important to consider. Ian Maitland argues that it would be possible for business to operate more fully in the public interest if it goes beyond the level of trade associations to a "peak organization." He asks: Can a peak organization be responsible to the whole business sector? Can a peak organization socially guide and monitor business activity without interfering improperly with the freedom of the market? Maitland answers that it is possible for a democratic organization to do so even though it will probably not happen in the United States at the present time. He is still convincing as to the usefulness of such an organization for promoting self-regulation and for reducing the need for government intervention.

Maitland points out that peak organizations exist in the private sectors of West Germany, Japan, and Sweden, and play an effective role in self-regulation. He cites research that shows their value in advancing the public good. For example, David Bresnick studied the role in six countries of the national confederation of employers and trade unions in forming youth employment policies. In each country a peak association was able to operate effectively to further the public good. Esra Vogel studied the peak organization of Japanese business, the Keidanren, and came to a similar conclusion. It has worked successfully on many public issues without being partial to any single group or industrial sector.[17]

Steven Kelman investigated the activity of a peak organization in Sweden that dramatically showed its contribution to the public welfare, in contrast to the lack of peak activity in the United States in the same field, occupational safety and health rule-making. He found that the contents of the regulations were similar but there the resemblance ended.

> The regulations were fought persistently in the U.S. but accepted meekly in Sweden.
> OSHA was bound by a detailed set of procedural requirements while ASV [its Swedish counterpart] was bound by virtually none.
> OSHA adopted a far more punitive approach to compliance than ASV did.
> Lawyers and courts were pervasively involved in both rule-making and compliance in the United States, and were virtually uninvolved in Sweden.[18]

Kelman concluded that industrial self-governance was promoted in the Swedish case without the costly government rule-making and interference observed in the United States. The main reason was that business was able to reach agreement on health and safety standards itself through the influence of its peak organization, the Swedish Employers Federation.

Maitland posits that a democratically constituted peak organization in the U.S. private sector should be able to obtain compliance with its rules with some adjustment in antitrust legislation. It would need to offer firms some private benefits or "selective incentives" unavailable outside the organization but still sufficiently attractive to induce compliance. On the other hand, the government could give the peak organization mildly positive and negative limited powers. They might include granting the organization the right to special information on technical development, the right to regulate certain jurisdictional disputes between members, the right to act on predatory price cutting, the power to criticize corporate misconduct, the right to issue fines, or some combination of these and other powers. In other words, Maitland suggests that some degree of government support might be needed for the peak organization to be fully effective, including a requirement that all organizations be members, as is true in Japan.

The properties of rule making in such peak organizations as the U.S. Chamber of Commerce require more research. We have argued that norms are already established in the activities of trade associations at the level of the locality, region, state, and nation in particular industries. More research is required at these levels to add to an understanding of what is needed in the context of the whole business community. Furthermore, research is required on the intersections between countervailing trade associations to contribute to our understanding of what should constitute the jurisdiction of a peak organization. Finally, we have added labor and consumer organizations to the list of businesses; they are usually omitted in defining the business community but they have their own self-interests to advance toward the public good.[19]

The deliberation over these issues regarding the power of a peak organization rests on maintaining a proper balance between freedom and justice in the system of enterprise. Social investors – including the government – must balance these values. We have noted that a creative resolution is often found through the introduction of a democratic structure. The final question is: Can a democratic peak organization administer justice while promoting greater freedom in the system of enterprise?

Institutional investors

Institutional investors represent the main body of stockholders in the corporate economy and can play an important role in determining the direction of corporate policy. Even though they are not in a direct line of decision making in the hierarchy of business associations, they help shape corporate policy by way of their investment decisions. We have noted that pension funds control well over $1 trillion of investment capital today and can expect to control over $4 trillion in the 1990s. Put another way, employees (pension beneficiaries) now own over 50 per cent of corporate stock in America and will become the primary owners of all major corporations in the 1990s. This change in the structure of ownership suggests that a new public role may be forthcoming for workers in helping to shape the direction of investment policies in the economy.

Many pension fund managers already see the significance of their public role and have organized the national Council of Institutional Investors to discuss the basis for an overall investment policy. The council comprises about twenty-five public and union pension funds, currently with more than $100 billion in assets. Membership is growing rapidly and it looks as though it will become the peak organization for pension fund managers. It not only claims to represent the interest of its constituencies (employees) but also expresses concern about the *overall performance* of the economy. Because many council members have begun to apply social criteria in decision making, overall performance is admittedly measured in more than economic terms.

Social investors have also organized their own national Social Investment Forum. The forum includes pension funds, mutual funds, banks, and individual stockholders, all of whom combine ethical and financial criteria in their investment practice. The forum represents billions of investment dollars and its members meet regularly to discuss policies for allocating capital in the public interest.[20]

Although corporate self-interest has been altered by the development of vertical trade groups, employee self-interest has been affected by the development of pension funds. Workers have traditionally sought higher wages in their own interest, but this practice today can interfere with the corporation's capacity to pay dividends to its owners, now the workers. Thus, the workers (owners) face a contradiction in the simple pursuit of higher wages because success can yield lower returns for themselves in the dividends paid to pension funds. In some corporations pension funds are in trouble, and the future of all pensions could be in jeopardy if a serious recession takes place. Therefore, workers must find a broad interest base for their decision making in the light of the fact that they benefit from corporate profits. A day of reckoning appears to be close in which worker-representatives and pension managers will work with other stakeholders such as employers and the government to determine investment policy in the best interest of everyone. The logic of history is leading toward democratic structures of decision making that will be guided by a concept of the public good.

The invisible hand becoming visible

If the trends toward peak decision making evolve, Adam Smith's notion of an invisible hand may find new grounds for debate. Smith believed that the pursuit of self-interest would by itself lead the economy to act for the public good without requiring government regulation. But we know from the historical record that corporate self-interest actually led to many problems like pollution and monopoly that led Congress, in turn, to demand government regulation.

We have argued that at the same time the business system began to regulate itself in some measure. Given the development of countervailing trade associations, unions, and consumer groups, we can see real possibilities for advancing self-regulation from a social perspective. An invisible hand becomes visible in what we have called the social sector. We believe that a social structure with the potential for helping the economy to operate the public interest has been emerging in the private sector. Admittedly, this social structure has much need for development of its capacity to lead naturally toward the public welfare and become more self-regulating. But this is exactly what constitutes the task ahead for investment research and eventually for legal reforms.

Our discussion of the invisible hand of interest groups' affecting corporate policy toward the public good is of course only one dimension of the larger problem. Among other important institutional dimensions of the public good are the intensity of demand for a product, the amount of the product that is available in the light of the need, the current state of technology, the manner of distributing the product, the manner of consuming the product, and the manner of charging for the product's use. Social investors and researchers will want to examine the literature on this topic.[21]

In summary: the social economy

There is an important distinction to be made between social and economic variables in empirical research. From one perspective a variable is "economic" and from another perspective it can be "social." This distinction has important implications for public policy when people see only one side of reality. For example, some investors see "social" programs such as the quality of working life, labor–management committees, and even worker ownership as "economic" because they can improve productivity and profits. Some economists interpret trade associations and unions as economic entities, even though they are designed as nonprofit corporations with social purposes. Economists say that trade groups exist primarily for the purpose of advancing the profits of member firms, and unions for advancing wages and economic benefits. The *bottom line* in this view *is the economic factor*.

Nevertheless, there is a social factor in every economic variable and trade organization. Discerning how this social factor operates is vital to investment policy. The capitalist system needs to be recognized as socially motivated and socially structured. It is therefore important to recognize the social factor analytically as a separate component in a research design. It weaves a pattern throughout the economic order in subtle and intricate ways to make it productive and profitable. This pattern is so powerful that we can argue theoretically that *the bottom line is the social factor*.[22] The "social factor" plays a subtle role in our lives and a vital part in policies leading to industrial self-governance. In policy-making, it means simply *an awareness of how we orient ourselves toward one another and are interdependent in the corporate economy*. This awareness is critical to any serious effort to reduce government controls over the economy.

Financial investors are important to the stimulation of the social awareness needed for implementing new measures of accountability and productivity. The awareness must also develop among leaders in the business community and the government for effective action to take place. Business leaders must ask how one business can affect another in such a way as to result finally in an industrial recession. Conversely, they must ask how they can work together to reverse recessive trends and revitalize industrial life. Primarily, they must *want* the economy to recover socially, that is, move from sunset to sunrise industries without mass unemployment and to have industrial organizations solve their own problems together. In sum, the achievement of self-regulation requires a great awareness and sensitivity to the social variables involved in the process of development.

The purpose of industrial research, then, is to provide the data that yield a consciousness of these social relationships. This research paradigm – crude as it may be in its present form – symbolizes a direction for new studies to help create this consciousness. Studies along these lines, it is hoped, should develop the information and the framework necessary to stimulate U.S. industry to move profitably toward the development of a productive and stable economy.

7 Investment in community development

Scholars have said that the local community in the United States is perilously close to extinction. Many studies describe its "decline" and even its "eclipse." Some observers interpret the phenomenon as an inevitable and irreversible part of modern development. The idea that a residential group could develop a fair degree of economic self-determination is perceived as a fiction in contemporary society.

The loss of economic self-determination at the local level is mirrored now by the disappearance of community studies in the professions. The local community was a major focus of sociological research in the first half of this century but today it has lost its appeal. Because it has declined in its power of self-direction, it no longer has the same significance. Similarly, community planning was a major interest of city planners and architects, but the concept is no longer discussed in their journals. The idea of constructing autonomous communities is regarded by many planners today as hopelessly utopian. The notion of community development thus has little appeal for those in a position to encourage it in postindustrial society.

The concept of developing self-reliant communities was first questioned by city planners facing urban sprawl but now it is wholly eclipsed from the work of planners looking at the megalopolis. The megalopolis is a vast stretch comprising metropolises developing without plan in a particular region. The Eastern seaboard is one example, described by Jean Gottman as a metropolitan agglomeration reaching from southern New Hampshire to northern Virginia. He ascribes to it a personality of its own and poses it as a legal entity of the future; the megalopolis "stands indeed at the threshold of a new way of life" and contains the "outlines of tomorrow's world." Evidence shows that its likely future does not include a vision of community.

The rise of the metropolis has coincided with the decline in power of the local community, and has been accompanied by both progress and destructiveness in human organization. The organization of the city is, hence, a source of confusion as well as concern for social investors who must make decisions about its future. The causes of the decline of community life and

147

the basis of envisioning a new direction for community development are therefore central issues for social investors. The criteria for a new investment in community life are our subject as we discuss whether or not people in a modern locality can become genuinely self-determining and capable of governing their own lives and future.

The problem: disappearance of the local community

The decline in power of the local community is a complex process, one factor of which is clearly the market economy. If we can understand the loss of local self-determination as being a function of the market system, we can perhaps better judge the focal points for future investment in the purposeful redesign of community life.

The causes behind relentless and seemingly uncontrollable urban growth may well be summarized in Max Weber's definition of the city as essentially a settlement with a market. It was the market, much more than its size, its impersonality, or its intense social problems, that characterized the city. The city was basically created by the need to exchange goods and money within a limited geographical area in order for people to make a livelihood together. Other sociologists have examined the characteristics of the city but none has so strongly advanced the market as its defining feature.[1]

Weber's definition is important because it explains a cause of both the city's progressive development and its destructive direction. The market is the creative force in the city's evolution and simultaneously a basis for its loss of humanity and self-determination. The expansion of the small village into town, city, metropolis, and finally megalopolis with multiple commercial centers is largely a function of the market. Our hypothesis is that the shape of the city is significantly determined by the market forces of commerce and capital exchange. The market is not the only determinant of city size and direction, but it is such a critical factor that it is essential for us to understand it as the basis for investing in the future of human settlements.

The expansion of the village into the metropolis has also been determined significantly by the new technology of transport and communications. It was in part the invention of the automobile and telephone that helped city populations explode into suburbia, and the invention of passenger airlines and television that helped stretch cities farther into the hinterlands. But technology is socially determined, and remains basically a function of the market. It acts on the market system in certain ways but is also itself determined by market forces. Our hypothesis is that the market has been responsible for not only the direction of city growth but also the imminent extinction of the community as a way of life. Restoration of the community, then, means acting directly on the market.

The market as a cause of social problems

Data on how the market creates social and economic problems are too extensive and diverse to introduce here, but we want to illustrate the point because our argument is that people in localities cannot be in command of their own lives until the market system is altered at that level. The data show that key decisions affecting local life are increasingly made in distant places, sometimes thousands of miles away. The subject of plant dislocation illuminates the loss in local self-determination.

In the past decade hundreds of plant shutdowns severely disrupted local economies and community institutions. In Ohio alone we can observe the extensive impact of decisions made elsewhere. In Youngstown the shutdown of a sheet and tube company put 5,000 employees out of work, and Libby-Owens-Fords Aeroquip closed out 390. In Akron Goodyear Tire terminated 1,384 workers; Firestone, 1,000. In Cleveland 2,000 jobs were lost when White Motor moved truck production to Virginia, and 230 jobs went in a Westinghouse shutdown. In Dayton Sherwin-Williams closed out 110 workers. In Canton Ferro-Allos shut down 210 jobs. The pattern repeated itself throughout the country, devastating community life. It is easy to see why planners have lost hope for self-determination in the locality.[2]

When the Chance-Vought Division of United Aircraft moved an entire industrial complex from Bridgeport, Connecticut, to Dallas, Texas, local people had no voice in the decision. When one discovers that the company had assistance from the federal government for the relocation, the reality of a lack of community self-determination is even more clearly realized. Barry Bluestone and Bennett Harrison call such moves "capital flight." They estimate that during the 1970s up to 650,000 jobs were wiped out by runaway shops. When other affected businesses are considered, it appears that more than 32 million local jobs were destroyed in the process.[3] Capital flight does not simply create unemployment but adversely affects much else. The deleterious effects on local businesses and the social infrastructure bring on a multitude of social ills and the necessary attendant government spending.

The consequences of capital flight are disastrous for local communities in social, economic, political, and personal terms. Sidney Cobb and Stanislav Kasl have conducted longitudinal research on the health and behavioral effects of job loss from plant closures. Among the workers studied over a thirteen-year period, they found a suicide rate about thirty times the national average. They also found higher incidences of heart disease, hypertension, diabetes, peptic ulcer, gout, joint swelling, dyspepsia, and alopecia in the displaced workers than among control groups of employed workers. They found too, that the closings had serious psychological effects: extreme depression, anxiety, tension, insecurity, and loss of self-esteem.[4]

Workers lose their health insurance benefits when they lose their jobs. Fewer than 30 per cent of the unemployed have any health insurance at all; those who do, must spend 20 to 35 per cent of unemployment benefits merely to continue their former coverage, but generally the unemployed go without. The displaced worker has greater medical needs than the employed worker but the former answer to those needs is no longer available.[5]

More data and reasons for the cause of community decline and the festering problems of crime, divorce, drug addiction, and mental disorder could be marshaled here, of course. It is a complex process in which capital flight and the rise of cities are causal factors. Our argument is that behind all these interrelated factors is the most significant factor, the market system. The point is that the problems are extensive enough to warrant consideration of a serious alternative to the market as a basis for community development.

The market as a cause of progress

It is important to understand the market forces that destroy the community in order to initiate an alternative, but it may also be argued that the market has been a progressive force. The proponents of city life are no less in number than the community sociologists who criticize it. Their argument must be briefly presented here because their points are also critical to an alternative.

Celebrants of city life argue that without the rise of the city we would have no cultural progress: no symphonies, no great universities, no great theater or opera, and none of the great corporations that have given us the technological advances we enjoy today. They say that great museums and ballet companies do not come into being in the small town. The city has brought us culture as well as wealth. We now have a new level of consciousness of who we can be as people.[6]

The proponents of city life and the market as it now exists go still further. The city has made possible our social progress. It has broken down the provinciality of rural society and the smothering prejudice, boredom, and backwardness of the small town. The sense of community may have declined, but it is more important that the city has helped destroy the moral repressiveness and local elitism of the small town.

Others declare that the city is the economic engine of the nation. Jane Jacobs states that cities, as settlements that consistently generate new economic growth, have been the source of economic renewal in modern nations. Cities become larger because they are able to replace imports with their own modes of production through improvisation and innovation, which in turn generate new exports. In effect, the city grows on the basis of reciprocating systems of work. We will return to this point in our alternative plan for investment, but the question remains as to whether all these good things need to be lost in the reconstruction of community life.[7]

Jacobs admits that there are dynamic forces of destruction that will lead to the end of cities unless there are revolutionary steps taken to give them the power of self-determination. She believes that the only way by which cities can be saved is by converting them into sovereignties with their own currencies. Our argument is not inconsistent with her plea for greater self-determination, but our plan involves a local reconstruction of city life based on a concept of community development. The perpetuation of market forces uninfluenced by social planning is no longer a viable course to take in the solution to city problems.

A sociological interpretation of the problem

Community sociologists portrayed the developing problem in case studies begun before the midcentury, like *Democracy in Jonesville, Middletown*, and the Yankee City series. In 1947 Lloyd Warner described labor unrest and disruption in Newburyport, Massachusetts ("Yankee City") when the local owners of a shoe factory sold out to owners in New York.

Two fundamental changes have been occurring concomitantly, in recent years, in the social organization of Yankee City shoe factories. The first is the expansion of the hierarchy upward, out of Yankee City, through the expansion of individual enterprises and the establishment by them of central offices in distant large cities. The second is the expansion of the structure outward from Yankee City through the growth of manufacturers' associations and labor unions, also with headquarters outside Yankee City and with units in many other shoemaking communities in New England and elsewhere. Both ... decrease Yankee City's control over its own factories by subjecting the factories or segments of them, to more and more control exerted from outside Yankee City.[8]

The case studies were representative of what was described as the "great change" in community life across the nation. Various sociologists have sought to conceptualize its meaning. Roland Warren, for example, has been a leading interpreter of the change in terms of "vertical–horizontal relationships" in the locality. *Vertical relationships* are formal links between local organizations and their parent organizations outside the community. Examples would be the connections of the local YMCA or Girl Scout troop to their national offices. *Horizontal relationships* are formal links in the locality, such as between the Scouts and the YMCA in the local community welfare council. Similarly, the local subsidiaries of General Motors and Xerox have a vertical relationship to their national headquarters and trade associations, and a horizontal relationship with the local Chamber of Commerce. The same vertical and horizontal relationships exist with churches, trade unions, and other voluntary organizations.[9]

The "great change" is in the power of external linkages to shape the direction of community life. The basic decisions regarding each local unit are made in the national headquarters. The power of local horizontal relations has thereby been weakened, and thus there is a decline in real community life. The locality can no longer function as a planning unit with true self-direction; it is no longer a community.

Other sociologists have described the problems of the city as stemming from neighborhood disorganization. The problems of crime, delinquency, and drug addiction have been laid to the lack of neighborhood controls. Many attempts have been made to recultivate neighborhood life so as to solve these problems,[10] but again this is difficult or impossible as long as the neighborhood is disrupted by changing market forces.

Sociologist Robert Nisbet has taken a more global view of the decline of community life in modern nations, describing it in terms of a breakdown in primary groups and the institutions of communal life. The enduring face-to-face group has disappeared from the life of the factory, the church, the neighborhood, and the family itself. The primary group, once characterized by Charles Cooley as the nursery of human nature, was where original values of integrity, honesty, and social responsibility were developed. Without primary groups functioning in the basic institutions of the locality, the values are placed in jeopardy and sometimes distorted or lost in the process of socialization. They might be rediscovered in the "integrity" of the street gang, but they are not integrated into the round of institutional life. They can be lost in the organization of a factory's assembly line, the bureaucratic church, and people moving in and out of the neighborhood. The enduring primary relationships cannot be rediscovered through government welfare agencies and the divorce courts.[11]

These important analyses of the "modern problem" did not normally root themselves in the market system itself. The market was rarely connected to the rising rates of crime, suicide, drug addiction, divorce, and mental disorders. A severe neurosis in the adult would be traced psychologically to family instability or the absence of a father during childhood but not to the market system that caused the family break-up in the first place. Nor was the question of why people had to keep moving out of the neighborhood really addressed at its root. The market system was not examined in connection with personal problems. The time has come to make these connections, to answer these questions, and to take a new look at the importance of community life. This means that we must first look at the market as a political creation, not as a natural phenomenon outside human control and beyond our management.

The market myth

Karl Polyani wrote a classic treatise on "the great transformation" from feudalism to capitalism that took place centuries ago. His study is most applicable to our understanding of "the great change" taking place today because he demonstrates that the market system was not a spontaneous creation but was brought into existence by government laws and policies. It was not the purely natural phenomenon conceived by nineteenth-century economists as operating outside the legal domain, but had come into being by alteration of the legal framework of the medieval period. It was a creature of the new democratic state that wanted to destroy the bondage of serfdom and replace the estate system by changing the feudal laws governing use of *land, capital, and labor.*[12]

The myth of the Middle Ages was destroyed and a new myth of the modern period was created. The new myth brought forth new values and selectively ignored other values; it celebrated freedom and individuality in the economy but said nothing about social justice and equality in the economy. It provided for the right of workers to quit their jobs but provided no right to a job; it offered people the right to buy corporations but offered no protection to consumers who came to be dominated by corporations in the marketplace; it gave the right to owners to produce unsafe products but no right to consumers to obtain redress for injury; it gave the right to employers to speak harshly to employees but no right to employees to speak back without being fired. The myth of the market gave rights to people with capital but gave no heed to its impact on people in the local community.

We are today in another transition. We have gained the freedom of the market but have lost the base of our communities, gained the values of individualism and competition in the economy but lost the values of fellowship and mutual aid. We are now proceeding to redress the imbalance. Polyani has told us that to make such a transition effectively we must pay attention to the "laws" undergirding the market economy.

If we take the laws of the market as the primary cause of rapid change in residence, domination in work life, and the many other problems to be discussed later, we can begin to find ways of altering the market. The question is: What are the legal methods for reversing community decline? How can we begin to provide a legal basis for overcoming the market forces? Put another way: How can we regain control over local *land, capital, and labor* without involving government ownership? How can we restore life to the community without state controls over the market? How can we provide a social foundation to the private economy? And, how can we invest in new patterns of community development that will increase opportunities not only for individuality and freedom but also for justice?

Toward a solution: autonomy, viability, and polity

Some social planners believe that reconstruction of the local community can be accomplished by taking charge of the market mechanisms that have so long played havoc with local control. It is conceivable today for local people to control their land, labor, and capital without recourse to government ownership and regulation. The government can help facilitate the process but the objective is to gain social (not state) control and reduce the necessity for formal government. It means altering the social structure of the private sector so that people become more important than the market.

Let us think of the solution in terms of three attributes of community life: autonomy, viability, and polity. We cannot engage in all the legal arguments on social policy but we can look at this nonmarket pattern of community development so that the details can be debated and discussed as part of the decisions of social investment.[13]

Autonomy: local control

By *autonomy* we mean the capacity for people in a locality to be relatively independent of outside controls. The concept is best interpreted as a continuum in degrees of independence from outside controls over the economy. All communities have some autonomy and some have more than others. Our purpose is to see how autonomy can be increased by altering the legal system of the market.

If we take the market as the central element to be controlled in land, capital, and labor, we have a starting place for optimizing local autonomy. We shall see that legal devices are already in place for changing the system, and that the main problem is how they are best put together in an investment plan for community development.

Land: the community land trust (CLT)

When local land is on the market, all sorts of problems arise leading to community decline. We mention only one problem here because our task is describing alternatives.

Speculation in city land is a function of the market fostering slums and their related problems. Slums have often been created on the edges of a central business district because landlords speculate on rising market values. When city businesses decide to construct new buildings, adjacent land increases rapidly in value and can become more valuable than the buildings on it. Buildings on land with such potential appreciation are allowed to deteriorate. Absentee landlords do not care about tenants or maintenance because anticipated future profits outweigh such considerations. The city government then tries to solve the problem with housing codes, safety regulations, zoning ordinances, and enforcement agencies policing enforcement. The cost of government goes up but essentially the problem is usually unresolved.

There is a solution to the problem that could do away with both market and government controls. Communities have begun experimenting with what is called a community land trust (CLT) as an alternative to land speculation (Leesburg, Georgia; Clairfield, Tennessee; Hancock County, Maine; Columbia Heights, Washington D.C.; Cincinnati, Ohio; Minneapolis, Minnesota; and various other locations). The CLT is a nonprofit cooperative that buys land and holds it in the community interest and the wider public interest. It is designed not only to avoid speculation and the rapid turnover of land, which destroys its productive capacity, but also to create a democratic foundation to the local economy.[14]

The CLT owns land through a trusteeship with a democratically selected board, a third of which is representatives of lessees, a third representatives of the local community, and a third representatives of the public interest (often professional people). Local people are given the opportunity to lease the land for life as long as they maintain it in the public interest; lessee representatives defend their interests in policy making on the board. The CLT differs from the land conservation trust, which is primarily concerned with the retention of natural resources. The U.S. tax structure provides a framework for promoting the conservation of natural assets for the common good, and the latter kind of trust land is held by an organization that is not necessarily representative of the locality.

The charter of the CLT states principles of general use rather than specific uses, so lessees have a great deal of freedom. Free enterprise is encouraged. The charter may state that the land is not to lie fallow, that it must be kept in productive use. In rural areas land trust charters may emphasize the prevention of soil erosion; in cities charters may state that a lot is not to remain unused, that it must be put to some recreational or productive use. The lessees therefore can utilize the land in many ways to make profits that do not violate the public interest, and may keep their profits as long as they pay the fees. The CLT encourages individual incentive within a broad framework of community interest.

The lease fee can be used for the purchase of more land, hence the trust must have its own mechanism for self-expansion. Ideally, as CLTs broaden their ownership bases, they federate in order that one board does not gain control over too large an area. A board consists of people who live in a city neighborhood or a rural community who are not there to build land empires. Thus, a CLT expands on the basis of creating new trusts through a democratic federation. The central board of the federation has very limited powers in respect to local use of land. It functions very much on the principle of subsidiarity: the larger body should not govern any activity that can be governed better by the local community.

Not all land uses should be locally controlled. Certain land resources require the oversight of a regional trust board. For example, it is more appropriate to assign control over natural resources like rivers to regional or federal organizations rather than to a local community. In the Northeast water might be a resource under purely local control, but in the West, where water can be a scarce commodity, allocation of water rights should be determined by a democratic federation operating on a wider geographical basis. And certain regions are more subject to outside exploitation and control than others. For example, land in Appalachia is largely owned by a few dozen gigantic corporations in fuel, transportation, and lumber. A study of land ownership in eighty rural West Virginia counties found that the corporations owned 40 per cent of the land and 70 per cent of the mineral rights, that 75 per cent of the land and 80 per cent of the mineral rights were held by outside people or corporations. Further, the property taxes paid by the owners were extremely low. The resource wealth has been slowly drained out to absentee corporations while the communities themselves have remained poor.[15]

The CLT is designed to eliminate these inequities. It can act more effectively than the local government in many cases because local officials often refrain from interfering with the "free market." The CLT can lease the land to local developers and require its proper use and a fair return. The board sees to it that the land is not destroyed by outside corporations, that the land continues to make a contribution to local development. It could recommend that outsiders contract with a local corporation for resource extraction, which then makes a fair profit that along with fees paid to the land trust means that capital circulates in the local community.

If the leaseholder terminates a lease, owned improvements (e.g., buildings) may be sold or removed. The CLT typically retains a first option to buy the improvements at the owner's original cost, adjusted for inflation, depreciation, and damage during the ownership period. Such property can be sold to the next leaseholder. Thus the first leaseholder is guaranteed equity in the improvements and the succeeding leaseholder is able to buy the improvements at a fair price. Nobody profits from unearned increases in market value; no buyer is priced out of the market by such increases. Any increase in value not due to a leaseholder's efforts remains with the CLT. Neither the CLT nor the leaseholder holds the land itself as a commodity.

Lease fees represent a fair return to the community for use of the land and resources. They are similar in principle to local property taxes but with a special difference: they are based on the value of the land alone. Many municipalities not only tax improvements but tax them at a higher rate, and tax undeveloped land and extracted natural resources at considerably less than their full value. The CLT corrects these injustices.

The CLT is still experimental. Its first U.S. use occurred about twenty years ago, and only in the past few years has the model begun to achieve public recognition. It has a longer tradition in other countries. The Jewish National Fund of Israel was founded in 1901 as a land trust and operates today on a national scale, a nongovernmental institution that predates the founding of the nation. It is more centralized than in the United States; the fund owns most of the productive land and considerable additional land in both rural and urban areas. Land is held in the public interest and leased out for use, with improvements owned by leaseholders. Land trusts have also been developed in Mexico and Tanzania, where the governments are more closely associated with the land trust movement than is the case in the United States. The central governments have given land trusteeships to village communities that in turn grant use rights to individuals. Leaders in the U.S. celebrate the fact that the land trust movement is operating independent of government controls.

Capital: community development finance institutions

We have noted the deleterious impact of capital flight on communities, but this is only part of the story. The capital market has been harmful to communities in other ways. Indeed, the need to find methods for gaining control over local capital did not grow out of the runaway plants but, rather, out of the struggle of people in neighborhoods discriminated against by city banks. The capital market has not been any more favorable to the poor than the land market has been, and they have found it necessary to devise an alternative system for democratizing capital. They have organized community development credit unions and other types of community development finance institutions (CDFIs).

One of the reasons for setting up CDFIs was the conventional banks' "redlining," that is, their refusal to invest in certain neighborhoods because of perceived credit risks. (The term *redline* originated in the custom of drawing red lines on maps around ethnic, racial, or low-income neighborhoods deemed off limits.) Redlining leads to deterioration and eventually abandonment of the neighborhood. The slow decay is of course attended by crime and other social ills. The residents who are branded credit risks have to turn to loan sharks for personal loans, which costs them still far more than they would have paid to the banks and more than borrowers with "better" addresses. The local community deteriorates while the banks improve their creditor status. In other words, lending institutions use the savings of local depositors to make loans elsewhere. The money is diverted to build up other areas (e.g., new suburbs) instead of applied to local mortgages, home improvements, and personal and business loans. The residents are hence doubly victimized: their neighborhoods decline and they are deprived of the rightful use of their savings.

The first step toward what has become known as greenlining was taken by older residents of an Italian neighborhood in Chicago in the early 1970s when they discovered that they could not obtain mortgages but their children in the suburbs could. The group had very little capital power, combined assets of only $36,000 compared to the target bank's $88 million. Because it requires approximately 5 per cent of an institution's assets to wipe out its liquid assets, withdrawal of the $36,000 would be unavailing as a protest. The group decided on a "bank-in"; people lined up at all the tellers' windows to make minor transactions during the bank's busiest hours. The irritations eventually pressured the bank into committing $4 million to the community for mortgage loans.

The real greenline alternative was discovered later when residents found that they could establish their own banking system, a community bank organized under credit union legislation. A credit union is a nonprofit cooperative incorporated under state or federal law for people with a common affiliation, such as a profession or an occupation. It was only a step further to a credit union based on the common bond of residence in a particular community. This new type of credit union was to be based on locality.

The community development credit union (CDCU) is a nonprofit cooperative incorporated under state or federal law for low-income people living in one locality. Its purpose is to promote thrift among its members and to make loans to its members at reasonable interest rates for community development. The CDCU is controlled by the member-residents, each of whom has one vote regardless of the amount of savings. Although it may accept deposits by nonmembers outside the locality, loans may be made only to members. Money not currently on loan may be invested in federal and state government securities and other CDCUs. The earnings of the CDCU are not federally taxed. Some earnings are retained as a reserve for loans; the remainder are returned to members in services, dividends on savings, or loan-interest rebates. The money that the CDCU keeps within the community can in turn be mobilized as capital for cooperatives and other locally owned businesses.

The CDCU is defined simultaneously as a financial institution, a neighborhood institution, and an institution of learning. As an institution of learning, it deepens its members' understanding of finance and community economics, inspires members to see how it can expand its influence, and develops members' skills in keeping records, conducting meetings, contracting, financing, collecting data, hiring and firing, and in relations with other CDCUs.[16]

The CDCU is legally designed for low-income neighborhoods but other types of community-oriented finance institutions have also developed. For example, the Institute for Community Economics in Greenfield, Massachusetts, has a revolving loan fund (RLF) available to finance community land trusts. The capital volume increased by almost 200 per cent in 1982 and is now over $1 million. The RLF has placed forty-five loans with community land trusts, worker-owned businesses, and community service groups in eleven states.[17]

The South Shore Bank is a prominent example of how local people can turn around neighborhood deterioration. The "South Shore" is an area eight miles south of Chicago's Loop whose residents were determined to pull themselves out of a local depression. They created a bank that in ten years is outstanding in socially responsible investment. By mid 1984, it had reached $50 million in development loans and developed affiliated companies to carry on its work independently. The affiliates include the City Lands Corporation, a real estate development company managing the investment of $24 million in the rehabilitation of 340 units in five multi-family housing projects; the Neighborhood Institute, a not-for-profit firm packaging loans for energy retrofitting with its own Housing Center and currently managing a $1.4 million project developing 137 low-income housing units; and the Neighborhood Fund, with investments of $761,000 in minority-owned businesses.

Some communities are too small to sustain a local bank and therefore pool capital and coordinate efforts with other communities. In Birmingham, Alabama, Neighborhood Services, a coalition of more than a dozen neighborhood organizations, has established a revolving loan fund to finance the acquisition and development of local housing. The coalition has been developing cooperative housing in the city and has recently become interested in land trusts as a part of its method for increasing local control over capital.

The Industrial Cooperative Association in Somerville, Massachusetts has a million-dollar RLF for the purpose of investing in producer cooperatives.

All such financial institutions localize and democratize capital, taking capital out of the traditional market system. We shall note later how community finance institutions can create the basis for their investees (enterprises) to own them. Newly capitalized enterprises may come to own the bank that created them in the first place.

Labor: worker cooperatives

The labor market has been the subject of critical study since Karl Marx's first interpretation of "alienation" under capitalism. In Marx's view, *labor* had been reduced to a commodity, like *capital* and *land* in the economic system. In the original meaning used by Hegel, *alienation* referred to a divergence between human existence and human essence. *Existence* refers to the actual reality of people living in the world; *essence*, the human potential of the individual. Marx saw the potential of human beings as creative, free, and self-determining in their labor, but people could not realize this potential when treated as objects for hire within the market system.

The process of creating a system that allows people at work to realize their full potential is complex and has not been solved in either capitalist or socialist nations. Most recently this critical concern has been raised among Marxist workers living under state socialism. Marxist writers describe the Soviet system as domination of a bureaucratic apparatus over labor; the state has replaced capital as the manipulator. Clearly, the need in both state socialism and capitalism is to create a corporate system with greater degrees of worker participation and self-management.

Marx foresaw the worker cooperative as a stage in the process of eliminating the alienating forms of capitalism, but he did not foresee other stages of worker participation that would develop in capitalism. Today we can observe a slow reformation of business enterprises through quality-of-working-life projects, labor–management committees, and increasing degrees of worker ownership with labor participating at new levels of corporate governance. Recent cases of worker buyouts and labor–management agreements in the U.S. are reshaping the traditional role of labor. With labor representation on the boards of directors of Weirton Steel, Hyatt-Clark of General Motors, Chrysler Motors, Eastern Airlines, the former A & P Stores in Philadelphia, and other U.S. corporations, the possibility exists for a gradual shift toward the worker-cooperative model. We have noted that employee stock ownership plans have led to an increase in worker ownership to over 8,000 corporations, of which about 10 per cent are majority-owned by employees. These trends show a direction developing in U.S. enterprise that is taking more account of workers as a human part of the enterprise. The trends reduce tendencies in the capitalist system to treat labor as a commodity, but the movement has a long way to go.

The major point to be made here is that employee ownership means very little unless the stock is arranged in such a way that it cannot be purchased by outsiders. To maintain local control over the corporation, the stock must be taken out of the market. If not, the worker-owned business may be purchased by a conglomerate and once again become subject to capital flight, unnecessary layoffs, and the attendant problems of community decline.

Studies show that it is important for worker cooperatives to separate membership rights from ownership rights. Membership rights give employees the opportunity to vote for the board of directors and to receive a portion of the net income from the company, but ownership of the company is located in the company as a whole. The workers simply have collective rights to the final disposition of property. This important arrangement then removes labor from the marketplace and localizes control over the corporation.

We can now see more significance in Polyani's interpretation of the "great transformation" from feudalism in land, capital, and labor. Just as the market system was slowly divested from the feudal system by a series of legal and political changes, we are talking now about divesting legally from the market system, and developing a social economy out of local community life. (See figure 7.1.)

Figure 7.1

Community autonomy

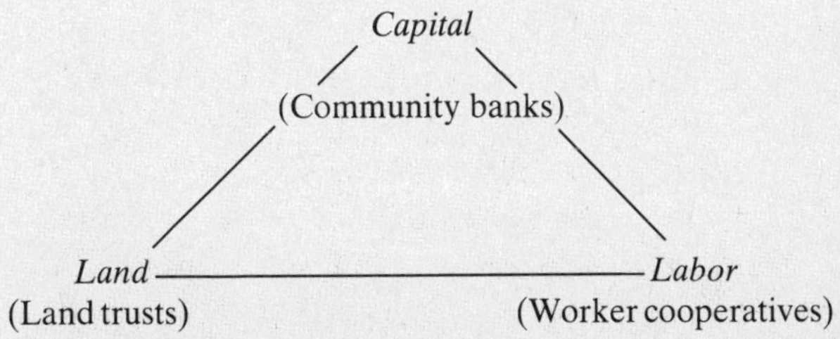

Capital
(Community banks)

Land ——————————— *Labor*
(Land trusts)   (Worker cooperatives)

Our point is that *the creation of local autonomy is a feasible goal for social investment*. There are many social and economic advantages in shifting from absentee ownership to local controls. First, jobs become more stabilized and income is more secure in the locality. People do not need to worry about plant relocation. Second, the community is in a better position to negotiate for the provision of services such as schools, churches, and public utilities. It can assume that companies will remain part of their future. Third, the local government can be more certain of tax revenues. Fourth, local control contributes to a better cash flow for localities and a stable commercial base; the income of local employees can be counted upon to circulate through local banks and businesses. Local control thus increases the probability that a company's retained earnings and distributed profits will also be held and spent within the community. Employee ownership and control advances the possibility that local profits will remain within the locality. Fifth, local ownership increases the opportunities for workers to lead and thus to experience personal development in the firm. Also, employees can feel more pride in their work. The ultimate advantage is that social problems and the devastation left in the wake of market forces – unemployment, crime, delinquency, family instability, mental illness – can now be more effectively treated in the context of the community. For all these advantages, it is feasible and important to take steps toward increasing local autonomy. The question remains whether such steps can be viable in the face of market forces still operating on local communities.

Viability: *local self-reliance*

We have said that the degree to which a community can become economically viable and self-reliant is no longer a matter of serious interest to planners. We define viability as the degree to which people can handle their own economic problems with human and material resources. Viability is different from autonomy in the sense that it is one thing to be formally independent and another thing to be able to solve one's own economic problems. The idea that localities can solve their own economic problems has become so far removed from reality that planners do not take it into consideration. New England, for example, is dependent on other regions for 80 per cent of its food, and it seems impossible that a community could approach any self-reliant capability for producing its own food, much less other major areas of industry.

Yet, self-reliance is not wholly irrelevant because localities can become overly dependent upon outside entities and thus lose their capacity for problem solving. Company towns, one-industry cities, and sleeper-suburbs illustrate such dependency; they have legal autonomy yet can be quickly destroyed by their need for outside sustenance and support. People living there may not have the knowledge, skills, resources, and industry to sustain the life of the locality. It is important, therefore, to invest in some degree of economic viability as part of the goal of restoring community life.

We shall speak here of economic viability and self-reliance as more realistic than the radical concept of self-sufficiency. Economic viability is concerned with issues of community survival, and is best conceived on a continuum from high to low degrees of capability for a community to solve its economic problems. Self-sufficiency may develop in the future with the aid of new technology, but a practical concern today is to restore a new degree of local viability in the face of the market forces that destroy it.

Detroit is a city with a limited degree of viability. It was so dependent upon the automobile industry that when that industry declined in 1975, the city declined. The unemployment rate went up dramatically, as did crime, delinquency, and drug addiction. The city almost went bankrupt and is still attempting to restore itself. Some Detroit leaders argue that the process of gaining economic viability should not be dependent upon the comeback of the auto industry.

Dan Luria and Jack Russell have described a new plan of economic self-governance for Detroit through a more diversified economy and new structures of local autonomy similar to these we have been describing. They believe that new enterprises should be organized to maximize social accountability to employees and the community, which means organizing companies in which workers participate in ownership and management, and creating a nonprofit, tax-exempt community corporation structured for local accountability to provide capital for new worker enterprises. Individual investors would be offered stock but without disturbing local control. New capital investment would include the use of local pension funds. Michigan-headquartered private pension funds include five of the hundred largest, with nearly $20 billion in assets. Luria and Russell say that unions must win joint control over an area-wide investment bank that guarantees a minimum rate of return to pension funds while targeting a portion of the funds to city enterprises. They also project a new conception of the land-assemblage process in which public-worker-community authority dominates. These recommendations are close to what we have described as creating local autonomy and they go a step further, toward what we now want to describe as local viability.[18]

The self-directed steps of a locality toward establishing greater viability involve what we call a series of contractions and expansions. By *contraction* is meant a movement to bring economic resources closer to home, which requires developing (1) ecological loops, and (2) economic diversity. *Expansion* means getting in touch with a wider scope of resources outside the locality, in the region, the nation, and the world at large, which requires (1) developing export/import trade, and (2) institutions of research and development. Finally, we will discuss social inventions in business that make possible the simultaneous action of these opposing tendencies.

Contraction (centripetal action)

Ecological loops Ecologists have a theory of closed loop systems wherein the wastes of one production system become the raw materials for another. For example, the carbon dioxide that human beings breathe out as waste is needed by plants and trees. Green plants combine the carbon dioxide with water and light energy to make food. All our food comes eventually from this important activity: animals eat the plants and humans eat the animals; in turn, humans and other animals give off their waste, which is taken by plants as food to survive. Thus, we have a closed loop.

Some cities are beginning to invest in closed loop systems. To illustrate, garbage is a waste material but it is also a mix of raw materials that have value. Discarded aluminum is worth about 17 cents a pound to community recycling centers, and recyling has the indirect benefit of reducing garbage disposal costs. Compressing the aluminum lowers the shipping cost to the central manufacturing plant, raising the value by 25 per cent. Then, when cans are smelted and formed into ingots, the aluminium's value rises to more than 50 cents a pound. If the ingot becomes, say, bicycle handlebars, the value of the aluminium is more than a dollar a pound. *A city that invests in this type of loop takes a step toward economic self-reliance.*[19]

Careful investors can look for innovations in technology that lead to loop systems. One instance is the increased use of steel-belted radial tires, which has made it uneconomical to use conventional mechanical shredding processes for worn-out tires, but new techniques are using liquid nitrogen to freeze the tires to hundreds of degrees below zero and the rubber is then pulverized. The rubber is then converted into a wide variety of products, from shoe soles to floorboard or road surfacing agents. Again, a waste product becomes the supply for a production process. Another instance of innovative technology has to do with city sewage being turned into useful products.

Certain communities are exploiting their special environments. Oceanside and Davis, California, require solar hot water systems in all new homes. Springfield, Vermont, is completing a hydroelectric facility that will allow it to sell power to the utility from which it had been purchasing power for thirty years. Clayton, New Mexico, gets 15 per cent of its electricity from a wind turbine; Burlington, Vermont, gets about the same percentage from wood. The Harbor School District in Eire, Pennsylvania, developed two wells of natural gas between 1979 and 1980, and converted thirty-four vehicles, including twenty-five buses, to compressed natural gas. The wells paid for themselves in seventeen months, and because the gas burns cleaner than gasoline, vehicle maintenance is much reduced.

All communities can make better use of their environment. Buildings can tap the warmth of the soil and ground water by means of heat pumps. The heat lost in burning oil and gas is usually wasted: 30 per cent in most residential burners to over 55 per cent in some industrial processes. An alternative exists in cogeneration systems that halve electricity bills. Massive cogenerators provide virtually all the heat and power needs of multiplant industrial complexes, but the smallest units look like small compression engines for cars. For example, FIAT introduced the Total Energy Module System (TOTEM), that sells for $15,000 and generates heat and electricity for up to eight houses. The household power plant is almost here.

In sum, investment in closed loop systems helps to increase the economic viability of the community. It reduces local dependency on outside technology and it gives support to people seeking to maintain local autonomy.

Economic diversity Cities are like developing nations in that they can become dominated by one industry. When the industry fails, the whole city declines. This has been the fate of hundreds of cities as well as Detroit. People in Weirton, West Virginia, have experienced a successful worker takeover of the steel plant, which gives them more autonomy but not viability. Their single industry is still dependent upon the market for steel; in spite of a major step toward worker control, they could be destroyed as a community by a change in steel prices on the national or world market.

It is important, therefore, for social investors to take a careful look at the economic diversity of a community, including the structure of the economy relative to basic human needs. The summary below covers what anthropologists generally consider to be the physical needs of people. We are interested in how economic activities develop around these needs as well as how they are taken out of the market system. The community may gain in local autonomy but investment in these products and services is a mark of its viability.

1. Food – local access to varied food supplies, starting with agricultural production and moving through distribution to retail outlets.
2. Housing – availability of diverse construction firms to build housing for everyone in the community.

3.   Clothing – local access to textiles and seasonal garments from production to distribution.
4.   Transportation – local access to different sources for production and delivery of transport vehicles.
5.   Communications – availability of adequate media technology for everyone in the locality.
6.   Health – local provision of sufficient care for mind and body.

There are other important human needs, in religious life, recreation, and so on, but the above activities supply physical needs related to survival. A small community concerned with achieving relative self-reliance should be concerned with optimizing the local *production* of these goods and services.

Most communities and large cities are simply concerned with maintaining a minimum degree of viability. It is rare to aim for relative self-sufficiency in the production of housing, clothing, food and transportation. To do so means avoiding overdependency on one type of business as the foundation of the community and, rather, emphasizing a broad production base and not becoming a "retail city" or a "recreation city" or a "government city." It means creating more diverse production. At the very least, it means providing adequate housing, water, sewerage, and electrical facilities. Each step that a community takes to develop diverse production increases its viability. In this way it underwrites an interest in maintaining local autonomy.

A community can gain in legal autonomy and lose its economic viability. The aim of community development, therefore, is to increase economic viability so that the locality will become less subject to the destructive forces of a national market.

Expansion (Centrifugal action)
Import–export trade Jane Jacobs looks at the city as a settlement that consistently generates economic growth from its own local production. The city begins with its own production and then develops a "reciprocal dynamic" through trade with other cities.

Detroit began as a settlement in the early 1800s with a small flour trade. Then small shipyards developed to enable a flour trade with other lake cities. By the 1840s the yards had found customers for their ships in other lake ports and even along the coast. Machinists from the flour mills were transferring their skills to create some of the first steamships. The export work grew and the yards were supporting a collection of engine manufacturers, parts makers, and suppliers of fittings and materials. By the 1860s marine engines were a major export, and some were being sold in Europe. This basic mode of production had a multiplier effect in the economy.

There were also refineries and smelters that supplied copper alloys made from local ores to manufacturers of valves and engine brightwork. Between about 1860 and 1880 copper was Detroit's biggest export.

Jacobs says that a city like Detroit develops by two mechanisms. The first is *import replacement*. As imports are received and become known, consumers demand that they be produced locally. Local people devise their own techniques of production and are often able to supplant imports because of the saving in transport cost. The second mechanism is *innovation*. Continuing effort to develop new products for export means that their production can generate a new multiplier effect and bring in new imports that are eventually supplanted by local products. When this creative cycle is broken, the city begins to decay. This is what happened in Detroit.

The Detroit study by Luria and Russell (*Rational Reindustrialization*) aims at the recreation of the cycle of import replacement and innovation. Without having read the recent work of Jacobs, they write:

A rational economic development agenda must be centered on replacing the declining private activities of the city – auto assembly, parts and machining – with new activities that take maximum advantage of the existing industrial linkages. There are many activities that produce desirable goods and services for a national as well as a local market that fail to exploit these linkages. For example, a bakery may produce bread for the Midwest market, but it doesn't salvage the tool and die shops whose auto industry orders are drying up.

They then advance a set of social criteria for determining the direction for Detroit's community development and find four types of products that meet all the criteria: (1) deep natural gas and heavy oil production and upgrading equipment; (2) residential and industrial steam/electric cogeneration units; (3) large, and diesel-fuel-fired industrial process engines; and (4) mine-mouth coal gasifiers. The authors are recommending principles that would help restore the economic viability of Detroit.

Detroit has begun to follow some of these principles in its attempts at recovery, but it is not the only city that is vulnerable to the forces of a national market and capable of recovery. Any city could institute periodic self-studies of the local economy in this manner and then establish agencies to encourage product innovation and import-replacement. The city government could do this through its own agencies but at best it should sponsor community corporations in the private sector to assume this responsibility. We will discuss later the role of such corporations in the "polity" of community development.

A city should institute self-studies not simply for the city at large but also for its neighborhoods. If neighborhoods themselves are not innovating and engaging in import–export trade, they will suffer their own decline. The history of the city then repeats itself as depressed neighborhoods produce crime instead of commerce. *The challenge of investment today is to restore neighborhood viability.* It can be part of the larger plan of city development designed to revitalize community life. When cities invest in community development, they support the needed transformation toward local autonomy, and help reduce the power that the national market has gained over their fate.

Research and development Another way in which a community develops is by expanding its knowledge base. Knowledge is a critical factor in the development of a postindustrial society, and is increasingly important with the rise of new technology frontiers. It is no less important an economic factor today than are land, labor, and capital. Knowledge is a marketable item. It can also be localized and socialized in order for a community to maintain its viability.

A program in community development that seeks to restore local viability requires an educational and scientific foundation to keep in touch with the latest developments in technology and product research. For this reason, it is vital that communities expand their connections with institutes of technology and universities that can maintain ongoing studies of the development process.

A model strategy in this direction is the Greenhouse Compact devised in Rhode Island. Even though the plan was voted down largely on tax issues, it remains useful as a design for community economic development. The compact includes the creation of programs to enhance the contribution made by institutions of higher education to social and economic development in Rhode Island communities. If implemented, it would have involved creation of a general research institute at the state university to assist companies in special areas of research, product development, and product testing; the creation of an academy of science and engineering, for industrial development; and the authorization of the use of public pension funds for venture capital. The goals of the compact were to reduce unemployment to levels 25 to 30 per cent below the national unemployment rate, and to raise the average wage to within 12 to 13 per cent of the national level.

The "Greenhouses" were planned as independent nonprofit institutions for conducting research and consulting with government and industry; they would have helped to identify products and services, locate entrepreneurs, and finance new companies or product development efforts. The compact recommended that a customized training program be established for an expanding market in knowledge that would be localized through contracts with the institutions of higher education and thus create a more viable base for community development.[20]

Social inventions: decentralizing business

The expansion of the local economy toward national and world trade is essential at the same time that local people "contract" their control over land, labor, and capital. This appears to be a contradiction under the present system of business, but it becomes possible through business management based on decentralized systems of authority.

The decentralizing process in business has already begun by economic necessity. Many executives today have found that sheer bigness does not pay off. This was first observed in the wreck of the Penn Central and the cost overrun catastrophes of Lockheed and Douglas Aircraft. It was seen to be still more serious in the decline of the A & P and many conglomerate failures. W. T. Grant was once the third-largest U.S. variety store, but had to file for bankruptcy after amassing debts of $1.8 billion, largely from overexpansion. The cofounders of the Daylin retailing empire found that their huge bureaucracy could not respond adequately to new technology and the changing world market and their fortunes waned. The big airline companies – TWA, Eastern, and Pan American – became victims of overordering costly jumbo jets. The reality is that corporations can become too big to be managed effectively on a command system. Although the Reagan administration has encouraged conglomeration, every industry has also been in process of adjusting to overbigness by dismantling or decentralizing.

Some industrial decentralization has taken place through increased worker participation. We have mentioned that employees in the Philadelphia stores of the ailing A & P purchased and are now managing the stores. Employees in the subsidiary of General Motors in Hyatt, New Jersey, have purchased the local plant and contracted for production with their former Detroit employer. Employees of other firms have acquired stock in the company and some representation on the board of directors. Worker management in a big firm is good for decentralizing authority but not sufficient in itself unless it becomes more locality based.

Peter Drucker's concept "federal decentralization" is a process of altering the management system so that the corporation becomes a number of autonomous businesses. Each has responsibility for its own performance, its own results, and its own contribution to the total company. Each unit has its own management and can have its own board of directors. "Federal decentralization has great *clarity* and considerable *economy*. It makes it easy for each member of the autonomous business to *understand his own task* and to understand *the task of the whole business*. It has high *stability* and yet is *adaptable*."[21] One of federal decentralization's greatest strengths is "manager development." Each manager is close enough to business performance to get immediate feedback on his own task. This humanizes the work force, increases employee authority, and is more efficient. Drucker says: "The federal principle therefore enables us to divide large and complex organizations into a number of businesses that are small and simple enough so that managers can know what they are doing and can direct themselves toward the performance of the whole instead of becoming prisoners of their own work, effort, and skill."[22] Drucker points to some of the efficiencies of decentralized systems. He describes how Alfred Sloan first experimented with decentralizing within General Motors; a new level of autonomy and efficiency developed in the management of its car manufacturing divisions. He notes that a bigger step toward decentralization occurred in Sears, Roebuck and Company that eliminated the need for middle management. A Sears vice-president oversees three hundred stores, each an autonomous unit responsible for marketing and profits. Each store manager may have thirty section managers, each running an autonomous unit and responsible for meeting marketing and profit goals. Hence there are only two levels between the lowest management job (section manager in a store) and the president: the store manager and the regional vice-president.

Johnson and Johnson, a mammoth multinational producer of health care products, has taken still one more step in federal decentralization. For many years it has limited the size of each autonomous local business to 250 employees. Each has its own management and board of directors, and reports directly to a small, parent-company top-management team. Even with sales of over a billion dollars and more than 40,000 employees, Johnson and Johnson states that there is a need to operate in such a fashion.

The *Milwaukee Journal*, discussed above, is not mentioned by Drucker but it has taken the next qualitative leap toward federal decentralization. It developed as a worker-owned company in the 1950s when the original owners sold their stock to the employees. As the company expanded and bought other companies, it used the conventional form of command management. Employees in the new subsidiaries have now been given the right to purchase stock and can place representatives on the central board of directors. This is a true federation of autonomous businesses.

The overall direction of management decentralization can be schematized on a gradient of increasing controls for local businesses (figure 7.2).

General Motors is on the far left of the gradient; it was decentralized significantly under Sloan but still retains a relatively strong central command

Figure 7.2

Decentralizing authority

Command system ————————→ Federation ————————————→ Confederation

(GM)   (Sears)   (Johnson and Johnson)   (*Milwaukee Journal*)   (NAM)

system. Sears is more decentralized than GM in regard to local outlets and marketing functions. Johnson and Johnson is still more decentralized, with local boards of directors. All these firms, nonetheless, remain within the category of a command system. It is a qualitative leap from this system to the *Milwaukee Journal*, whose local firms have representatives on a central board of directors. This would be the next logical step for Johnson and Johnson if it wished to decentralize into a true federation.

The next qualitative step in decentralization involves the confederation, in which local corporations are given full power to operate independently without any top-down controls, as in a trade association. This does not necessarily make the organization weak. Modern methods of communication make the confederation in many ways more effective and efficient than the more centralized forms of control. For example, the National Association of Manufacturers (NAM) can communicate quickly with the 14,000 plants owned by its member companies through computerized mailing. NAM mobilizes political and economic information rapidly on issues of common concern in the manufacturing field. All trade associations are confederations of independent yet cooperating businesses. Many of them are, in their own way, more powerful nationally than large businesses operating under a command system. Indeed, computer networks manifest the enhanced power that loose alliances acquire in an information economy.

Federal decentralization is a social invention that encourages the simultaneous forces of contraction and expansion for local communities. A local business can expand its market through franchises and autonomous businesses in other cities and nations. A national business may decentralize its subsidiaries into federated local units. Experience has shown that the decentralized enterprise can often be a more efficient and effective way of doing business.

If Johnson and Johnson were to develop a national board of directors on which representatives of its local boards would participate, the local firms would gain in power and reduce the likelihood of shut downs. *They would increase their local viability by virtue of their representation at the national level* and also increase their motivation to succeed as profit centers within the federation.

The democratic federation is a common form of management in the non-profit sector of the economy and has served well in the economic affairs of such varied organizations as the Presbyterian church, the YWCA, the Rotary Club, trade unions, and the Chamber of Commerce. It could be the next step in the organization of the profit sector, giving local people greater control over the locality while maintaining access to national and international trade. This may become an important direction for social and economic development in the years ahead.

Polity: *social accountability*

The concept of *polity* refers to the way power is distributed in the community, not simply the formal distribution of power through the local government but rather through the *total community* with its various organizations and variegated class structure. Creating a democratic polity in this larger sense is more difficult than creating a democratic government. It means undoing the class inequities in the local economy while maximizing the overall community income; it involves overcoming the destructive forces of the market without succumbing to an economic decline.

We are interested in the issues of polity in the local system of enterprises in part because we think it is connected to the resolution of social problems. The creation of greater equity in the economic organization of the locality should offer a better opportunity to treat the problems of slums, crime, delinquency, divorce, mental disorders, and so on.

This new step in community development will require investing in a system of local corporations so that people can share power more responsibly in the round of local life, and require as well supporting structures of social accountability in the business sector within the context of the whole community. The social mechanisms for achieving the objective of sharing power have already been legally created but have not yet been implemented as part of a coordinated plan. We have already discussed some of these mechanisms, such as community corporations and worker-owned firms. A new planning strategy requires imagination on this legal and social frontier. The question is whether we are ready today for a coordinated plan of development.

Social investment groups, such as churches, universities, and pension and mutual funds, can come up with a common strategy for supporting a mode of development that overcomes the destructive market, but they cannot do it alone. They also need the help of government at every level. Government has not entered into our discussion of investment planning, partly because our whole design of development is based on a policy of building a local economy that reduces the need for government. The goal of this investment policy is to create a self-governing economy that requires less government regulation and fewer monitoring agencies.

At present, government is in a central position to help advance this mode of self-development. No other institution could assume the leadership role as well. Of course, doing so would place government in a paradoxical position. It would be authorizing and encouraging a method of planning that would reduce its own power; that is, it would be setting up organizations in the economy that would take government out of solving the problems of the city and initiating a method of nonmarket development that could stabilize growth and local self-management. The municipal government must look outside itself for community groups to perform this task. It cannot act entirely on its own or it becomes self-defeating. It must support private corporations in a position to promote a social economy.

A key corporation created by law to represent the whole community outside the government is the community development corporation (CDC). The government would do well to examine the grounds for supporting this structure to act on its behalf as an agent of social change.

The community development corporation The Community development corporation (CDC) is a democratically organized corporation designed to operate in the interest of the locality. All citizens in its geographic area are given, by means of their purchase of a low-cost share (e.g., $5.00), the right to vote for a board of directors that sets corporation policy. The board is in a unique position to provide a coordinating plan for establishing a more equitable economy in the locality.

The CDC was created as a legal structure in 1967 by the 90th Congress as a method for overcoming pockets of poverty in communities across the nation. Congress was responding to city riots that were reactions to the destructive forces of the market. CDCs began to organize slowly with marginal support from the Office of Economic Opportunity in various cities. A few CDCs, such as those in Bedford-Stuyvesant in New York City and the Hough Area of Cleveland, Ohio, have become known nationally for some of their efforts, but CDCs never reached a point of take-off. About 1,000 have been created in the nation, and with only limited resources. They have been evaluated at different times for effectiveness and have been given moderate marks of success, but they have never been notable for making revolutionary changes in the local market economy.

Our argument is that CDCs never had a methodology for overcoming the

excesses of the market. A few people envisioned them with the signal purpose of overcoming the destructive effects of the market, but the vision had
no overall plan. Consequently, the CDC has always been considered a relatively insignificant entity for treating local problems associated with
poverty. It operates within the market to create jobs, with no larger purpose of economic conversion. CDCs have at times been embroiled in local
politics, which slows them down, but their growth and effectiveness have
mostly been checked by the national market's acting against the social development of city neighborhoods.

The CDC has taken small but helpful steps toward initiating a wide
variety of local enterprises, including shopping plazas, housing construction, electronics plants, supermarkets, restaurants, factories, and job-
training programs. The enterprises, however, have been established largely
within the market framework of land, capital, and labor, and hence subsequently subject to the same damaging process as all other local enterprises. CDCs have *not* systematically acted to introduce the legal
frameworks we have been discussing: land trusts, community banks, and
worker cooperatives.

The next step in the development of the CDC, therefore, involves a new
plan of social development. It also involves providing broader support
nationally through long-term planning, equity capital, debt financing, and
technical assistance. CDCs are in a position to provide the thrust for formation of a system of local corporations operating outside the market
forces. They represent the functional equivalent to formal government
operating in the private sector of the local economy (see figure 7.3).

Figure 7.3

The local economy: an alternative model

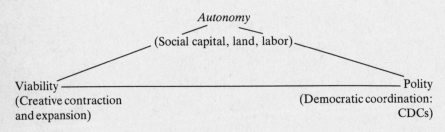

Autonomy

(Social capital, land, labor)

Viability ———————————————————————— Polity
(Creative contraction   (Democratic coordination:
and expansion)   CDCs)

A coordinated plan: CDCs

The new direction for the CDC involves planning for the simultaneous contraction and expansion of the community economy. It involves on the one

hand localizing (contracting) controls through community land trusts, community finance institutions, and worker-owned firms, as well as developing ecological loops and a greater diversity for the local economy. On the other hand it means broadening (expanding) its resources through import–export trade, and forging a new link with higher education. Finally, it means negotiations for both expansion (local firms becoming globally connected) and contraction (global firms developing local controls) through corporate federations.

We have spoken about how knowledge must be added as an economic factor along with land, labor, and capital. Knowledge has always been a latent factor in the market system, but today it has become a significant force as the professions become a central part of the service economy and essential to the development of new technology. The CDC is a channel through which communities may "localize" and "democratize" knowledge. The Greenhouse Compact plan is one example of how this new force of knowledge might become harnessed for local advantage. The CDC is the logical agency to help implement it, with the aid of university faculties in its region. This becomes part of its central role in reconstructing the foundations of the local economy.

There are innovative experiments under way today for investors to examine. The City of Burlington, Vermont, has initiated a program of investment that combines community land trusts and employee ownership along the lines we have been suggesting. It has begun to implement a model plan for developing new private ventures based on the following criteria:

1. *Market/Viability*: judging the capacity of new businesses on traditional standards of market needs and business skills of the principals.
2. *Quality local employment*: creating jobs having better than median regional wages, potential for skill enhancement, and for employee participation in company decision-making.
3. *Traded export goods or services*: giving preference to ventures that export their products in outside markets to encourage an inflow of new dollars.
4. *Local ownership*: assuming that the more "equitably held the local ownership structure – with full employee ownership as the ideal – the more likely the firm will maintain local roots, and the more equitable will be the sharing of rewards and responsibilities."
5. *Diversity of economic base*: spreading investments "across diverse industrial or service groups."[23]

Especially noteworthy is the creation of a "nonprofit Local Ownership Development Corporation" (LODC). The function of the LODC is to receive funds for investment in employee owned firms and to stimulate the development of such enterprises. Social investors will learn by investigating the Burlington venture.

The innovative enterprises we have been discussing are not normally part of any concerted plan for community development. The members of local cooperatives, land trusts, and CDCs are not commonly aware that together they are a legal system for overcoming the destructive forces of the market. There is no central agency to consult with them about their common purpose, to build the locality into a more self-governing community. The CDC could help develop local autonomy and viability by organizing these firms in business and commerce. It could help create worker-owned businesses and promote their products on a national and international market without losing autonomy and viability. The new role for the CDC could be to promote the development of the locally oriented enterprises in the context of an overall community plan. The CDC is in a special position to assume this role because of its democratic base and overall purpose for development outside city government. In fact, it could help unite these seedling enterprises into a local movement. The CDC could call together representatives of the enterprises to explore their common goals and policies in the locality, and together they could implement policies having statewide and national implications.

Let us look at what a CDC might do as a model experiment for social investors. When employees purchase shut-down plants, the CDC staff talk to employees about how a community land trust is important to develop because it can keep the property from becoming a marketable item; it preserves local control over land use in case future employees decide to sell to an outside corporation. A land trust board would give the employees the right to use the land in perpetuity.

Let us follow the model experiment further. The new worker cooperative may need capital to start the enterprise, and the CDC would tell it about community finance institutions. A CDCU may be available locally for capital, or there may be a special revolving loan fund such as the ones created by the Industrial Cooperative Association and the Institute for Community Economics in Massachusetts. When the workers get their enterprise going, they may want to provide a percentage of their profits as a charitable (tax-exempt) contribution to a land trust or CDCU. In these ways they contribute to the larger local movement to build community-oriented enterprises.

The CDC itself may have a way to go in accommodating to the new plan because it has not been oriented in this direction. The CDC and the CDCU have both lent money regularly to traditional capitalist enterprises, which then become part of the national market. They have not capitalized shopping centers with a land trust charter or normally funded new enterprises as worker cooperatives. Their capital has been simply an instrument of the market system. The CDC has often been separate from the cooperative movement at both the local and the national level.

One of the tasks of the CDC in the new plan is to help community finance institutions localize capital while expanding export–import trade. A key problem of impoverished localities is the outflow of capital without an adequate return to residents. This type of capital outflow could be redirected and localized.

Much rethinking of CDC goals must go into the new, more coordinated plan. The CDC has made mistakes in capitalizing the market system and thereby limited its own potential as a force for social development. For example, it customarily buys conventional enterprises and maintains ownership; this simply plays into the capitalist process of stock ownership and outside control. It is regressive for two reasons. First, purchase of the firms ties up CDC equity so that it cannot continue to utilize its capital for start-ups or other constructive purposes. Second, management in the CDC-owned enterprise is appointed from the outside by the CDC; the CDC thereby can dominate the workers in the same manner as an outside capitalist. It is better for the CDC to capitalize and support independently operated business cooperatives, still aiding as a business consultant but not acting in an ownership capacity (Figure 7.4).

The CDC would inform community banks about the methods for successfully spawning socially owned companies in Mondragon, Spain, where cooperatives have been created effectively for over forty years. The Mondragon Bank has devised a method for making small business cooperatives succeed. Bank staff utilize a special system of supervision and training in the development of a cooperative, and its success is part of the bank's highest priority. The cooperative later becomes involved in the bank's self-management, as part of a federation of cooperatives created by the bank for its governance.[24]

In the light of the new plan for local development, the CDC could consider added functions for itself:

1. Encourage employees to purchase cooperative equity in the firms they now own.
2. Sponsor new businesses on principles of worker ownership and self-management.
3. Facilitate linkages between cooperatives, land trusts, community banks, and other democratically based groups.
4. Establish a center for new entrepreneurship, with venture capital directed toward the cooperative movement.

Figure 7.4

Model of community development

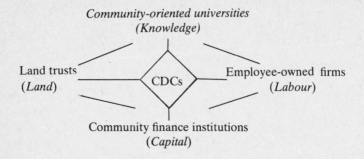

Community-oriented universities
(Knowledge)

Land trusts   Employee-owned firms
(Land)   CDCs   *(Labour)*

Community finance institutions
(Capital)

5.   Support programs combining skill training and cooperative education for the
      unemployed, former convicts, minorities, young people, drug addicts, and
      delinquents in the neighborhood.
6.   Cultivate relationships with local colleges and universities to institute
      community self-studies directed toward the social development of the local
      economy.

Final arguments

The source of capital investment

Some investment analysts have argued that there are no funds available to
risk toward a new direction in community development, but others point
out that the real problem is the proper placement of investable funds, that
is, how to redirect existing capital flows. The greatest potential for socially
redirecting capital flows is in the pension funds. Their advantages are their
size, their long-term perspective, and their established use of social criteria.
State pension laws and ERISA have relaxed the prudent-investor rule in
the past few years, allowing more flexibility in placement of funds. Thirty-
one states have undertaken socially targeted pension investment for economic development.[25]

Patrick McVeigh writes that overcoming a capital shortage does not
mean seeking easier access to pension-fund capital but rather finding more
efficient vehicles for its deployment. He points to three major movements
in the targeting of pension funds to illustrate the potential for redeploy-
ment: one involves housing; another, small business development; the
third, equity financing. He argues that although social investors have
placed capital in all three directions, they have simply tended to displace

private capital and therefore still represent new sources for socially directed capital investment.[26] Let us follow his argument.

First, housing investment has been a high priority for social investors. In June 1983 thirty-one states held $14.7 billion in housing securities through their state-administered pension funds, but it is doubtful that they have had any effect on increasing the level of affordable housing. The bulk of the investments are in mortgaged-backed securities of the Government National Mortgage Association (GNMA, called "Ginnie Mae"). GNMA guarantees payment of principle and interest on privately issued securities that are backed by pools of government-issued or government-guaranteed mortgages. "Ginnie Maes" yield competitive rates, are liquid, and are relatively risk free. They are popular with managers of pension funds seeking to achieve social goals through the development of local housing.

Studies show that by investing in "Ginnie Maes" pension funds have merely displaced private investors.[27] The Federal Reserve of Boston has concluded that the purchase of GNMA securities by pension funds apparently does not increase the supply of mortgage money. *A withdrawal of pension funds from GNMA would not affect the home mortgage market because private investors would quickly fill this gap.* These funds, therefore, could be available for a new cooperatively based plan for community development. There is still a need to investigate further where that replacement funding will come from, and what organization might be temporarily short of capital in the transfer process.

Second, managers of public pension funds frequently purchase Small Business Administration (SBA) loans, partly to support the values of local development but also because 90 per cent is guaranteed by the federal government. The loans have a competitive rate and little risk. Again, it is doubtful that the SBA loans are responsible for an infusion of money for economic development. Pension fund investments simply displace private capital, and continue to finance conventional business and perpetuate the problems of the market. But this is an important source of capital because SBA loans permit support for employee-owned businesses and other community-oriented firms while remaining relatively 'risk-free' for the investor.

Third, the equity market has been a prominent vehicle for pension funds. ERISA regulations have sometimes been interpreted so as to restrict equity investments to only the largest and most successful firms, but a current restructuring of the market is producing a significant change in the rationale for this vehicle. The restructuring began with a movement to restrict investments in companies doing business in South Africa. There are today twenty-eight states, eight cities, and various private pension funds (for instance, the United Auto Workers and the International Ladies Garment Union) that have taken action to divest funds from companies in South Africa. This capital is available to middle-sized non-blue-chip firms.

In sum, capital is available for investment toward frontiers in community development. First, the funds for GNMA housing can be redirected experimentally toward cooperative housing with no higher risk of investment; these investments may also include community land trusts under the guidance of CDCs. Second, funds available for typical small business loans can be redirected toward employee ownership and self-management and other community-oriented corporations without increasing the risk of investment. Third, the funds for equity investment in big corporations involved in South Africa can be redirected toward middle-sized firms taking steps toward employee-ownership. These steps might be taken through a cooperative oriented stock ownership plan; the equity could also be sold gradually to the employees under the guidance of the local CDC. In general, these funds would then encourage the development of an economy which is still competitive but increasingly based on principles of cooperation.

Finally, big corporations that undergo some reduction in stock prices have the option of decentralizing so that their subsidiaries gain local autonomy and the entire administration becomes governed more directly on the principles of a federation. We have noted how this pattern of administration can be economically beneficial to a company, but it is also advantageous to investors interested in local development because the national market helps to insure their liquidity. Also, for social investors it suggests a greater balance in the flow of funds from overcapitalized areas to undercapitalized areas. The administration of a federation tends to equalize the distribution of internal capital among its units in wages, investments in new technology, and expansion. Greater local control increases the likelihood that capital does indeed flow to necessary local projects and does not just displace private capital. The investment does not then lead to more deindustrialization. For local employees, it increases job security, provides greater control over their own economic resources, and allows them to gain the benefits of a national market. Put another way, the decentralized firm can help increase the viability and the autonomy of the local economy as well as its own vitality and profit-making ability. In sum, if the changes are made effectively, everybody wins.

An experimental approach

The pattern of social investments recommended here is a starting place for experiments in overcoming the effects of the market. This plan is designed to test the transformability of the market where it leads to undesirable ends.

It is intended as a way to break the national market's stranglehold on the locality, but it should be seen as a pattern to be constantly studied and evaluated as the changes are made.

The new policy could mean concentrating investments in neighborhoods or sections of the city without attempting a massive metropolitan change, testing each alternative corporation for its capacity to localize labor, land, capital, and knowledge. It also means testing how the corporations work together effectively in the contexts of particular localities. *Dozens of social, legal, and political issues must be settled as these four components of the market are simultaneously introduced in a suburb, a ghetto, or a central business district.* If changes are made too rigidly or massively, they could result in more problems than they are intended to resolve.

Altering these four components of the market to any significant degree could also have a major effect on the local power structure and local culture. The plan implies a slow reversal in the "great change" toward vertical power. It means reintroducing a new form of horizontal power through the work of the CDC and other community organizations. Furthermore, under employee ownership and democratic banking, the business sector may begin to change in its values. It may begin to look more like the nonprofit sector. The process will require systematic observation so that adjustments can be made from time to time because the social and cultural effect of the structural changes cannot be easily anticipated. Therefore, it is important to have continuing studies conducted with the aid of local colleges and universities.

The multi-leveled community

One argument against increasing the power of the local community is based on what the community was like a century ago. It was not all friendliness, cooperation, and amity. The early community often contained prejudice, discriminatory practices, and elitism, which could be seen as the danger in returning controls to the locality. The argument has merit but is countered by two fundamental changes that are introduced in this plan.

First, the old community was under a local market system. Much of the elitism and discriminatory practices arose from the fact that a few families controlled the land and the businesses. The *new community* suggested here is based on democratizing patterns of ownership and management; former patterns of elite ownership and control are less likely to be reproduced.

Second, the expansion of the local community through business federations reduces the likelihood that the former conditions of localism will repeat themselves. The top boards of federations located outside the community (e.g., churches, YMCAs) have often taken positive steps in recent times to reduce discrimination and prejudice at local levels of their organization. Also, the mass media have had a positive effect in broadening the local acceptance of ethnic and racial differences in corporate life. Similarly, transportation today carries people out of their localities frequently enough to reduce tendencies toward extreme provincialism that characterized the village in the past century.

Third, the recreation of community life in the modern locality reduces the intense search for a community at the level of the nation. When a sense of community is not found in the locality, people seek primitive identities in the nation, so loss of community at local levels has its price in an extreme identification with the nation-state. Erich Fromm in *Escape from Freedom* noted the danger of this drive for a national community in the midst of the changing and collapsing forms of capitalism in Nazi Germany. Emile Durkheim clarifies the meaning of this danger in the tribal totemism and intense collective identity that develops in the "sacred community." The sacred community today is the nation-state. People do not sacrifice their lives fighting for their locality or their church, they do so for their country.

The danger today is not so much in localism as in nationalism. In the nuclear age the risk of continuing the destructive effect of the market on local life and permitting its course toward centralizing power in the nation-state is greater than the risk of augmenting power in the local community. The loss of the local community to the market forces of modern nations can result in a still more intense form of national community going beyond patriotism to idolatry and war.

Our argument for a new plan to restore local autonomy and viability is really a call for balance in the search for community. This step toward a new balance is an attempt to overcome what Durkheim once called the "egoism" and "altruism" developing in modern nations. He found these deviant forms of social relationship pervading especially the life of modern cities. Egoism (weak solidarity) led to suicide, crime, and family instability. At the level of the nation, altruism (intense solidarity) led to war based on self-sacrifice. The sociological problem was to find a balance between these two extremes.

Durkheim believed the *anomic* (normless) forces of the market system to be a central cause of these problems. He was concerned about the chaotic and cyclical nature of capitalism and called for a new balance in community through a movement for "solidarity." It may be on this speculative theory of a needed balance through the search for solidarity that the argument for investing in community development must rest its case.

The local community thus becomes the final focus for decision making in the field of social investment. It is the "final criterion" for judging fiduciary decisions at every level of administration: the corporation, the industry, and the economy as a whole. At every level the question arises as to how investment decisions will affect the local community, which is where the philosophy underlying social investment is finally judged. The community can be the locale for creating new forms of enterprise that are both profitable and accountable to the people they affect; where free enterprise need not be restrained but can be enhanced by norms of justice and democracy; and when economic freedom can reign without government domination. So, it remains for social investors – churches, universities, unions, banks, mutual funds, state pension funds, and loan agencies – to chart a new path for business in the context of the community. The continued social transformation of business secures a better future for all of us.

Part III Global social investment

8 International investment

The need to utilize social criteria for investment in developing countries is vitally clear. The singular use of economic criteria in world banking has been an abysmal failure in solving the basic problems of the Third World. The sum of money invested in developing nations is enormous, but extreme hunger and poverty continue unabated. One reason is that international investors continue to base their decisions on financial and economic criteria, while the problems are increasingly recognized as social and political. If it is true that the real barriers to doing away with world poverty are in the way people organize in society, investment requires a sociological perspective to provide the information needed for decisions that will be effective in overcoming poverty and hunger in the world today.

When Robert McNamara became president of the World Bank in 1967, he began to see the serious gap between the amount of money invested by the bank and its ameliorative effect on poverty. In 1973 he took major steps to alter the situation. He changed bank priorities to attack poverty directly, brought in staff to deal with the changes he needed, and increased the bank's research budget for the poverty problem. During the McNamara years, the amount loaned annually to developing countries rose from less than $1 billion to $12 billion, yet the high levels of poverty continued. The bank's *World Development Reports* in 1978–9 projected that there would still be 600 million people in absolute poverty by the year 2000. McNamara's limited success is illustrative of the complexity and depth of the problem. The World Bank is only one of many institutions investing in the Third World with some purpose in attacking poverty, but their efforts seem unavailing.

We will examine the problems that investment has engendered in the Third World, but our main task is to determine why they persist and how they can be overcome. We will point to social problems existing in the organization of finance, production, and exchange as a basis for developing a set of corrective investment guidelines. Our main contention will be that the failure to include social criteria in the investment process is a principal cause for the social problems remaining unchanged.

185

Put another way, the economic problems associated with developing nations are rooted in social problems. Economic problems are what we see and analyze in such terms as profits, debts, and exchange rates, but they rest on a more fundamental problem that has to do with the way people are organized in the economic order. Our reasoning is that economics should not be the only discipline determining the direction of investment policy. As important as economics is, it is not sufficient by itself to deal with Third World problems. Sociology and related disciplines are fundamental to the investment process. Furthermore, our argument is that social development must be included with economic development as the goal of investment. A program of economic development cannot really be successful without the resolution of social problems in emerging nations. The social factor is intricately intertwined with economic development; in fact, it is critical when the investment goal is overcoming hunger and poverty.

The two perspectives: social and economic

It is essential to understand the difference between the economic and sociological perspectives of development, for the difference is critical to our theoretical framework for global investment.

The most famous definition of economics has been that of Lionel Robbins: "the science which studies human behavior as a relationship between ends and scarce means which have alternative uses."[1] The widely respected economist Paul Samuelson also stated it simply: "How ... we choose to use scarce productive resources with alternative uses, to meet prescribed ends ..."[2] Economics does not study the values and the culture of a people but begins with an acceptance of the values ("prescribed ends") of the people who use economics as a science.[3]

Economics emerged within the capitalist system and has gained much of its direction within that system, so it serves the values of business. Economists function in the higher councils of business and government and their values usually coincide with business values. For example, economists generally take the concept of efficiency as a basis for measuring the relationship between means and ends in economic planning partly because efficiency is important in the business system. Such concepts exhibit intrinsic value, but economics is not designed to study them as human values. Mainline economics raises no systemic questions about human nature and human values in society. Economic values are not examined for their standing in a larger cultural context, for the impact they have on people's lives in society.[4]

Central economic concepts formulated within the capitalist system include savings, interest, exchange, capital, land, rent, gross national product, profits, supply and demand. Economists quantify these concepts (for instance, exchange rates) as a basis for measuring the relationships between them as "variables" in economic analysis, but economists do not study the variables of social structure that become the major determinants of how economics' variables function in society.

The focus of economics is on the development of material wealth in a nation. The concept of economic development is associated with the optimization of the material well-being of people. Within the values of the capitalist system this has meant policies that perpetuate the disparities between wealth and poverty. Economists who measure economic development cannot tell us how to solve the problems of poverty; their concepts do not provide the insight. A common measure of economic development includes growth of the GNP and annual per capita income, but these figures can increase while the class structure remains the same or poverty worsens and people starve. Most economists know this but still do not integrate social statistics into their research or incorporate a theory of social development into their findings.

A sociological perspective consists of a relatively coherent picture of the human variables of community life. Sociology often lacks the mathematical precision of economics but gains in its relevance to human realities. Through its concern with the norms, customs, mores, and symbols guiding people's choices in everyday affairs, it reveals the social processes underlying group life, such as competition, cooperation, and accommodation. It requires a basic understanding of economic organizations, such as banks, trade associations, trade unions, farm cooperatives, and consumer federations, which are studied for their impact on people, and for the manner in which people within organize to establish standards of justice and create conditions of freedom. Thus, sociologists study the symbolic life of the culture and the contradictions of group life along with the effect these factors have on the social well-being of people.

The perspectives of economics and sociology, then, yield different interpretations that may contradict one another but, we believe, need to be reconciled and integrated in regard to investment policy. An economic perspective focuses on the material well-being of people; a social perspective, on their personal well-being in society. The goal of economic development is usually defined as the cultivation of material resources; that of social development, as the cultivation of human resources. The separation of perspectives has not been useful because the latter goal is ignored with serious consequences, as we shall see. Therefore, we define social development as the synergistic cultivation of human and material resources.

A social perspective is fundamental to the formulation of investment policy because *all* development is rooted in human interaction, and the symbolic life of people. What people see to be a social problem is what motivates them to act. *The social factor is the real engine of development.* A social problem is defined by people on the basis of what they believe interferes with their fundamental values, that inhibits or prevents fulfillment of a way of life. The problem is not interpreted simply by professional sociologists, but grows from the life of people living in community. The problem may not be interpreted similarly by everybody in the community, but there is generally consensus about broad areas of interference. Consensus is essential for development to take place effectively.

Social and economic problems intermingle. Such problems as low profits and high interest rates are causally related to crime, prisons, and high welfare costs. Even though the connections are not always made, our contention is that there are no economic problems without associated social problems. This is why it is so essential to add the social perspective and to integrate social criteria into a global investment policy.

A gap in economic expectations and social realities in the Third World

The importance of adding a social perspective is made apparent at the outset by studies that show a gap between investor expectations and the social expectations of people in developing nations. For example, many international agencies, such as the World Bank, the Asian Development Bank, and the Agency for International Development (AID) in the United States, have emphasized programs to increase agricultural output and commodities that count in the gross national product. Their investment criteria are largely economic and success is measured in monetary terms, so they often overlook the power of the social factor at local levels and assume people will respond to their definition of the core problem in economic development.

People in Third World nations do not always have investment criteria in mind; local people are looking at social problems. They see social amenities that they want but that do not provide short-term profits. Their interest in development is more local and is based on more socially immediate returns. Studies show they want to improve the quality of life in their communities: better roads, good water supplies, health and educational facilities, and public buildings. They would like to have some of the luxury goods they see appearing in the cities. It is such things that more often concern local people, rather than an increase in crop production and industrial productivity for the nation as a whole.[5]

When people in rural Nigerian communities were asked what projects they would want to work for, farming came near the bottom; they preferred to work on roads, bridges, schools, civic centers, marketplaces, motor parks, water supplies and health centers.[6] In other nations there have been similar answers. Kenyans put irrigation last on their list of preferences.[7] Tanzanians cooperated most easily in building schools, dispensaries, and shops, and they did not want to participate in agricultural projects until the government compelled them to do so.[8]

Many Third World people regard farming as unprofitable and having less value than other activities. The fact is that small-scale farming has been devalued and made unprofitable by patterns of outside investment, among them in big-scale farming projects by big banks, as we shall see. Such farming has been funded because without taking account of the social consequences, they deemed it more *economically efficient*.

There are other gaps between investor expectations and Third World people. Investors sometimes expect local organizations to be democratically structured. In reality, local groups are generally motivated by special interests that are variously ethnic, religious, and political, and they exclude other members of the community. The problem for social development is to make the transition to democratically based groups. Suddenly to create structures that have a wide geographic scope and that represent interests of the whole community is no simple matter. It is not as easy to identify with a democratic organization as it is with a temple, caste, or tribal group. The change involves a social process of some complexity, and is first a matter in *social* (not economic) development, and the economic failures in such ventures should really be understood as socially caused.

Studies show that when amenities such as roads or schools are constructed, there is often a local expectation that the government will repair and maintain them over time. Also, there is often a local belief that the government has a pool of resources to undertake new construction. These are problems in social development and must be resolved before the economic problems can be resolved. Let us look in more detail at the social problems behind economic problems in developing nations.

There are several positions in regard to what constitutes Third World problems. One position holds that the problems of the capitalist Third World are rooted in the external dependency caused by the investment patterns of multinational corporations, and that the central problem is the imperialism of a system of world corporations whose primary interest is profits. A second position examines the internal dependency resulting from the investment patterns of international banks. It suggests that internal elitism in Third World nations is due to economic criteria that emphasize large-scale technology. A third position holds that the crucial issues are financial and are identified with the Third World debt. It suggests that the problem originates in uncoordinated world investment and mismanagement of funds. A fourth position focuses on civil violence and political revolution, pointing to the violent reaction against capitalism that results in statism and bureaucratic centralization with its own patterns of dominance and exploitation.

Third World problems

External dependency: multinational corporations

According to empirical studies conducted in the Marxist tradition, nations of the Third World exhibit dependency patterns that are based on *exploitation*, *distortion*, and *suppression*. This research has been directed largely at capitalist nations related to multinational corporations.[9]

The studies demonstrate that capitalist development involves *exploitation* because of an economic drain toward the core nation of profits and interest on loan capital. Multinational companies have gained advantageous positions in developing nations through their power to accumulate profits under.the protective wing of domestic elites.[10] Some studies have shown that exploitation is rooted in disparity between the pricing and wage structures of the core nation and peripheral nations. For example, low wages in developing nations have provided high market returns on goods sold in the home nation of the multinational.[11] Other studies show that exploitation is rooted in transfer pricing between subsidiaries located in countries with different tax rates, enabling executives to hide profits that otherwise might be taxed where production takes place.[12]

Dependence theorists also argue that the economics of Third World nations become *distorted* through trade that prevents genuine local development.[13] An outward-oriented economy specializes in a limited number of products (e.g., bananas or sugar) designated by an outside power for its own use. Under these conditions, the host economy does not diversify to meet the needs of its population. The economy is structured around cities with ports of exit for trade with the big nations, leaving a deprived rural economy. Peasants swarm to the port cities and there create massive slums.[14] The strong link with the foreign power thus retards the economic growth by lowering capital formation.[15]

Finally, dependence theorists argue that Third World nations are *suppressed* by foreign investment. A national elite is formed in the developing nation to support the export–import trade; the existence of this elite helps to curtail the growth of local enterprise.[16] Domestic elites prevent the imposition of tariffs that would protect new enterprises from the competition of outside corporations. They encourage local banks to lend money to multinationals rather than to local companies because they have more confidence in foreign enterprise and because of personal ties developed with foreign executives. The "bridgehead" created between domestic elites and foreign investors blocks local leaders from mobilizing for new manufacture and production.[17]

A vicious circle of exploitation, distortion, and suppression, then, keeps developing countries from experiencing genuine development along alternative paths of social development.

Internal dependency: international banking

The problems of capitalist dependency in Third World nations are not due solely to multinational corporations that are seeking profits. They are also due to the investment patterns of international banks whose economists seek to reduce dependency but whose investment criteria have resulted in producing sets of elites inside emerging nations. Hence, the investments simply perpetuate a system of internal colonialism. This has happened in part because many international investors have sought to speed up the process of development through financing of large-scale projects with complex technology. The attempts have been successful in some respects in economic terms, but they have created many social problems in regard to further economic development. Studies show the reasons that this is true.

First, large-scale projects like big-tractor farming have led to a strengthening of local elites. The larger landowners have benefited from the projects partly because they are more educated and can lead in the development process. The outside support for existing elites angers the less affluent farmers and the peasantry, for it leads to devaluation of their kind of farming. Second, small cultivators have lost land to this kind of investment and have become increasingly impoverished. There is no development plan that takes them into account. In addition, agricultural laborers have lost their livelihoods in the mechanization of farming. The application of high technology, then, simply benefits the rich, and this brings on political unrest and even more vexing economic problems in the nation as a whole.[18]

The Green Revolution seemed to be a promising program by the standards of international investors. It was a large-scale effort to intervene in the struggle against hunger with high-yielding cereals, but social problems interfered with its economic success. Its difficulties can be attributed in part to competing politics among big nations and the need to control the direction of development on the basis of capitalist ideology, which in effect meant the dependency of host elites on big-nation equipment, replacement parts, feed-mixing formulae, food specialists, special varieties of wheat and rice, and "breakthrough" fertilizers. The outcome was a widening of the distance between the well-to-do and the poor.[19]

It is important to observe the intertwining of social and economic problems in these efforts. Irrigation schemes and road-building projects relied on massive technological inputs which were not as cost effective as were less expensive projects.[20] Large-scale programs often displaced agricultural labor and caused small farmers to view their level of farming as less valuable, and thus encouraged a flight of people from rural areas to the slums of the cities.[21]

Governments in Third World nations have made attempts to correct these problems to no avail, for example, giving major representation to small farmers on local boards designed to carry out land reform.[22] But such efforts did not succeed as a rule in the face of threats of big landlords and wealthy cultivators who maintained power in the regions beyond the reach of the law.[23] Any break at all in strong backing from central governments resulted in the local poor's becoming virtually powerless. Mandatory committees organized within villages were even limited in what they could do. In India local managers would collaborate with elites to drain development funds from those who could not protest.[24] In Niger elites threatened to sabotage programs that challenged their power. Even when the main government demanded participation of the poor in local programs, the landlord entrenchment has often been countervailing.[25] In Senegal Islamic leaders who controlled large rural followings were able to expand their power and preempt new rural cooperatives sponsored by the government. The same pattern of elitism can be seen around the world. In Asia and the Near East as well as in Latin America countries trying to hasten the process of development based on strictly economic criteria, that is, on the efficiency found in advanced technology, ended by strengthening local elites.[26]

The Third World debt: overburdened Third World budgets

In the past two decades, the official capital of multilateral banks has grown rapidly. For example, the World Bank Group consists of the International Development Association (IDA), the International Finance Corporation (IFC), and the International Bank for Reconstruction and Development

(IBRD). Together these entities provided $12,568.6 million in loans and credits, 77 per cent of all development bank lending in 1980. The IBRD is the parent body of the World Bank Group and extends loans on near-market terms primarily to middle-income developing countries. Since it began operations in 1946, it has loaned about $60 billion. IDA was created to provide concessional resources to the poorest nations, with a current per capita GNP of $80 or less in 1979 dollars. Credits are interest-free but have a 0.75 per cent service charge. Maturities are fifty years with ten years' grace. The IFC encourages growth of private enterprises in developing nations through loans and equity investments financing about 20 per cent of project costs. In 1980 the IFC loaned $680 million, and had plans to double that level of investment over the next five years.[27]

Regional banks are no less important for their international impact on development. The Inter–American Development Bank committed $2,168 million of its resources in 1980. The Asian Development Bank was created in 1966 and has since loaned a total of $6,696 million. The African Development Bank in 1980 committed $247.7 million to twenty-three countries.

Loans from multinational banks are on more liberal terms than those from commercial banks and are therefore important to the structure of the external debt. External capital from multilateral sources comes primarily from these banks, but assistance is also obtained from United Nations agencies such as the U.N. Development Program, the Internal Fund for Agricultural Development, and regional organizations such as the Arab Fund for Economic and Social Development or the OPEC Special Fund.

In the past decade the Organization of Petroleum Exporting Countries (OPEC) has played a key role in providing development assistance. During the four-year period starting in 1973, OPEC aid increased rapidly, reaching $5.9 billion in actual disbursements in 1977. Disbursements declined to $3.7 billion in 1978 but increased by one-fifth in the following years. This is when the problems began to mount.[28]

The debt of the lesser developed countries (LDCs) in 1970 was primarily with multilateral banks and governments. It was a serious situation but not yet critical because the international economy was still expanding with investments, experiencing a growth in commodity prices, and responding to plans of the LDCs for development and new interest among commercial banks in participating in the investment process. In 1973–4, however, OPEC tripled and quadrupled oil prices and thereby brought on a world-wide economic crisis. This led to a steep decline in trade; a drop in export demand and an increase in the import prices for petroleum, fertilizer, and capital goods. Third World nations were in trouble. LDC governments found that high levels of unemployment, lower living standards, and broken promises about prospective development intensified political instability, so they asked for more money from outside banks.

At the same time, commercial banks were depositories for OPEC dollars even as their normal sources of funds for investment in MNCs and domestic programs were drying up. They turned for replacement customers to the LDCs, who were being caught in a foreign exchange shortage and needed financing for their balance of payments. The new round of loans exacerbated the debt problem in the Third World.

By 1980, one out of every two dollars borrowed abroad by LDCs was being used to repay old debts. The economies of LDCs were now in deeper trouble, and the governments could not have enough money to get out of debt in the foreseeable future. They saw that they would be dependent on the capitalist banking world for longer than they had ever imagined. The question remaining is whether there is any alternative to maintaining long-term dependency on outside banking institutions.

Bureaucratic centralism: the socialist state

Although problems in the capitalist world are deplorable, some scholars argue that alternatives seem no better. Revolutions in the Third World often lead to the dominance of a centralized state apparatus. Indeed, the successful socialist state can create its own forms of internal elitism and external dependency that are not easy to dismantle.

Speaking of this development problem in Eastern European nations, the former East German Rudolf Bahro says:

Where the aim was the reabsorption of the state by society, we are faced with a desperate attempt to adapt the whole of living society into the crystalline structure of the state. Statification instead of socialization, in other words, *socialization in a totally alienated form* . . .

Again:

the state cannot disappear as domination over men, it cannot be reduced to the administration of things, without the traditional division of labor being overcome. The abstract centralist form of the state, by which the administration of things is entoiled, will only become positively superfluous to the extent that a system of social self-organization grows up from below into this inorganic scaffolding . . .

Still again:

The bureaucratic centralist form of planning, in which what those at the top receive from below is principally only passive factual information and "questions" while what they hand down are active imperatives, stamps the mechanism by which tasks are allowed to individuals . . . [29]

The problems of rural development and farming have been particularly acute in socialist states. In the Soviet Union since the sixties, the *Kolkhoz* (collective farm) has declined relative to an expanding private sector. Yugoslavia and Poland have acknowledged the failure of collectivization and restored private agriculture to a position of dominance under a system of restricted marketing and purchase practices. China has been the most successful socialist nation, but it too has recently introduced a range of new managerial and marketing systems that some observers argue is a prelude to the abandonment of collective agriculture as part of a wider set of changes in the nation. The study of failures in imposed collectivization and similar state-directed efforts within socialist nations has led Marxist Mark Selden to conclude:

> That alternative vision of a socialist agrarian policy that we found articulated in various ways in the writing of Marx, Engels, Lenin and the early Mao has yet to be seriously tested. Though perhaps China's experience prior to the autumn of 1955 constitutes its fullest implementation thus far. Since the late fifties each of the [socialist] countries studied here and many others have sought solutions to the problems generated by imposed collectivization. Most have experimented with attempts to redefine the relationship between plan and market and among state, collective, and private sectors. In each of these cases, we observe the search for greater latitude for the market and private sectors... A fresh consideration of the essential promises of socialist agriculture is long overdue.[30]

Efforts to overcome the problem of dominance in capitalist Third World nations through revolution result in new kinds of dominance. A violent socialist takeover can bring the opposite of what was expected by theorists and dreamed about by guerillas in the hills. The problem of state dominance is being attacked in some socialist nations, but the resolution of development problems involves a subtle and creative action that goes beyond the standard revolutionary methods of implementing social change. It also goes beyond standard capitalist investment.

A state-dominated economy is not what is intended by capitalist lending banks, but it is becoming the unintended outcome of their investment patterns. It is not simply the result of their tendencies to create social problems, and thus lay the seeds for revolution, but it is, rather, the result of their emphasis on investment solely from an economic perspective. The first and last concern of bank investment is with economic returns, even though larger political concerns may lie in the background of their decisions. The irony of capitalist investment is the creation and proliferation of centralized controls through Third World governments. The reason for such controls is that bank executives feel more comfortable dealing with government authorities than with private firms in LDCs; governments do not go bankrupt. Bank loans are based on the belief that a nation-state would not repudiate its debts, and a private firm could easily declare bankruptcy. Thus, the state sector has grown enormously in the capitalist process, and now controls most or all of Third World development banking, telecommunications, electric power production, petroleum, steel production, and many other basic industries.

The basic question for both the capitalist and socialist Third World nations is: What is the alternative to present circumstances?

Sociological causes: the noneconomic factor

From a sociological viewpoint, the causes of these four problems can be located in the social organization of finance, production, and exchange. We do not go into detail on causes here because our primary concern is with solutions, but we can indicate that the complexities go beyond economics and finance to suggest a perspective that will lead us toward social solutions. Let us look first at the social structure of the multinational corporation and the role it has played in causing economic problems. The way the MNC has caused problems in world finance sheds light on how the omission of social criteria in investment results in harming the interests of all nations.

In the 1960s and 1970s MNCs were doing very well in overseas investments. A 1973 Senate Finance Committee report put it in the following critical terms:

> It is beyond dispute that the persons and institutions operating in these markets have the resources with which to generate international monetary crises of the sort that have plagued the major central banks in recent years ... $268 billion, all managed by private persons and traded in private markets virtually uncontrolled by official institutions anywhere ... more than twice the total of all international reserves held by all central banks and international monetary institutions in the world...[31]

Even so profits began to decline and in the 1980s there was economic despair about the ability of U.S. MNCs to compete in the world market. The U.S. share of the world's manufactured exports had fallen from more than 25 per cent to less than 1 per cent in the previous two decades. Why did this occur?

The structure of the multinational corporation

One reason for the precipitous drop in the U.S. share of total world exports is that the MNC is designed to act first in its own self-interest and only secondarily in the interest of those with whom it does business. As a result it has caused social problems that have led to economic problems, problems that may be partly understood as patterns of exploitation, distortion, and suppression but also in terms of the costs of host-nation strikes, political payoffs, sudden tax hikes, rebel attacks against plantations and factories, and the nationalization or expropriation of land, equipment, and buildings – economic problems preceded by social problems.

Executives in MNCs began to treat social problems, partly because of profit losses and partly because of competition from foreign firms developing innovative structures in response to the problems. They began to share control and profits with people in the host society, including selling stock in foreign subsidiaries to host-nation citizens. We discuss these adaptive changes further in chapter 9 on "solutions", but the point here is that the *social organization* of the MNC is critical to its economic success.

The Third World debt is also related to the structure of MNCs, even though that is not included in the analysis of economists. The sudden rise in OPEC oil prices, which pushed surplus capital to commercial banks and which in turn led to overlending in the Third World, originated in the structure of the world cartel in the petroleum industry. The capitalist structure of oil companies known as the "seven sisters" clearly played a major role in exploiting oil-producing nations. It was not interpreted by everyone as exploitation in the beginning, but that is what a cartel eventually does. The oil companies were a monopoly and fixed prices in their own interest. Recognition of this by oil-producing nations led to the formation of OPEC to fight against the perceived social injustice. They saw that they could act collectively, as did the big oil companies, and recover or avenge their losses. Their political action then had the financial repercussions that economists are still analyzing.

The logical solution from a sociological perspective is to look toward multinational structures that reduce the tendency toward monopoly and increase the possibility of benefit for all nations. But such is not part of the thinking in the realm of finance and economics. The World Bank explains the causes of the debt-problem as "substantial fluctuations in the world market prices of primary commodities, sharp increases in the prices of energy products, the slowdown of economic activity in the industrial countries ... sharp increases in the real interest rates in the international capital markets ..."[32]

Ignored in economic and financial analysis is the fact that the social structure of world business is a basic part of the problem. The ultimate irony is that untreated social problems keep causing new financial troubles for advanced nations. The overseas losses of MNCs were a factor in the decline of industrial activity in the U.S. The debt burdening the Third World nations today has economic repercussions in the advanced industrial nations. *Business Week* declared that a debt moratorium in LDCs would not plunge the U.S. into a depression but could slow growth and increase unemployment enough to swing a presidential election. According to Chase Econometrics in 1983, if both Brazil and Argentina were to have stopped payments on their debts, the Federal funds rates would rise by over 1.5 per cent to around 11 per cent. If a moratorium were to spread to all of South America, it would cripple many banks, shrink their lending capacity, and push the economy to the brink of a recession.[33]

In the summer of 1985, it became clear that Latin America's big debtor nations were importing more and exporting less, so that they had less cash to repay loans. As a result of smaller trade surpluses in 1985, such nations as Argentina, Brazil, Mexico, and Venezuela could need new loans to pay off some of their older debt, and successful resolution of the debt crisis seemed more distant. William R. Cline, a senior fellow of the Institute for International Economics in Washington, D.C., said the worsening trade performance could lead both Mexico and Brazil to seek new loans in 1986.[34] Creditor banks know that they must loan new money if they want the older loans paid off. The financial problems continue to simmer while no serious examination of the underlying social problems is formally proposed in banking circles.

The structure of the World Bank

We have said that the social problems created by the MNC are caused in part by its organizational structure, and the same may be said about international finance. The voting power of individual members in the World Bank is determined by the size of each member's capital subscription: 250 votes for each share of stock held. A share is worth $100,000 (1944 dollars). This formula means that the United States had 21.11 per cent of the total number of votes in 1980; the United Kingdom, 7.82 per cent; West Germany, 5.32 per cent; and so on down to countries like Ecuador, with 0.18 per cent. The big socialist nations of course are not represented. World Bank policies are clearly dominated by the United States and its allies, which explains why the bank refused loans to socialist-leaning governments such as Chile under Allende, Peru under Velasco, and Vietnam during its reunification. The bank favors capitalist business and nations that support U.S. policies. It uses political criteria in investment policy in spite of the fact that it states publicly that it uses only economic criteria. Political criteria were dominant in decisions during the initial years of the Pinochet regime in Chile; this is not the creative mix of social-economic criteria we have been proposing. Chile was a terrible performer on social-economic and financial grounds, and the bank itself produced a report that showed Chile to be in its worst depression since the 1930s. Yet two weeks after the report was issued, in January 1976, bank staff recommended a loan of $33 million, and two additional loans followed.

The bank is clearly organized to accent capitalistic and nationalistic (U.S.) interests. It is not staffed to study systematically the social problems causing the economic problems in developing nations, nor is it organized to apply principles of social development or to utilize data based on social studies of development in the same sense that it utilizes financial studies. Instead, the bank supports a trickle-down policy of development that generally preserves the class structure and leaves social problems untouched, even while showing statistical signs of economic progress for the nation as a whole.

The Brandt Commission report on North–South relations states that the World Bank has a deficiency in its social organization: the power of the bank is too concentrated in the United States, where it has a professional staff of about 2,400, of whom over 95 per cent work in its Washington, D.C., headquarters. The commission points out that the bank's Articles of Agreement anticipated an administrative, decentralization but this has not happened. The commission recommends, first, that the developing countries be given more of their own people as representatives in both the World Bank and the International Monetary Fund. Second, the bank's regional offices should be placed around the world to assess and respond better to problems in the field. The offices should have regional advisory councils, as originally provided for in the articles. Third, the commission concludes that the relationship among the executive board, the central administration in Washington, the regional advisory councils, and regional operating staff should "encourage autonomy and genuine decentralization."[35]

Our task now is to look toward organizational solutions. We want to move more definitively to the kind of social criteria that it is hoped would spell more success in overcoming hunger and poverty in developing nations. The reader should continue to take note of the critical importance of both social and economic factors in the following discussion of global investment policy.

9 Social development in the Third World

The concept of social development is common to both capitalist and communist ideologies. We have defined it as the synergy that occurs in the cultivation of human and material resources together. Human resources include the individual's reserves of intelligence, intuition, sensitivity, imagination, and for our purposes, a capacity to learn technical knowledge, skills, and responsibilities needed for advanced states of economic development. It also includes the larger social domain, that is, a potential for institutions (e.g., courts) and organizations (e.g., schools) essential to the life of an advancing economy. Development means the cultivation of the personal and social resources of people so they can increase their capacity to work effectively in a more complex society. For social investors it means the formation of new patterns of social governance in the economic order of society.

Put another way, social development may be seen as the cultivation of a responsible use of power in the institutions of the economy. This means the unfolding of human potential among people governing economic organizations, the opening of inherent possibilities of social authority and responsibility among people working in the governing centers of the economy, and the creation of a new system of accountability of productivity for corporations. It involves the construction of a growth economy with a social foundation. To be successful, the process requires the expression of a new degree of human sensitivity for both the rich and the poor. This demands that creative action be taken by the rich in centers of power and by the poor in peripheral zones of the economy. And finally the formation of a social economy that is relatively self-regulated and independent of state controls is necessary.

The goal of social development is not inconsistent with the original beliefs of capitalism and socialism. The founding fathers of each system, Adam Smith and Karl Marx, were both interested in the development of a society with a minimum amount of internal monopoly and state control, that is, the kind of development characterized by neither corporate monopoly nor state dominance. Smith abhorred the rise of large corporations that he saw beginning to dominate the economy of his time. Marx abhorred the existence of unequal classes of people where corporate exploitation ran rampant. They were both interested in the idea of some degree of self-determination within the economic order.

Both founding fathers fell short of understanding the whole process of achieving this end through social development. Smith never fully anticipated the difficulty of small entrepreneurs competing without the eventual formation of monopolies and then state regulation. On the other hand, Marx never fully anticipated the difficulty of moving from a revolutionary "dictatorship of the proletariat" to a socialist economy in which, he believed, the state would "wither away."

Given this background, the social goal of capitalist and socialist countries could be to create that which was expected (or hoped for) by the founders but never adequately formulated in their work. The goal could be to develop a social system in the economy that reduces the necessity for state control.

Developing nations may yet find a path toward social (nonstate) regulation which the big nations so far have not been able to find. They have yet to develop effective methods for destatification and deconcentration without shortening their stride toward economic development. The question is: How can an effective system of social governance be developed in the economic order of Third World nations?

We have said that social governance is explained by two interrelated concepts: self-governance and mutual governance. Self-governance refers to the degree to which people in different organized levels of work (i.e. workplaces, departments, corporations, and whole industries) can be autonomous and capable of managing their own system of work. It is measured by the *degree* to which people can be effective together within their own organized level of work without regulation and supervision by outside authorities. The basic proposition in this development policy is that the more people in the organized levels of work who can become self-governing, the more the economy as a whole should be capable of functioning with a minimum of state regulation.

Mutual governance refers to the degree to which people work cooperatively and accountably together within a competitive environment. It is measured by the degree to which they participate equitably in the governance of industry and by the degree to which they become accountable to one another in the economic context of society. Put another way, the challenge is to introduce governing institutions into the nonstatist sector that are functionally equivalent to those of the state without interfering with productivity and fair competition. This means introducing democratic institutions

into the economic order, including private legislative and judicial institutions. The basic proposition is that the more people are able to participate
equitably and accountably in these different levels of work, the less likely it
is that they will need government regulation.

Developments in this direction have already been taken in both capitalist
and socialist societies. For example, we have discussed movement toward
self-management for workers in capitalist nations at all levels of corporate
life, reducing strikes, labor turnover, and the need for agencies of mediation in the government. We noted how trade associations in the United
States have developed hundreds of tribunals to handle commercial conflicts
without the need for the Justice Department to settle them. They also
handle problems of product standardization, develop ethical codes, engage
in self-monitoring of trade practices, establish consumer departments to
handle complaints from customers, and engage in a great number of other
activities that reduce the need for state regulation. In socialist nations there
have also been steps toward self-regulation within the economic order. In
Cuba relatively autonomous mass organizations have emerged, like the
Women's Federation and peasant organizations. And Cuba has taken steps
toward democratization through new electoral practices that began in
Matanza Province and have been spreading elsewhere in the country.
There is also the creation of neighborhood tribunals that function apart
from direct state control.[1] The development of economic enterprises that
operate independent of government controls and other organizations with
autonomous democratic forms is most advanced in Yugoslavia, but is occurring as well in many socialist nations, including Tanzania, Nicaragua,
Poland, Zimbabwe, and Vietnam.

We can observe some measure of social governance in the economic
order of both capitalist and socialist nations. The point for investors and
planners is that there is always room for social development toward higher
levels of self-governance and accountability. The question for investment
planning is: How can business firms, trade unions, and trade associations
become more socially governed in capitalist nations? On the same principle, how can state enterprises, trade unions, and ministries of industry
become more socially governed in socialist nations? How can they demonstrate a higher level of self-regulation and higher standards of accountability (justice) in their organization?

These abstract principles of social governance are a starting point for
planning among politicians in less-developed countries (LDCs). They are
significant at the outset because the goal of social development needs to be
clear in the investment process. The purpose of social investment is to culti-

vate programs that maximize these principles in the organizational development of the economy.[2] It is with the assumption that these principles can be a starting place that we can point to the way in which they can be implemented.

Global social investment

To achieve a socially governed economy, we need to reverse some of the modern trends toward imperialism, statism, and elitism. In capitalist nations this means aiming for a greater degree of economic independence, economic diversity, and self-sufficiency as well as a strong democratic polity. These same goals are applicable to socialist nations, but the strategies have a different emphasis. In socialist nations, the primary goal is to reverse the tendency toward bureaucratic centralism and statification of the entire society. The need is to devolve state controls in the economic order by developing new systems of social accountability and self-regulation.

Our task now is to formulate some guidelines for patterns of social investment that can work toward more effective routes to the goals. The process is too complex to discuss in detail here, but let us look at some examples of how to put these principles into practice.

Social policy

1. Investing in programs of decentralized development (avoiding bureaucratic centralism and national elitism)

The concept of decentralized development does not mean eliminating central controls in society, but simply that investment capital should be used to cultivate resources in the undeveloped regions of society. This should be done with two principles in mind. First, investors should aim to optimize social and economic development together. The ideal is to find a synthesis that enhances both the social and economic factors in host-nation projects. A guideline for this is to assume that the basic purpose of economic development is to optimize human resources. Second, the social process by which resources are cultivated within developed regions is an important part of the investment decision. An unwise investment that leads toward civil war or revolution can lead toward new forms of political dominance and exploitation. The method that optimizes social and economic development, and that alters political life nonviolently, is central to the discussion throughout this chapter.

In a highly centralized state economy, it is important to know that invest-ment funds can stimulate development towards a self-governing economy. Thus, it is helpful to be conversant with the following social mechanisms for decentralized development.

From a unitary system to a federal system of polity. Transition from a uni-tary government to a federal government requires the transfer of certain powers of authority from a central state to the constitutional states. Great Britain has a unitary system while the United States is a federal polity of constitutional states. More power is given to regions under a federal system. The process can also take place within the economy. A big corpor-ation may devolve its powers to newly constituted subsidiaries; this was done with Fagesta AB, a specialty steel maker in West Germany. The cor-poration devolved its operations into separate profit centers of subsidiaries that now have their own boards of directors within the larger firm.[3]

From a concentrated system to a deconcentrated system. This means a shift of administrative power to lesser bodies while spreading out the authority among them. For example, the dismantling of AT&T in the U.S. into a number of independent and competing corporations involved a deconcen-tration of the telecommunications industry. A preferable alternative would be the devolution of the industry into a confederation of enterprises that co-operate as well as compete with one another in the interest of their consti-tuencies.[4]

From a direct command department to an autonomous agency. This means giving special authority to separate bodies to fulfill the goals of the central administration. For example, the creation of public corporations has transferred power from the state to external bodies for the financing, construction, and management of physical projects. The transition requires care that such bodies retain public accountability and that recall powers are available for top officers. This same type of decentralized development may take place in mammoth business corporations. It simply means giving more authority to divisions of a corporation that have been under a direct line of command.

From state agencies to nonprofit corporations. This means giving powers of government to nonprofit organizations, such as trade unions, trade as-sociations, and professional groups. For example, socialist and capitalist nations have often delegated authority to professional societies to establish procedures for licensing practitioners in such fields as medicine, account-ing, law, religion, social work, and physiotherapy.

From state agencies to socialized enterprise in the private sector. Socialized enterprises are corporations that are in some significant measure accountable to their stakeholders, people whose personal lives are importantly affected by the enterprises. Such enterprises include community development corporations, labor-managed enterprises, cooperatives, and land trusts. We have noted that land trusts exist in various regions of the United States as well as in other countries.

From private management to worker ownership/control. This means transferring management authority to labor through training programs in the administration of corporations. This practice has been taking place in both socialist and capitalist nations around the world.

From government regulation to corporate self-regulation. Government deregulation means trimming or eliminating state controls over an industry. This practice is illustrated in the deregulation of the airlines industry in the U.S. and the deregulation of food prices at one point in Poland. But deregulation is not sufficient without new structures of self-regulation within the private sector. Otherwise the original purpose of regulation is not fulfilled and it is likely that new state regulations will again appear at a later date. Yugoslavia is the most notable case of a national government divesting control over its entire enterprise system. Greece is an example of a government that has divested control over certain public agencies by including representatives from labour and communities on their boards of directors.[5]

These decentralizing mechanisms are illustrated and described further in guidelines that follow.

2. Investing in experiments that socialize global corporations (avoiding imperialism and nationalism)

Business executives have become increasingly conscious of the social repercussions of the MNC when it is based solely on a command system whose primary objective is to make profits for the corporation and its home country. They have been encouraging a greater degree of local participation in the governance of the corporation in the host society. Leaders of host societies have also taken steps toward a greater degree of self-direction. For example, instead of the MNC's providing the foreign capital, technology, personnel, and managerial expertise to build and run a new factory, these elements of industrial expansion have been divided more recently between a variety of foreign firms, consultants, and banks, on the one hand, and the local government and local private firms on the other. Instead of inviting a big MNC to buy land and establish a factory, the host society will purchase the know-how from the foreign firms, buy the necess-

ary equipment from a variety of suppliers, hire foreign consultants to help
set up the project, and use domestic resources – such as private suppliers
and local training programs – to help develop the project. U.S. business is
finding arrangements with host leaders based on a new social contract.

Invest in democratically oriented MNCs

The MNC is also beginning to become localized and socialized in its overseas relationships. The trend began with reducing the number of U.S. managers and increasing the number of host managers, and continued by
opening stock ownership to people in the host nation. It developed in part
from host society resistance to outside dominance and in part because the
new structures were economically rewarding. The MNC has most recently
been forced to include host labor on the board of directors of its subsidiaries. In West Germany, for example, the subsidiaries of General
Motors (Opel) and Xerox have worker representatives on the boards; they
constitute 50 per cent of the board with U.S. owners having the other 50 per
cent. Labor can now participate in decisions on profit sharing and indirectly
on international policies of the MNC related to revenues of the subsidiaries.
The structure of the MNC appears to be moving toward becoming a social
federation.

Social federations have begun to appear on the world scene in the form of
multinational cooperatives. This means that the subsidiaries of the multinational are fully autonomous participants in the governance of the main
corporation and have representatives on the board of directors of the main
corporation, providing direction on policies of international development.[6]

Invest in social development (case: South Africa)

Social investors have begun to have a significant influence on the conduct of
U.S. corporations overseas in selected instances, of which South Africa is
one. Investors demand that these firms follow a policy of racial integration
and social justice. We have noted that some state pension plans have withdrawn their investments from corporations involved in South Africa regardless of their fair conduct, but other pension plans have agreed to invest in
companies following the Sullivan Principles.

The Sullivan Principles represent a major advance in the socialization of
the multinational corporation. They require that firms maintain "nonsegre-
gation of the races in all eating, comfort, locker room, and work facilities";
provide "equal and fair employment practices for all employees"; offer
"equal pay for all employees doing comparable work"; initiate and develop
"training programs that will prepare Blacks, Coloreds, and Asians in substantial numbers for supervisory, administrative, clerical, and technical

jobs"; increase "the number of Blacks, Coloreds, and Asians in management and supervisory positions"; and improve "the quality of employees' lives outside the work environment in such areas as housing, transportation, schooling, recreation, and health facilities."

There is some debate about the extent to which firms are advancing the Sullivan Principles, but the process is monitored and rated openly for investors to make their own judgments. About 125 of the biggest U.S. firms are signatories. They range in type from Abbott Laboratories to the Xerox Corporation. Like the phenomenon of codetermination in the subsidiaries of U.S. corporations in West Germany, this practice suggests that social development is possible under the right management without losing profits. Indeed, social practices can be quite profitable when combined with good business practices.

The social issue is a thorny one. The demand for divestment of the stock of all firms operating in South Africa is criticized because it is said that a lack of U.S. support would lead to violent revolution and an African dictatorship. Others argue that divestment would not amount to much because if U.S. firms were to pull out in consequence, multinational firms from other nations would simply take their place. On the other hand, social investors who maintain their support of firms adhering to the Sullivan Principles are criticized in that the firms do nothing to alter the political state of affairs in that nation; they are supporting a racist regime, it is argued, while not really gaining much progress through affirmative action programs internal to the firms.

Some self-management theorists have asserted that it is possible for investors who have withdrawn support from companies operating in South Africa to formulate a new strategy. The strategy would add a new set of principles to the Sullivan Principles that would provide a firmer social-economic basis for minority development within the network of U.S. firms in South Africa. This plan would encourage divestors to reinvest in South Africa.

The new principles would be implemented through company-conceived plans for subsidiary self-management backed by social investors and U.S. policy. First, a plan would be formulated for an MNC to increase the level of employee participation in the interracial governance of the subsidiary over a specified period of time; this should involve establishing worker councils in the European tradition of corporate administration. Management training programs would be introduced in accordance with the Sullivan plan. Second, a plan for eventual *interracial employee ownership of the subsidiary* and incorporating a management training program would be formulated by the MNC to be carried out over a period spanning from three to ten years, depending upon the nature of the business, its size, and permanent position in South Africa. Third, the company would contribute a percentage of its profits to a program of community development. The new principles would be no less controversial than the Sullivan Principles, but the fact that it was possible originally to implement a policy so radically different from the South African government's desires suggests that a concerted effort by social investors might be successful.

MNCs following the Sullivan Principles in a racist nation offer an image in contrast to those that have distorted and suppressed social development in the Third World. The exploitive behavior of big firms in developing nations have led world leaders in the past to call for ethical codes and world charterment of MNCs. Some social economists see signs that MNCs could become chartered within the United Nations, which has already established a Commission for Transnational Corporations to help develop an ethical code by which they should operate. The need is clearly to establish world charters that can set limits on the exploitative behavior of some MNCs. In the absence of such a charter, the MNC continues to roam a lawless domain much differently constituted than is its regulated home terrain. The concept of global charters is a part of a thrust toward a stronger United Nations and the foundation for world law.

3. Investing in decentralized programs with support from opposing factions (avoiding loss of national unity)

Decentralized development can be supported by relatively radical and conservative factions at the same time because decentralization serves a variety of political ends. It is important, therefore, to encourage a bridging of factions and to monitor the process. The main question in investment is whether it can serve the objectives of social development. Some of the selective arguments that persuade different political factions to decentralize include the following.[7] Decentralization offers

A greater diversity of experience and freedom of beliefs within society.

A better input of ideas from local citizens into national planning.

A greater variety of solutions to problems based on felt need and personal knowledge of people in localities.

A greater capacity of people as a whole to adapt to changes when they have been involved in the planning.

The likelihood that people will contribute more toward the upkeep of local projects and amenities that benefit them directly.

Better monitoring of national projects under conditions where local people want to participate.

Useful strategies for the main government to mobilize popular support and to achieve stability within the country.

Greater respect for political, ethnic, and religious diversity within the larger polity.

Methods to bypass local elites for greater empowerment of people in undeveloped regions and communities.

The introduction of intermediate technology that is most appropriate to the needs of local populations.

An interest in labor-intensive projects and self-help development in localities.

Greater emphasis on self-reliance, which expands the control of individuals over their own lives.

Increases in the level of involvement of people in communities and offering them more power over their local organizations.

Leaders in both socialist and capitalist nations have acted upon the need for decentralized programs. Socialist leaders have wanted at times to limit the power of state ideology imposed on all the organizations of society. This is one reason Yugoslavia began to decentralize and develop structures of self-management. It sought to remove itself not only from the command bureaucracy of the Soviet Union but from command dominance by any one of its provincial regions.

Revolutionary socialist governments have also sought to restrict the total politicization of the economy compromising with business opposition. It is essential to keep capitalist managers and professionals within the country because their exodus can cripple an economy. Such decisions have been made by revolutionary leaders in many new governments, including Zimbabwe in Africa and Nicaragua in Central America. Also, socialist leaders have opened private markets in limited areas of business after they had been closed. For example, rural markets have been opened in Cuba and Tanzania. Leaders sometimes see that a state bureaucracy can interfere with social innovation and productivity. This was one of the arguments of Mao Zedong in the cultural revolution. There are moments in socialist development when leaders see the importance of letting "a hundred flowers bloom."

Policies supporting decentralization have certain advantages, but they can have terrible disadvantages if the steps are misguided. Misguided steps could strengthen elitism and create great problems of local dominance. They could increase the strength of old tribalisms and bigotries or the rigidity of castes, and lead to provincial discord and civil war. The loss of political unity could make the country vulnerable to invasion from the outside.

For these reasons, it is important to examine the methods of decentralization in more detail.

4. Investing in community-oriented projects (avoiding local elit tribalism, and bigotry)

Studies show a variety of ways in which investment can avoid promoting local elites, village tribalism, and bigotry. Some of the following guidelines are helpful:[8]

Support projects whose products can be shared with the whole community rather than privately distributed in the market

Investment should be designed so that results can be shared. For example, it is easy for local elites to gain disproportionate benefits from a water system piped to individual dwellings, but not so easy from one piped to communal use points. Also, investment in special training schools or subsidized credit for private schools (even when intended for everyone) usually reinforces the privileges of the more powerful. But the organization of community-based schools chartered for use by every child decreases the likelihood of unequal distribution. Similarly, investment in community development credit unions and retail cooperatives have a higher likelihood of widespread availability of benefits than would investment in a conventional bank or retail establishment.

Invest in quantity of products rather than in quality alone

An attempt to improve the quality of life in less-developed countries (LDCs) often contributes to a greater disparity between the rich and the poor. To illustrate: investing in the quality of medical, veterinary, and educational services may result in making them available only to the well-to-do while funds for inexpensive basic services are depleted. Investing in methods that have been developed for the widespread distribution of simple (but adequate) services seems to be the wiser course. The literacy campaigns in Cuba and Nicaragua reveal a method of basic education that can be instituted for everyone in undeveloped regions. The training of barefoot doctors to handle basic health problems in China is an example in the field of medicine.

Invest in public goods that have widespread benefits

Investment incentives for private enterprise can result in reinforcing the old elite. Providing incentives for public facilities is the better course for social development. The construction of a public road that all citizens can enjoy is preferable to a road constructed for private plantations and factories. The construction of village sanitation systems that reduce the vulnerability of everyone to disease is preferable to private systems of (unaccountable) enterprise intended to provide sanitation for everyone.

Invest in goods that are needed to a point where supply exceeds demand

When the market is flooded with a commodity, it is almost certain that the poor will be able to get it. On the other hand, if a commodity is in short supply, only the wealthy will get it. It is possible to anticipate demand in certain cases where only one item is needed per person. For example, a child need be provided with primary education only once. Smallpox vaccinations are required every three years. With such measured types of investments, a product or service can be subsidized until it reaches its saturation point.

Invest in publicly oriented professional services

Modern professions differ in the extent to which they are oriented to practices of decentralized development and aiding the poor. For example, most Western-based medical practices have been oriented toward high-technology, hospital-based forms of treatment, so agencies controlled by doctors are less likely to give priority to the preventive services that mean most to the poor. On the other hand, public health practitioners tend to value these alternative services.

The clinic and village systems are alternatives that seem to work better in certain stages of development. They are based on the premise that health is more dependent on the social and environmental conditions under which people live than on high-technology medicine. Changing the adverse environmental conditions in a community (e.g., polluted water) and local dietary practices can often quickly reduce the rate of disease.

Clinic and village systems use auxiliary health workers who have several advantages over doctors. One advantage is that they do not cost as much. Another is that they are less likely to move to an advanced nation and leave the area without any medical assistance. More important, the training of auxiliaries is flexibly designed to fit the needs of local communities. Western-trained M.D.s have been known to find themselves incapable of applying their skills in the bush without technical equipment and supplies.

The training of civil engineers is usually associated with big capital-intensive projects. Western engineering is not oriented to small-scale technology. In fact, the labor-intensive roadbuilding needed in rural areas can seem professionally unrewarding and not technically challenging to Western engineers. Without adequate funding for Western-oriented professional work, the project may never get off the ground.

5. Investing in decentralized, linked cooperatives (avoiding centralized independent cooperatives)

Investment in enterprises in which owners have one vote is preferable to conventional business systems whose voting stock can be purchased easily by wealthy people. When cooperatives are organized and managed properly, they make a special contribution to social development. One value of the cooperative rests in the fact that it is a functional part of both capitalist and socialist states and does not contradict the values of these competing economic systems. Its prevalence affords a developing nation the opportunity to negotiate investments with competing big nations. This structural neutrality offers LDCs more autonomy because they need not be bound to one ideology. LDCs can increase their capacity for national independence by diversifying their trade relations with both socialist and capitalist countries.

Cooperatives are supported by capitalist nations because they serve as a buffer between the state and its direct control over the private sector; they can strengthen the free enterprise system on new grounds. On the other hand, they are supported by socialist nations because they provide a more equitable basis for people to produce and distribute goods and services. They help to socialize the economy, that is, they cause people to become conscious of the needs of one another and they provide a structure through which people can collaborate to meet common ends.[9]

Cooperatives are organized in production, distribution, banking, professional, and retail activities. They tend to develop in the periphery of power in advanced capitalist and socialist nations, which has caused them to assume some of the characteristics of each system. Some cooperatives are large, bureaucratic, and competitive; they can look very much like any other capitalist business. Cooperatives have sometimes functioned as an arm of the government. They can also look like a department of the state. But they were not originally designed for these purposes and if given their own independence and linked together from production to retail, they can serve as the basis for a different type of economy. For emerging nations, therefore, it is important to observe how investment in cooperatives may strengthen them to avoid weaknesses caused by their partial and peripheral participation in advanced economies. The following guidelines can assist in the direction of that support.

Invest in producer cooperatives and land trusts as a starting point

In advanced industrial countries, marketing cooperatives are usually organized by small farmers to combat business oligopolies, but in LDCs they have different origins. They are sometimes organized and promoted by the state and sometimes designed by relatively wealthy members of small-farm communities who are emerging from subsistence into export agriculture. They are at times tightly regulated by the state and at times do not function on behalf of the poor unless they are connected to production cooperatives.

Production cooperatives are harder to organize than marketing and service cooperatives. For example, farm cooperatives often threaten large landowners and state policies. Production cooperatives are difficult to organize in cities when poor laborers have no skills in management. When organized; they seem most effective when membership is kept small.

It is important to distinguish in rural areas, between farm cooperatives, where the individual ownership of land is retained but the use of implements and production is coordinated, and cooperatives based on collective ownership. The most common form of the farm cooperative allows for individual ownership of land with collective management of services ranging from simple pooling of equipment to complex management of production decisions. Farm cooperatives based on collective ownership often develop for specific purposes within contrasting systems. They can be a method for dealing with uncultivated areas in a capitalist system through communal management of pasture or forest land, or they may develop from an effort to promote socialist agriculture. They have also developed from a need to pool small farms into a size more suitable for production, and have also facilitated land reform programs dealing with large estates where former employees want to continue farming the land together.

The land trust, composed typically of a set of trustees who own large tracts of private land in the community interest, is a recommended type of territorial organization for farm production. We noted in an earlier chapter that the charter of the land trust sets forth certain principles under which the territory is to be utilized. The principles promote community development as opposed to merely private development. For example, the land cannot be sold for speculative purposes; farm land must remain in production and not lie fallow; it must be protected from soil erosion; its crops must be nutritious or useful to the consuming public. (Some charters prohibit raising tobacco, drugs, and so on.) The trustees lease parcels of land to farmers, who are then represented democratically on the trustee board to help in determining policies. The rent is used to purchase more land or equipment for the farms. Farmers have the option to purchase their own equipment, which is retained by them if they leave the farm. They can raise whatever crops they wish as long as they fit charter principles and serve the public interest. Private profit is still a motivating factor for lessee farmers; they operate in the community interest but may keep their profits. The land trust has been acclaimed for the way its structure balances individual interests with community development and the public interest.[10]

Invest in industrial cooperatives with internal capital accounts

Studies of producer cooperatives show that certain internal structures are most important to their success. Many worker cooperatives, such as the common ownership firms in England and self-managed firms in Yugoslavia, are structured like nonprofit corporations in the sense that there is no recoupable claim on the net worth of the firm. This eliminates any incentive to finance capital investment by retained earnings as opposed to borrowing. Other cooperative structures have attached capital rights to membership rights so that the worker must purchase capital rights in stock to become a member of the firm, which may put membership beyond the reach of the poor. The plywood cooperatives in the northeastern region of the U.S. are based on this structure, which outprices new members. The new U.S. firms based on the employee stock ownership plan also have this type of ownership structure. The more effective cooperatives, however, maintain separate membership rights (e.g., voting) and capital rights (e.g., stock purchase); each member has an internal capital account representing the capital value due to the member upon retirement. This account is separate from membership rights; workers may have differing amounts in their accounts (for instance, based on seniority) and still have the same right to one vote.[11]

In addition to the individual capital account, there is also a collective account that is unindividuated. The sum of the balances is the net book value or net worth of the cooperative. The collective fund is allocated in different ways: some cooperatives spend 10 per cent of the fund on community development; an additional 20 per cent may stay in the firm; the remainder, up to 70 per cent of the net surplus, is allocated among the workers' individual capital accounts. In this way, both the individual and the collective interests of workers are preserved in the accounting system.[12]

Invest in experimental programs supporting cooperative linkages (producer to wholesaler to consumer)

Production cooperatives may become linked to wholesale cooperatives, which in turn can be linked to retail cooperatives – this is a new area of social experimentation. A system of voting in some cases has become connected to trading exchanges in cooperative systems, but the effects are yet to be made clear in studies. For example, in England *consumer* cooperatives have representatives on the boards of the *wholesale* cooperatives from which they purchase goods, and their voting power is linked to the amount of purchases. A wholesale cooperative can have a representative on the top board of *production* cooperatives.[13] The best manner of linking has yet to be ascertained but it is clear that the organization of cooperatives from their origin in supply and production through distribution to retail services is an important part of the process of social development.

Investment in cooperatives with skilled management operating under the proper social conditions

Studies show that the success of a cooperative is dependent upon certain factors: (1) staff with good management skills; (2) internal mechanisms that make information on managerial performance available to members in understandable terms; (3) membership that is relatively homogeneous (socially and economically) so that people can work easily together; (4) relationships with other cooperatives from supply to retail; (5) some competition; (6) a friendly political environment; (7) independence from government controls.[14]

6. Investing in social controls leading toward self-governance. (avoiding organizational dependency)

Social investors need to be aware of how linkages between their capital and recipients may function to encourage social governance. At the outset any investor (or government) develops certain controls over the investment through some regulatory or monitoring mechanism. This could include auditing, administered prices, required ratios of credit to savings, registration and certification of local organizations, recruitment standards, inspections, evaluations, and so on.

If investment is designed to bring about self-governance, then outside auditing must be done for a limited period, with the understanding that it will eventually be conducted internally and in conjunction with other professional authorities. Similarly, if organizations are certified to operate (e.g., medical clinics), local leaders must be trained for granting certification. Likewise, when inspections and evaluations are necessary to maintain quality of product (e.g., grading of lumber or meat), local leaders must then be taught in the standards of evaluation.

Research suggests that outside controls can be creatively exercised to assist the poor and less-educated members of a community. Some of these controls designed for self-governance are summarized below:

Coercive controls are the most difficult to apply effectively. They may be designed to punish a local organization or to prune out exploitative operations. Coercion includes placing high credit rates on an organization that exploits the poor, refusing to register the organization, and withdrawing professional services (e.g., accounting) until remedial action is taken.

Limiting controls are intended to restrict exploitative practices. They include providing legal protection for innocent members who are attacked by the elite or placing a restriction on the range of functions to simplify management for less-educated members.

Supportive controls are designed to improve the administrative strength of the local organization. They include support in bookkeeping, management, and regulations that assist members to bring sanctions against oppressive practices by members of the organization.

Equalizing controls are intended to assist the poor directly by imposing limits on elite access to resources, limiting monopoly of benefits by the wealthy, placing ceilings on credit and establishing fertilizer quotas and acreage limits. They can also include limits on salary ratios and patronage, and establishing recruitment standards valuing skills of applicants before politics or friendships. Finally, they can equalize but not exclude elite use of goods and services. Examples are seeds for crops that elites prefer not to produce; rudimentary implements that best serve small producers; extension advice on nonmechanized small production techniques; and pump wells that provide wide access to irrigation.

Redistributive controls may exclude elites from obtaining greater advantages by reaching directly to the small producer. Examples are highly subsidized credit with asset limitations on recipients; extension advice solely for the small farmer; fertilizer quotas based on land holdings; and direct grants to small producers. This type of assistance is more costly to provide and generally requires extensive monitoring on a smaller scale.[15]

7. Investing in marginal organizations apart from formal cooperatives (avoiding exclusion of the very poor)

Studies suggest that in societies where inequality is very serious, investment in limited organizations for the poor (with congenial leadership) is preferable to formal cooperatives. An example is the Fundación in Guatemala, which organizes and links marginal producers. It stands in contrast to the two public-sector programs in Guatemalan agriculture, FENACOAC (credit unions) and FECOAR (regional agricultural cooperatives). Four services are provided by Fundación exclusively for poor farmers: group credit, assistance in small-group organizing, supplying fertilizer, and purchase of land. The primary criticism is that it fails to insure the transition from a precooperative organization to a cooperative.[16]

The arguments for supporting such groups among the very poor can be summarized as follows: (1) a big cooperative must cultivate national elite support to become effective, and this is not always in the interest of the very poor; (2) local people should not be forced into a more complex organization before they are ready; (3) local group development should be evolutionary and not determined by a national blueprint; and (4) a group seeking to organize marginal producers can best concentrate on a few tasks (e.g., land purchase) rather than introducing the complexities of rural commerce and a large cooperative.

8. Investing in redundancy (avoiding cooperative monopolies)

Developing nations show a great need for redundant and competitive enterprises that can take up the slack in case one fails. Redundancies are back-up enterprises capable of performing the same function as do other enterprises. Their existence helps stop monopolies that can inhibit the capacity of an economy to be self-regulating. For example, an East African cooperative was organized with monopoly rights over the marketing of certain export crops, and, both the state and the peasant producers became highly dependent on it. Because the state could not afford to let the cooperative fail, signs of weakness led to increasing controls. The peasants grew alienated from the cooperative and eventually lost out to the state.[17]

Two methods of organization would have avoided the East African outcome. First, a competing firm could have taken up the slack and reduced the concern of the state about the cooperative's success. Second, a federation of cooperatives could have developed the skills for supporting the cooperative when it was failing. Such federations provide consulting services for their members in time of need so that the state is not needed to save the situation.

9. Investing in social banks (avoiding capitalist or state banks)

A variety of social banking arrangements avoid the pitfalls of capitalist banks and state banks. One such arrangement developed in Mondragon, Spain. In the 1950s cooperatives began farming under the innovative leadership of a priest, José Maria Arizmendi, and these grew rapidly to include eighty-five industrial cooperatives as well as many agricultural, consumer, educational, and housing cooperatives. The Mondragon system is recognized today as one of the most advanced examples of a self-governing economy in the developing world.

One of the unique social inventions of the Mondragon system is its bank, the Caja Laboral Popular (CLP), designed to create worker self-managed enterprises. It is the twenty-sixth-largest bank in Spain: 120 branches, 1,000 employees, and a half-million customers.

The CLP has a general assembly, a board of directors, a social council (composed of worker representatives), watchdog council (three internal auditors), management council (president and department heads), and other administrative bodies. It has initiated over a hundred successful producer cooperatives which have proportional representation in the general assembly. In effect, the bank has become a hybrid confederation of the business enterprises that it has created.

The bank's own success as an ordinary savings institution is important because it has utilized the savings as a basis for investment in socialized enterprise. In effect, it has helped spawn a new system of social governance in the private sector of the economy of northern Spain that serves as a model for social development in the Third World.[18]

10. Investing in educational systems for cooperative managers and social engineers (avoiding management failure and inappropriate technology)

The educational system offered within the Mondragon is considered a vital part of social development in the region. The leaders of the cooperatives found that it was essential to develop training schools for cooperative managers and engineering schools to keep abreast of the technology appropriate to their ventures. From its beginning, Mondragon has had a polytechnical school associated with its cooperative form of management; the founders saw it as essential. In the 1970s research in the school was deemed inadequate to cope with explosive developments in electronics and computer science, and an advanced applied research institute was established, Ikerlan. Ikerlan has over sixty researchers and works in close collaboration with the technical college and the enterprises.

There are nineteen educational centers in Mondragon, including five in secondary education, five in professional and technical education, two in adult education, and two in language studies, 140 faculty teaching over 8,000 students. There is also a cooperative factory where students work to finance their education and learn firsthand about cooperative work.

The Mondragon system is a social experiment that draws increasing numbers of Third World leaders for study. It probably cannot be replicated in other cultural settings but it does serve as an important stimulus for social ideas in building new economies.

11. Investing in democratic federations for mutual aid (avoiding isolated enterprises and communities)

One of the most significant experiments with worker and community owned enterprises has been taking place in Israel. Israeli kibbutzim are well known throughout the world but their methods of support for survival and growth have remained unpublicized. They are actually organized through a system of regional and national associations that have developed with them over the decades. The associations are relatively independent of one another but together they compose a web of crucial support for the kibbutzim in an otherwise hostile capitalist environment.

The associations linking kibbutzim together are many, but four types appear noteworthy. First, kibbutzim have established federations that bring them together on religious, ideological, and political grounds as movements. Second, kibbutzim have brought their separate federations together into a super-federation that provides the necessary support and guidance for the whole diversified movement. Third, kibbutzim have established regional councils and enterprises, in some cases on the uninhabited land between them. Fourth, kibbutzim are members of a national labor economy organized largely through Histradut, a labor organization that provides a still wider base of support for kibbutzim.[19]

Innovative enterprises need mutual support in a competitive or hostile environment. In the nineteenth century capitalist enterprises organized trade associations and local unions organized state and national federations to survive. They were the innovators of their time. The social innovations developing in Third World nations today are in a similar position of vulnerability. Seedling enterprises like cooperatives, community development corporations, community credit unions, social banks, neighborhood tribunals, and similar self-managed enterprises require support from social federations. The federations in turn need support from investors who see the significance of a new economic order coming into being on the fringes of the supernations today.

New international investment systems: in retrospect

Robert L. Ayers, a senior research fellow with the Overseas Development Council, presents a fascinating portrait of what happened when Robert McNamara sought to fight poverty through the World Bank. He describes the bank's economic perspective in a manner that clearly demonstrates the problems we have been discussing, revealing how McNamara's efforts were resisted by bank staff who believed that the bank's function was to be a bank in the financial sense only and that it should not become involved in development. Formal research and country reports were done by economists in the framework of finance and economics; no sociological data or anthropological assessments were included. Ayers points out that staff believed poverty existed "because [people] lacked jobs. Because they were unproductive. Because they produced insufficient output."[20] Clearly there was no social theory in staff thinking during the McNamara years.

A social perspective is becoming more evident in recent policy studies. Increasingly formal arguments are made to alter the structure of world banking. The first step involves shifting the major percentage of investments from bilateral to multilateral banking. It is said that multilateral banking has a better foundation for utilizing objective criteria based upon scientific findings. Bilateral aid by governments is more frequently tied to political interests, and continues to account for almost three-quarters of the total aid from official sources. Over 50 per cent of bilateral financing is concessional in nature but it becomes linked to the purchase of goods and services from donor countries. Political strings that hamper completion of projects are attached to aid, and conditions under which aid is continued are determined by the politics of the donor nation.[21]

It is becoming apparent that steps must be taken to overcome the political obstacles to a new international order. These steps include investments. First, we have noted that developing nations should assume a more prominent role in decision making within international institutions of finance. This means a greater minority representation in the World Bank and the International Monetary Fund in particular. Second, there is a need for increased political security for developing nations to be protected from the threats of core nations. This includes new regional accords, with additional use of the UN's capacity to guarantee peace within regions. To be effective, the accords require the joint support of competing big nations like the Soviet Union and the United States. Firmer national security allows funds budgeted for military purposes to be reallocated toward development. Third, the flow of financial resources to the poorest countries must be stabilized so as to enable long-term planning and development. This means undertaking measures to even out massive fluctuations in exchange rates of foreign currencies. Fourth, multinational corporations must continue to develop structures based on principles of social governance, including structures that broaden the responsibilities and authority of subsidiaries and their employees in developing nations. We have seen that democratic adjustments in corporate governance have been necessary for the survival of MNCs, and there are signs that this trend elicits a greater economic return for all members of the corporations. At the same time, this step means greater regulation of MNCs in accordance with a code of ethics nego-tiated through the United Nations. Fifth there is a need to reduce market restrictions, including trade barriers that deny access to world markets. This step becomes more possible as MNCs become socially governed and more nations are committed to work together toward mutually beneficial ends.[22]

International investment that is grounded in a social perspective means that economics still plays a central role. The decision-making process simply requires data from both social and economic research. Social theory offers the added insight needed to overcome poverty in developing countries. If the perspective of only economics and finance enters into the investment process, elitism, imperialism, and statism will continue to plague the Third World. The new nations will keep on reproducing the problems of the old nations. The patterns of history – hunger, poverty, and war – will not be broken.

The time is arriving for a new consciousness of how to invest socially in the Third World. The future of developing nations is clearly important to all nations that are closely interdependent with them. The use of social criteria in the investment process could become a critical factor in helping to make that future more secure as well as more just and profitable for everyone.

Epilogue: Social investment as a self-correcting movement in the market system

The practice of social investment is becoming more evident to the public and more organized among fiduciaries in banks, universities, cities, states, churches, mutual funds, and multinational organizations. It shows signs of increasing its momentum as more agencies become interconnected and conscious of a common cause. What appears as a trend in the 1980s may become a social movement in the 1990s.

At the same time, investment practices based solely on the profit motive have been showing a collective trend toward instability and crisis. Stock market speculation on the one hand and on the other hand debt accumulation in major institutions of the economy – corporations, banks, farms, households, and the federal government – are revealing a fault in the financial system. Sparked partly by policies of government deregulation without compensatory arrangements of self-regulation and social standards of investment, the system of finance in the United States has become overburdened with debt that can no longer be backed by real capital. Debt today rests on a very small capital base, and some economists argue that any major stress in the financial system could bring the system toward collapse.

The question is whether there may be a connection between this growing trend toward establishing social standards and self-regulation in the market system and solutions to the disastrous trend toward unregulated speculation and indebtedness. Are the new patterns of social investment developing sufficient strength and sense of direction that they may provide sensible alternatives to the purely profit-based patterns of finance now threatening the security of the national economy? Let us look briefly at each of these trends developing concurrently in the middle of the 1980s.

The growing trends toward social investment

We have discussed the trend toward social investment in earlier chapters, but let us illustrate how it may gain strength in a social movement during the coming decade. According to Zald and Ash, a social movement maintains itself over time to the extent that it acquires a "societal interest," that is, a public awareness of its legitimate place and purpose in society. It must also establish a support base and a strong movement organization with clear linkages to individual supporters as well as maintain goals broad enough to remain flexible in the changing environment.[1]

We have already noted signs of a growing public acceptance of social investment as a legitimate practice in the field of finance. There is also the appearance of a support base and movement organization as well as evidence of strong individual linkages to investor-clients. In addition, there is evidence that participants are developing a broad vision of their future and are not becoming trapped in a narrow set of goals that limit their growth as a movement. It is not our purpose here to evaluate this evidence in detail, but we do want to review a few current events and subtrends leading social investment in the direction of a national movement.

The seeds of a social movement can be seen in the growth in fiduciary organizations for social investment and their common purposes in allocating capital in the United States.

Increasing levels of nationwide organization for the practice of social investment

Social investors have been learning more about one another's work and formulating common purposes for their activity. They have also been organizing to pool resources and share social screens in a common cause. This has been happening at local and regional levels, but the process gains significance when it occurs at the national level.

ITEM: *The Social Investment Forum* was incorporated in January 1985 as a national professional association. It shows signs of being a movement organization with widespread support from fiduciaries in every sector of the economy. Its members include *advisers* (brokers, investment managers helping clients use social screens to select publicly traded securities), *bankers* (financial institutions with loan funds that help clients direct capital and deposits into local development), *analysts* (journalists and academics who provide data to guide social investment), and *investors* (corporations, foundations, churches, public interest groups, universities, and other institutions that practice social investment in their own portfolios). The criteria for social investment mentioned in the forum's brochure includes such familiar concerns as the environment, renewable energy, labor relations, South Africa, the military, and other items we have discussed. Among the choices of corporate types favored by the organization are worker-owned firms, community development corporations, land trusts, and other firms designed to be accountable to their constituencies. The use of capital is clearly aimed at an economy that is both productive and accountable to the people in society whom it affects.[2]

ITEM: *The Clearinghouse on Alternative Investments* was formed in 1985 by fifteen Protestant denominations and over two hundred Roman Catholic religious communities and dioceses with the assistance of the Interfaith Center of Corporate Responsibility. It is designed to increase communication among religious orders and denominations making alternative investments. Clearinghouse members have been discussing the idea of extending the usual pattern of investment based on selective criteria of avoidance (for instance, South Africa; environmental pollution) toward the positive encouragement of an alternative system of enterprises designed to be accountable to their constituencies. Members meet regularly and circulate bimonthly packets on the latest developments in alternative investing, discuss the problems of leveraging and debt, analyze investment proposals, and monitor past investments.

The Clearinghouse has published a 1985 Directory of Organizations in which churches have invested and are planning investments. It has been hosting a series of brokering meetings at which church treasurers and staff have been meeting with alternative investment organizations.[3]

ITEM: *The National Council of Institutional Investors* was formed in January 1985 to assert the rights of pension fund shareholders around issues of corporate change affecting their investment. Over thirty pension funds and assets of more than $132 billion are represented. The council began early in the year to discuss the impact of corporate mergers on shareholders. T. Boone Pickens, Jr, Carl Icahn, and other reputed "corporate raiders" participated in a televised meeting, a "first" for this set of fiduciaries exercising fiscal responsibility over a major portion of the largest source of wealth in the world today.

The council expects to take up other issues in the coming years, such as corporate compensation, money management fees, election of corporate boards, incentive bonuses for management when a company is losing money, insider trading, golden parachutes, money manager fees, and performance measurement. Social issues are already an implicit part of its agenda and seem destined to become more visible because of the composition of the membership. Many member-funds are already engaged in utilizing social criteria in regard to such questions as South Africa and labor relations.

The council is composed largely of public and union pension funds but other types of funds show interest in joining. A corporate fund, U.S. West, has applied for membership, along with the International Union of Operating Engineers, International Brotherhood of Electrical Workers, and the Los Angeles County Employees' Retirement System. Future issues on the agenda should include the role of labor unions in meeting social criteria and issues of corporate governance. The council has three cochairs: Jesse Unruh, California treasurer; John Konrad, chairman of the Wisconsin State Board of Investments; and Harrison Goldin, New York City comptroller and trustee of the New York City Employees Retirement System.[4]

Increasing numbers of support groups behind social investors

Support groups are organizations that offer resources to social investors and are friendly to their purposes. They provide vital information to investors and rally quickly to their defense. They represent their interests to the public and facilitate communication on the legitimacy and purpose of the movement. The variety of support groups is extensive, but examples can suggest their crucial position in creating a foundation for the field of social investment in the decades ahead.

ITEM: One variety of support group provides information and does research for social investors. Among such groups are the Council on Economic Priorities (publishes a monthly newsletter focusing on issues of corporate responsibility, defense policy, and the environment, as well as three to six books each year based on its research); the Center for Economic Revitalization (publishes a bimonthly newsletter, *Good Money*, and in alternate months, *Catalyst*, plus *Netback Quarterly* for investors and the public to communicate with each other); the Resource Publishing Group (publishes a complete guide to 1,400 New York Stock Exchange companies and makes reports on individual companies upon request); and Pagan International (publishes *The International Barometer* to inform business, government, and investors of the objectives and activities of issue-oriented organizations, and publishes its own newsletter monthly).[5]

ITEM: An important set of support groups comes from organized stockholders. They regularly submit resolutions to corporations to influence their behavior on such matters as environmental pollution, defense policies, and employee-ownership. They include such varied organizations as Accuracy in Media, Committee of Concerned Shareholders of Northern States Power, Clergy and Laity Concerned, Foundation for the Study of Corporate Philanthropy, GE Stockowners Alliance Against Nuclear Power,

Greenpeace, League for Industrial Democracy, Methodist Board of Pensions, the United Auto Workers, and hundreds more. In 1984 eighty church-related agencies and individuals filed fourteen shareholder resolutions on the issue of military production alone.

> *Increasing institutional connections in the practice of social investment*

The practice of social investment is becoming more connected among vastly different institutions such as cities, churches, banks, universities, and business corporations. These connections are being diffused in new modes of cooperation, contract, and competition. The close connections are bringing a wider citizenry toward awareness of the significance and importance of the movement.

ITEM: In April 1985 New York City Mayor Ed Koch presented Thomas G. Labrecque, president of the Chase Manhattan Corporation, with a check for $1.6 million of city funds to deposit in exchange for the bank's making available $10 million in loans for the Energy Loan Financing Program to rehabilitate low- and moderate-income apartments through the city. The program had been proposed originally to Chase Bank in a 1982 shareholder action sponsored by the Interfaith Center on Corporate Responsibility (ICCR) through its member Roman Catholic Women Religious. The city funds will total $3.3 million and will be used to reduce Chase's lending rate for the project to below-market rates. The program will enable owners to replace heating plants, roofs, plumbing, windows, and other building systems on about 100 apartment buildings in the city's poor neighborhoods. The Northwest Bronx Community and Clergy Coalition helped urge the arrangement, along with the Sisters of Charity of St Vincent de Paul, the community of Sisters of St Dominic, and the Society of the Holy Child Jesus, after concluding that the bank had a less-than-satisfactory community reinvestment record.[6]

ITEM: The Brooklyn Ecumenical Cooperatives (BEC) is a community economic development organization owned by thirty-one Catholic and Protestant churches that serves 35,000 low- and moderate-income families. It originated with an interest in energy conservation, and is now addressing the housing needs of its community in competition with area realtors. BEC's geographic base (the downtown Brooklyn area) contains about 700,000 people and is suffering from a disastrous pattern of speculation and displacement caused by conventional business driving out thousands of families. Operating on cooperative principles, BEC has initiated a five-year housing rehabilitation effort involving 8,800 units, and organized a federal credit union "mustard seed fund" as a long-term source of development capital made available at slightly below the market rate of interest.[7]

Increasing acceptance of social responsibility as legitimate for business

There appears to be a growing acceptance of corporate social responsibility as a motive for business policy. More executives are including reports on the public and community involvement of their firms in annual reports, business and management schools are developing courses and centers on business ethics, and business journals are including favorable articles on corporate responsibility and social investment.

ITEM: The number of companies participating in the Center for Corporate Public Involvement has increased steadily each year for a decade. The center is associated with the American Council of Life Insurance and Health Insurance Association of America and promotes corporate social responsibility. A record number of 342 companies reported their public involvement activities in the industry's thirteenth annual *Social Report* (1985). *Social Report* reflects corporate community activities of member companies in contributions, equal employment, social investment, health and welfare, and community projects. Contributions reached $108 million in 1985; social investments increased in the same period, with over two-thirds of the companies reporting some type of formal energy policy in their decision making and over $1.4 billion allocated to family housing.

The social goals of the council have remained broad and flexible in response to the changing interests of its membership. In 1985, 91 per cent of the companies reported involvement in some type of community project; about 13,000 company employees reported volunteering over 330,000 hours for community work; 326 firms reported operating health and well-ness programs.[8]

ITEM: The Catholic Bishops' Pastoral Letter on the U.S. Economy brought a moral argument to the nation for corporate social responsibility. The *Letter* contained specific references to problems in such areas as environmental pollution, job safety, consumer protection, and other issues of social investment. It accented the importance of managing a proper mix of social and economic criteria in decision making. Special to the letter were references to the need for alternative investing in firms accountable to their constituencies, such as cooperatives and community development corporations. The basic intent of the letter was to seek a reconciliation between pursuit of profit and the "common good" in the corporate system.

ITEM: The Sixth National Conference on Business Ethics was held at Bentley College in October 1985, and it attracted hundreds of guests from business schools nationwide. Speakers noted the mounting interest in business ethics, while exhibits gave testimony to a growing number of research centers on business ethics. Many journals on display carried articles on social investment and business ethics. According to a recent study by W. Michael Hoffman, director of Bentley College's Center for Business Ethics, at least 224 companies on the Fortune 500 list of industry and service companies have taken steps to introduce ethics into the business process.

Increasing investment in the development of a social sector

We have described the private sector as a social sector in the sense that it represents a nonstatist economy capable of becoming developed to operate more directly in the public interest. It consists of profit and nonprofit corporations that are interrelated through loans, gifts, commerce, and politics. Innovative investors have been interested in how such corporations can work together to advance their social purposes and contribute to the well-being of the larger society.

Put another way, the social sector includes democratic federations such as churches, professional associations, trade associations, and voluntary associations designed for social purposes operating in the private sector beside command-based corporations like General Motors designed for economic purposes. The nonprofit corporations are learning how to improve their management systems and make money to survive with their democratic constitutions and social orientation, while profit corporations are learning to introduce workplace democracy and develop a social orientation. Social investors have shown an interest in supporting creative connections between them to help build a social foundation to the private economy.

Some steps in this direction of investment can be seen in the response to the President's Task Force on Private Sector Initiatives. State and local governments have become more interested in constructing relationships between profit and nonprofit organizations "to help meet the needs of America's communities" and "to fulfill a broad public purpose." They are seeking "public–private partnerships" to stimulate social-economic development in the "broader community." For example, the Governor's Task Force on Private Sector Initiatives was formed in Massachusetts to stimulate partnerships where "two or more organizations can each bring to bear their unique skills and resources in the planning or pursuit of a goal of mutual and public interest." Massachusetts has developed approximately 120 partnership programs in education, employment and training, economic and community development, public safety, and health and human services.[9]

ITEM: The Riverside Cambridgeport Community Development Corporation, a partnership of neighborhood groups with the city of Cambridge, Massachusetts, was formed to advance housing rehabilitation and job training programs.

ITEM: The Westmass Area Development Corporation is a nonprofit industrial development corporation that uses private-sector funding to set up development packages in partnership with the city of Springfield, Massachusetts, and other local communities. The arrangement makes possible local improvements in the private sector by providing funds through no-maturity/no-interest notes.

National organizations are also being initiated to promote the collaboration between the profit and nonprofit sectors and thereby advance the well-being of communities.[10]

ITEM: The Local Initiatives Support Corporation (LISC) has forged a nationwide private partnership whose total funding commitment for community development investment activities was over $50 million in 1983. LISC puts capital to work at below-market rates to build self-supporting, income-producing ventures in real estate, housing, industry, and commerce. A total of 148 corporations and fifty-four foundations have taken the initiative (with fifty-three donors giving $100,000 or more) to create pools of investment funds in twenty-four cities and regions and to make loans and grants to 197 community development organizations.

The nonprofit sector is becoming organized on its own to advance the cause of development in the common good. It has its own support groups for the movement toward investment in the social sector.[11]

ITEM: The Independent Sector was launched as a national organization in 1980, replacing the Coalition of National Voluntary Organizations and the National Council on Philanthropy, and has a membership of 200 organizations. Its purpose is to create a positive climate for social development in public education, communication, research, and effective management. Independent Sector has an organizational interest in "civil rights, women's rights, historic preservation, conservation, consumerism, neighborhood theater, mental retardation, services for the aged, and international under-standing." President John W. Gardner has been concerned especially with the promotion of corporate responsibility and social investment.

> *Increasing interest among social investors in evaluating whole industries*

Social investors began by focusing on the behavior of corporations but today are also developing social screens for whole industries. This broadens the basis for judging the performance of individual firms and enables investors to see how sectors of the economy are operating in the context of society.[12]

Investment agencies are also analyzing the relationships among government, profit corporations, and nonprofit corporations in their studies of the health care industry, the housing industry, the arts, and education. They have found that human values may be cultivated by investing in these sectors of the economy.[13]

ITEM: The report on the transportation industry by Franklin Research reveals contrasts between "companies wedded to the past and those adapting to the expanding horizons that lie ahead." It discusses, among other things customary in such reports, the social advantages and disadvantages of change. For example, deregulation has meant savings for customer groups with economic muscle but higher costs for weaker customers in small towns. The report raises such questions as, Does a carrier continue to treat its customers well without regulation? Does it continue to provide service even though no longer required to do so? Does it charge reasonable rates no matter the kind of customer?

Are companies increasing the level of employee ownership? Franklin presents the data in the table below.

Although ESOPs are sometimes recommended for their economic benefits, they do not represent the most desirable form of ownership from a social standpoint. Franklin Research, itself a cooperative, advocates the principle of ownership based on one person, one vote. Conventional voting by shares is seen as a low level of employee democracy but deserving of some merit. Franklin evaluates the trucking industry as fragmented but excelling in employee ownership in some degree; industry actively promotes employee ownership and employee participation. Franklin suggests that in trucking there is generally "a feeling of common mission in a firm, rather than adversarial relations." This represents a relative advantage.

Table 1. *Transportation companies with high employee ownership*

	% of common stock held by employees	Date plan started
Transcon Trucking Corporation	49	1983
People Express Airlines	33	1981
Western Airlines	33	1983
Eastern Airlines	25	1983
Chicago and Northwestern Railroad	22	1972
Republic Airlines	18	1985
Roadway Systems (trucking)	16	1966
Pan American World Airways	13	1983
Southwest Airlines	13	1972
America West Airlines	9	1983
Viking Freight	*	1976

* Considered significant, but the company does not disclose this figure.
Adapted from *Insight: Report on Vital Industries*, # 8, August 1985, p. 10.

Increasing local to global connections in social investment

Social investment agencies in the United States are connecting with agencies in other countries and also international agencies to promote a common cause. This current of interest in global investment shows signs of growing in the coming decade.

ITEM: Churches and religious institutions worldwide have joined to create social alternatives to the World Bank. They have begun with the Ecumenical Development Cooperative Society (EDCS) to make long-term, low-interest loans to poor communities that own and manage self-development projects. Fred Bonkema, an official of the EDCS, reports that individuals and local parishes and congregations can purchase EDCS subvention certificates (special shares). Securities administrators in forty-four states have given approval for a $10 million offering of such certificates through the U.S. Conference for the World Council of Churches. The focus of investment is on cooperative, self-managed, community-based enterprises that are accountable to the people they affect in villages, cities, and the larger society.[14]

ITEM: The Ethical Investment Research and Information Service (EIRIS) began in London in April 1983 with the mission to provide more information on the ethics of investment, especially its social aspects. Although it does not provide advice on commercial or financial aspects of investment, its aims are (1) to provide information to assist investors to determine whether particular companies conform to their ethical criteria; and (2) to promote a better understanding and awareness of corporate responsibility issues.

EIRIS provides fact sheets on a range of publicly traded corporations that include information on their involvement in the manufacture and trading of armaments, or in defense contracts, as in South Africa.[15]

ITEM: The year 1984 saw launched four vehicles for social investing in Great Britain as well as two sources of advice and information. Two investment agencies had been operating theretofore. The Mercury Provident Society, founded in 1974, has become increasingly involved in loans to community-based and cooperative firms with social and economic goals. The Ecology Building Society lends money toward the development of "properties and projects that are in harmony with or improve the environment," the most rapidly developing of which is Traidcraft, designed to advance its objectives of increasing "love, justice and equity in international trade." Unity Trust was organized by the trade union and cooperative movements "embracing the philosophy of the common good." The Stewardship Unit Trust is similar to mutual funds in the United States; its policy is to invest in companies that support long-term community interests and to avoid investments in companies with operations in "undesirable parts of the globe or the economy." It avoids investing in firms having connections with vivisection or factory farming, as well as in those with links with South Africa, tobacco, alcohol, gambling or armaments. Financial Initiative is a venture capital fund seeking to invest in "socially and ecologically worthwhile enterprises" that "have been conceived for the good of the whole."[16]

The growing crisis in finance

The profit-based system of finance in the United States is in trouble. *Business Week* describes it as a serious national crisis: "The U.S. has evolved into what Lord Keynes might have called a 'casino society' – a nation obsessively devoted to high-stakes financial maneuvering as a short-cut to wealth." The problem is first visible in the stock market, which is increasingly based on speculation and in which an incredible number of transactions occur each day. Second, it is visible in the mind-boggling debt mounting in government and the corporate sector. Some economists believe that the profit-oriented system of finance is rapidly approaching collapse. The question is whether alternative systems of finance based on social standards as a framework for profit-making may be a corrective.

Business Week criticizes the "unconscionable proportions" of speculation on the stock market, part of which is attributable to leveraging mechanisms like the "stockless market" that allows the investor to play big on the market with very little real capital. The "leveraged takeover" allows the investor to buy a small amount of stock in a big corporation and offer to buy the rest of its shares. Then an investment firm is persuaded to line up the needed money to buy "junk bonds" (issued by companies with a credit rating of BB or lower but that can pay five percentage points more than conventional bonds) after the tender offer succeeds. The bonds are paid off from the big corporations' treasury. Such schemes and many others render the stock market very tempting to actual and would-be high rollers.

The number of shares that change hands on the New York Stock Exchange runs at 108 million each day, and keeps going up. The trading volume in government securities is running at $76 billion daily and mounting. The daily volume in Treasury-bond and T-bill futures is $26 billion and shows no sign of slacking off. Trading volumes like this are utterly new. The only other time transactions peaked so excessively relative to the past record was before the Great Depression. Many financial analysts believe the volume has soared beyond any economic purpose.[17]

Debt in major U.S. institutions is also approaching major proportions. The federal government's annual budget deficit is running at $200 billion, and it topped $2 trillion in 1986. Corporate debt was over $2 trillion in 1985; we have discussed some of its complexities in such areas as foreign competition, unfunded pension liabilities, and poor management. Farm credit is so unmanageable that it has required legislation to support the banking system. Household debt through credit cards is inordinately high. The total debt of governments, corporations, and households reached $7.1 trillion in 1984. Many economists predict that the house of cards will fall before the 1990s.

We have discussed the Third World debt to U.S. banks and the fact that nonpayment can jeopardize the viability of world banking. The irony is that current efforts to renegotiate dept payments have turned many profit-making dreams into dust. Some profit-motivated investments in the Third World have been transformed into no-interest loans, and the system-burden threatens international finance.

The federal government has had to move quickly to save major U.S. corporations in trouble. It bailed out the eighth-largest bank, Continental Illinois Corporation, at a cost of $11 billion lest the bank undermine a string of other financial institutions. But the "feds" ability to cushion new shocks is diminishing because of its own debts. The list of financially troubled firms has been lengthening in the past five years, and includes Drysdale Securities and a half-dozen other government securities dealers that have failed to the tune of nearly $2 billion in investor losses.

The financial-legal system supporting corporate takeovers has worsened the problem. The $140 billion business in mergers, acquisitions, and leveraged buyouts in 1984 exceeded its previous mark in 1983 by $54 billion, and the pace continues. The merger movement is of course based on many questionable procedures and simply adds to the corporate debt-equity problem. Bank lenders provide the capital and make exorbitant profit in the process. In 1982 investment bankers participated in takeover transactions that cost their clients more than $20 billion and brought them over $100 million. Four of the First Boston Corporation's four transactions in 1982 earned it over $31 million in 1982.[18]

The banking system is in trouble even though some big banks are making money. Banks have always depended upon depositors' funds for investment, but the advance of money market funds has drawn bundles of deposits out of the banking system. Some 800 thrift banks have closed in the last five years; a third of the remaining 3,200 thrifts have zero net worth or are insolvent, according to generally accepted accounting principles, rather than the lax accounting methods allowed by regulators. The banking industry's profitability has declined for twenty years, and in 1983 seventy-nine banks failed, the greatest number since 1937. The failure rate can be expected to increase unless there is congressional action to stop it.

Congress and government agencies are beginning to introduce stopgap measures to address overactive financing. The Federal Reserve can change the percentage required to buy stock on margin, can reduce the percentage required to buy stock index futures, can "chill" the purchase of junk bonds, and so forth, but such measures do not get to the root of the problem. The causes are more complex than can be fixed by changing financial regulations. There is good reason to believe that they arise in the social organization of the market. Social research is needed along with financial studies to help find the cure.

Sensible alternatives: researching the future

Social researchers must look carefully at the structure of the market system itself. It comprises interlocking roles and organizations that contain the seeds of serious conflict and contradiction, auguring the pressing need for systemic changes. One type of conflict is manifested daily in the arguments between investment professionals. At one extreme is Hugh Calfins, an attorney with Jones, Day, Reavis, and Pogue, who proposes that trustees of pension funds could devote as much as 20 per cent of their portfolios to buying shares of a few publicly held companies, placing their own representatives on the board of directors. His argument is that funds should look out for the long-term welfare of companies because it eventually benefits members. The idea is anathema to Joseph Auerbach at Harvard University and others, who are totally opposed to pension trusts having anything to do with management. Auerbach is of course in the clear majority.[19]

It is not the normal practice of investment fiduciaries to manage a corporation. In fact, legal questions can be raised about the extent of their involvement in a corporation. Their purpose is to make money for their clients on the stock market. As investors, they do not customarily care about the welfare of workers in the corporation or even about the corporate system itself, nor are they concerned about maintaining the productivity of the system or advancing the well-being of its employees. The contradiction rests in the fact that their individual decisions in the aggregate do affect employees and the corporate system.

Social investors must be included as part of the deep problem in the market system even though they show a greater readiness to act toward it as a social system. Predicating investing behaviour on social issues like environmental pollution has merit at certain ethical levels, but careful assessment suggests that the overall system is in such trouble that more is needed than a finger in the dike, so to speak. Major revisions in its social organization must be made. By not understanding more fully the nature of the system, social investors unwittingly become part of the forces leading toward cycles and serious downturns in the market. Social investors are becoming organized nationally, but they are still too decentralized to study the deeper issues together. They may be a beacon across a dark sea, but they are still getting acquainted with one another and only beginning to set the ground rules for entering into a highly competitive market with a set of social standards.

When social investors do become better organized and are ready to study the systemic problems, what should be done? What areas of research can help point to solutions to the problems of the market as a social system? The many areas we have discussed so far must be reviewed, but in the context of corporate debt and speculation, we can note four areas.

First, studies are needed on employee ownership as a basis for reducing the amount and kind of corporate stock traded on the market. If greater stress were put upon advancing a cooperative model of stock ownership by employees, a substantial portion of stock would gradually be removed from sale. This would reduce disaster-prone market speculation and merger mania. It would cut down on the excessive number of transactions taking place and go far toward removing the "casino climate" from the market. Alternative forms of nonvoting stock would need to be created and studied for their capacity to yield economic returns for institutional investors.

Second, studies are needed to determine the effectiveness of other enterprise models in expressing social standards along with profit standards. Such models include land trusts designed to reduce land speculation, and community banks designed to be accountable to their constituencies.

Third, studies are needed to provide greater uniformity in pension plans so that unfunded liabilities and corporate debt can be more carefully monitored and funds allocated appropriately to the benefit of employees and enterprise development in key industries.

Fourth, studies are needed to examine methods for advancing social self-regulation in the business system, to stop the clamor for power through monopoly, and thus reduce government costs and legal controls over the economy. Structural limits can be set on moneymaking within the business system itself so that energy may be channeled more productively into the fulfillment of human values and realization of cultural life in its broader aspects.

The above areas can also become the focus of congressional research and legislation. This focus becomes timely and feasible during downswings in the market, high unemployment, and other publicly visible consequences of debt and speculation. The fact that Congress is not ready to take action on root causes of corporate and government debt in the organization of the economy and spends its time treating symptoms does not alter what the present portends. It behooves us, therefore, to look at the future of social legislation and go into our argument for research in more detail.

Legislation and national policies

In the light of the four areas for research in the field of social investment, what forms of national legislation could help settle financial problems in the market system? And could the legislation advance the cause of social-economic development and self-regulation within the national economy?

A national policy for employee ownership (stopping market speculation, merger mania and paper entrepreneurialism while advancing opportunities for social development)

Legislation supporting employee ownership as in the cooperative model could follow in the footsteps of ESOP legislation, with corrections based on that experience. This would allow corporate changes to be made slowly enough to be experimental, yet rapidly enough to begin treating problems of market overstimulation and corporate debt.

In our opinion, the cooperative model of employee ownership is best suited to treat the market problem while advancing opportunities for human development. It is based on a voting system valuing the integrity of the individual rather than on a financier's ability to purchase voting shares. But to reach a point where a firm is worthy of cooperative ownership is not easy. To be successful, it should have an agreement with employees to take such a step and should institute a training program that insures that management can handle the change without disrupting business. Firms typically need a new administrative system that includes *internal mechanisms of mediation and judicial hearings for employees, profit-sharing and internal accounting for their savings, departmental councils, employee representation on the board of directors*, and in very large companies, *a system of co-managed newspapers and ombudsmen*. The change could be slower than in ESOPs because it involves a self-studied process of organizational development within the firm.

A major change toward co-operative ownership requires an altered infrastructure supporting the business system, tax incentives to support professional consultation in organizational development, and training programs in worker participation in management. It also means a new emphasis in the curriculum of business schools to take account of the trend in human-resource management. It means, as well, looking toward the modifications in the law so corporations may become chartered according to the cooperative model of business.

Self-management advocates recommend various methods for introducing the cooperative model into the national marketplace, but two can be mentioned here. One is to require the top fifty corporations to become federally chartered and socially constituted. New mergers reaching the asset size of the smallest of the top corporations would automatically be required to charter themselves federally and become employee-owned. The stock would be purchased by employees over time, and the majority of the stock would be removed from the stock exchange. Such congressional action would place a limit automatically on the number of megamergers because financiers would no longer have an incentive to play games on the market. Banks would not be tempted to make financial killings and corporations would tend toward decentralization. We have noted the structural tendency for worker-managed firms to value greater self-direction in departments and the workplace.[20]

The second method to stimulate employee ownership is based on the experience of ESOPs. ESOPs opened the door to the idea of employee ownership for business leaders and has had its period of testing. The effects of ESOPs have been studied extensively and legislation can be formulated to provide incentives for the cooperative model. This approach seeks full support from a national administration that would provide the assistance of government agencies. The following summary condenses certain points emphasized by William F. Whyte and Corey Rosen:[21]

A national policy supporting employee ownership and participation could be undertaken by means of an amendment to the Full Employment Act. Such a law or presidential executive order would direct each federal agency to report annually on what it had done to carry out the policy. Agencies that support research on work and the economy might fund studies on these issues; agencies that regulate stock ownership could review their regulations to make sure they do not unintentionally raise barriers against broadened employee ownership; agencies that hold conferences for business and labor could include these subjects in their agendas; agencies that make loans and loan guarantees could make them available for employee ownership. These actions represent an important first step because the legislation's very enactment helps to provide legitimacy for the concept of employee ownership.

A specific federal agency can be mandated to provide technical assistance and promotional services for efforts in self-management. Certain states – Michigan, Illinois, New Jersey – have already assigned such agencies to do so. One federal program, the Labor–Management Cooperation Act, already authorizes the Federal Mediation and Conciliation Service (FMCS) to provide grants to area labor–management committees and joint union–management cooperation programs in individual companies. The program has been underfunded ($500,000) and would require support. The Act could be expanded to include a broader technical assistance and promotion program to fund research, innovative labor–management cooperation, and outreach programs. In addition, the FMCS could develop its own technical assistance expertise, with technical publications and the formation of a resource center to help facilitate the process toward self-management.

Various incentive plans could be formulated, such as allowing owners of small businesses who sell their stock to employees to defer taxes on their gains if they reinvest the stock in another business. At present, capital gains taxes encourage owners to sell to large firms instead of remaining independent.

Employee buyouts of companies that might otherwise shut down are a small percentage of the employee ownership movement, but they do involve a large number of employees and are often widely publicized. All the government-supported projects so far have succeeded. By making loans in these cases, the government has avoided the enormous costs that would otherwise result from a plant shutdown. Instead of an empty factory and hundreds or thousands of unemployed workers, there is a tax-paying corporation and tax-paying workers.

Still other types of tax incentives can encourage corporations to develop employee ownership. One is to eliminate all taxes on corporations that choose to become based on the model of cooperative employee ownership. Legislation could strengthen the process by providing incentives for employees to purchase stock collectively on a wage salary deferment arrangement. A portion of the income of all employees would be automatically directed toward the purchase of stock in their company. The stock would then be retired out of the market and could not be publicly traded.

New nonvoting stock can be issued for institutional investors needing to make returns on their capital by firms wishing to raise capital. The nonvoting stock would not be a basis for manipulation on the market because it would not permit outsiders to gain control over the corporation. A specific percentage (e.g., 20 per cent) of voting stock could still be maintained on the market without interfering with employee control, for it could still be traded without encouraging paper entrepreneurialism.

There are several good reasons for maintaining an outside influence over employee-owned firms. One is to share in the risk undertaken by the employees; another is to provide outside judgments about the direction of the firm in the context of society.

The model of worker cooperatives assigns a claim on residual profits (positive or negative) to the employees because outside holders of stock are barred when only workers control management. In our model a cooperative's net worth is owned by employees individually, not collectively, i.e., workers have individual capital accounts, with the firm, entitling them to corresponding claims on the firm's net book value. This is important because evidence suggests that firms with collective ownership tend to invest too little in their future; internal accounts provide capital for retooling and expansion. In this case workers also bear the risk of fluctuations in the net worth of the firm. By sharing risk with outsiders, they reduce the economic impact on themselves if the firm fails but also must share the benefits if it succeeds. Outsiders can invest in a large number of firms, so overall risk is reduced by a balance of risk-bearing firms in the overall portfolio.

Many outside investors also want to press social issues in stockholder resolutions to employee-owned firms. These firms are still competitive and therefore profit oriented, so may fail to develop any social vision. Outside social investors may even win in instances where a percentage of employees become awakened and want to take action on such issues as product safety and environmental pollution.[22]

A typical pattern of ownership, then, could involve 20 per cent outside stock and 80 per cent employee stock, plus nonvoting stock according to the firm's need for capital. Outside stock would become composed typically of pension funds; this means that employees could eventually exercise control from within the firm and also from outside the firm through their representation on pension boards, depending on the direction taken by Congress in handling the growing dilemma of pension fund management.

It is conceivable that the thousands of firms now under ESOP law may develop employee voting rights and thus quicken the process toward the model of cooperative ownership and management. Upon careful analysis of ESOP law, Joseph Blasi concludes that "the right to vote all shares in closely held companies and democratically elect the trustees of the Employee Stock Ownership Trust must be mandated by federal laws." He sees the real choices of the future to be "to amend ERISA's section on Employee Stock Ownership Plans to provide some basic protections for workers' rights; to redefine the National Labor Relations Act to provide for these basic rights."[23]

If the cooperative model should become more prevalent in U.S. business, we can expect a trend toward worker buyouts and divestiture of subsidiaries among conglomerate corporations. The evidence is mounting that conglomerate management is inefficient because of its bureaucracy. Company plants and divisions can be operated more effectively by their employees in some cases than by higher management. William Foote Whyte offers cases in which worker buyouts have improved levels of company efficiency. For example, the Library Bureau, a subsidiary plant of Sperry-Rand in Herkimer, New York, did not earn profits high enough for its parent's norms and the plant was planned for shutdown. The employees and residents in the community, however, decided to buy the plant. Whyte tells how higher-echelon salespeople in Sperry-Rand had not responded to requests of Library Bureau lower management to sell library equipment only through the subsidiary. Also, the Library Bureau could not get any response from the international division of Sperry-Rand to its requests to sell overseas through export trade. The worker buyout allowed for more flexibility in product marketing. Whyte cites other cases of unresponsive conglomerate bureaucracy, and suggests worker buyouts as a creative solution in certain instances.[24]

Nonvoting stock would be issued by employee-owned firms for new capital, but it would not be the basis for "greenmail" or paper entrepreneurialism because outsiders could not gain control over the corporation. Mergers would still be possible but on a more rational basis. They would take place through negotiations between top executives who find the new corporate combination in the interest of everyone affected by it. Consent would be needed from employee-owners. The merger would then probably look more like a social federation than like a conglomerate command system. It would be much more decentralized and flexible in its system of authority.

Market speculation and merger mania should slow down as the system gradually changed over to employee ownership, and at the same time the potential for human development should increase. We have noted the potential benefits of employee self-management in the reduction of labor costs for the government and for the company in costly strikes; the tendency toward more local corporate control; the strengthening of work motives among a wider number of employees who gain in real profit sharing; the use of corporate capital saved by employees in their internal accounts for paying off corporate debts and for investment in new technology; savings to the company through the likelihood of a reduced wage differential; company savings by the elimination of executive frills (like "golden parachutes"); the reduction of employee theft; the greater potential for mobility among talented employees within the stratification of the firm; and many other advantages.

The changeover to corporate self-management does not resolve all problems. Management would still confront internal labor-management conflict, tension between departments, competition for higher-paid positions, and so on, but employees would struggle with these old problems on fairer grounds. There are new structures in the firm to develop relationships around principles of cooperation. The new pattern of ownership means that everyone must reconcile the social purposes of the corporation with making profits in the marketplace.

*A national policy for decentralized banking (avoiding bank
failures and small-firm bankruptcies by organizing a new system
for lending capital)*

We have discussed how social investors have begun to develop rotating loan funds to support enterprises accountable to stakeholders and the surrounding community. Providing legislative support for regional banks modeled after such funds should go far toward disciplining the speculative trend in banking and the tendency for firms to become overburdened with debts.

Social investors have set standards of control in alternative banking to optimize both social and economic returns. They have learned much from the Mondragon system in which each investment is carefully monitored. The system is based on a careful assessment of each firm's capacity to produce and market its wares effectively. It has been so successful that bank managers have lost only one enterprise out of more than eighty new starts. Profitable firms eventually participate in the governance of the bank itself. The bank and its enterprises have social objectives but they have a nononsense policy when it comes to finance.

Lester Thurow tells us that the U.S. banking system is in deep trouble. Banks' loan portfolios include more than $500 billion in farm and Third World debt, whose default is easily imagined. As oil prices fall, good oil loans are rapidly becoming bad ones. Major banks are sinking along with real estate values. Mergers and leveraged buyouts can barely meet interest obligations, and they could not meet them in a recession. "A nervous stock market booms while the economy sags. Stagnation, farm bankruptcies, financial speculation, nonperforming loans, large potential defaults, falling real estate values (remember the Florida land boom and bust of the 1920's) – the echoes of the Great Depression sound louder and louder."[25]

Alternative banking systems and different priorities can be seen in the trend toward social investment. Social investors are less interested in oil investments and more interested in cultivating renewable energy sources. In world banking the Ecumenical Development Cooperative Society is avoiding loans to governments (especially those with dictatorial politics) and making loans to socially accountable firms in the private sector. They point the way toward not only new priorities in making loans but a new system of world banking.

A financially responsible alternative in regional banking is found in what self-management experts call Local Ownership Development Corporations (LODCs), regional banks that can lend to cooperatives and community-based firms. This method of loaning would remove excessive profit-making schemes and the "casino climate" of underwriting, replacing them with a decentralized mode of investment in socially accountable enterprises.[26]

Legislation could provide funding to start socially oriented banks designed to become part of the private sector in the model of the Consumer Cooperative Bank. Conceived in the Carter administration but crippled in its launching period during Reagan administration cutbacks, this national bank had great promise of following closely the Mondragon model. It was to become owned by its successful businesses as it became organized in the private sector. Given the consequences of negligence in current banking systems, such legislation becomes significant to review again today.

A national policy for greater uniformity among pension plans through regional/industrywide holding companies
(Overcoming the problem of unfunded liabilities and offering an opportunity for higher social and economic returns)

When Peter Drucker presented his surprising statistics in *The Unseen Revolution* (1976) showing projections that workers would own over 50 per cent of the corporations in the United States through their pension stock, it created a stir in every quarter of the polity. He was criticized on the left for suggesting that it had anything to do with socialism and on the right for recommending reforms. He argued that the first priority for reforming the system of pension funds was to establish boards of directors and trustees that could satisfy three requirements:

1. to provide the effective organ of control and accountability that pension funds must have.
2. to provide representation of the "constituencies," and especially of the new "owners."
3. to reach the new "owners," the country's employees, and obtain their understanding and support.[27]

The first step in the reform would be the appointment of professional directors of public standing who could be truly independent of conventional management. The funds were too important to be put in the hands of banks that might not dispense them in the best interest of the beneficiaries or might even consider them of very little interest. Drucker called for independent management through a "public and community relations board, that is, a strong visible membership on the board by people who represent both true 'constituencies,' such as consumers and employers, and the future new 'owners' – the country's employees." He said that the Teachers Insurance and Annuity Association (TIAA) could be one model of an industrywide public and community relations board. The TIAA is governed by a board of distinguished university administrators and economists elected by its constituents, the nation's universities and faculty. The correct model, however, would require a "radical restructuring of the institution of governance: the board of directors or trustee."

Drucker said that adjustments would have to be made in the "prudent-man" rule. Pension funds have reached such capital importance in the nation's system of investment that the rule can no longer be applied inflexibly. It limits investment policy to past performance of corporations; the goal of prudent investment is to minimize risk. But pension funds are no longer a part of the capital market, they *are* the market. This means they must become responsible for stimulating new business and industry as well as responsible for preserving the old; otherwise, the nation runs the risk of "starving the new, the young, the small, the growing business." So we need a commitment on the part of the independent fund managers to place a significant share of their assets (perhaps 10 per cent) for investment in new entrepreneurial activities.[28]

Drucker argued further that the corporate income tax was punitive to workers as owners of corporations. For pensioners who receive all or most of their income from their corporate pension fund, the corporation income tax sharply raises the effective rate of tax on the income of which they are the beneficial owners and ultimate recipients. The corporation income tax is therefore a highly regressive tax that is paid increasingly by the employees.

Drucker also criticized the lack of uniformity among pension plans, which creates a major problem for employees who seek to move from one job to another without loss of their retirement plans. It is impossible for workers in some corporations to move to others without loss of pension; in fact, in some governmental jurisdictions, such as New York City, it has been impossible to move even from one department to another without a loss of pension rights. Hence, the need for a radical restructuring of pension fund arrangements at the national level.

Finally, pension liabilities and corporate debt are related to the demographics of aging. The increasing number of people reaching retirement age today (and in the coming decade) places an added strain on pension payments; this because pension funds do not represent capital formation but, rather, transfer payments or savings for retirement. When employees retire, the capital goes directly into consumption and its productive function is lost. The use of pension investments for productive activity among the elderly is therefore one of the most important fields of research today. The question is, how may these funds be used productively so that retirees who wish to work may do so? How they can contribute toward the circulation of productive capital and thus to the economic well-being of society?

In the light of these complexities, a legislative commission is needed to look into the process of restructuring pension funds in the interest of their beneficiaries and the larger society. It should work with the National Council of Institutional Investors, the International Foundation of Employees' Benefit Plans, the Social Security Administration, ERISA, and other appropriate bodies to recommend solutions.

Key areas for study in formulating legislation are the following:

1. Guidelines for the professional use of social and economic criteria in the allocation of capital.
2. The structure of a decentralized organization of industrywide or regional holding companies with fair representation of employees and other relevant

constituencies who together can act in the public interest as well as in the interest of their beneficiaries.

3.   Uniformity among pension plans in reference to income and mobility in the corporate-governmental system for retirees.

The plan for organizing pension funds in the United States is not the same as plans in other nations, and the differences are worth noting. The Swedish Social Democratic Party adopted a plan developed by Rudolf Meidner in the research bureau of the national trade union organization (or LO) that would require the largest firms (about two hundred of them) to set aside 20 per cent of their profits each year in the form of "wage-earner shares" with voting rights. As a result, ownership of the firms will gradually pass to the employees. The Swedish plan does not give control directly to the employees of the firms. The shares and voting rights would be transferred to various national and regional funds, which would be governed by representatives elected by all wage earners in the country. A company's employees would never control more than 20 per cent of the voting rights in their own firm; the main control would reside in the larger representative body.

A proposal introduced in parliament by the Danish Social Democratic Party in 1973 proposed that the proceeds of a payroll tax covering most Danish firms (about 25,000) would be divided into two parts. One part would go to a national investment and dividend fund to be used for investment and to provide dividends to Danish workers. Workers would receive certificates from the fund in amounts proportional to the number of years worked but not to wages or salaries. The certificates would be nonnegotiable, but an employee would have the right to withdraw the value of the certificates after seven years or at age sixty-seven with the posthumous amount paid to the employee's estate. The larger part of the proceeds of the tax would remain in the firm as share capital owned collectively by the employees. Employees would vote on the basis of one person one vote, but voting rights would not be permitted to increase beyond 50 per cent to reassure private investors of their property rights.[29]

The national plans follow the currents of tradition and power uniquely constituted in each nation. The Danish plan finds kinship with the tradition of codetermination in West Germany, where corporate control by employees is limited to 50 per cent on the top boards. The power of outside investors to influence legislation in both countries was juxtaposed against a limited yet strong union power. The Swedish union was stronger yet, and is today moving toward worker control on a more centralized basis. The plan seeks ultimate authority in regional and national funds in order to make better use of capital for overall social-economic welfare.

The power of unions in the United States has been declining, but the growing power of pension funds has brought workers back into national significance with reference to their legal rights to ownership. If the trend toward a convergence of worker ownership and participation in management continues, a qualitative change in the character of free enterprise will take place. The U.S. trend of development suggests a decentralized pattern of control by mostly nonunion employees, with limited union participation in the industries where they remain strong. It also suggests a pension-management structure that includes representation of all employees (most would be nonunion) as well as other constituencies representing the larger public domain.

Self-managed firms in the United States therefore will not be influenced so much from the outside by union hierarchy, as in Europe, but rather by the structure of trade associations and consumer organizations. Future antitrust legislation must take account of the balance of power among intercorporate associations – from supply to production to wholesale to retail to consumers – so that trade representatives can better take account of their corporate constituencies. Thus, the Government sets the conditions for the economy to become structured in the public interest.

> *A national policy for greater degrees of social self-regulation in the enterprise system (controlling debt resulting from declining industries and foreign competition, and acting on household debt by strengthening the consumer movement)*

Even if employees continue to gain positions of responsibility and authority in governing their firms, the firms will still operate in a competitive market. The struggle for corporate power goes on, and profit and tendencies to exploit outside constituencies is a natural ingredient of the market system. The need for a higher order of governance and accountability to protect consumers, the environment, and small firms from big firms will still be present. The government has long played the protector through its regulatory departments and agencies, but we have noted that trade associations and consumer organizations are beginning to take on the role through ethical codes, judicial systems, and their countervailing power. Our argument therefore continues that the root causes of speculation and debt can be treated by self-correcting mechanisms socially constructed within the private sector of business.

The climate for creating a self-regulating system of enterprises develops with the advent of two other trends. First, the increasing power of employees in the governance of corporations leads normally toward a decentralized system of corporations. This changes the structure, composition, and purpose of trade associations in the larger polity. Second, the trend toward social investment is carrying with it an interest in the development of the social sector, with broader analyses of industry in which trade groups play a part, and an increasing acceptance of social responsibility as legitimate for business.

We have noted how the special power of big corporations in trade associations interferes with the industry's becoming fully self-regulatory. Big corporations act in their own self-interest and frequently dominate the smaller firms in an industry's trade association. We can offer two examples of trade associations that have acted against what Congress defines as the public interest before we suggest a self-regulatory role for these associations in resolving the problem of corporate debt.

The Business Roundtable is an elegant exemplar of the organized power elite in the United States. It contains no small firms and represents no single industry. It is composed of the biggest 192 corporations in business and operates more as an alliance of corporate oligarchies than as a democratic federation. It is managed by a policy committee of forty-six CEOs who meet every other month to thrash out political positions in the interest of the members. Their interest is to help formulate public policy, but the structure and composition of the association leads them in reality to defend their commanding power in the economy. The members have private data accessible to no other political body. To illustrate, Chase Manhattan has collected statistics on the oil industry throughout the world for the past fifty years. The statistical data point toward the possibilities for expansion to new energy sources. Chase makes this information available to the Energy Task Force of the Roundtable, which, in turn, uses it in testimony before congressional committees. Such data are vital to the formation of public policy but the structure of the association biases their communication.

This kind of resource, multiplied in variety and scope within the remaining constellation of big companies, represents a valuable resource in treating the problems of global competition. The Business Roundtable could have an important role in preserving the self-governing power of the economy in the context of world capitalism. It is needed in the battle against the breakdown of domestic industry, but Congress has yet to see how to help the Roundtable fulfill its legitimate public purpose.

The Business Roundtable is organized to resist any "unreasonable" attempt by Congress to hold it accountable to the public on domestic matters. It has vigorously opposed congressional efforts to hold managers criminally liable for their subordinates' felonies. It has supported total decontrol of oil prices, successfully turned aside any windfall profits tax, and has fought consistently against the labor movement. Neither Congress nor the Roundtable has studied how business can structure itself to be accountable to its constituencies on these issues, much less how it can help to reverse the tide of foreign competition. It is a perpetual contest between an unimaginative Congress and the unsocialized private sector.

The U.S. Chamber of Commerce has more redeeming value because it is more decentralized, but it also tends to be controlled by big corporations. It is a federation of corporations, trade associations, and local Chambers of Commerce. It has 94,000 members, a staff of 1,200, and an annual budget of $30 million. Much of its time is spent lobbying Congress, and its Capitol Hill battles are similar to those of the Roundtable. It has opposed antitrust legislation, federal mass transit subsidies, the minimum wage, public housing, and many other bills that would seem to be in the public interest. When threatening legislation is proposed, Chamber staff send informational computerized mail to every plant with more than five employees, whereupon plant managers ask employees to organize and "write their Congressmen" before it is too late. The Chamber also has the power to fight foreign competition threatening the survival of its members but does not know how to do it effectively in partnership with Congress. Its relationship to Congress is defensive rather than cooperative.[30]

Peak organizations like the Roundtable, the Chamber, and the National Association of Manufacturers (NAM) have a legitimate right to work toward the public interest, but Congress has yet to help them do so. To do so requires legislation conferring the power to act on foreign competition without interfering with domestic competition.[31] Let us look more carefully at the problem in order to assess their public role in solving it.

The U.S. trade deficit of $150 billion and the overvalued dollar are related to the decline of exports and the poor performance of U.S. industries. Foreign goods have swamped U.S. industries. For example, between 1972 and 1984, foreign imports have overtaken more than two dozen industries, with resultant major corporate losses. The percentage of imports in the U.S. market in blowers and fans went from 3.6 per cent to 29.2 per cent; in dolls, 21.8 per cent to 54 per cent; in luggage and personal goods, 20.7 per cent to 52 per cent; in shoes, 17.1 per cent to 50.4 per cent; in radios and television sets, 34.9 per cent to 57 per cent; and so on.[32]

The peak organizations should be actively helping to restore these industries and reducing corporate debt, but they need government support. We have discussed (in chapter 5) methods for acting on global competition without introducing trade restrictions. This includes the reduction of labor costs through compensatory agreements with employees to increase their participation in the governance and ownership of firms. It includes the government's working closely with peak organizations to lower interest rates for investment in retooling. It means adjusting corporate law in some cases so that trade associations can combine member resources (e.g., in machine tools) for research and development. It means government departments working with trade associations to sharpen their ability to predict the onset of global competition. Although trade associations need legislative support and social investors' help to decentralize their authority on the domestic scene, they need to centralize their authority for the specific task of meeting the challenge presented globally by other central authorities like Japan's MITI and the European Economic Community.

In the 1960s Japanese steel production grew from 24 million to over 100 million net tons. Consultation between the government's planning agency (MITI) and private industry was critical to this propitious development. Tax incentives for expanding industries were part of a national plan. Capacity for industrial growth was financed largely (up to 80 per cent) by long-term, low-interest loans. Japanese industry was thus able to construct large, technically advanced, integrated plants in modern deep-water port locations. By 1977 U.S. Steel's Edgar Speer, chairman of the American Iron and Steel Institute, was pushing for U.S. government protection, asserting that the "national security" and "health of the economy" were in jeopardy.[33]

This story can be repeated for other U.S. industries. The fact is that Congress can stimulate trade associations to help their members to restructure themselves. Instead of crying for protection, trade associations can work with Congress to predict world trends in industry more accurately, to develop new technology, to invest in industrial frontiers, and to reorganize corporately to reduce costs with labor participation.

Congress has the task of looking more carefully at how the competitive system of industries can protect itself not only from incursions from overseas but also from itself as a social system causing corporate debt. The petrochemical industry can serve as an example of how domestic competition can lead to decline of an industry and cause corporate debt in a manner similar to foreign competition.

Petrochemical products have been invading industries and causing a collapse in their markets as serious as Japan's invasion of U.S. industry from the outside. For example, since synthetic detergents appeared in the 1940s, they have captured about 80 per cent of the market once held by soap. Since 1950 synthetic fibers have taken over about 70 per cent of the U.S. textile market, once held largely by cotton and wool. The production of plastics has grown at the rate of 16 per cent per year, while that of competitive industries has grown much more slowly: leather, 1.2 per cent, and paper,

4.8 per cent. Lumber production has *decreased* at a rate of 0.5 per cent per year.[34] These changes seem at first to be a good thing because innovative technology in petrochemicals lowers prices for consumers, but the real costs are more hidden and subtle, for the petrochemical industry has been developing a kind of economic imperialism. While petrochemicals have been invading these established markets, the social and economic costs have been mounting. The costs to competing businesses can be measured in debt and bankruptcies, and the government debt can be measured in the costs of welfare and unemployment compensation, environmental protection, conservation, and product safety.

Food dyes and fire retardants for children's sleepwear had to be banned by the government because they are carcinogenic. Indeed, a major cause of cancer is officially related to petrochemicals like PCB. The highest incidence of bladder cancer is found in Salem County, New Jersey, an area dense with refineries and petrochemical plants. The list of public costs is endless. Pesticides have killed fish and wildlife. Plastic building materials produce toxic fumes when they burn and have had to be banned. Beaches have become blanketed by debris since nonbiodegradable synthetics replaced hemp cordages, wooden spoons, and paper cups, which decay quickly. The government pays these costs, and its debt keeps mounting.

Congress can lay the basis for competing trade associations to conduct joint studies in the public interest. If they are given an opportunity to work together for the public welfare, the government does not need to pay the costs of actions counter to the public welfare, and business costs can be saved as well. For example, the insurance industry is a countervailing power to the petrochemical industry, and the two have a shared interest in reducing public costs – this because they want to protect themselves against damage suits. The insurance industry in this case acts as a leverage against public dangers. A survey of the skyrocketing insurance premiums in the petrochemical trade journal, *Chemical and Engineering News*, is an inside account of the future. Insurance policies are being canceled, and many are not being renewed. Both industries therefore have reason to curtail their losses in their mutual interest. But when insurance companies are canceling policies, the damage has already been done. The task of Congress is to bring industries together to anticipate problems and avoid future costs.

A congressional plan to encourage social self-regulation would involve a new role for government agencies: to help balance the power of trade associations and consumer groups to reduce their costs in the public interest. It can be done without interfering with free trade. The Antitrust Division can remain the watchdog of the economic concentration of competing industrial associations. It should move *first* to clarify how corporations have crossed between industries in the movement toward conglomerates. The division's permissiveness in the past toward conglomeration has tended to confuse corporate responsibilities in vital industries. Big conglomerates are less interested in maintaining a vital industry than in making profits. Trade associations are weakened as conglomerates lose their interest in an industry and focus only on paper profits. The division needs to define competition so that industries can be recognized for their public importance and retain their competitive character. Second, the division should help to keep concentrations of power from developing between industries from supply to production to wholesale to retail. The assumption is that such a balance will eventually reduce costs to businesses themselves, and the government's protection costs as well. The concept of balance between economic sectors should include consumers as part of the business economy.

Consumers are usually the weakest link in the chain leading from supply to production to retail sales. They are not traditionally organized as a business, but Congress can help support the final link through tax incentives for consumer organizations in a way that does not diminish the power of retailers or producers. Consumers can act to check the power of a petrochemical industry as well as other countervailing businesses in the interest of reducing the federal debt and government regulations.

Ralph Nader currently points toward the development of new corporations for consumers that allow them to establish buyer–seller contracts with producers. The idea follows the model of the American Association of Retired Persons (AARP), a nonprofit corporation with 19 million members, who can obtain special discounts on pharmaceuticals and health insurance. AARP has power because it can deliver volume sales. Nader has organized a fuel-buyers' corporation called Buyers-Up that pools buying power and lets contracts to bid by local fuel companies. Nader says that car buyers could organize in this manner and demand fifty miles to the gallon and air bags. Nader envisions 15 million members negotiating installment-loan contracts with Citibank at the national level and renegotiating health and other types of insurance policies with Prudential.[35]

Consumers are a part of the countervailing powers that regulate the business system. They are themselves a growing enterprise that contributes to social self-regulation and discourages monopolies from developing in trade areas. They are part of the balance wheel that Congress must consider in judging how the system itself can lead toward a reduction in corporate and government debt.

In conclusion: beyond the market and the state

The trend toward social investment is fraught with risk as it gathers momentum and bids for national recognition, but if it deals wisely with its own problems it may not only advance solutions to market speculation and corporate-government debt but also move toward altering the very character of the market system itself.

Social investors are aware of some special dangers ahead as they organize nationally to promote a common cause. One is that some fiduciaries could begin to fall behind the standard market returns and become objects of ridicule. Some may even lose sight of the importance of their fiduciary responsibilities. The conventional investment scene has certainly shown the ease with which fraud and deception can enter and also where mistakes can be made quite innocently. The National Association of Security Dealers has sought valiantly over the years to establish its own ethical codes and professional standards of practice so as to avoid any extensive malpractice among its ranks.

Another real danger is defined by opponents of social investment who claim that the practice will become politicized. Proponents agree that if politics were to enter significantly into decision making, social investment would suffer a major setback. The National Council of Institutional Investors has been especially subject to outside criticism on this point because politicians are heading the pension fund agencies. But the term *political* is also used in reference to unions investing in their own interest without regard to the public interest. The term refers pejoratively to the use of any criteria to advance special interests. It could refer to the special interests of a church, a state, or even a bank.

This is not what we are suggesting should develop in the movement, even though some cases have already shown that it happens. A confusion occurs partly because "political" criteria are of course "social" in the analytical use of the term. The terms overlap. In one sense, *political* can be conceived as contained within the broad concept of *social*, but the normative meaning of the term for our purposes refers to the allocation of capital in the balanced interest of beneficiaries, investors, and the needs of the larger society. The practice of social investment is justified on these grounds. We have recommended a theory of social-economic development that can provide priorities and guide decisions for investors, but it is also subject to research and correction. It is not designed as political dogma.

The challenge ahead for social investors is to lay the institutional foundation for fiduciary practice and research. The practice must be guided by an informed set of managers and a decentralized governing structure that can allow for the freedom to experiment within the larger context of society. It means not only establishing professional standards for combining social and economic criteria but finding new relationships with schools of management and business as well as with social science departments in universities to help implement programs of study in this field.

If these challenges are met successfully and social investment becomes a movement in the 1990s, we should then see its subtrends spearheading changes in the character of modern capitalism. The subtrend of alternative investment especially questions the roots of capitalist belief as it points toward a new path of social development within the economy.[36] Alternative investors are challenging the assumption that state regulation is necessary to maintain a free market system. They have been proposing a business system based on self-accountability and social self-regulation. The theory implicit in this subtrend goes still further to question the belief that the market must be predominantly competitive in order to maintain a system of free enterprise. It suggests that cooperation can occur effectively among competitors without collusion. Indeed, the process of cooperation appears at least as important as competition in leading the market to operate in the public interest.[37]

If we define capitalism sociologically as a competitive market system in which firms maximize profits in their own self-interest, and psychologically as a system in which individuals compete to increase their income, status, and power within the command management of business, we can say that alternative investors have been working with a different model. They are instead encouraging the development of an exchange system characterized by cooperation within which the competition among firms becomes less significant and takes place within a framework of social justice. They are encouraging an interest in systems of accountability, profit sharing, and social equity in the context of building stronger local communities.[38]

We have taken this argument further by claiming theoretically that the system of balanced power evolving among competing firms in the same industry, and between competing trade associations from supply to production to distribution to retail, is an important new direction for investment. A relatively balanced system of power is needed between each trade area for the development of a self-governing economy.

The trend toward social investment may seem insignificant in the context of the larger forces of business today, but evidence is accumulating that it could become a significant movement in the near future. Congressional leaders claim that it should gain strength and become politically important to address in legislation.[39] But the trend should also be observed as simply one component in the larger sea change taking place in market economies around the world today. It is interacting with other trends in political, religious, and educational institutions that are affecting the economy. It is important therefore to study it in the decades ahead, as part of the institutional development of modern society. This larger picture of change is likely to contain even more surprises than history has shown to be part of our past evolution. It could include major recessions, depressions, and even a nuclear war with all its implications for national and world decline. However, it also contains the possibility of a future based on a greater system of social justice in the business economy. Let us hope that the tragic consequences of another Great Depression or a nuclear war will not be the source of change, but that the slow movement of people experimenting with self-directed reforms may be the future course of our evolution toward a new society.

Apart from a social movement: the field itself

At the outset of the book we said that social investment could be defined from a descriptive, normative, analytical, and theoretical viewpoint. We have emphasized the normative trend in this epilogue, but there is every reason to believe that all these dimensions remain relevant to the future of this field. Various departments of the university have a stake in studying the dimensions of investment in the decades ahead.

We said that all business investments have a socially *descriptive dimension*; the social factor is embedded in all economic investments. It can be found in the structure and concentration of power among fiduciaries and the subtle organizational interests that affect decision making. It can be found in the impact of financial decisions on people apart from whether it was intended or observed by the investors. Research is needed on all investments recognizing the fact that the social and economic factors are closely intertwined. The consequences of decisions to allocate capital need to be studied in the context of society.

The *normative dimension* should also be studied for the manner in which investments actually contribute to the well being of people in society. The ethical patterns of investment developing among selected colleges, universities, pension funds, mutual funds, churches, and banks require study by philosophers, theologians, and political scientists to help assess not simply the impact of decisions on people but how the decisions themselves are based on the broad standards in their disciplines. The universality of the principles employed need to be examined in addition to the question of whether they show results.

The *analytical dimension* remains important to this field because comparative studies of investment in different societies will demonstrate how a social framework interpenetrates with an economic framework. We need to see how business investors take account of the social behavior of a company in order to make profits in comparison with how government investors in other countries take account of profits in order to improve the well-being of people in their society. Comparative analyses of investment behavior in different nations should be enlightening to financial managers.

Finally, the *theoretical dimension* remains important to future studies because a conceptual framework for interpreting investment policy needs continuous examination. We have said theoretically that investments confer power and value to people, but the meaning of power and value requires conceptual interpretation. The field of social investment needs connection with the meaning of concepts like community, freedom, and justice, as the social implications of capital allocation become more widely understood by the public.

It is clear that the field of social investment is more than a social trend or movement in society. The social factor is embedded in the nature of investment itself and should therefore come of age in the evolution of business. It should also become a subject of study in schools of management and various departments of the university in the decades ahead. The field is a part of the changing character of capitalism, which is destined – like state socialism – to evolve in new directions before the end of this century.

Notes

1 The meaning of social investment

1. Ford Foundation, *New Options in the Philanthropic Process*, 320 East Forty Third St (New York: N.1967).
2. Charles Powers, *Social Responsibility and Investments* (New York: Abington Press, 1971), p. 122.
3. Michael Hillard, *Towards a Union Label Investment Policy* (Boston: SEOC, 294 Washington St, Boston, 1979), p. 2.
4. Marc Weiss, *Pension Fund Investments: The Issue of Control* (Washington, D.C.: Conference on Alternative State and Local Policies, 1978), p. 488.
5. A. F. Ehbar, "Index Funds – An Idea Whose Time Is Coming," *Fortune*, November 1977.
6. Randy Barber and Jeremy Rifkin, *The North Shall Rise Again* (Boston: Beacon Press, 1978).
7. *Labor and Investments* (Industrial Union Department, AFL-CIO), Vol. 1 (January 1981).
8. Carol O'Cleireacain, "Towards Democratic Control of Capital Formation in the United States: The Role of Pension Funds," in Nancy Lieber, ed., *Eurosocialism and America* (Philadelphia: Temple University Press, 1982). These pension funds are growing at an annual rate of about 11 per cent. If we assume that about one-quarter of these funds turnover annually, then new money (in 1982, it was about $60 billion) plus turnover ($140 billion) would finance about half of the $400 billion gross private investment in the United States.
9. Ibid., p. 48. Carol O'Cleireacain calculates that 70 per cent of pension fund assets lie within the present bargaining or legislative reach of workers.
10. Quoted in Weiss, *Pension Fund Investments*, p. 25.
11. *Harvard College* v. *Amory*, 26 Mass. 446, 9 Pick. 446, 461 (1830).
12. Michael T. Leibig, "Social Investments and the Law," *Studies in Pension Fund Investments*, Conference on Alternative State and Local Policies, 3 August 1980.
13. Revenue Ruling 70–536, 1970–2 C.B. 120 (1970).
14. "Investment," *International Encyclopedia of the Social Sciences* (New York: Crowell Collier and Macmillan, 1968), p. 185.
15. Ibid., p. 194.
16. Leibig, "Social Investments and the Law," pp. 3–4.
17. Amy L. Domini with Peter Kinder, *Ethical Investing* (Reading, Mass.: Addison-Wesley, 1984), pp. xii–xxiii.
18. Ibid., pp. xii, 133

2 The activity of social investment

1. In theory, the field of social investment may include the provision of capital for any purpose because social factors are always analytically intertwined with any investment. Thus social investment could include government outlays to the departments of education, welfare, and defense; the practice of taxation, in which citizens and corporations make an investment in their government; and even the conventional activities of banks and loan agencies investing ostensibly with only an economic objective. A social purpose can be found analytically in all business and government investments, but we are not interested here in studying the social dimensions of capital outlay in the conventional sense. We are interested in how a pattern of corporate loaning, "gifting," and stock purchasing is appearing in the *private sector* designed primarily for social and economic development. The new mix of social and economic incentives offers a fascinating study within the investment field.

2. New Jersey was the first state to begin socializing its law in the 1930s, but it was not until 1950 that its legislature passed a law stating that it was "public policy" for corporations to be empowered to contribute money "to improve social and economic conditions" of society. In the following year the famous case of A. P. Smith Manufacturing Company cleared the way for corporate gifts. A. P. Smith's attempt to make a gift of $1,500 to Princeton University was opposed by stockholders who claimed it was not in their economic interest. In his decision the judge stated that the two "corporations" were highly interdependent and "the only hope of survival" of higher education was in "the willingness of business to furnish financial support." For a discussion of this case, see Clarence Walton, *Corporate Social Responsibilities* (Belmont, Calif.: Wadsworth, 1968), p. 48.

3. *Response* (Center for Corporate Public Involvement, Washington, D.C.) 11 (July 1982) 12. (The numbers do not add up perfectly because apparently some small "family foundations" are not included in the Registry. The total number is estimated (pp. x–xi).)

4. *Annual Register of Grant Support 1981–82*, 15th edn.

5. *Response* (Center for Corporate Public Involvement, Washington, D.C.) 11 (September 1982).

6. National Economic Development and Law Center, 2150 Shattuck Ave., Berkeley, Calif. 94704.

7. *Business week*, 28 March 1983, 72–3.

8. James H. Heard and David C. H. Johnston, *Socially Responsive Investing* (Washington, D.C.: Investor Responsibility Research Center, September 1982), p. 33.

9. *Social Report, 1982* (Washington, D.C.: Center for Corporate Involvement).

10. Ibid., p. 29.

11. Martin Larson and C. Stanley Lowell, *Praise the Lord for Tax Exemption* (Washington, D.C.: Robert Luce, 1969). See also Martin Larson, *Church Wealth and Income* (New York: Philosophical Library, 1965).

12. Lynn Rhenisch, "Community Capital," paper prepared for the Program in

Social Economy and Social Policy, Boston College and Rural American Women, Inc., Washington, D.C., June 1982.

13. Ritchie Lowry, "The Crisis in Fund Management," adapted from *Doing Good While Doing Well* (in progress) 9 August 1981, Department of Sociology, Boston College.

14. Heard and Johnston, *Socially Responsive Investing*.

15. AFL-CIO Investment Study, prepared for the AFL-CIO Executive Council Committee on Investment of Union Pension Funds, by Ruttenberg, Friedman, Kilgallon, Gutchess, and Associates, Inc.

16. Ritchie Lowry, "Doing Good While Doing Well," *Social Report* (Boston College) 3 (June 1982), 2–3.

17. Severyn T. Bruyn, *The Social Economy* (New York: Wiley, 1977), Appendix.

18. Robert Schwartz, "The Blue Diamond Coal Company Case," *Social Report* (Boston College) 3 (June 1982), 5.

19. Steven Lyndenberg, "SEC Proposes New Shareholder Rules," Council on Economic Priorities Publication N83–1, February 1983.

20. Lowry, "Doing Good While Doing Well," pp. 3–5.

21. Eugene Glover, "Social Investment: Directing Union-Negotiated Funds to Social Purposes," *Employee Benefits Journal* 7, September 1982, 15.

22. Harold L. Johnson, *Disclosure of Corporate Social Performance* (New York: Praeger, 1979), ch. 3.

23. *Directory of Socially Responsible Investments*, prepared by the Funding Exchange and Bread and Roses Community Fund, 1983.

24. Milton Moskowitz, "How to Rate Companies on Social Responsibility," *Insight*, Winter 1983.

3 A theory of social investment

1. A theory of social investment is formulated inductively and deductively. It can begin inductively with data from systematic observations of fiduciary practices. On the basis of empirical observations, researchers formulate hypotheses about the process of investment decisions and the impact they have on people in the corporate system. Researchers then continue to build a factual foundation around variables defining the investment process and its impact through controlled field studies. The concepts that are drawn from interpretations of field data are then formulated into a coherent logic and connected with more generic concepts in the social sciences. A theory may also begin deductively after observing the practice of investors. It begins with the most generic concepts and then moves logically toward middle-range concepts that help explain investment activity. Middle-range concepts then yield hypotheses about investment activity that can be tested in the field.

   We are formulating a theoretical framework about the development of social organization. The framework begins in this chapter and continues in the remainder of the book in terms of premises and propositions about the domain of social development. We create our framework in part from sociological thought and in part from the data we have discussed on current investment practices. Our aim is to offer a conceptual framework for research on social criteria for investment.

2. This analytical priority is most clear in Talcott Parsons and Neil Smelser, *Economy Society: A Study in the Integration of Economic and Social Theory* (Glencoe, Ill.: Free Press, 1956).

3. The problem of economics as a field separate from the study of society and its values is addressed most adroitly by John Kenneth Galbraith, *Economics and the Public Purpose* (Boston: Houghton Mifflin, 1973).

4. An excellent review of theoretical currents in economics and the problem of the social factor is found in Ben Seligman, *Main Currents in Modern Economics* (New York: Free Press, 1962).

5. This close interdependency of economy and society is discussed in Neil Smelser, *The Sociology of Economic Life* (Englewood Cliffs, N. J.: Prentice-Hall, 1963).

6. See Lionel Robbins, *On the Nature and Significance of Economic Science* (London: Macmillan, 1935), p. 16; also Paul Samuelson, *Economics*, 8th edn (New York: McGraw-Hill, 1970), p. 13.

7. Severyn T. Bruyn, *The Social Economy* (New York: Wiley Interscience, 1977); also "Social Economy: A Note on Its Theoretical Foundations," *Review of Social Economy* 39 (April 1981), 181ff.

8. A paper by Herbert Spencer, "The Developmental Hypothesis," dating from 1852, seven years before Darwin's *Origin of Species*, advocated a theory of progressive evolution that was later incorporated into his work on the historical development of society; see Lewis Coser, *Masters of Sociological Thought* (New York: Harcourt Brace Jovanovich, 1977), p. 104; and Petr Kropotkin, *Mutual Aid: A Factor of Evolution* (Boston: Extending Horizons Books, n.d.; first published 1888).

9. A conceptual framework for conducting research into creative conflict is found in Severyn T. Bruyn and Paula Rayman, eds., *Nonviolent Action and Social Change* (N.Y.: Irvington, 1981), ch. 1.

10. Creative conflict does not show itself through the agency of investors who emphasize only one side of the opposition. Investors who stay on one side simply prolong the resolution of problems usually related to the class structure. Such investors can be typified as "realists" or "idealists."

We have noted that "realists" today argue against applying social criteria because they reduce profit returns, the only acceptable motive for allocating capital. Investing capital to replace slums with new cooperative housing means that one will lose one's money in a poor market. It is better to invest in high technology, where the profits are better. At the other extreme are "idealists," who argue that profit is unethical; the real aim of investment should not be profit returns but the promotion of human development. Placing one's capital into the construction of gambling casinos or even into high tech firms simply takes it away from the rehabilitation of slums. The idealists are willing to lose money on slum rehabilitation so as to correct the injustice slums inflict. The underlying problem of the class structure is active behind both investment decisions. In the case of "realists," the conflict is not visible until much later when the costs of crime, welfare, and riots become known. In the case of "idealists," the consequences are not seen until losing the investment money leads everyone into poverty. The deeper dialectic continues to operate in both extremes. The costs are higher and the pain is greater in the long run. In principle, social investors work at the heart of the problem by combining social and economic factors in developing community resources. They are not on one side or the other, they are on both sides. They are promoting a creative opposition.

11. Thomas J. Peters and Robert H. Waterman, Jr, *In Search of Excellence* (New York: Harper & Row, 1982). See also William Abernathy, Kim Clark, and Alan Kantrow, *Industrial Renaissance* (New York: Basic Books, 1983).

12. William Ouchi, *Theory Z* (New York: Avon Books, 1982). See also Richard Pascale and Anthony Athos, *The Art of Japanese Management* (New York: Simon & Schuster, 1981).

13. George Webster, *The Law of Associations* (Washington, D.C.: American Society of Association Executives, 1971). When the business system does not develop its own forms of equity, the federal government steps in to provide it through regulatory commissions and bureaus, interventions that supply the needed "power balance." Agencies such as the Federal Reserve Board and the Federal Housing Authority help regulate aggregate demand; the Bureau of Mines, the Interstate Oil Compact, and the Department of Agriculture equalize supply and demand; the Interstate Commerce Commission, the Civil Aeronautics Board, and the Federal Power Commission regulate economic activities to protect business from its own competition.

14. Max Weber, *Economy and Society*, ed. Guenther Roth and Claus Wittich (New York: Bedminster Press, 1968), pp. 49–50.

15. Peters and Waterman, *In Search of Excellence*, pp. 216ff. See "Who's Excellent Now?" *Business Week*, 5 November 1985, 76ff.

16. Rosabeth Kanter, *The Change Masters* (New York: Simon & Schuster, 1983), pp. 79–82, 146–8. Kanter describes the difficult transition of employees moving from a vertical system of authority to a horizontal system based on lateral communication. For example, "Ed Quiller," a district sales manager at a company called Med Systems, operated effectively under a vertical command system but ran into trouble adjusting to a matrix system of management. As district manager Quiller had reported to the regional manager, who reported to the national sales manager, who reported to the divisional marketing manager, who reported to the general manager. The structure became overloaded and unresponsive as technical sophistication increased among employees, and in the overhaul to a matrix system, Quiller was placed in a status equal to that of service manager formerly under his command. It appeared to Quiller that he had lost authority, and this affected his sense of authority and self-confidence. When other former subordinates came into positions parallel to his, Quiller resisted losing the authority derived from his earlier position and did not perform well and his job ratings went down. It took time for him to adjust to the horizontal system, but he finally began to see the benefits in cooperating across sales and service boundaries and "got on board." He became his old self, and his performance returned to its normal high. The case illustrates the subtle connection among principles of social governance. The change from a command system

caused Quiller to lose independence and self-confidence temporarily, and required that he develop a new set of skills and attitudes so as to participate in more equitable relationships. The greater mutuality in corporate governance meant anxiety and a slowdown in Quiller's work, but he dropped his former dictatorial style as he learned to work collaboratively with his new colleagues.

17. David Montgomery, *Workers' Control in America* (London: Cambridge University Press, 1981); John Naisbett, *Megatrends* (New York: Warner Books, 1982), p. 187.

18. The correct translation of *Herrschaft* has scholars puzzled. Nicholas Timascheff translated the word as "imperative control"; Talcott Parsons preferred the term *leadership* but used the term *authority* for more specific purposes; Guenther Roth used the term *domination*. Roth concludes that it is best interpreted as a form of rulership, a structure of superordination and subordination, a system of rulers and the ruled; *Herrschaft* is a combination of "legitimacy" and force used in obtaining obedience. The combination of meanings led Roth to translate the word as *domination* while acknowledging its ambiguity. The meaning of *authority* in this sense, however, does not easily fit the charismatic types depicted by Weber himself. It is difficult to interpret the authority of Buddha or Christ or artists like Beethoven as simply based on force. Similarly, the force exhibited in a command bureaucracy is qualitatively different from the force exhibited in participative management and worker ownership. Guenther Roth, ed., *Economy and Society* (New York: Bedminster Press, 1968).

19. Keith Bradley and Alan Gelb, *Worker Capitalism and the New Industrial Relations* (Cambridge: MIT Press, 1983), pp. 102–3. An evaluation of ESOPs can be found in "ESOPs: Really a Revolution?", *Business Week*, 15 April 1985, 94ff.

20. Connections are sought in Bengt Abrahamsson, "On Form and Function in Organizational Theory," *Organizational Studies* 6, no. 1, (1985), 39–53; John Simmons and William Mares, *Working Together* (New York: Knopf, 1983).

21. The governance of the self-managed firm is discussed in Paul Bernstein, *Workplace Democratization: Its Internal Dynamics* (Kent, Ohio: Kent State University Press, 1976; New Brunswick, N.J.: Transaction Books, 1980); Frank Lindenfeld and Joyce Rothchild-Whitt, eds., *Workplace Democracy and Social Change* (Boston: Porter Sargent, 1982).

22. The evidence for increasing the responsibility of workshops and departments as a basis for enhancing corporate self-governance is currently being studied under different names, including "quality of working life" and "enterprise self-management." See Louis F. Davis, Albert B. Cherns and Associates, *The Quality of Working Life: Problems, Prospects, and the State of the Art* (New York: Free Press, 1975); Jaroslav Vanek, *The Participatory Economy* (Ithaca: Cornell University Press, 1971); Jaroslav Vanek, ed., *Self-Management* (New York: Penguin, 1975); Arnold Tannenbaum et al., *Hierarchy in Organizations* (London: Jossey-Bass, 1974).

Research so far demonstrates investing with these social criteria in mind combines with the profit-making interests of investors. E. H. Bowman, "Corporate

Social Responsibility and the Investor," *Journal of Contemporary Business*, Winter 1973, 21–43; E. H. Bowman and M. Haire, "A Strategic Posture toward Corporate Social Responsibility," *California Management Review*, Winter 1975, 49–58. Ritchie Lowry's studies are reported in the newsletter *Good Money* (Center for Economic Revitalization, Box 363, Worcester, Vt.) See also Ritchie Lowry, *A Good Money Investor Handbook* (Center for Economic Revitalization).

23. Management theories can be seen as conceptual attempts to overcome the traits of command governance in large-scale corporations: the steep hierarchical structure versus the flattened structure, vertical versus horizontal communication, formal versus informal distribution of tasks. See Douglas McGregor, *The Human Side of Enterprise* (New York: McGraw-Hill, 1960); Chris Argyris, *Integrating the Individual and the Organization* (New York: Wiley, 1964); Erik Rhenman, *Industrial Democracy and Industrial Management* (London: Tavistock, 1968). Mintzberg's recent concept of "Adhocracy" is in the same tradition, denoting an innovative organization designed to avoid "sharp divisions of labor, extensive unit of differentiation, highly formalized behavior, and an emphasis on planning and control systems." Henry Mintzberg, *The Structuring of Organizations* (Englewood Cliffs, N. J.: Prentice-Hall, 1979).

24. Severyn T. Bruyn, "The Community Self-Study: Worker Self-Management versus The New Class," *Review of Social Economy*, March 1984. See also Billy B. Joiner, "Searching for Collaborative Inquiry: The Evolution of Action Research," Ed. D. dissertation, Harvard University, 1983.

25. Anthony F. Buono and Lawrence T. Nichols, *Corporate Policy Values, and Social Responsibility* (New York: Praeger, 1985).

26. The concept of "stakeholders" is discussed in Bengt Abrahamsson, *Bureaucracy or Participation* (Beverly Hills: Sage Publications, 1977). See also R. Edward Freeman and David L. Reed, "Perspective on Corporate Governance," *California Management Review* 25, no. 3 (Spring 1983), 88–106.

27. The first count is from data of the U.S. Department of Commerce; the second, from Udo Staber and Howard Aldrich, "Trade Association Stability and Public Policy," ch. 10 in *Organizational Theory and Public Policy*, ed. Richard Hall and Robert Quinn, Beverly Hills: Sage Publications, 1984.

28. Kenneth Hance, *Association Management* (Washington, D.C.: U.S. Chamber of Commerce, 1958).

29. George P. Lamb and Sumner S. Kettele, *Trade Association Law and Practice* (Boston: Little, Brown, 1956); Chamber of Commerce of the United States, *Association Activities* (revised 1958).

30. Margaret Fisk, ed., *Encyclopedia of Associations*, 10th edn, vol. 1, *National Organizations of the U.S.* (Detroit: Gale Research Co., 1976); Roy Foltz, "Why You Must Talk Up to Employees," *Textile World*, November 1975, 153–54.

31. Joel R. Evans, *Consumerism in the United States* (New York: Praeger, 1980), p. 353.

32. "ITC to Seek Protection for Footwear Industry," *Boston Globe*, 23 May 1985, 57.

33. David Ellerman, *The Union as the Legitimate Opposition in an Industrial Democracy* (Industrial Cooperative Association, 249 Elm Street, Somerville, Mass., 02144).

34. William Foote Whyte, Tove Hellend Hammer, Christopher Meek, Reed Nelson, and Robert Stern, *Worker Participation and Ownership* (Ithaca, New York: ILR Press, Cornell University, 1983).

35. Derek Jones and Jan Svejnar, eds., *Participatory and Self-Managed Firms* (Lexington, Mass.: Lexington Books, 1982).

36. Milton Friedman, "A Friedman Doctrine – The Social Responsibility is to Increase its Profits," *New York Times Magazine*, 13 September 1970, 126; see Ami L. Domini and Peter D. Kinder, *Ethical Investing* (Reading, Mass.: Addison-Wesley, 1984), pp. 194–5.

37. Milton Friedman and Rose Friedman, *Free to Choose* (New York: Harcourt Brace Jovanovich, 1980), p. 224; see also Domini and Kinder, *Ethical Investing*.

38. Joel A. Devine, "State and State Expenditure: Determinants of Social Investment and Social Consumption Spending in the Post-War United States," *American Sociological Review* 50 (April 1985), 150–65. The original theorizing on this subject can be found in James O'Connor, *The Fiscal Crisis of the State* (New York: St Martin's, Press, 1973). Note that the term *social consumption* is used to refer to public spending on education, health, housing, and urban renewal. Other relevant Marxist writings on state capitalism include Nicos Poulantzas, *Classes in Contemporary Capitalism* (London: New Left Books, 1975); Theda Skocpol, "Political Response to Capitalist Crisis: Neomarxist Theories of the State and the Case of the New Deal," *Politics and Society* 10 (1980), 155–201; Claus Offe, "Advanced Capitalism and the Welfare State," *Politics and Society* 1 (1972), 479–88.

39. Suzanne Strickland studied a welfare system in Halifax, Nova Scotia, in which professional social workers were upset about the effect of the public dole on recipients and asked higher administrators for funds to support self-managed enterprises for their clients. This request was granted, and the welfare recipients were then invited to participate in organizing business enterprises with the capital supplied by the welfare administration. They were successful in organizing numerous small businesses and, off welfare, became employees and owners of the businesses. Suzanne Strickland, *HRD Enterprises Limited: A Case Study in Productive Alternatives for Public Transfer Payments* (Cambridge, Mass.: Institute for New Enterprise Development, 1982).

40. The task of government officials in this case is to avoid privatizing as a method for "busting" municipal unions. Officials can take responsibility for encouraging the development of self-managed firms in the private sector and help negotiate a role for unions in the new firms. Unions can also take the leadership in this process of privatization. Martin Tolchin, "More Cities Paying Industry to Provide Public Services," *New York Times*, 28 May 1985, pp. A1, D17.

41. Our use of the term *nonstatist* refers to an economy not controlled directly by the government. Its antinomy, *statist*, refers to an economy strongly regulated and controlled by the government. These terms are "sensitizing concepts" in

the same sense as *primary group* or *mores*. They point to a dimension of society that is significant to social development but are not defined for our purposes in more operational or ideal-typical terms.

Our use of the term *statist* has a different empirical reference than Bronko Horvat's use of *etatist*. The terms *statist* and *etatist* have much in common but also differ in that our primary reference is to a capitalist society, and Horvat's primary reference is to a socialist society. The two terms, then, express different connotations at times even though they are similar in many respects.

Horvat describes a society as *etatist* when the ruling strata profess the basic tenets of traditional socialist ideology but then "revise the socialist approach" in regard to the role of the state. He documents how socialists have traditionally viewed the state as an instrument of repression consisting of "government over people," to be replaced by the "administration of things," and proposed that the "proletariat must overthrow the state" and that the state should "wither away" so that society becomes based on "communes" and "associations." Horvat then asserts that in an *etatist* society "all these ideas are replaced by a totally opposite ideology in which a strong, centralized, authoritarian state becomes the main pivot of society." His primary reference is to the Soviet Union. Bronko Horvat, *The Political Economy of Socialism* (New York: M. E. Sharpe, 1982), p. 21.

We are not using the term *statist* in the same pejorative manner that Horvat uses *etatist*. We do use *statist* to designate an excessiveness in state control over the economy, but primarily in reference to the idea of a continuum of control and then only as one variable of social development. The statist variable (government control over the economy) is just one factor in evaluating stages of social development, and that one factor is evaluated in turn by degrees of government decentralization and democracy. We would not claim generically, therefore, that the capitalist state represents a higher stage of development than the socialist state simply because it may have less government control over the economy. The conditions of exploitation and domination can be strong in societies claiming to be capitalist as well as socialist. The structure of a capitalist economy has its own capacity to exploit people beyond the confines of the state. A definitive theory of the state is needed to differentiate more exactly the position of government in determining a society's stage of development.

42. Richard Nielson, "Strategic Piggy-Backing: A Self-Subsidization Strategy for Nonprofit Institutions," *Sloan Management Review* 23 (Summer 1982), 65–9.

43. European conferences and journals have been exploring the question of how profit enterprises can function in the public interest and how a "public corporation" can be structured outside the state sector. W. Streeck, "Private Organizations as Agents of Public Policy" (paper prepared for a conference of the European Group for Organization Studies, EGOS), *EGOS News*, April 1984. See also articles in *Annals of Public and Cooperative Economy* (Editorial Offices: 45 quai de Rome, 4000 Liege, Belgium); Praxy Fernandes and Pavle Sicherl, eds., *Seeking the Personality of Public Enterprise: An Enquiry into the Concept, Definition, and Classification of Public Enterprise* (papers prepared

for Expert Group Meeting, International Center for Public Enterprises in Developing Countries), held in Tangier, Morocco, 15–19 December 1980, and Ljubljana, Yugoslavia, 1981.

44. Harold L. Johnson, *Disclosure of Corporate Social Performance* (New York: Praeger, 1979).
45. Bruyn, *The Social Economy*, pp. 51ff., 108ff.

4 Social investment in business corporations

1. Adolf Berle and Gardiner Means, *The Modern Corporation and Private Property* (New York: Harcourt, Brace & Jovanovich, 1968).
2. For a discussion of this case and the wider changes in corporate behavior, see Clarence C. Walton, *Corporate Social Responsibilities* (Belmont, Calif.: Wadsworth, 1968).
3. Andreas Papandreou, "Some Basic Problems in the Theory of the Firm," in *A Survey of Contemporary Economics*, vol. 2, ed. B. F. Haley (Homewood, Ill.: Irvin, 1952), p. 208.
4. Profit maximization became dismissed as a nonoperational concept. See J. Feldman and H. E. Kanter, "Organizational Decision-Making," in *Handbook of Organization*, ed. J. G. March (Chicago: Rand-McNally, 1965). B. C. Miller and F. A. Schull, "The Prediction of Administrative Role Conflict Resolutions," *Administrative Science Quarterly*, September 1962), 143–60, found that managers depend upon the needs of departments at the expense of optimal profits.
5. R. N. Anthony, "The Trouble with Profit Maximization," *Harvard Business Review* (November–December 1960), 126–34.
6. Herbert Simon, "On the Concept of Organizational Goal," *Administrative Science Quarterly* (1964), 1–22. Other writers had suggested earlier that the firm maximized different goals. See O. E. Williamson, "A Model of Rational Managerial Behavior," in *A Behavioral Theory of the Firm*, ed. R. M. Cyert and J. G. March (Englewood Cliffs, N.J.: Prentice-Hall, 1963), pp. 237–52.
7. R. M. Cyert and J. G. March, *A Behavioral Theory of the Firm* (Englewood Cliffs, N.J.: Prentice-Hall, 1963).
8. John Simmons and William Mares, *Working Together* (New York: Knopf, 1983), pp. 49–79.
9. David Jenkins, *Job Power* (New York: Doubleday, 1973).
10. Rogene A. Bucholz, *Business Environment and Public Policy* (Englewood Cliffs, N.J.: Prentice-Hall, 1982).
11. "Assessing ESOP's" (New York: Research Institute of America, 1979); *Employee Ownership: Report to the Economic Development Administration of the Department of Commerce*, Project 99–6–09433 (Ann Arbor: Survey Research Center, Institute for Social Research, University of Michigan, 1978). For the latest information on these integrative trends, see Corey Rosen, Director National Center for Employee Ownership, Washington, D.C.
12. Thomas R. Marsh and Dale E. McAllister, "Esop's Tables: A Survey of Companies with Employee Stock Ownership Plans," *Journal of Corporation Law* (Spring 1981), 619–20. See also House Select Committee on Small Busi-

ness, "The Role of the Federal Government and Employee Ownership of Business" (Washington, D.C.: Government Printing Office, 1979).

13. L. W. Porter and E. E. Lawler III, "Properties of Organizational Structure in Relation to Job Attitudes and Job Behavior," *Psychological Bulletin* 64 (1965), 1; J. Zupanov and A. S. Tannenbaum, "The Distribution of Control in Some Yugoslav Industrial Organizations as Perceived by Members," in *Control in Organizations*, ed. A. S. Tannenbaum (New York: McGraw-Hill, 1968).

14. Robert Blauner, "Work Satisfaction and Industrial Trends in Modern Society," in *Labor and Trade Unionism*, eds. W. Galenson and S. M. Lipset (New York: Wiley, 1960).

15. Rensis Likert, *New Patterns of Management* (New York: McGraw-Hill, 1961); Arnold Tannenbaum, *Social Psychology of the Work Organization* (Belmont, Calif.: Brooks/Cole, 1966).

16. S. Kasl and J. R. French, "The Effects of Occupational Status on Physical and Mental Health," *Journal of Social Issues* (1962), 3.

17. Chris Argyris, *Personality and Organization* (New York; Harper, 1957).

18. A significant study of the positive effects of increasing the degree of occupational self-direction on conception of the "self" among workers can be found in Melvin L. Kohn, *Class and Conformity: A Study in Values* (Homewood, Ill.: Dorsey Press, 1969). A basis for studying the effects of raising the level of worker authority in firms can be found in Severyn T. Bruyn and Litza Nicolaou-Smokovitus, "A Theoretical Framework for Studying Worker Participation: The Psychological Contract," *Review of Social Economy* 37 (April 1979).

19. Karl Frieden, *Workplace Democracy and Productivity* (Washington, D.C.: National Center for Economic Alternatives, 1980).

20. David Ellerman, "The Question of Legal Structure," and "What Is a Cooperative?" (Somerville, Mass.: Industrial Cooperative Association, 248 Elm St.; n.d.). For legal details, see David Ellerman and Peter Pitegoff, "The Democratic Corporation," *Review of Law and Social Change* (New York University), forthcoming. One argument here is that "profit" should be interpreted as a source of capital to the firm rather than a "use." Although profit can be used to buy machinery, pay dividends, etc., it does not necessarily exist as liquid cash. Therefore, it is helpful to think of the balance sheet as made up of a "right side," representing the sources of capital (i.e., outside debt financing, outside equity financing, and retained earnings from past operations); and a "left side," representing the uses (i.e. applications of capital in cash, inventory, accounts receivable, machinery, buildings, and land). The two sides of the ledger should then balance. See also Robert Oakeshott, *The Case for Worker Coops* (London: Routledge & Kegan Paul, 1978).

21. Paul Bernstein, *Workplace Democratization* (Kent, Ohio: Kent State University Press, 1976; New Brunswick, N.J.: Transaction Books, 1980); William P. Anthony, *Participatory Management* (Reading, Mass.: Addison-Wesley, 1978); Henk Thomas and Chris Logan, *Mondragon: An Economic Analysis* (London: Allen & Unwin, 1982).

22. Lyman D. Ketchum, "A Case Study of Diffusion," in *The Quality of Working Life*, Vol. 2, ed. Louis E. Davis, Albert B. Cherns and Associates (New York: Free Press, 1975).

23. Severyn T. Bruyn, "On Becoming a Democratically Managed Firm," *The Social Report*, Vol. III, Program in Social Economy and Social Policy, No. 2, June 1983, Boston College.
24. Edwin Mansfield, *The Economics of Technological Change* (New York: Norton, 1968):
25. Jerald Hage and Michael Aiken, "Program Change and Organizational Properties: A Comparative Analysis," *American Journal of Sociology*, 72 (1973), 503–99.
26. Empirical studies suggest that when organizations grow by innovation their rate of innovation also increases, but that there is a limit. The number of patents secured by large firms in the United States is not proportionately greater than that secured by smaller ones, and their quality is on the whole lower. There are threshold effects for innovation and monopoly power. Modest size and power are associated with more innovation than are giant size and high monopoly power – as assessed by industry concentration. See Frederic Scherer, *Industrial Market Structure and Industrial Performance* (Chicago: Rand McNally, 1970).
27. Bruyn, "On Becoming a Democratically Managed Firm," pp. 7–9; see also Judith Blanton and Sam Alley, *Program Development: A Manual for Organizational Self-Study*, NIMH Contract No. 42–72–143, August 1975.
28. John Child and Alfred Keiser, "Development of Organizations Over Time," in *Handbook of Organizational Design*, ed. Paul Nystrom and William Starbuch (New York: Oxford University Press, 1981). Business consultants suggest that the treatment for these problems includes increasing spans of control and a new delegation of responsibility for employees. Management should redirect its attention from close supervision and information processing with the focus on how people do their jobs toward an emphasis on overall results. Instead of utilizing a Taylor-like system of computer controls to measure individual work, it is wiser to concentrate on final output and have it discussed by all employees. Group discussions can become the source for change without having to tighten bureaucratic controls from top management.
29. Fred Blum, *Work and Community: The Scott Bader Commonwealth and the Quest for a New Social Order* (London: Routledge & Kegan Paul, 1968).
30. Thomas and Logan, *Mondragon*.

5 Social investment in industry: a new social policy

1. Lester Thurow, "Revitalizing American industry: Managing in a Competitive World," *California Management Review*, 27 (Fall 1984); also *Zero Sum Society* (New York: Basic Books, 1980). Thurow's solutions are directed toward innovations in management. Our argument is that innovations also need to be made in the relationship among corporations and other associations in the industry.
2. Robert Reich, "The Next American Frontier," *Atlantic Monthly* (March 1983), 43.
3. Ralph Nader, Mark Green, and Joel Seligman, *Taming the Giant Corporation* (New York: Norton, 1976); Rogene Bucholz, *Business Environment and Public Policy* (Englewood Cliffs, N.J.: Prentice-Hall, 1982).
4. "Making Our Money Work for Us" (editorial), *Labor and Investments* (AFL-CIO Industrial Union Department, n.d.), p. 4.

5. Ibid., p. 1.
6. Paul Lawrence and Davis Dyer, *Renewing American Industry* (New York: Free Press, 1983), p. 10.
7. George Gilder, *Wealth and Poverty* (New York: Bantam Books, 1981), pp. 62–3.
8. Reich, "The Next American Frontier," p. 52; see also Robert Reich, *The Next American Frontier* (New York: Times Books, 1983).
9. Samuel Bowles, David Gordon, and Thomas Weiskopf, *Beyond the Wasteland: A Democratic Alternative to Economic Decline* (New York: Anchor Press, 1984).
10. There is no solid proof that a greater degree of efficiency is produced in the private economy. But even if a state economy could be shown to be more efficient, Gilder would argue for a private sector on other, noneconomic grounds; one would be freedom for the individual and for private initiative. Again, these are issues of sociology and politics rather than finance and economics.

    In the last analysis, these studies lead to a debate over the social order of industry. The issues involve social governance at every level of its organization. At the other "progressive" end of the continuum, a sociological perspective is equally discernible.
11. See Barry Bluestone and Bennett Harrison, *The Deindustrialization of America* (New York: Basic Books, 1982).
12. The research of Bowles et al., *Beyond the Wasteland*, demonstrates most persuasively that a causal relationship exists between low productivity and the adversarial structure of labor and management. They argue for a new social contract that includes labor in the governance of corporations. Many others have also stressed a causal connection between the adversariness and poor productivity. The studies noted here of Reich, and Lawrence and Davis, argue that increasing labor participation in corporate governance is an important route to increased productivity. The same issue has been behind the studies of Japanese management; see William Ouchi, *Theory Z* (Reading, Mass.: Addison-Wesley, 1981). Robert Cole, *Work Mobility and Participation* (Berkeley: University of California Press, 1979), estimated that one out of eight workers in Japan are participating in quality circles, which makes a difference in productivity. Ezra Vogel, *Japan as Number 1* (New York: Harper & Row, 1979), p. 151, pointed out how featherbedding and labor's inflexible insistence on work rules contrast with Japanese styles of participatory management; he says low productivity in the U.S. is due partly to workers' fear of losing their jobs in contrast with Japanese workers, who eagerly seek technological change because they have a guarantee of permanent employment and a high level of participation in corporate governance. Such policies applied in the U.S. would of course radically change the structure of labor–management relations. William Abernathy, in William J. Abernathy, Kim B. Clark, and Alan M. Kantrow, *Industrial Renaissance* (New York: Basic Books, 1983), concludes that Japan's edge in labor productivity is not due to a substitution of capital for labor. For example, in the auto industry, "the unpleasant truth is that Japanese producers use less capital to produce a vehicle than do their U.S. competitors and can sus-

tain a given volume of production with much lower levels of investment," (p. 62).

13. For example, Carl A. Gerstacker, chairman of the Dow Chemical Company, argues that a new concept of "corporate democracy" must be introduced into industry. "The adversary system of labor vs. management has about run its course. As an adversary system it is often destructive rather than constructive ... I would suggest that because of the scope, complexity, and potential benefit to be accrued a special government commission might fruitfully explore the vast possibilities of this subject. And I would suggest that farsighted unionists themselves ought to take the lead in fermenting the new and bloodless revolution that we need, and that I firmly believe will take place." (Address, White House Conference on the Industrial World Ahead: A Look at Business in the 1990s, Washington D.C., February 1972.)

Curt Tausky, a well-known social scientist in the field of industrial relations, concludes: "It is doubtful, however, that we can collectively continue to afford the results of antagonistic relations – sluggish or nonexistent productivity increases accompanied by wage and price boosts. This is not merely gloomy speculation. There are, unfortunately, solid reasons for suggesting that collaboration among all parties to raise productivity is now a necessity." (*Work and Society* (Itasca, Ill.: F. E. Peacock, 1984), pp. 147–8.) See also Martin Weitzman, *The Share Economy* (Cambridge: Harvard University Press, 1985).

14. Paul Bernstein, *Workplace Democracy* (Kent, Ohio: Kent State University Press, 1976; New Brunswick, N.J.: Transaction Books, 1980); Louis E. Davis et al., *The Quality of Working Life*, vols. 1, 2 (New York: Free Press, 1975); David Jenkins, *Job Power* (New York, Doubleday, 1973); Gerry Hunnius et al., *Workers' Control* (New York: Random House, 1973); B. Pettman, *Industrial Democracy: A Selected Bibliography* (New York: State Mutual Books, 1978).

15. Paul Blumberg, *Industrial Democracy* (New York: Schocken, 1969); Karl Frieden, *Workplace Democracy and Productivity* (Washington, D.C.: National Center for Economic Alternatives, 1980). These studies do not evaluate the Hawthorne effect, which suggests that the special attention given to workers in the studies is an important factor in bringing positive results. See also: Alvin Gouldner, *Industrial Patterns of Bureaucracy* (Glencoe, Ill.: Free Press, 1954).

16. Stephen Hill, *Competition and Control at Work: The New Industrial Sociology* (Cambridge: MIT Press, 1981).

17. The evidence for some of the following arguments come from examples of successful self-managed firms and therefore must be taken with caution until more evidence is forthcoming for new firms developing on a large scale. See Chris Mackin *Strategies for Local Ownership and Control: A Policy Analysis,* (Somerville, Mass.: Industrial Cooperative Association, 58 Day Street, Suite 200, Somerville, Mass., 02144); Carole Pateman, *Participation and Democratic Theory,* (Cambridge: University Press, 1970); Donald V. Nightingale, *Workplace Democracy: An Inquiry into Employee Participation in Canadian Work Organizations* (Toronto: University of Toronto Press, 1982); Corey Rosen, *Employee Ownership in America* (Lexington, Mass.: Lexington Books, 1986).

18. For an evaluation of studies behind these arguments, see Severyn T. Bruyn, "Studies Guiding Legislation for Self-Management," unpublished paper, 1986. For studies on the economics of self-managed firms, see Frank Stephen, *The Performance of Labor-Managed Firms* (N.Y.: St Martin's Press, 1982).

19. To keep abreast of new research on self-managed firms, see annual volumes of the *International Yearbook of Organizational Democracy*, (N.Y.: Wiley).

20. Studies show a significant reduction in the number of working days lost in countries that include labor on the boards of directors of corporations. For example, the number of working days lost per 1,000 employees due to strikes for the period 1964–73 in the United States averaged 1,247; in Britain, 633; in France, 277 – but in countries in which labor shared authority at top levels of corporate governance, the hours lost were significantly lower; in Sweden and West Germany, the hours averaged 43 in this same period. L. Forseback, *Industrial Relations and Employment in Sweden* (Stockholm: Swedish Institute, 1976), p. 67. Until the mid thirties, Sweden had one of the highest rates of strikes among all the developed countries. After the Social Democratic government assumed power in 1932, new levels of labor participation began to be encouraged and legalized. Sweden then came to rank lowest in the frequency of industrial disputes. W. Korpi, *The Working Class in Welfare Capitalism* (London: Routledge & Kegan Paul, 1978), pp. 95–6.

When labor is trained and prepared to participate significantly at top levels of governance in corporations, productivity is increased and labor unrest is reduced significantly. For this reason, the European Economic Community has taken West Germany as a model for other nations to follow. For comparative studies on labor participation in higher management, see Charles D. King and Mark Van De Vall, *Models of Industrial Democracy* (New York: Mouton, 1978); David Jenkins, *Industrial Democracy in Europe* (Geneva: Business International, 1974).

21. John Simmons and William Mares, *Working Together* (New York: Knopf, 1983), ch. 13, "Middle Managers in the Middle."

22. William F. Whyte et al., *Worker Participation and Ownership* (Ithaca N.Y.: IBP Press, 1983); Gail Sokoloff, "The Creation of an Employee Owned Firm: A Case Study of Hyatt Clark Industries," Monograph 3, Comparative Worker Ownership Study Group, Harvard University, 1982.

23. Keith Bradley, *Worker Capitalism: The New Industrial Relations* (Cambridge: MIT Press, 1983).

24. The philosophy underlying these current changes is discussed in Ronald Mason, *Participation and Workplace Democracy* (Carbondale: Southern Illinois University Press, 1982). The economics of the change are discussed in Jaroslav Vanek, *The Participatory Economy* (Ithaca: Cornell University Press, 1971).

25. Robert Reinhold, "Stanford and Industry Forge New Research Link," *New York Times*, 10 February 1984, A22.

26. Lawrence J. White, "Clearing the Legal Path to Cooperative Research," *Technology Review* 88 (July 1985), 38ff. The National Cooperative Research Act was passed by Congress in 1984 to permit firms in a collective-research venture to register with the Antitrust Division and the Federal Trade Commission as a

gesture of good intent, thus protecting themselves against the treble damages that might be won by private plaintiffs in antitrust suits. It also allows them to be heard in court on the "rule of reason." This means that the court must weigh the public benefits of the cooperative research against its possible anticompetitive effects.

27. In 1941 Philip Murray of the CIO introduced the Industry Council Plan. It had considerable support from Catholic leaders; Bishop Francis J. Haas and Bishop Karl Alter called for "industry councils." My thanks to John Cort for bringing this to my attention; see his article in *The Commonweal*, 19 March 1948.

28. International Association of Machinists and Aerospace Workers (Grand Lodge Heights, 1300 Connecticut Avenue, N.W., Washington, D.C.), *Let's Rebuild America* (1983), pp. 134ff.

29. Max Weber, *Economy and Society*, ed. Guenther Roth and Claus Wittich (Bedminster Press, 1968), p. 224.

30. Peter Drucker, *Management* (New York: Harper & Row, 1973), ch. 46. "Result Focused Design: Federal and Simulated Decentralization."

31. Will C. Conrad, Kathleen Wilson, and Dale Wilson, *The Milwaukee Journal* (Madison: University of Wisconsin Press, 1964); also "Partners in Ownership" (published periodically by the Journal Company).

32. The concept of decentralizing the large corporation is discussed in Bruyn, *The Social Economy*.

33. Wolfgang Friedman and George Kalmanoff, *Joint International Business Ventures* (New York: Columbia University Press, 1961). The bourgeois democratization of MNCs continues today through joint ventures, and each step is surrounded by practical politics and economics. The internationalization of the auto industry is a case in point. The mix of ownership in production and sales of U.S. and Japanese automakers is partly due to the power of Japan's efficient production playing against the threat of exclusion from the U.S. market by protective tariffs. See "The All-American Car Is Fading," *Business Week*, 12 March 1984, pp. 88ff.

34. J. R. Craig, *Multinational Cooperatives* (Saskatchewan: Western Producer Prairie Books, 1976).

35. The average *corporate* pension fund experienced an annual return of 3.9 per cent on its stock investments for the period 1970–9. The stock market as a whole, measured by Standard and Poor's 500, showed an average annual return of 5.9 per cent. This same study showed that for the period 1965–79, corporate pension funds had a total annual return on all investments averaging 4.1 per cent; inflation for that period averaged 6.2 per cent. AFL-CIO, Industrial Union Department (1980) *Pensions and Investment Age*, 17 August 1981.

36. This is a perfect example of how social policies might have turned the industry around. Labor and management could have collaborated to beat their outside competitors by (1) cooperating to reduce wages and salaries during the period of crisis; (2) developing a plan for labor participation in corporate governance as a management concession for deep wage cuts; (3) decentralizing corporate operations to energize a new management at lower levels in collaboration with labor; (4) investing pension funds for new technology; and (5) establishing a

new relationship with engineering schools to keep ahead on the technology frontier. The first company to take the new steps toward labor-management in the steel industry was Weirton Steel, but the whole industry could move in these directions through studies and recommendations made by an industry council.

37. The Corporate Data Exchange (CDE) studied 142 large pension funds in 99 companies, and found that the funds were directed to either predominately non union companies, major violators of equal opportunity or occupational health and safety laws, or major investors in or lenders to South Africa.

38. For this reason and others, the California legislature appropriated $400,000 for the creation of the Pension Investment Unit to develop criteria for investment in the interest of the state.

39. Randy Barber, "Pension Funds in the United States: Issues of Investment and Control," *Economic and Industrial Democracy* (London: Sage Publication, 1982).

6 Social research on industrial policy

1. Supply-side economics is criticized in Samuel Bowles, David Gordon, and Thomas Weiskopf, *Beyond the Wasteland* (Garden City, N.Y.: Doubleday 1983), pp. 182–96. See also George Gilder, *Wealth and Poverty* (New York: Bantam Books, 1981).

2. W. Lloyd Warner, ed., *The Emergent Society* (New Haven: Yale University Press, 1967), pp. 349–407. In 1966, Warner surveyed more than 1,000 federations in such fields as transportation, communications, utilities, finance, insurance, real estate, agriculture, and manufacturing; over a third had annual incomes above $500,000 and staffs of more than thirty employees, and about 10 per cent had staffs of more than 100.

3. H. Assad, "The Political Role of Trade Associations," In *Interorganizational Relations*, ed. William Evan (Philadelphia: University of Pennsylvania Press), 1978, pp. 202–18.

4. William Scott, *The Management of Conflict* (Homewood, Ill.: Irwin, 1965); H. Vollmer, *Employee Rights and Employee Relationships* (Berkeley: University of California Press, 1960).

5. Ivan Hill, ed., *The Ethical Basis of Economic Freedom* (Chapel Hill, N.C.: American Viewpoint, 1976), pp. 353ff. Many other federations also have ethical codes, among them such diverse groups as the Direct Selling Association, the National Association of Broadcasters, the American Society of Newspaper Editors, and the Orthopedic Appliance and Limb Manufacturers (OALM). The codes are established in the interest of competing businesses and their customers. For example, the OALM has a set of mandatory rules covering such malpractices as "deception." This includes unwarranted guarantees that the product will fit, misuse of the term "custom made," and the word "free," as well as false advertising and invoicing.

6. Joel Evans, ed., *Consumerism in the United States: An Inter-Industry Analysis* (New York: Praeger, 1980), pp. 51–64.

7. Edgar Heermance, *Can Business Govern Itself?* (New York: Harper & Bros,

1933); George D. Webster, *The Law of Associations* (Washington, D.C.: American Society of Association Executives, 1971); Joseph Bradley, *The Role of Trade Associations and Professional Business Societies of America* (University Park: Pennsylvania State University Press, 1965).

8. Our theory places social self-governance as a primary goal in the context of economic goals. It assumes that the goal of high economic performance is essential though not sufficient to achieve self-governance. Put another way, if an industry is performing poorly, it becomes subject to government controls and loses its capacity for self-regulation. The government steps in through federal commissions, loans, and subsidies. The government must act because a dying industry can affect other industries adversely and bring about a general economic recession (dying industries can also be purchased by foreign corporations, which, again, leads to a loss of self-governance). Furthermore, if an industry dies, government must enter with welfare payments, public aid, unemployment compensation, and other subsidies to save communities from disaster. A dying industry increases government controls, and thus economic goals become essential to achieve self-governance.

9. Robert Coulson, *Labor Arbitration: What You Need to Know* (New York: American Arbitration Association, 1973). The researcher must be aware of the degree to which power groups change the performance scores. First, a rise in opposition groups like labor or consumers can cause an increase in the legal violations of an industry without any change in corporate behavior. It is simply that these opposition groups have raised the consciousness of the public by pointing to the "problems." Second, a change in the politics of Congress and the White House also affects performance without any change in corporate behavior. A strong Democratic Congress and White House administration, for example, may strengthen the staff of regulatory agencies, which, in turn, increases the number of violations in an industry. The performance score is thus adversely affected. Changes must be taken into account in data that are dependent upon politics and the rise of opposition groups to management.

10. Paul Lawrence and Davis Dyer, *Renewing American Industry* (New York: Free Press, 1983).

11. Robert Reich, *The Next American Frontier* (New York: Times Books, 1983).

12. Lawrence J. White, "Clearing the Path to Cooperative Research," *Technology Review* 8 (July 1985), 43.

13. There is always a contradiction in the conduct of these democratic federations. Trade unions, for example, have acted to improve the lot of labor and helped increase productivity in corporations and at the same time have caused production slowdowns and worsened conditions by supporting "dictators" in their union organization as well as by becoming deeply involved in crime and racketeering. Trade associations have reduced the need and cost of government by organizing activities in the public interest and have helped their member firms survive in a competitive environment; at the same time they have caused an increase in government regulations, and have acted against the public interest, and have dominated trade areas, keeping new firms from joining their association.

14. Karl Frieden, *Workplace Democracy and Productivity* (Washington, D.C.: National Center for Economic Alternatives, 1980). For a discussion of some of the problems in worker ownership, see William Foote Whyte, Tove Helland Hammer, Christopher Meek, Reed Nelson, and Robert Stern, *Worker Participation and Ownership* (Ithaca: ILR Press, Cornell University, 1983).
15. Severyn T. Bruyn, *The Social Economy* (New York: Wiley, 1977), p. 53. The concept of power is redefined as "the capacity to realize human values through social authority within the economic order of society."
16. The kinds of normative questions we need to ask in research on trade associations are becoming clear. The philosophic question is: How are competing firms and associations best able to express the values of democracy and justice in a competitive market? Other researchable social questions on self-regulation among trade associations:

    1. *Business Competitors*
       How can trade associations help competing firms
       solve their own problems and operate in the public interest?
       1. What are the best mechanisms for conflict resolution among members (e.g. trade tribunals, private arbitration, joint committees)?
       2. How can trade associations respect the autonomy of competing associations while advancing their own interests?
       3. How can associations encourage the entrance of new enterprises into their industry while their members still maximize profits?
       4. How can associations organize themselves better democratically and still operate effectively?
       5. How can associations improve communications and the basis for advancing research together without violating the law?

    2. *Buyer vs Sellers*
       How can effective working relationships be cultivated
       between federations of buyers and sellers in each industry –
       suppliers, manufacturers, wholesalers, distributors, retailers, customers?
       1. What are the best mechanisms for conflict resolution between associations of buyers and sellers?
       2. How are prices determined justly within the structure of competition and cooperation?
       3. How do buyers and sellers work together and still remain independent in their businesses?
       4. How do the federations act to reduce the need for regulatory agencies?
       5. How can competing associations be chartered with principles and by-laws leading them to operate in the public interest?

    The answers are vital to inform policies leading toward the development of a social sector in the economy. They are part of the rationale for building a research paradigm.
17. Ian Maitland, "The Limits of Business Self-Regulation," *California Management Review* 27 (Spring 1985), 132ff.
18. Steve Kelman, *Regulating America, Regulating Sweden*: *A Comparative Study*

of Occupational Safety and Health Policy (Cambridge, Mass.: MIT Press, 1981), quoted in Maitland, p. 141.

19. It is important to note that a concept of the public good (or public interest) is not synonymous with the concept of human values or a universal ethic. We are discussing human values only as they are implied in what we are describing as the social organization of business and only within a national context. We are saying that the public good is constituted in part by the social organization of business within the United States as a nation. We are not examining human ethics. It must be remembered that all nations compete with other nations in their own self-interest, as do businesses. Without stronger "transcending bodies" than exist now in the United Nations, or the General Agreement on Tariffs and Trade (GATT), world business will fall short of supplying the kind of organization yielding high ethical principles beyond national confines. The world system of commerce also includes the public corporations of socialist states, which compete capitalistically on the world scene. They are also involved in advancing their national self-interest. The tragic picture of big corporations producing nuclear weapons within this world system of competing nations should caution the reader to limit what we are discussing here in the concept of the public good.

20. Fred Bleakley, "A Trustee Takes on the Greenmailers," *New York Times*, 10 February 1985; "Council Heading for the Crossroads," *Pensions and Investment Age*, 25 November 1985; *Directory of Socially Responsible Investments* (Funding Exchange and Roses Community Fund, 1983). The Council of Institutional Investors and the Social Investment Forum are discussed in more detail in the Epilogue.

21. Tyler Cohen, "Public Goods Definitions and Their Institutional Context: A Critique of Public Goods Theory," *Review of Social Economy* 43 (April 1985), 53–63. See also James Buchanan, *The Demand and Supply of Public Goods* (Chicago: 1968); Harold Demsetz, "The Private Production of Public Goods," *Journal of Law and Economics* 13 (October 1977), 293–306; William Loehr and Todd Sandler, "On the Public Character of Goods," in *Public Goods and Public Policy*, ed. William Loehr and Todd Sandler (Beverly Hills: Sage Publications, 1978).

22. Most people can accept today that a social purpose (as well as an economic purpose) exists in the new experiments on labor participation in management, but it is always said that the bottom line is profits. It is more difficult for people in a business society to see the *power of the social factor* operating throughout the economy and as a force for development. This social power can be explained from an analytical perspective even though it does not fit the context of business.

First, we can say analytically that all economic action is rooted in social action. Similarly, every economic exchange is based in a social exchange; this can be demonstrated in the forms of symbolic discourse and interpersonal exchange that are essential to the life of the corporation and the marketplace. In this analytical context it can be argued that social action is the real "engine" of the economy; the enterprise system could not exist without it. Furthermore, classic studies like the Hawthorne experiment by Elton Mayo have shown that people are motivated by their orientation to one another and their beliefs about work life more than by money, even in a capitalist setting. The pattern of social life empowers the economy. It gives the economic enterprise system its élan and its legitimacy in society. *The social factor* thus becomes the *bottom line* in the economy.

Second, the economy is a functional part of society. It is the material basis by which the broad purposes of the society and its culture are advanced. The social factor remains a critical part of this material foundation as well as critical factor in other institutions interdependent with the economy. The social organization of business is essential to the success of business as well as its connection to the organization of universities, churches, and other nonprofit corporations. It follows that social and economic development are intimately interwoven in the activity and direction of the business system in society. This type of analysis does not lend itself easily to public discourse in a business environment. The idea of profit making as the *motif* of business reigns supreme in the public mind. Nevertheless, these broad assertions become manifest in the identification of social variables in a research paradigm and are eventually tested through empirical studies.

7 Investment in community development

1. Max Weber, *The City* (New York: Free Press, 1958).
2. Every state has experienced shutdown plants. In California during 1980 at least 150 major plants closed their doors permanently, displacing more than 37,000 workers at all occupational levels. By the spring of 1982 four Salinas plants (Firestone, Peter Paul-Cadbury, Walsh, and Spreckles Sugar) accounted for the loss of 2,400 jobs. California Association for Local Economic Development, *Economic Adjustment Report* 1 (August–September 1981), quoted in Barry Bluestone and Bennett Harrison, *The Deindustrialization of America* (New York: Basic Books, 1982), p. 40.
3. Bluestone and Harrison, *The Deindustrialization of America*, pp. 25–6.
4. Sidney Cobb and Stanislau Kasl, *Termination: The Consequences of Job Loss*, Research Report Publication No. 77–224, (National Institute of Occupational Safety and Health, June 1977). See also Alfred Slote, *Termination: The Closing at Baker Plant*, (New York: Bobbs-Merrill, 1969).
5. Paula Rayman and Barry Bluestone, *Out of Work* (Chestnut Hill: Boston College, Social Welfare Research Institute, October 1982).
6. Lewis Mumford, *The Culture of Cities* (New York: Harcourt, Brace, 1938).
7. Jane Jacobs, *The Economy of Cities* (New York: Random House, 1969); Jane Jacobs, "Cities and the Wealth of Nations" and "The Dynamic of Decline," *Atlantic Monthly*, March and April 1984.
8. Lloyd Warner, *The Social System of the Modern Factory* (New Haven: Yale University Press, 1947), p. 108.
9. Roland Warren, *The Community in America* (Chicago: Rand McNally, 1963).
10. Robert E. L. Faris, *Social Disorganization* (New York: Ronald Press, 1948); Martin Neumeyer, *Juvenile Delinquency in Modern Society* (New York: Van

Nostrand, 1961). Many of the studies of the Chicago school were in this tradition: *The Hobo*, *The Gold Coast and the Slum*, *The Ghetto*, and *The Gang*. See Robert Ezra Park, *Human Communities* (Glencoe Ill.: Free Press, 1952).

11. Robert Nisbet, *The Quest for Community* (New York: Oxford University Press, 1953).
12. Karl Polanyi, *The Great Transformation* (Boston: Beacon Press, 1965).
13. Roland Warren, ed., *Perspectives on the American Community* (Chicago: Rand McNally, 1973); see also Severyn T. Bruyn and Paula Rayman, *Nonviolent Action and Social Change* (New York: Irvington Press, 1979), pp. 53ff.
14. Robert Swann et al., *The Community Land Trust* (Cambridge, Mass.: Center for Community Economic Development, 1972).
15. The Institute for Community Economics, *The Community Land Handbook* (Emmaus, Pa.: Rodale Press, 1982), p. 4.
16. Brad Caftel, *Community Development Credit Unions* (Berkeley: National Economic Development Law Project, 1978), p. 38.
17. Ian Keith and Chuck Mathei, "New Developments in Social Investments," *Community Economics*, (Greenfield, Mass.: Institute for Community Economics), No. 1, Summer 1983.
18. Dan Luria and Jack Russell, *Rational Reindustrialization: An Economic Agenda for Detroit* (Detroit: Widgetripper Press, 1981).
19. David Morris, *The New City States* (Washington, D.C.: Institute for Local Self Reliance, 1982). The examples of ecological loops are drawn from this book.
20. The Greenhouse Compact carried a tax plan that was defeated in a referendum by voters, but the plan remains as a model of development for other states and communities ready to undertake it.
21. Peter Drucker, *Management* (New York: Harper & Row, 1973), p. 574.
22. Ibid., p. 575.
23. Vermont Community Economic Development Office, *Jobs and People*: *A Strategic Analysis of the Greater Burlington Economy* (Montpelier: December 1984). On LODCs, see Christopher Mackin, "Strategies for Local Ownership and Control: A Policy Analysis" (Somerville, Mass.: Industrial Cooperative Association, 58 Day St, Suite 200, Somerville, Mass., 02144, 1983). The LODC functions like a trade association of producer cooperatives and serves as another community-oriented corporation worthy of consideration for social investors.
24. Similarly, other types of community-oriented banks can be devised experimentally with the creation of consumer cooperatives, land trusts, and CDCs themselves. The National Consumer Bank was chartered in 1979 to aid consumer cooperatives but 10 per cent of its loans were reserved for producer cooperatives. The bank was designed to become owned by the business cooperatives to which it made loans. As the loans were paid off, the businesses participated in the governance of the bank. Also, the CDC itself has need for capital support. National legislation had been proposed in 1967 with the original legislation to create the CDC and to create also a community development bank. The bank would become owned by the CDCs it helped to form. That part of the legislation, however, was never enacted into law; pending its revival, the CDC must develop local banks to help capitalize its expansion.

25. Alicia Munnell, "The Pitfalls of Social Investing," *New England Economic Review*, September/October 1983, pp. 20–37.
26. Patrick McVeigh, "Pension Funds and Industrial Policy: Are the Vehicles Worthy?" (unpublished paper, Program in Social Economy and Social Policy, Boston College; based on field research with Franklin Research and Development Corporation, Boston, Mass.).
27. Michael Clorves, "Social Investing without Any Tears," *Pension and Pension Age*, 12 May 1980, 10, quoted in McVeigh, "Pension Funds and Industrial Policy."

8 International investment

1. Lionel Robbins, *An Essay on the Nature and Significance of Economic Science* (London: Macmillan, 1935), p. 16.
2. Paul Samuelson, *Economics*, 8th edn (New York: McGraw-Hill, 1970), p. 13.
3. Thorstein Veblen argued in *The Engineers and the Price System* (New York: Harbinger, 1965) that the direction of an economy is not determined by the price system but rather by the values of the culture.
4. The most complex argument here is that economics is really a theoretical orientation (or subsystem) of sociology. This point's premise is that all economic variables are rooted in the culture of a society and shaped by its social structures. Economic variables are always conditioned by sociological variables.

   Economics has been interpreted as a behavioral theory within the social sciences based upon a premise of utility maximization. When such a theory becomes tightly developed with definitive and related concepts, it becomes relatively separate from society and autonomous in itself, more abstractly formulated and related to mathematics. As it becomes more mathematical, it loses touch with social reality. On the other hand, the more practical it becomes, the more dependent its direction is upon the web of norms in society; Robert A. Solo recognized this fact in *Economic Organizations and Social Systems* (New York: Bobbs-Merrill, 1967.) But the choice need not be between abstraction and normative policy. The field of sociology makes a fundamental connection to the categories of economics through its categories of study. Robert M. Solow made this basic point when he struggled with a theory of "wage stickiness" during his presidential address to the American Economic Association in December 1979. He concluded most profoundly, "Economic man is a social ... category."
5. A. H. Bunting, "Change in Agriculture, 1968–74" in *Policy and Practice in Rural Development: Proceedings of the Second International Seminar on Change in Agriculture* (New Jersey: Allanheld, Osmun & Co., Sept 1974), ed. Guy Hunter et al. (printed in association with the Overseas Development Institute) pp. 30–41; Barbara Huddleston and John McLin, eds., *Political Investments in Food Production* (Bloomington: Indiana University Press, 1979); 1980 Annual Report of the World Bank (Oxford University Press).
6. Donatus Okpala, "Towards a Better Conceptualization of Rural Community Development: Empirical Findings from Nigeria," *Human Organization* 39,

(London: Heinemann), no. 2 (1976): 161–9; H. I. Ajaegbu, *Urban and Rural Development in Nigeria* (London: Heinemann, 1976).

7. Philip Mbithi, *Rural Sociology and Rural Development: Its Application in Kenya* (Kampala: East African Literature Bureau, 1974).

8. Dean McHenry, Jr, *Tanzania's Ujamaa Villages: The Implementation of a Rural Development Strategy* (Berkeley: University of California Press 1979). These last three studies were identified by the Institute of International Studies at the University of California, Berkeley in a literature-review project resulting in three monographs called *Project on Managing Decentralization* (1981). The research was performed pursuant to Cooperative Agreement AID/DSAN CA–0199 between the university and the Agency for International Development.

9. The interpretation is found in Christopher Chase-Dunn , "The Effects of International Economic Dependence on Development and Inequality," *American Sociological Review* 40 (December 1975), 720–38.

10. André Gunder Frank, *Latin America* (New York: Monthly Review Press, 1969); Samir Amin, *Accumulation on a World Scale* (New York: Monthly Review Press, 1974).

11. Arghiri Emmanuel, *Unequal Exchange* (New York: Monthly Review Press, 1972).

12. John Gerassi, *The Great Fear* (New York: Macmillan, 1963).

13. Teotonio Dos Santos, "The Structure of Dependence," *Papers and Proceedings of the American Economic Review* 60 (1970), 231–6.

14. Philip Ehrensaft, "Semi-industrial Capitalism in the Third World," *Africa Today* 18 (1971), 40–67.

15. Keith Griffin and J. L. Enos, "Foreign Assistance: Objectives and Consequences," *Economic Development and Cultural Change* 18 (1970), 313–27.

16. Dale Johnson, "Dependence and the International System," in *Dependence and Underdevelopment*, ed. J. D. Crockroft et al. (New York: Anchor, 1972.)

17. Johan Galtung, "A Structural Theory of Imperialism," *Journal of Peace Research* 8 (1971), 77–81.

18. Eugene Havens, "Diffusion of New Seed Varieties and Its Consequences: A Colombian Case," in *Problems of Rural Development*, ed. Raymond Dumett and Laurance Brainerd (Leiden: Brill, 1975); David Guillet, "Reciprocal Labor and Peripheral Capitalism in the Central Andes," *Ethnology* 19 (1980), 1511–7; Robert Maguire, "Bottom-up Development in Haiti," Inter-American Foundation Paper. no. 1 (1979).

19. Eugene Havens, "Green Revolution Technology and Community Development: The Limits of Action Programs," *Economic Development and Culture Change* 23 (1975), 469–82. For those who claim successes in the Green Revolution, see Vernon Ruttan, "Induced Institutional Innovation and the Green Revolution" (Paper presented at the Conference on Strategic Factors in Rural Development in East and Southeast Asia, sponsored by the Council of Asuab Manpower Studies, Pasay City, Philippines, December 1976; Lester Brown, *Seeds of Change* (New York: Praeger, 1970).

20. Elliot Morss, "Strategies for Small Farmer Development," *International Development Review/Focus* 1 (1976), 7–11.

21. James Anderson, "Rapid Rural Development and Socio-economic and Ecological Imbalances in the Philippines," in *Too Rapid Rural Development*, ed. Colin MacAndrews and L. S. Chia (Singapore: McGraw-Hill, International Book Company, 1980); Peter Lloyd, *Slums of Hope? Shanty Towns of the Third World* (Harmondsworth: Penguin, 1979).
22. L. C. Arulpragasam, "Some Basic Issues in the Implementation of Agrarian Reform: Lessons from Cooperative Experience," *Land Reform, Land Settlement and Cooperatives*", 1 (1979), 11–33; Erik Eckholm, "The Dispossessed of the Earth: Land Reform and Sustainable Development," Worldwatch Paper 30, 1979 (Washington, D.C.: *World Watch Institute*).
23. Mary Hollnsteiner et al., "Development from the Bottom-Up: Mobilizing the Rural Poor for Self-Development" (Paper presented at the World Conference on Agrarian Reform and Rural Development, UN Food and Agriculture Organization, Rome, 1979).
24. Marcus Franda, *India's Rural Development: An Assessment of Alternatives* (Bloomington, Indiana: Indiana University Press, 1979).
25. Robert Charlick, "Induced Participation in Nigerian Modernization," *Rural Africana* 18 (1972) 5–29.
26. H. Chenery and M. Syrguin, *Patterns of Development, 1950–1970* (London: Oxford University Press, 1975). My thanks to the University of California, Berkeley, Project on Managing Decentralization for reference to these studies on elitism.
27. Marilyn J. Seiber, *International Borrowing by Developing Countries* (New York: Pergamon Press, 1982), pp. 57–61. See also Eugene Versluysen, *The Political Economy of International Finance* (New York: St Martin's Press, 1981).
28. Seiber, *International Borrowing by Developing Countries*, p. 54.
29. Rudolf Bahro, *The Alternative in Eastern Europe* (London: NLB and Verio Editions, 1978), pp. 38, 137, 213.
30. Mark Selden, "Imposed Collectivization and the Crisis of Agrarian Development in Socialist States," in *Crises in the World System*, ed. Albert Bergesen (London: Sage Publications, 1983), p. 249. See also Carl Rosebergand and Thomas Callagby, eds., *Socialism in Sub-Saharan Africa* (Berkeley: University of California, Institute of International Studies, 1970).
31. "Implications of Multinational Firms for World Trade and Investment and for U.S. Trade and Labor," Hearings before the Senate Committee on Finance, February 1973.
32. Mohsin S. Khan and Malcolm Knight, "Sources of Payments Problems in LDCs," *Finance and Development* 20 (December 1983). Marilyn Seiber (*International Borrowing by Developing Countries*, p. xii) adds a helpful note on the structure of the debt in the new commercial bank loans; this shift means shortened maturities, raised interest rates, and bunched repayments. For further reading, see Emar Lisboa Bacha and Carole F. Dias Alejandro, *International Financial Intermediation* (Princeton: Princeton University Press, 1982). For a well-informed journalist's description of the corridors of power, see Anthony Sampson, *The Money Lenders* (New York: Viking, 1982).

33. "How an LDC default Would Hit the U.S. Economy," *Business Week*, 7 November 1983, 118.
34. Nicholas Kristof, "Latin Trade Surpluses Shrink," *New York Times*, 13 June 1985, pp. D1, D5.
35. Willy Brandt, *North–South: A Program for Survival* (Cambridge, Mass.: MIT Press, 1980), pp. 248–9.

9 Social development in the Third World
 1. Michael Albert and Robin Hahnel, *Socialism Today and Tomorrow* (Boston: South End Press, 1981).
 2. The principles of social governance are discussed in more detail in Severyn T. Bruyn, *The Social Economy* (New York: Wiley, 1977).
 3. David Jenkins, *Industrial Democracy in Europe* (Geneva: Business International, 1974).
 4. We have noted that Peter Drucker discusses "federalizing" the command system of a corporation in *Management* (New York: Harper & Row, 1973).
 5. Milovan Djilas, *The Unperfect Society*, (N.Y.: Harcourt Bracet Wald, 1969); Severyn Bruyn and Litsa Nicolaou Smokovitis, *International Issues in Social Economy* (N.Y.: Praeger, forthcoming).
 6. J. R. Craig, *Multinational Cooperatives* (Saskatchewan: Western Producer Prairie Books, 1976).
 7. A similar list of advantages can be found in G. Shabbin Cheema and Dennis Rondinelli, eds., *Decentralization and Development*, (London: Sage Publications, 1983), pp. 14–16.
 8. These guidelines are informed by data in *Project on Managing Decentralization* (Institute of International Studies, University of California, Berkeley, 1981); David Leonard, Introduction, *Decentralization and Linkages in Rural DevelopmentProject on Managing Decentralization*, Berkeley: February, 1981, pp. 9ff.
 9. James Warbasse, *Co-operative Democracy* (New York: Harper, 1936). Information about cooperatives around the world can be obtained from the International Cooperative Alliance, as can a booklet about workers' productive societies: Bruno Catalano, Secretary, International Cooperative Alliance, Via Torino 135, 00184, Rome.
10. Robert Swann et al., *The Community Land Trust* (Cambridge, Mass.: Center for Community Economic Development, 1972).
11. David Ellerman, *Worker Cooperatives: The Question of Legal Structure*, and *Theory of Industrial Cooperatives* (Somerville, Mass.: Industrial Cooperative Association, 1982).
12. The technical details of these accounts are discussed in Robert Oakeshott, *The Case for Workers' Co-ops* (London: Routledge & Kegan Paul, 1978).
13. E. Topham and J. A. Hough, *The Cooperative Movement in Britain* (London: Longmans Green, 1948).
14. John W. Bennett, *Agricultural Cooperatives in the Development Process: Perspective from Social Science*. Monograph no. 4, California Agricultural Policy Seminar, Department of Applied Behavioral Sciences (University of California, Davis, 1979). The difficult conditions under which one nation worked to develop agricultural cooperatives is told in James F. Petras, *Class, State and*

Power in the Third World (London: Zed Press, 1981), ch. 13, "Urban Radicalism in Peru."

15. This is my summary of information gathered from studies reported in *Project on Managing Decentralization*, ch. 3 (by Stephen Peterson).

16. William Rusch, et al., *Rural Cooperatives in Guatemala*, vol. 1, report prepared for the A.I.D. (1976), discussed in *Project on Management Decentralization*, ch. 4, p. 9.

17. Goran Hyden, ed., *Cooperatives in Tanzania: Problems of Organization* (Dar es Salaam: Tanzania Publishers, 1976), pp. 17–19, discussed in David Leonard, "Introduction, Decentralization and Linkages in Rural Development", *Project on Managing Decentralization*, p. 45.

18. David P. Ellerman, *The Socialization of Entrepreneurship: The Empresarial Division of the Caja Laboral Popular* (Somerville, Mass.: Industrial Cooperative Association, 1982); cf. Thomas Henk and Chris Logan, *Mondragon: An Economic Analysis* (London: Allen & Unwin, 1982).

19. Severyn T. Bruyn, "Behind the Kibbutz: Mutual Aid Societies" (unpublished paper, 1983).

20. Robert L. Ayres, *Banking on the Poor: The World Bank and World Poverty* (Cambridge: MIT Press, 1983), p. 79.

21. Ervin Laszlo, *The Obstacles to the New International Economic Order* (New York: Pergamon Press, 1980), p. 68.

22. This is my summary of key points on social development often noted today by progressive economists and diplomats. I should mention that the revised report of the Brandt Commission (*Common Crisis North–South: Cooperation for World Recovery* [Cambridge: MIT Press, 1983]) brings important technical arguments to bear on social issues in international finance. The report could have a significant influence on future investment policy because it has been discussed by parliaments in several countries and has been widely circulated in banking circles.

Epilogue: Social investment as a self-correcting movement in the market system

1. Mayer Zald and Roberta Ash, "Social Movement Organizations: Growth, Decay and Change," *Social Forces* 44 (September 1966), 327–41.

2. The Social Investment Forum, 222 Lewis Wharf, Boston, MA 02110.

3. The Directory is available from the Interfaith Center on Corporate Responsibility, Room 566, 475 Riverside Dr., New York, N.Y. 10115.

4. Fred R. Bleakley, "A Trustee Takes on the Greenmailers," *New York Times*, 10 February 1985, p. F6; Steve Hemmerick and Alan Krauss, "U.S. West Joins Investors' Council," *Pensions and Investment Age*, 8 July 1985, "Council Heading for the Crossroads," ibid., 25 November 1985. My thanks to Marcy Murninghan for these sources.

5. Council on Economic Priorities, 30 Irving Place, New York, NY 10003; Center for Economic Revitalization, Box 363, Worcester, Vt., 05682; Pagan International, 1120 Connecticut Avenue, N.W., Suite 330, Washington, DC 20036. Many more sources could be listed, e.g., *Inform*, 381 Park Avenue, New York,

NY 10016; *Corporate Responsibility Monitor*; 464 19th Street, Oakland, CA 94612; *Solar Industry Bulletin*, Harrisville, NH 03450.

6. *Corporate Examiner* 14, no. 7 (1985), 1.

7. *Insight* 2 (Spring 1985). For more information contact Richard Harmon, BEC, 562 Atlantic Avenue, Brooklyn, NY 11217.

8. *Response* 14 (November 1985), 6.

9. *The Report of the Governor's Task Force on Private Sector Initiatives* (Boston: Commonwealth of Massachusetts, 1983), pp. 52–3.

10. *Response* 12 (May 1983), 19.

11. Ibid., 9 (November 1980), 15.

12. Center for Economic Revitalization, Box 363, Worcester, Vt. 05682, has focused its research and its reports on selected industries. See *Good Money* 2, for a summary review of firms in such industries as publishing, food processing, banking, railroads, and air freight. For a study of performance in the utility industry comparing twelve nuclear, five mixed, and eight nonnuclear utilities, see Ritchie P. Lowry, *Is the Peaceful Atom a Good Investment?*, A Center publication, n.d.

13. *Insight: Report on Vital Industries*, 8 August 1985. Prepared by Darrell Reeck and Scott Klingers, Franklin Research and Development Corporation, 711 Atlantic Avenue, Boston, Mass., 02111.

14. Fred Bonkema, Ecumenical Development Cooperative Society, 475 Riverside Drive, New York, NY 10115.

15. *Corporate Examiner* 12, 11 (1983), 5. Also see *Newsletter of the Ethical Investment Research and Information Service*, 9 Poland Street, London.

16. Martin Stott, "Social Investing in Britain," *Insight* 2 (Summer 1985).

17. Anthony Biance et al., "Playing with Fire" (cover story), *Business Week*, 16 September 1985.

18. Kenneth M. Davidson, *Megamergers* (Cambridge, Mass.: Ballinger, 1985), p. 12. Davidson summarizes the findings on how mergers are not more efficient (p. 319); innovations actually occur in smaller firms (p. 291); big firms are less efficient (p. 294); and tax laws encourage mergers and the leveraging mechanisms for buyouts (p. 298). The big mergers have shifted centers of business decision making away from cities such as Buffalo, Syracuse, Utica, Scranton, Toledo, Dayton, and Youngstown. These areas were once the birthplace of new businesses and industries but have now lost regenerative capacities as much of their economic life has come under the dominion of distant corporate executives.

19. Joel Chernoff, "Corporate Issues May Be Next for Council Members," *Pensions and Investment Age*, 28 October 1985.

20. The legal and historical argument for federal charterment of the largest corporations is made in Ralph Nader, Mark Green, and Joel Seligman, *Taming the Giant Corporation* (New York: Norton 1976). The argument for its association with worker-ownership and decentralization is made in Severyn T. Bruyn, *The Social Economy* (New York: Wiley, 1977).

21. The following summary is a selected account condensed from an article by Corey Rosen and William Foote Whyte, "A Federal Catalyst for Employee

Ownership," in *The Big Business Reader*, ed. Mark Green (New York: Pilgrim Press, 1983).

22. The unique fact about cooperatives is that the level of profits can be controlled more easily by raising or lowering wages. This adds to the capacity of the firm to survive during a recession without laying off workers, but it also allows workers to raise wages in good times to make money as well as to add to their internal accounts. There is then less incentive to pay dividends to outside investors, which makes it difficult to link stock payments to profit levels. Richard Cornwall ("New Instruments in Finance Worker-Cooperatives" [unpublished manuscript, Middlebury College]), has offered a proposal to solve this problem: issuing certificates entitling holders to a share in the surplus, defined by combining profits and wages as the revenue net of all expenses. This includes fixed interest payments on bonds and also net of interest due to workers individual capital accounts and base wages. Such certificates, called "surplus shares," are tradeable and apply only when the surplus is "nonnegative," that is, shareholders are not required to pay money to the firm when its surplus is negative.

23. Joseph Blasi, "Labor Policy and the Changing Role of Government," in *Industrial Democracy: Strategies for Community Revitalization*, ed. Warner Woodworth, Christopher Meek, and William Foote Whyte (Beverly Hills: Sage Publication, 1985).

24. William F. Whyte, "The Potential for Employee Ownership," in Woodworth, Meek, and Whyte, *Industrial Democracy*, pp. 189ff.

25. Lester Thurow, "The 20's and 30's Can Happen Again," *New York Times*, 22 January 1986, p. A23.

26. Christopher Mackin, "Strategies for Local Ownership and Control: A Policy Analysis" (Somerville, Mass.: Industrial Cooperative Association, 58 Day Street, Suite 200, Somerville, Mass., 02144, 1983).

27. Peter Drucker, *The Unseen Revolution: How Pension Fund Socialism Came To America* (New York: Harper & Row, 1976), p. 91

28. Drucker's argument is made in full knowledge of the fact that the ERISA standard is based on the common law "prudent-man" rule, that is, "trustees in investing fund assets must consider the same factors that a reasonable prudent man would take into account in investing his own money." It differs from this prudent rule only by substituting an "institutional standard" of conduct for the old personal standard. The Labor Department recognized, for example, that the manager of a plan with assets of $50,000 need not employ the same investment management techniques as would a fiduciary of a plan with assets of $50,000,000. Dallas L. Salisbury, ed., *Should Pension Assets be Managed for Social/Political Purposes?*, EBRI Policy Forum (Washington, D.C.: Employee Benefit Research Institute, 1980), pp. 49, 97

29. Robert A. Dahl, *A Preface to Economic Democracy* (Berkeley: University of California Press, 1985), pp. 125ff.

30. More details on the Roundtable and the Chamber can be found in Mark Green and Andrew Buchsbaum, "The Corporate Lobbies: The Two Styles of the Business Roundtable and Chamber of Commerce," in *The Big Business*

Reader, ed. Green. Business opinion, of course, cannot be fully represented through these peak organizations. For example, the Chamber argued against Senator Edward Kennedy's criminal code bill that included corporate malpractices, but the Federation of Independent Businesses opposed the Chamber's position because the bill made it easier for small firms to band together to sue big firms in court.

31. Our argument is that staff time in peak organizations is misdirected toward protective reactions against congressional legislation on domestic issues when the organizations could be dealing with the problem of imports decimating their corporate members. For example, peak organizations want permission to use polygraphs to question employees regarding the theft of store goods. The $22 billion cost claimed in store theft is important, but the solution is symptomatic and does not get to the root of the matter, which is related to a lack of employee participation in management and ownership. Employees who participate in ownership and management are less likely to steal their own goods. This is perhaps less true in big corporations, but even in these cases it becomes more possible to develop inside-training programs that reduce thefts. A self-managed firm can organize peer pressure to keep delinquent fellow-employees from ripping off the firm. But Congress can address these issues when it begins to take action toward a national policy for employee ownership.

32. Lee Walczak et. al., "The New Trade Strategy," *Business Week*, 7 October 1985, 94–5.

33. Michael Borrus, "The Politics of Competitive Erosion in the U.S. Steel Industry", in *American Industry in International Competition*, ed. John Zysman and Laura Tyson (Ithaca: Cornell University Press, 1983), p. 88.

34. Barry Commoner, "The Promise and Perils of Petrochemicals," in *The Big Business Reader*, ed. Green, p. 109.

35. "(Still) Unsafe at Any Speed," *Inc.*, (December 1985), 33ff.

36. We have noted that many of the alternative businesses supported by social investors reduce the competitive factor as the dominant characteristic of the exchange system and introduce a greater emphasis on the cooperative factor. The worker self-managed firm removes labor from the competitive market to a large extent. Labor is no longer treated as an object in the market by big capital, and a greater degree of self-direction comes into the hands of labor itself. This means that the nineteenth-century picture of the conflict between labor and capital is reduced or eliminated and the twentieth-century picture of competition between labor and management is changed qualitatively through this interest in capitalizing cooperative firms. The structure of the Mondragon Bank and the introduction of the Consumer's Cooperative Bank and CDCUs in the United States begin to remove capital from its traditional control in the hands of an elite and pass it into the hands of people in localities. It becomes removed from the competitive market for profit insofar as people seek to use their capital for community development.

In the Consumers Bank, capital is directed toward a system of cooperatives that by their nature involve sharing power and profits more than individual private gain. The land trust also begins to take land out of the competitive market and away from speculators who treat it as a basis for maximizing profits. These investment priorities – small as they may be in the contemporary currents of national investment – point toward the development of a new system of economic exchange rooted more firmly in what we have characterized as a social economy.

37. The capitalist economy has been developing modes of cooperation within the competitive market for over a century. In the nineteenth century competing railroad enterprises had to cooperate to arrange the physical connection of the many roads; they had to devise uniform operating, accounting and other organizational procedures; and they had to agree on the use of a standardized technology. The cost of loading and reloading freight between Boston and Chicago in 1865 required interfirm cooperation of the highest order. As technology became more sophisticated and as markets expanded, administrative coordination replaced market coordination in an increasingly larger portion of the economy. Modern business enterprise took the place of market mechanisms in coordinating the activities of the economy and allocating its resources. This is the central theme of Alfred Chandler Jr's recent study of business history (*The Visible Hand: The Managerial Revolution in American Business* [Cambridge, Harvard University Press, 1977]). "In many sectors of the economy the visible hand of management replaced what Adam Smith referred to as the invisible hand of market forces."

38. New modes of cooperation continue to develop today without the incentives of social investors. U.S. companies, facing stiff competition from abroad and relaxed antitrust regulations at home, are banding together to cooperate in research and development at an unprecedented rate. Government officials state that "for the first time, the cooperation has gone beyond dealing with such industrywide issues as controlling pollution to projects that could result in new products with broad commercial potential. Proponents argue that cooperative research allows companies to pool resources and avoid duplication of effort and thus enhances the competitiveness of large U.S. companies while allowing smaller companies without huge resources to compete as well. We have yet to see whether collusion can be avoided in this new step toward cooperation." Andrew Pollack, "A New Spirit of Cooperation," *New York Times*, 14 January 1986, pp. D1.

39. Senator Howard Metzenbaum (D–Ohio) believes that the issue of social investment will be with us for some time. At a Senate hearing he said: "I believe that this trend, this questioning of the process by which pension fund investments are made, is likely to continue to gather strength, and I believe further that Congress will have to address the complex issues this trend will inevitably bring to the floor." Opening statement before the Subcommittee on Citizens' and Shareholders' Rights and Remedies, 21 November 1979, p. 1.

Bibliography

My thanks to Franklin Research and Development Corporation, Boston, Mass., for helping to prepare this bibliography.

Books

Adler, Patricia and Adler, Peter, *The Social Dynamics of Financial Markets*, Greenwich, Connecticut: JAI Press, 1984

Berger, Renee and Moy, Kirsten et. al., *Investing in America*, President's Task Force on Private Sector Initiatives, 1982

Boldgett, Richard, *Conflicts of Interest: Union Pension Fund Asset Management*, New York: The Twentieth Century Fund, 1977

Domini, Amy and Kinder, Peter, *Ethical Investing*, Boston: Addison Wesley, 1984

Drucker, Peter F., *Unseen Revolution: How Pension Fund Socialism Came to America*, New York: Harper, 1976

Greenough, William C. and King, Francis P., *Pension Funds and Public Policy*, New York: Columbia University Press, 1976

Harbrecht, Paul P., *Pension Funds and Economic Power*, New York: The Twentieth Century Fund, 1959

Knight, Sharon and Knight, Deborah, *Concerned Investors' Guide*, Arlington, Virginia: Resource Publishing Group, 1983

Kohlmeier, Louis M., *Conflicts of Interest: State and Local Pension Fund Asset Management*, New York: The Twentieth Century Fund, 1976

Levin, Noel Arnold, *Social Investing for Pension Funds: For Love or Money*, Brookfield, Wisconsin: International Foundation of Employee Benefit Plans, 1982

McGill, Dan M., *Social Investing*, Homewood, Ill.: Wharton School, Pension Research Council, 1984

Marcus, Bruce W., *The Prudent Man*, New York: ESP Corporation/Pensions and Investments, 1978

Pension Investments: A Social Audit, CDE Handbook, New York: Corporate Data Exchange, 1979

Rifkin, Jeremy and Barber, Randy, *The North Will Rise Again: Pensions, Politics and Power in the 1980's*, Boston: Beacon Press, 1978

Salisbury, Dallas, *Should Pension Assets Be Managed For Social/Political Purposes?*, Washington, D.C.: Employee Benefit Research Institute, 1979

Silk, Leonard and Vogel, David, *Ethics and Profits*, New York: Simon & Schuster, 1976

Simon, John G., *Ethical Investor: Universities and Corporate Responsibility*, New Haven, Connecticut: Yale University Press, 1972

Vogel, David, *Lobbying the Corporation: Citizen Challenges to Business Authority*, New York: Basic Books, 1978

Articles and monographs

General

"Accounting for Corporate Social Performance," *Management Accounting*, February 1974, 39

"An Assessment of Socially Responsible Investing," *The American Banker*, 30 March 1983, 4

Bok, Derek, *Beyond the Ivory Tower*, Cambridge, Mass.: Harvard University Press, 1982

Brody, Michael, "Pure Play Investments: Socially Sensitive Portfolios are Gaining in Popularity," *Barron's*, 24 January 1983, 13–15

Brownstein, Ronald and Easton, Nina, "Ethical Investing: Putting your Money Where Your Heart Is," *The Amicus Journal*, Winter 1984, 16–19

Darby, Rose, "Social Investing: Meeting the Needs of Socially Conscious Clients," *Registered Representative*, April 1984, 85

Foltz, Kim, "Doing Well by Doing Good," *Newsweek*, 11 June 1984

Friedman, Jeffrey, "Dreyfuss' Do-Gooder," *Financial World*, 15 February 1981, 57

"Good Ways to Invest in Do-Good Companies," *Changing Times*, December 1982, 61–3

Gould, Harry M. and Divens, Terry, "Help on Putting your Money Where your Principles Are," *Philadelphia Inquirer*, 13 September 1983

"Governor Brown pushes for Social Investing," *Pensions & Investments*, 14 April 1980, 11

Hansen, Larry, "Doing Well with Do-Good Funds," *Fact*, June 1984, 58

Hundley, Kris, "Investing Without Guilt," *Hampshire Life*, 17 September 1983, 4

"Investment Advisers Seek 'Socially Acceptable' Mutuals," *Manchester Herald*, 17 July 1983

Kane, Joe, "Making Money in Good Conscience," *New Age Journal*, November 1983, 41ff

Knight, Sharon, and Knight, Deborah, *The Concerned Investors' Guide*, Resource Publishing Group, 1983

Lawrence, Jill, "Social Investing: Making Money Without Guilt," *Bangor Daily News*, 26–7 November 1983, 24

Leger, John M, "Socially Responsible Funds Pique Interest, but Results have Often been Unimpressive," *The Wall Street Journal*, 18 November 1982, 33

Lipnack, Jessica and Stamps, Jeffrey, "Finance: Putting Your Money Where Your Heart Is," *Esquire*, October 1983, 162

Louthan, Shirley, "The Ethical Investor," *Ms.*, August 1984, 20

Lydenberg, Steven, "Making Money in Step with Conscience," *Christianity & Crisis*, 28 May 1984, 1–5

Michak, Don, "Capitalists with a Conscience," source unknown: FRDC has copy

"Mutual Funds with a Social Conscience," *Black Enterprise*, November 1983, 35

Olson, Mark ed., "The Money Guide," *The Other Side*, July 1984, A–O

Pacey, Margaret D., "Investment Do-Gooders: A Look at a Dogged Trio of Socially Conscious Mutual Funds," *Barron's*, 21 July 1980, 9ff

"Pax World Fund," *The Christian Century*, 24 October 1984, 978

"Politically Correct," *Boston Business Journal*, 2 November 1981

"Public Responsibility of Corporations," *Harvard Business Review*, May–June 1977, 60ff

"Reprise of the Ethical Investors," *Harvard Business Review*, March–April 1981, 159

Rollman, Gordon L., "Ain't Misbehav'in: Investments with a Cause," *Plowshare Press*, May–June 1983, 3

Schlesinger, Arthur, "Social Responsibility: It's a Must for Capitalism," *New York Times*, n.d.

Schlesinger, Jacob M., "Investing Based on Social Issues is Gaining Adherents Among the Children of the 60s," *The Wall Street Journal*, 11 July 1984

Shapiro, Harvey, "Doing Well While Doing Good," *New York Times*, 7 August 1983

Smart, Donald A., *Investment Targeting: A Wisconsin Case Study*, Madison, University of Wisconsin Press, 1979

Social Investment Information Packet, available from Co-op America 2100 M St. NW, Washington, D.C. 20063 (cost: $5.00)

"Social Investors Irked," *Business & Society Review*, Fall, 1984, 69–71

"Social Responsibility: Base of Three Market Funds," *National Catholic Reporter*, 20 April 1984, 8

"Socially Committed Investments," *Turst & Estate*, October 1984, 56–8

"Socially Responsible Investment: Putting Your Money to Work for Social Change," *Our Marketplace* (Co-op America newsletter), Sept.–Oct. 1984

"The Socially Responsible Investor Comes of Age," Women's Foundation Newsletter, Spring 1984

Stock, Craig, "More Investors Turn to 'Socially Responsible' Mutuals," *Philadelphia Inquirer*, 13 September 1983, 8E

Tooley, Doug, ed., *The Hampshire College Report on Socially Responsible Investment*, Resource Publishing Group, 1401 Wilson Blvd Suite 101; Arlington, Va. 22209

Train, John, "Responsible or Irresponsible: Making Wise Investments," *Forbes*, 6 July 1981, 176

Truasch, Susan, "A Business Book that Might Spoil Your Day" (review of Edward Herman's *Corporate Control, Corporate Power*), *Boston Sunday Globe*, 10 May 1981

Wallace, Beatson, "A Mutual Fund that has a Social Conscience," *Boston Glove*, 4 January 1983, 46

"Warding Off the Big Chill: Ethical Investing for Profit," *Barron's*, 21 May 1984, 49

South African divestiture (apartheid)
Publications on the financial effects of divestiture

Baldwin, Brooke and Brown, Theodore, *Economic Action Against Apartheid: An Overview of the Divestment Campaign and Financial Implications for Institutional Investors*, New York: The Africa Fund, 1985

Cheru, Fantu, *The Financial Implications of Divestment: A Review of the Evidence*, New York: Interfaith Center on Corporate Responsibility, 1984

Investor Responsibility Research Center, *Does Signing the Sullivan Principles Matter?*, Washington, D.C.: Investor Responsibility Research Center, 1985

Investor Responsibility Research Center, *The Impact of South Africa-Related Divestment on Equity Portfolio Performance*, Washington, D.C.: Investor Responsibility Research Center, 1985

Litwak, Lawrence, Estrella, Julia, and McTigue, Kathleen, *Divesting From South Africa: A Prudent Approach for Pension Funds*, Oakland: Community Economics, 1981

Love, Douglas A., "On South Africa," *Financial Analysts Journal*, May–June 1985, 14

Tell, Lawrence J., "The Apartheid Factor: It Could Have a Big Impact on U.S. Stocks," *Barron's*, 19 August 1985, 18

General

"Acting Against Banks," *Business Week*, 16 April 1981, 40

"American Lutherans Sell Stock Linked to South Africa," *Jet*, 18 October 1982, 32

"Anti-Apartheid Pension Fund Policies Criticized by some Fund Managers," *The Wall Street Journal*, 18 April 1984, 33

Austin, Charles, "Diverging Views on Divestment," *The Christian Century*, 28 October 1981, 1084

"Codes of Conduct: South Africa and the Corporate World," *The Canadian Forum*, August–September 1983, 33

"Companies that Hide behind the Sullivan Principles," *Business & Society Review*, Spring 1984, 15–18

"Divest: Labor shows the Way: Unions Withdraw Investments from South Africa," *Labor Today*, May 1981, 3

"Divesting from South Africa: A Prudent Approach for Pension Funds," *Community Economics, Inc.*, September 1981

"Divestiture Guidelines," *The Christian Century*, 12 December 1984, 1168

"GE Withdraws," *Business Week*, 25 October 1982, 40

"Harvard Asked to Divest of South African Stock," *Jet*, 28 May 1984, 35

"Hearing held on Bank Loans: Legal Aspects of Anti-Apartheid Campaign," *U.N. Chronicle*, May 1981

"Is Withdrawing the Best Way to Fight Apartheid?," *New York Times*, 28 October 1984, section 1, 6

Lyles, Jean Caffey, "Putting Pressure on Pretoria" (editorial), *The Christian Century*, 7 October 1981, 979

"Missionary Funds out of South Africa," *New Statesman*, 13 November 1981, 3

Olson, Martha J., "University Investments with a South African Connection: Is Prudent Divestiture Possible?," *New York University Journal of International Law and Politics*, Winter 1979, 543–80

"Pension Play on Apartheid," *Black Enterprise*, March 1982, 19

"Politics among Friends: For the Quakers it was a Tough Issue: Were their Investments Supporting Apartheid?," *Progressive*, April 1981, 20

Reidhaar, Donald L., "Memorandum: The Legal Implications of University Investments in Companies Doing Business in South Africa," *Journal of College and University Law*, 1980–1, 164–73

"Rising Risks: American Investment in South Africa," *Business Week*, 20 October 1980, 144

Rudd, A., "Divestment of South African Equities: How Risky?," *Journal of Portfolio Management*, Spring 1979

"South Africa Foot Dragging Vexes U.S: Companies," *Business Week*, 20 October 1980, 56

"States have Duty to Aid South Africa Liberation Movement, Say Experts," *U.N. Chronicle*, May 1981, 22

"U.S. Corporate Involvement in South Africa," *Labor Today*, November 1980, 2

Church related issues

"All that Money Can Buy: The Movement for Corporate Social Responsibility Affects You, Your Money, and Your Church," Toronto: Committee on Investing Church Funds For Social Purposes, United Church of Canada, 1973

"Corporate Responsibility & Religious Institutions: Information & Action Papers," Corporate Information Center, October 1971

Craig, Eleanor, S. L., *A Shareowners' Manual for Church Committees on Social Responsibility in Investments*, Interfaith Center for Corporate Responsibility 1977

Goodman, Walter, "Stocks Without Sin," *Harper's Magazine*, August 1971

Investing Church Funds for Maximum Social Impact," The United Church of Christ's Committee for Maximum Social Impact (1970)

Rolland, Keith, "The Second Wave of Church Social Investments," *The Entrepreneurial Economy*, December 1984, 2

"Should Churches Use Their Funds to Force Social Change?," *U.S. News & World Reports*, 20 September 1971, 71

Pension funds

Blakely, Edward J., Lynch, James, & Skurdna, Kenneth, "Creating Jobs Through Pension Fund Investments in Real Estate: Innovations from California" *California Management Review* 27, Summer 1985, 184

Control Data Exchange, Inc., *Pension Investments: A Social Audit*

"Controversy Raised Over Investment of Pension Assets for Social Purposes Instead of Solely for Performance," *Employee Benefit Plan Review*, December 1978, 64

Cooper, John W, "The Basic Trends Which Are Emerging in Social Investing," *Pensions & Investments*, 8 October 1979, 31

Eaton, William J., "Unions May Seek Pension Investment Power," *Los Angeles Times*, 20 September 1978, part III, 17

Glover, Eugene, "Social Investment: Directing Union-Negotiated Pension Funds to Social Purposes," *Employee Benefits Journal* 7, September 1982, 13

"How Pension Officers View Social Responsibility," *Institutional Investor*, April, 1979, 85.

Laurence, John F., "Use of Pension Power for Social Goals Can Backfire," *Los Angeles Times*, 8 October 1978, part 7, 3

Macina, Marianne, "Wisconsin Looks at Socially Beneficial Investing," *Pension World*, May 1979, 25

Minick, Clare, "Social Investing Sparks New York Fund Debate," *Pensions & Investments*, 24 September 1979, 1

Munnell, Alicia H., "The Pitfalls of Social Investing: The Case of Public Pensions & Housing," *New England Economic Review*, September/October 1983, 20

O'Neal, Vincent, "Pensions, Politics and 'Prudent Man'," *The New Englander*, September, 1978, 77.

"Prudence, Not Social Purposes, Must Control Investments," *Employee Benefit Plan Review*, April 1979, 52

Schotland, Roy A., "Social or Divergent Investments," *Investments Institute Proceedings*, 1980

Taylor, Tamsin & Parker, Richard, *Strategic Investment: The Case For Increasing Total Yield on Wisconsin's Pension Fund*, Strategic Management Advisers, 1979

Employee Involvement (ESOPs)

Rodgers, Wilfrid C, "A Stock Bill for Workers," *The Boston Globe*, 8 July 1980, 38

Scott, Maria Crawford, "Social Investing is Hot Issue at Madison Fund Conference," *Pensions & Investments*, 9 April 1979, 6

Wayne, Leslie, "Management Gospel Gone Wrong," *New York Times*, 30 May 1982, section 3, p. 1

Pensions

Blanton, Kimberly, "Control Data Funds 'Social' Experiment," *Pensions & Investments*, 9 November 1981, 3

Braver, Mary A., "Issues to Consider in Social Investing," *Pension World*, June 1983, 29–34

"Campaigners call for Pension Fund Housing Boost," *Pensions & Investments*, 13 September 1982

Hawthorne, Fran, "Shakeup at the Union Funds," *Institutional Investor*, February 1984, 123

Heard, Jamie, "Investor Responsibility: An Idea Whose Time Has Come?," *Journal of Portfolio Management*, Spring 1978, 12–14

"Investing in Ourselves: Strategies for Massachusetts," *Conference on Alternative State & Local Policies*, June 1979

Kaye, Jeffrcy, "Unions Map Investment Guidelines," *Washington Post*, 9 March 1980, p. G1

Landau, Peter, "Do Institutional Investors Have a Social Responsibility?," *Institutional Investor*, July 1970, 84

Litwak, Lawrence, Estrella, Julie, & McTique, Kathleen, "Divesting From South Africa: A Prudent Approach for Pension Funds, *Conference for Alternative State & Local Policies*, September 1981

McGill, Dan M., ed., *Social Investing*, Pension Research Council, Wharton School, University of Pennsylvania, 1984

Mach, Joseph D. "Can Pension Plans Make Socially Motivated Investments?," *The Political Account*, March 1985, 91

Malkiel, Burton G. and Quandt, Richard E., "Moral Issues in Investment Policy," *Harvard Business Review*, March–April 1971, 37–47

Moskowitz, Milton, "Profiles in Corporate Responsibility," *Business and Society Review*, Spring 1975, 28–42

"Origins of the Anti-Union Social Investing Report," *Labor & Investments*, June 1983, 2–5

Pension Funds and Ethical Investments, Council on Economic Priorities, 1980

Public Hearing on September 24, 1984 on State of New Jersey Assembly Bill 1308 (Establishes Principles for the Investment of State Pension Funds By the State Investment Council) & *AV 1309* (Require Divestiture of States Public Pension and Annuity Funds Directly or Indirectly Linked to the Republic of South Africa)

Purcell, Theodore V., "Management and the Ethical Investors," *Harvard Business Review*, September–October 1979, 24–44

Ring, Trudy, & Eddy, Christman, "S. African Divestiture Momentum Grows," *Pensions & Investment Age*, 27 May 1985, 1

Vieira, Edwin Jr, "Social Investing: Its Character Causes, Consequences, and Legality under the Employee Retirement Income Security Act of 1974," U.S. Department of Labor, Washington D.C., 1983

Financial studies

Bloch, Howard and Lareau, Thomas J., "Should We Invest in 'Socially Responsible' Firms?," *The Journal of Portfolio Management*, Summer 1985, 27

"Good Returns With Good Conscience," *Institutional Investor*, September 1981, 111

Legal issues

Leibig, Michael, *Social Investments and the Law: The Case for Alternative Investments*, Washington, D.C.: Conference on Alternative State and Local Policies, 1981

Marcus, Bruce W., *The Prudent Man: Making Decisions Under ERISA*, New York: Pensions & Investments, 1978

Ravikoff, Ronald and Curzan, Myron, *Social Responsibility in Investment: Policy and the Prudent Man Rule*, Arnold & Porter, 1979

Financial implications

Alexander, G. J. & Bucholz, R. A., "Corporate Social Responsibility & Stock Market Performance," *Academy of Management Journal*, 1978, #21, 479

Arlow, P. & Gannin, M. J., "Social Responsiveness, Corporate Structure & Economic Performance," *Academy of Management Review*, 1982, #7, 235

Baldwin, Brooke & Brown, Theodore, "Economic Action Against Apartheid: An Overview of The Financial Implications for Institutional Investors," published by the Africa Fund

Beresford, D. R., *Social Responsibility Disclosure – 1975 Survey of Fortune 500 Annual Reports*, Ernst & Ernst, 1976

Cochran, Phillip & Week, Robert A., "Corporate Social Responsibility & Financial Performance," *Academy of Management Journal*, 27, #1 March 1984

Folger, H. R., & Nutt, F., "A Note on Social Responsibility & Stock Valuation," *Academy of Management Journal*, 1975, 18, 155

Jobson, J. D., & Korkie, B., "Estimation of the Markowitz Efficient Portfolio," *Journal of the American Statistical Association*, September 1980, 544

Rudd, Andrew, "Social Responsibility and Portfolio Performance," *California Management Review*, Summer 1981, 55

Spicer, B. H., "Investors' Corporate Social Performance & Information Disclosure: An Empirical Study," *The Accounting Review*, 1978, 53(1), 94

Vance, S., "Are Socially Responsible Corporations Good Investment Risks?," *Management Review*, 1975, 64(8), 18

Industrial development

Abernathy, William J., Clark, Kim B. and Kantrow, Alan M., *Industrial Renaissance*, New York: Basic Books, 1983

Blauner, Robert, "Work Satisfaction and Industrial Trends in Modern Society," in Galenson, W. and Lipset, S. M., eds., *Labor and Trade Unionism*, New York, Wiley, 1960

Bluestone, Barry and Harrison, Bennett, *The Deindustrialization of America*, New York: Basic Books, 1982

Bowles, Samuel, Gordon, David and Weiskopf, Thomas, *Beyond the Wasteland: A Democratic Alternative to Economic Decline*, New York: Anchor Press, 1984

Cobb, Sidney and Kasl, Stanislau, *Termination: The Consequences of Job Loss*, National Institute of Occupational Safety, and Health Research Report Publication No. 77–224, June 1977

Cole, Robert, *Work Mobility and Participation*, Berkeley: University of California Press, 1979

Forseback, L., *Industrial Relations and Employment in Sweden*, Stockholm: Swedish Institute, 1976

Gouldner, Alvin, *Industrial Patterns of Bureaucracy*, Glencoe, Ill.: Free Press, 1954

Hill, Stephen, *Competition and Control at Work: The New Industrial Sociology*, Cambridge, Mass.: MIT Press, 1981

International Association of Machinists and Aerospace Workers (Grand Lodge Heights, 1300 Connecticut Ave., N.W., Washington, D.C.), *Let's Rebuild America*, 1983

Lawrence, Paul and Dyer, Davis, *Renewing American Industry*, New York: Free Press, 1983

Luria, Dan and Russell, Jack, *Rational Reindustrialization: An Economic Agenda for Detroit*, Detroit: Widgetripper Press, 1981

Rayman, Paula and Bluestone, Barry, *Out of Work*, Boston College: Social Welfare Research Institute, October 1982

Reich, Robert, *The Next American Frontier*, New York: Times Books, 1983

Scherer, Frederic, *Industrial Market Structure and Industrial Performance*, Chicago: Rand McNally, 1970

Thurow, Lester, *Zero Sum Society*, New York: Basic Books, 1980

Vogel, Ezra, *Japan as Number 1*, New York: Harper & Row, 1979

White, Lawrence J., "Clearing the Legal Path to Cooperative Research," *Technology Review* 88, July 1985

Organizational democracy

Abrahamsson, Bengt, *Bureaucracy or Participation*, Beverly Hills and London: Sage Publications, 1977

Anthony, William P., *Participatory Management*, Reading, Mass.: Addison-Wesley, 1978

Bernstein, Paul, *Workplace Democratization*, Kent, Ohio: Kent State University Press, 1976; New Brunswick, N.J.: Transaction Books, 1980

Blum, Fred, *Work and Community: The Scott Bader Commonwealth and the Quest for a New Social Order*, London: Routledge & Kegan Paul, 1968

Blumberg, Paul, *Industrial Democracy*, New York: Schocken, 1969

Bradley, Keith and Gelb, Alan, *Worker Capitalism and the New Industrial Relations*, Cambridge, Mass.: MIT Press, 1983

Bruyn, Severyn T. and Nicolaou-Smokovitis, Litza, "A Theoretical Framework for Studying Worker Participation: The Psychological Contract," *Review of Social Economy* 37, April 1979

Clark, Dennis and Groben, Merry, *Future Bread: How Retail Workers Transformed Their Jobs and Lives*, Philadelphia: O and O Investment Fund, 119 Cuthbert St, Phila., Pa, 1983

Conrad, Will C., Wilson, Kathleen and Wilson, Dale, *The Milwaukee Journal*, Madison: The University of Wisconsin Press, 1964

Ellerman, David P., *The Socialization of Entrepreneurship: The Impressarial Division of the Caia Labooral Popular*, Somerville, Mass.: Industrial Cooperative Association, 1982

(n.d.) "The Question of Legal Structure," Somerville, Mass.: Industrial Cooperative Association, 248 Elm St (n.d.) "What is a Cooperative?," Somerville, Mass.: Industrial Cooperative Association

Ellerman, David P. and Pitegoff, Peter, "The Democratic Corporation," *Review of Law and Social Change*, New York University, forthcoming

Frieden, Karl, *Workplace Democracy and Productivity*, Washington, D.C.: National Center for Economic Alternatives, 1980

Hunnius, Gerry and Garson, G. David, eds., *Workers' Control*, New York: Random House, 1973

Jenkins, David, *Industrial Democracy in Europe*, Geneva: Business International 1974

Job Power, New York: Doubleday, 1973

Jones, Derek and Svejnar, Jan, eds., *Participatory and Self-Managed Firms*, Lexington, Mass.: Lexington Books, 1982

Ketchum, Lyman D. "A Case Study of Diffusion," in Davis, Louis E., Cherns, Albert B. and Associates, *The Quality of Working Life*, Vol. 2, New York: The Free Press, 1975

King, Charles D. and Van De Vall, Mark, *Models of Industrial Democracy*, New York: Mouton, 1978

Lindenfeld, Frank and Rothchild-Whitt, Joyce, eds., *Workplace Democracy and Social Change*, Boston: Porter Sargent, 1982

Mackin, Christopher, "Strategies for Local Ownership and Control: A Policy Analysis," Somerville, Mass.: Industrial Cooperative Association, 58 Day St, Suite 200, Somerville, Mass., 02144.

Mason, Ronald, *Participation and Workplace Democracy*, Carbondale: Southern Illinois Press, 1982

Nader, Ralph, Green, Mark and Seligman, Joel, *Taming the Giant Corporation*, New York: Norton, 1976

Oakeshott, Robert, *The Case for Worker Coops*, London: Routledge & Kegan Paul, 1978

Pettman, B., *Industrial Democracy: A Selected Bibliography*, New York: MCB Publications, State Mutual Books, 1978

Simmons, John and Mares, William, *Working Together*, New York: Knopf, 1983

Thomas, Henk and Logan, Chris, *Mondragon: An Economic Analysis*, London: George Allen & Unwin, 1982

Vanek, Jaroslav, *Self-Management*, New York: Penguin, 1975

The Participatory Economy, Ithaca: Cornell University Press, 1971

Zupanov, J. and Tannenbaum, A. S., "The Distribution of Control in Some Yugoslav Industrial Organizations as Perceived by Members," in Tannenbaum, A. S., *Control in Organizations*, New York: McGraw-Hill, 1968

Organizational development

Anthony, R. N., "The Trouble with Profit Maximization," *Harvard Business Review*, Nov.–Dec. 1960

Argyris, Chris, *Personality and Organization*, New York: Harper, 1957

Bruyn, Severyn T., "The Community Self-Study: Worker Self-Management versus The New Class," *Review of Social Economy*, March 1984

Child, John and Keiser, Alfred, "Development of Organizations Over Time," in Nystrom, Paul and Starbuch, William, *Handbook of Organizational Design*, New York: Oxford University Press, 1981

Craig, J. R., *Multinational Cooperatives*, Saskatchewan: Western Producer Prairie Books, 1976

Cyert, R. M. and March, J. G., *A Behavioral Theory of the Firm*, Englewood Cliffs, N.J.: Prentice-Hall, 1963

Davis, Louis E., Cherns, Albert B. and Associates, *The Quality of Working Life: Problems, Prospects, and the State of the Art*, New York: Free Press, 1975

Drucker, Peter, *Management*, New York: Harper & Row, 1973

Feldman, J. and Kanter, H. E., "Organizational Decision-Making", in *Handbook of Organization*, ed. J. G. March, Chicago: Rand-McNally, 1965

Kanter, Rosabeth, *The Change Masters*, New York: Simon & Schuster, 1983

Kohn, Melvin L., *Class and Conformity: A Study in Values*, Homewood, Ill.: The Dorsey Press, 1969

Likert, Rensis, *New Patterns of Management*, New York: McGraw-Hill, 1961

Ouchi, William, *Theory Z*, Reading, Mass.: Addison-Wesley, 1981

Papandreo, Andreas, "Some Basic Problems in the Theory of the Firm," in Haley, B. F., ed., *A Survey of Contemporary Economics*, vol. 2, Homewood, Ill.: Irvin, 1952

Employee ownership

Marsh, Thomas R. and McAllister, Dale E., "ESOP's Tables: A Survey of Companies with Employee Stock Ownership Plans," *Journal of Corporation Law*, Spring 1981

Research Institute of America, "Assessing ESOP's," New York, 1979

Select Committee on Small Business, "The Role of the Federal Government and Employee Ownership of Business," Washington, D.C.: U.S: Government Printing Office, 1979

Sokoloff, Gail, "The Creation of an Employee Owned Firm: A Case Study of Hyatt Clark Industries," Monograph 3 in the Comparative Worker Ownership Study Group, 1–8 Vanserg Hall, Harvard University, Cambridge, Mass., 1982

Survey Research Center, "Employee Ownership: Report to the Economic Development Administration of the Department of Commerce, Project 99–6–09433," Ann Arbor: Institute for Social Research, University of Michigan, 1978

Corporate social responsibility

Bowman, E. H., "Corporate Social Responsibility and the Investor," *Journal of Contemporary Business*, Winter 1973

Bowman, E. H. and Haire, M., "A Strategic Posture Toward Corporate Social Responsibility," *California Management Review*, Winter 1975

Bucholz, Rogene A., *Business Environment and Public Policy*, Englewood Cliffs, N.J.: Prentice-Hall, 1982

Buono, Anthony F. and Nichols, Lawrence T., *Corporate Policy, Values, and Social Responsibility*, New York: Praeger, 1985
Johnson, Harold L., *Disclosure of Corporate Social Performance*, New York: Praeger, 1979
Walton, Clarence, *Corporate Social Responsibilities*, Belmont, Calif.: Wadsworth, 1968

Social and political economy

Bruyn, Severyn T., "Social Economy: A Note on its Theoretical Foundations," *Review of Social Economy* 39, April 1981
   The Social Economy, New York: Wiley, 1977
Gilder, George, *Wealth and Poverty*, New York: Bantam Books, 1981
Horvat, Bronco, *The Political Economy of Socialism*, New York: M. E. Sharpe, 1982
Korpi, W., *The Working Class in Welfare Capitalism*, London: Routledge & Kegan Paul, 1978
Tausky, Curt, *Work and Society*, Itasca, Ill.: F. E. Peacock, 1984
Weitzman, Martin, *The Share Economy*, Cambridge: Harvard University Press, 1985

Democratic community development

Craftel, Brad, *Community Development Credit Unions*, Berkeley: National Economic Development Law Project, 1978
Community Economic Development Office, *Jobs and People: A Strategic Analysis of the Greater Burlington Economy*, December 1984
Institute for Community Economics, *The Community Land Handbook*, Emmaus, Pa.: Rodale Press, 1982
Jacobs, Jane, *Cities and the Wealth of Nations: Principles of Economic Life*, New York: Vintage Books, 1985
   The Economy of Cities, New York: Random House, 1969
Morris, David, *The New City States*, Washington, D.C., Institute for Local Self Reliance, 1982
Whyte, William Foote, Hammer, Tove Hellend, Meek, Christopher, Nelson, Reed, and Stern, Robert, *Worker Participation and Ownership*, New York: ILR Press, Cornell University, 1983

Name index

Subject index

Other books in the series

J. Milton Yinger, Kiyoshi Ikeda, Frank Laycock, and Stephen J. Cutler: *Middle Start: An Experiment in the Educational Enrichment of Young Adolescents*

James A. Geschwender: *Class, Race, and Worker Insurgency: The League of Revolutionary Black Workers*

Paul Ritterband: *Education, Employment, and Migration: Israel in Comparative Perspective*

John Low-Beer: *Protest and Participation: The New Working Class in Italy*

Orrin E. Klapp: *Opening and Closing: Strategies of Information Adaptation in Society*

Rita James Simon: *Continuity and Change: A Study of Two Ethnic Communities in Israel*

Marshall B. Clinard: *Cities with Little Crime: The Case of Switzerland**

Steven T. Bossert: *Tasks and Social Relationships in Classrooms: A Study of Instructional Organization and Its Consequences*

Richard E. Johnson: *Juvenile Delinquency and Its Origins: An Integrated Theoretical Approach**

David R. Heise: *Understanding Events: Affect and the Construction of Social Action*

Ida Harper Simpson: *From Student to Nurse: A Longitudinal Study of Socialization*

Stephen P. Turner: *Sociological Explanation as Translation*

Janet W. Salaff: *Working Daughters of Hong Kong: Filial Piety or Power in the Family?*

Joseph Chamie: *Religion and Fertility: Arab Christian–Muslim Differentials*

William Friedland, Amy Barton, Robert Thomas: *Manufacturing Green Gold: Capital, Labor, and Technology in the Lettuce Industry*

Richard N. Adams: *Paradoxical Harvest: Energy and Explanation in British History, 1870–1914*

Mary F. Rogers: *Sociology, Ethnomethodology, and Experience: A Phenomenological Critique*

James R. Beniger: *Trafficking in Drug Users: Professional Exchange Networks in the Control of Deviance*

Andrew J. Weigert, J. Smith Teitge, and Dennis W. Teitge: *Society and Identity: Toward a Sociological Psychology*

Jon Miller: *Pathways in the Workplace: The Effects of Race and Gender on Access to Organizational Resources*

Michael A. Faia: *Dynamic Functionalism: Strategy and Tactics*

Joyce Rothschild and J. Allen Whitt: *The Co-operative Workplace: Potentials and Dilemmas of Organizational Democracy*

Russell Thornton: *We Shall Live Again: The 1870 and 1890 Ghost Dance Movements as Demographic Revitalization*

* *Available from American Sociological Association, 1722 N Street, N.W., Washington, DC 20036.*